LIBERALISM AND ITS DISCONTENTS: SOCIAL MOVEMENTS IN WEST AFRICA

Edited by

Ndongo Samba Sylla

Rosa Luxemburg Foundation

Published by the Rosa Luxemburg Foundation

West Africa Regional Office
Dakar, Senegal
http://www.rosalux.sn

© 2014 Rosa Luxemburg Foundation

ISBN-13: 978-1499324754
ISBN-10: 1499324758

The publication of this book was made possible with funds made available from the
German Federal Ministry for Economic Cooperation and Development.

Project Manager: Firoze Manji
Copy-editing: Patrick Burnett
Design and layout: Tidiane Oumar BA - SOGO BA
© Credit photos: Gallo images and Arona N'diaye

CONTENTS

ACKNOWLEDGMENTS

This book would not have been possible without the support of many individuals and institutions. The West Africa bureau of the Rosa Luxemburg Foundation, through its director Claus-Dieter König, agreed to support this research project. If this publication has been compiled and published in a relatively short time period, the credit must go to the contributing authors. Their openness, availability and cooperation were essential. My colleague Bruno Sonko helped me enormously in coordinating this research project. I also thank him for having read and commented on several chapters. Despite the relatively short time available, our team of translators (David Clement Leye, Mallé Kassé, Maimouna Diallo Ka, Carole Small Diop and Codou Mbassy Diene), as usual, showed understanding and professionalism. Firoze Manji devoted much energy towards the publication of this volume. His comments and suggestions, and those of the copy-editor, Patrick Burnett, have helped to improve the manuscript. A big thank you must also go to Abdoulaye Diallo, director of L'Harmattan Senegal, for the care with which he welcomed the project. I thank my colleagues at the Rosa Luxemburg Foundation (Ibrahima Thiam, Diallo Kolo Cissokho, Mariem Ndiaye, Clémentine Thiam, Maimouna Ndao, Yoro Fall and Damien Sarr) for their encouragement and for facilitating the administrative processing of the project. I would also like to thank our network of partners in West Africa for having provided valuable contacts and agreeing to lend their support. Finally, a special mention to Lila Chouli and Louisa Prause, whose comments and suggestions were of immense benefit. As it is customary to state, the views expressed in this volume are those of the authors and do not necessarily represent the views of the Rosa Luxemburg Foundation.

Ndongo Samba Sylla

AUTHORS' DETAILS

Ibrahim Abdullah is a Sierra Leonean historian and associate professor of history and African studies at the Fourah Bay College, University of Sierra Leone. He is the editor of *Between Democracy and Terror: The Sierra Leone Civil War* and the co-author of *A People's History of Sierra Leone* (forthcoming with Ismail Rashid). E-mail: ibdullah@gmail.com

Souley Adji is a socio-political scientist from Niger and a researcher and lecturer at the University Abdou Moumouni, Niamey. Author of numerous contributions to collective books and articles on Nigerian politics, he has co-authored a book on the trajectories and figures of the intelligentsia in Niger (forthcoming with CODESRIA). He is finishing a book on the re-Islamisation of the academic space in Niger. He is also very active in Nigerian civil society. Email: souley_adji@gmx.com

Kojo Opoku Aidoo is a Ghanaian political scientist, research fellow and coordinator at the history and politics section of the Institute of African Studies at the University of Ghana in Accra. His books include *Political Stability in Ghana since the 1992* Re-Democratization Wave and *Political Participation, Governance, and Neopatrimonial Rule in Africa: The Case of Ghana* (1990-2000). E-mail: aidoo77us@yahoo.com

Francis Akindès is an Ivorian sociologist and professor in the anthropology and sociology department of the Alassane Ouattara University. He is the editor of *Côte d'Ivoire: la réinvention de soi dans la violence* and the co-author of *Les Intellectuels ivoiriens face à la crise*. E-mail: f_akindès@yahoo.fr

Alpha Amadou Bano Barry is a Guinean sociologist and rector of the Winfrey Oprah University of Guinea. Among his publications are *La démocratie et le vote en Guinée* and *Les Violences Collectives en Afrique: le cas de la Guinée*. E-mail: barybano@hotmail.com

Fernando Leonardo Cardoso is a historian from Guinea-Bissau and author of numerous articles in scientific journals. A consultant for many international organisations, he is currently the principal technical advisor of the state secretary for culture, youth and sports. E-mail: leocard_090@yahoo.com.br

Lila Chouli is a French journalist and associate researcher at the University of Johannesburg. Chouli is the author of *Burkina Faso 2011: chronique d'un mouvement social.* E-mail: laly.lila@gmail.com

Modou Diome is a Senegalese sociologist and member of the Multidisciplinary Study and Research Centre of La Vallée (University of Gaston Berger, Saint-Louis, Senegal). Diome is the author of research works about media and communication, social movements, civil society, female domestic migrant work, political violence, the Muslim brotherhood, public sector reforms and school punishments and failures. E-mail: diomemodou13@yahoo.fr

Moussa Fofana is an Ivorian socio-economist, researcher, lecturer and assistant in the anthropology and sociology department at Alassane Ouattara University. He is head of the governance and ethics program development at the UNESCO chair on bioethics at the University of Alassane Ouattara and author of publications on youth engagement in political violence. Email: fofmous2003@yahoo.fr

Cláudio Alves Furtado is a Cabo Verdean sociologist, professor at the University of Bahia (Brazil), associate professor of sociology at the Cabo Verde University, member of the executive committee of the Council for the Development of Social Science Research in Africa (CODESRIA) president of the International Association of Social and Human Sciences and of the Portuguese Language. Amongst his publications are *Les Etats-nations face à l'intégration régionale en Afrique de l'Ouest, le cas du Cap Vert and Desigualdades sociais e dinâmicas de participação em Cabo Verde.* E-mail: cfurtado.unicv@gmail.com

George Klay Kieh Jr. is a Liberian political scientist and professor of political science at the University of West Georgia. Author of *Liberia's State Failure, Collapse and Reconstitution,* he co-edited *West Africa and the U.S. War on Terror, and The State in Africa: Beyond False Starts.* E-mail: georgekieh@yahoo.com
Claus-Dieter König is a German political scientist and the regional director

for the Rosa Luxemburg Foundation in West Africa, based in Dakar. He has published on social movements in Africa, including monographs on Nigeria and Kenya.

Severin Yao Kouamé is an Ivorian socio-economist and lecturer at the anthropology and sociology department at Alassane Ouattara University. His work focuses on issues of resilience and innovation in peasant economies experiencing the withdrawal and the weaknesses of the state, 'post-conflict' public policy community outreach, the fight against poverty and promoting access to basic social services. E-mail: kouame@gmail.com

Fodé Mané is a Guinea-Bissau legal expert and professor at the law department of the Bissau University. He is a militant and a leader of human rights organisations. He is the author of numerous scientific articles.

Issa N'Diaye is a Malian philosopher and professor at the University of Mali. He was formerly the minister of national education and the minister of culture and scientific research. He has written extensively on philosophy, politics, democracy and electoral processes, culture and national languages. He is the president of the Civic Forum, Space of Reflection and Action for Democracy. E-mail: issandiaye_flash@yahoo.fr

Zekeria Ould Ahmed Salem is a Mauritanian political scientist and professor of political science at the University of Nouakchott, Mauritania. He was the secretary general of the ministry of higher education (2005-2006) and of the ministry of rural development (2006-2007). He is the author of *Prêcher dans le désert. Islam politique et changement social en Mauritanie* and the editor of *Les trajectoires d'un État-frontière. Espaces, évolutions politiques et transformations sociales en Mauritanie*. Email: zakariadenna@yahoo.fr

Ndongo Samba Sylla is a Senegalese economist, programme and research manager at the West Africa office of the Rosa Luxemburg Foundation. Author of *The Fair Trade Scandal. Marketing poverty to Benefit the Rich* (translated from French by Pluto Press 2014), he is the editor of *Rethinking Development*. His recent research work deals with the history of the word 'democracy'. E-mail: n.sylla@rosalux.sn

Map of West African states

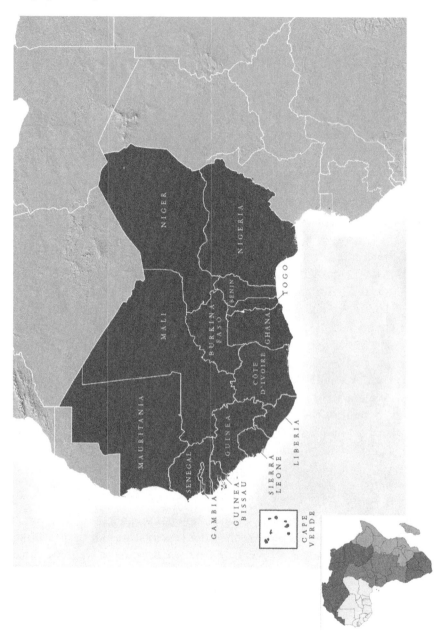

INTRODUCTION

DEMOCRACY, LIBERALISM AND SOCIAL MOVEMENTS IN WEST AFRICA

Ndongo Samba Sylla

This volume is a collection of studies on social movements in West Africa. It seeks to fill a research gap. In the wake of the 'Arab Spring', literature on social movements started to flourish in many regions, except in West Africa, where the 'social movement' entry was still not imposing itself as an analytical prism that could help to understand socio-political dynamics.[1] While one intuitively feels that 'things are happening', as evidenced by the many protest movements recently observed in most countries of the region, there is, in actual fact, very little research giving an indication of the inner dynamics of this apparent resurgence of social movements. What are the major socio-political struggles that have recently taken place in the countries of the region? What logic drives them? What forms do they take? What has been their political impact?

---

1   Due to the impressive literature on social movements from industrialised nations, a few summary works are available in French (Fillieule *et al* 2009, Fillieule *et al* 2010, Neveu 2011) and in English (Goodwin and Jasper 2009, Tilly and Wood 2012). In the global South, the following can be mentioned: Wignarajan 1993, Gills 2001, Motta and Nilsen 2011. As for Africa, the following are worthy of note: Mamdani and Wamba-dia-Wamba 1995, Harrison 2002, Prempeh 2006, Ellis and van Kessel 2009, McSween 2010, Manji and Ekine 2011, Dwyer and Zeilig 2012, Larmer 2010, as well as other articles in the same volume, Brandes and Engels 2011, as well as other articles in the same volume.

Can we speak of a resurgence of social movements? If so, are these a response to the 'representative democracy' crisis? Did they give rise to new forms of expression and democratic participation? What challenges do they bring? What are their limitations? Such are the questions that underpinned this research project. While the 2010-2013 period receives greater focus, the studies compiled in this volume generally cover a broader canvas. The situation in 12 countries of the region is analysed.[2]

The interest shown here for social movements is also the result of a methodological choice. One of the premises of this research project is that the 'social movement' entry provides a more heuristic analytical framework to help understand current political dynamics compared with the usual perspectives that focus on elections, political parties, power struggles at the highest level of the state and the shortcomings, actual or perceived, of African political systems. The main weakness of the analytical prism of 'politician politics', or politics 'seen from above', is that it overlooks the struggles, resistance and initiatives of ordinary citizens and the associations they create so as to improve their well-being, express their views and concerns, present a new public agenda and offer new perspectives in terms of public policies or even new social projects. In fact, the usual lack of interest in political activities by the *demos* lying beyond the electoral space is one of the reasons why indicators designed through this oligarchic prism are often at odds with the current socio-political dynamics and therefore struggle to predict the major changes that these can induce.[3]

---

2   In the context of this volume, West Africa includes the 15 Economic Community of West African States (ECOWAS) member states: Benin, Burkina Faso, Cabo Verde, Côte d'Ivoire, the Gambia, Ghana, Guinea, Guinea-Bissau, Liberia, Mali, Niger, Nigeria, Senegal, Sierra Leone, Togo as well as Mauritania. Benin, the Gambia, Nigeria and Togo are the four countries that are unfortunately not covered in this volume. See the table in the annex for a statistical outline of West African countries.
3   According to the 2011 Ibrahim Index of African Governance, Tunisia ranked first in Africa in terms of 'human development', while Egypt came second in terms of 'sustainable economic opportunity' (Mo Ibrahim Foundation 2011). Such attractive rankings were clearly not designed from the perspective of people like Mohamed Bouazizi, the informal worker at the origin of the protest that set North Africa and the Middle East on fire. They tell us more about the 'security' granted investors than about the economic 'freedom' of popular classes. Another example is Mali, which was considered the fifth democracy on the continent and the second in West Africa before the coup of March 2012 (Economist Intelligence Unit 2011). This shows that such ranking systems make their assessments of reality from the perspective of the 'elite'.

Table 1: Statistical brief of West African countries

Countries	Demographic Indicators					Socio-economic indicators					Political indicators	
	Population 2012 (in million)	0-14 years (% of total population in 2012)	Rural population (% of total population in 2012)	Projected population for 2030 (in million)	Life expectancy (in years)	2012 Rank on Human development index (out of 184 countries)	GDP 2012 current dollars, in billion	GDP per capita 2012 (current dollars)	Average annual GDP growth 2000-2012 (in %)	Average annual GDP per capita growth 2000-2012 (in %)	Number of successful coup attempts (1960-2000)	Number of successful coup attempts (2000-2012)
Benin	10.1	43.0	54.4	15.5	59.1	166	7.6	752	4	0.9	5	0
Burkina Faso	16.5	45.7	72.6	26.6	55.9	183	10.4	634	6.1	3.1	6	0
Cabo Verde	0.5	30.2	36.7	0.6	74.5	132	1.8	3695	5.9	4.9	0	0
Cote d'Ivoire	19.8	41.5	48.0	29.2	50.4	168	24.7	1244	1.3	-0.5	1	1
Gambia	1.8	45.9	42.2	3.0	58.6	165	0.9	512	3.3	0.1	1	0
Ghana	25.4	38.6	47.5	35.2	60.9	135	40.7	1605	6.7	4.1	5	0
Guinea	11.5	42.5	64.1	17.3	55.8	178	5.6	492	2.8	0.5	1	1
Guinea-Bissau	1.7	41.6	55.4	2.4	54.0	176	0.8	494	1.9	-0.4	1	2
Liberia	4.2	43.1	51.4	6.4	60.2	174	1.7	414	7.5	4.3	1	0
Mali	14.9	47.1	64.4	26.0	54.6	182	10.3	694	5.2	2	2	1
Mauritania	3.8	40.2	58.2	6.2	61.4	155	4.2	1106	5.1	2.2	3	2
Niger	17.2	50.0	81.9	34.5	58.0	186	6.8	395	4.9	1.1	3	1
Nigeria	168.8	44.2	49.8	273.0	52.1	153	510	2689	6.5	3.7	6	0
Senegal	13.7	43.5	57.1	21.8	63.2	154	14	1023	3.9	1.1	0	0
Sierra Leone	6	41.7	60.4	8.0	45.3	177	3.8	635	7.1	3.9	5	0
Togo	6.6	41.9	61.5	10.0	56.2	159	3.8	574	2.7	0	2	0
Total	322.5	43.8	54.5	515.7			647.1	2007	5.6	2.8	42	8

Sources: data on coups come from Ben Barka and Ncube (2012). About the population projections for 2030, see the United Nations population division: http://esa.un.org/unpd/wpp/unpp/panel_population.htm (accessed April 2014). The remaining data come from the World Bank development indicators database: databank.worldbank.org (accessed April 2014). In the case of Nigeria, data on GDP (Gross Domestic Product) have been updated to take into account the recent change of base year.

Unlike with the oligarchic prism, this volume adopts a more 'democratic' perspective by seeking to place a greater analytical focus on the dynamics stemming from 'below' and/or which lie beyond formal political institutions. New realities begin to surface as soon as we opt for a sociology of banners. We end up with a more complex image of Africa than the part-sordid, part-modernist image ('emerging Africa') conveyed by Western media and other 'experts on Africa'. Thus we seek to avoid the pitfalls of the approaches which assess the socio-political and socio-economic situation of a country solely on the basis of the show run by those at the top: such a country is corrupt because its elite is notoriously corrupt, another dislikes 'freedom' because its regime oppresses dissident voices, such a country is 'democratic' because it regularly holds elections considered free and transparent by the 'international community', another is on the right track because of a high growth rate, etc.

This volume follows in the footsteps of the Council for the Development of Social Science Research in Africa (CODESRIA) in its pioneering collective work entitled *African Studies in Social Movements and Democracy* (Mamdani and Wamba-dia-Wamba 1995). The view expressed then, and which remains relevant today, is that the study of social movements must be linked to the issue of democracy. Twenty years later, another issue that must be added is that of liberalism, in its economic and political dimensions.

Since the 1990s, the gradual adoption of the multi-party system by African countries was analysed from the angle of 'democratic transition'. This perspective must now be revisited in light of available factual elements. Further, the dominant theoretical approaches around the issue of democracy need to be assessed more critically. In retrospect, one may be under the impression that such analysis did not sufficiently grasp nor take into account what the French philosopher Jean-Claude Michéa (2007) called the original 'unity' of liberalism: political liberalism and economic liberalism start from the same underlying philosophical and moral principles.[4]

4   Initially, liberalism was an attempt to answer the following theological-political question: how can secular independence be achieved among Christian people? (Manent 1996, 2009). Deeply pessimistic about mankind's moral capacity, liberalism is the 'project of a minimal society' with 'right' defining its form, and economy its content (Michéa

The first mistake was to think that 'representative democracy' or 'liberal democracy' deserves its name; that it is democracy. The second was to think that the problems of contemporary Africa are due to economic liberalism (which allegedly had disastrous consequences) rather than to political liberalism ('representative democracy' institutions perceived a priori as 'good'). Hence the attitude consisting of lauding the very same principles that one criticises.

Like everywhere else in the world, West Africa certainly experiences highs and lows. Nevertheless, we should not make the wrong diagnosis. The problem in this region is not the lack or a deficit of 'democracy', but rather, the unbridled liberalism that prevails in the economic and political spheres. This statement may seem provocative or even counter-intuitive. In fact, provided that we distance ourselves from the mystification of bourgeois political language, unfortunately the language of contemporary political 'science' and its 'Africanist' branch, this is a self-evident conclusion. To 'representative democracy' or 'liberal democracy' or 'democracy for the master race' (Losurdo 2014), another approach to the democratic question should be proposed. That is the only basis on which we would be able to better gauge the issue of social movements in Africa today.

Democracy and 'representative democracy'[5]

A word of Greek origin, Demokratia was used for more than two millennia to refer to a form of government rather than a form of society. Suffice to recall that although it had a democratic government, Athens had been

---

2009:48). 'Right' refers to the impersonal mechanism that ensures coordination amongst individuals who do not share common values, whereas economy refers to market economy. For liberalism, what matters the most is preserving civil peace. In a liberal society, one does not seek to do good, but attempts to avoid evil. This is why a liberal society is a 'realm of lesser evil' (Michéa 2009). Besides, Losurdo (2013) demonstrates that in spite of their so-called love for 'liberty', liberal thinkers and liberal societies have often approved of slavery, racism and colonialism (see also Mills 1997). On the manner in which liberalism misrepresents the notion of liberty, see Skinner (1998).

5   This section on the history of the word democracy draws from as-of-yet unpublished research by the author. Some of these elements have been mentioned in other works (Sylla 2014a, 2014b). On this theme, a close reading of Dupuis-Déri (2013), as well as Dunn (2006), Canfora (2006) and Manin (2002) is recommended.

a slave-holding society in antiquity. While monarchy is a political regime in which sovereignty is held by a single person, and oligarchy one where sovereignty is in the hands of a minority of citizens, democracy is originally a political system where the *demos* (in other words the free men who hold neither power nor wealth and are generally excluded from any significant political involvement) are sovereign.

In a democratic regime, the concept of popular sovereignty means that ordinary people have the real possibility of devising the laws themselves (directly, without intermediary) and to make magistrates accountable, a political activity that starts at the local level, at the level of the deme (other meaning of *demos*). From antiquity until the 19th century, such was the prevailing conception in Western political theory.

Two significant elements should be added to this brief description. First of all, it ought to be pointed out that up to the beginning of the 19th century, there was hardly any Western thinker who would defend democracy, considered since antiquity as the 'worst of the best and the best of the worst form of government', as Plato argued. Neither the American nor the French Revolution celebrated the word 'democracy', which, due to all the hatred the idea attracted, was not to be found in the constitutions and in the most important documents of that period. Secondly, the representative system of government that gradually imposed itself from that point on was seen as an antidote to democracy, considered by the American founding fathers as 'the worst of all political evils' (Sylla 2014b).

At the start of the 19th century, in the post-revolutionary period, the principle of representation was promoted in order to exclude ordinary people from any form of political power. Initially, 'representation' did not mean that the 'representatives' should faithfully speak on behalf of the people. On the contrary, the people were portrayed as passionate and irrational, and the 'representatives' were therefore counter-powers with standing their destructive and tyrannical power.

'Representative democracy' as a concept is an oxymoron dating back from the last quarter of the 18th century. It was usually referred to as 'bourgeois government' and 'elective aristocracy'. John Dunn (2006) understandably argued that 'modern representative democracy has changed the idea of democracy almost beyond recognition', and to speak frankly, that no 'democracy' exists in the contemporary world. Regimes that describe themselves as 'democracies' are in fact liberal oligarchies. The point being made here is that a distinction must be made between the nature of political systems and the performances that these produce. Western 'liberal democracies' are oligarchies that succeeded in achieving a degree of *democratic performance*: in other words, a certain level of *constitutional performance* (relative upholding of the constitution, human rights, etc) and a certain level of *socio-economic performance* (good living conditions for the majority of their citizens). Beyond all-out propaganda, it is such democratic performance that tends to spread the erroneous idea that countries such as France or the United States are 'democracies'. Yet, one must acknowledge that this democratic performance relies to some extent on the inequalities and asymmetries created by the capitalist-imperialist system between countries of the North and countries of the South (Wallerstein 2001).

Three elements help to preserve this democratic 'front' for nations that claim to be 'democracies'. Firstly, the triad nations (United States, Europe and Japan), in the framework of the globalised capitalist system, are those that have appropriated for themselves the 'imperialist rent', which lies on monopolies in five areas: technological, weapons of mass destruction, financial, communication and the media, and access to natural resources (Amin 2010, Dembélé 2011). Secondly, thanks to the people's struggles in the triad nations, this imperialist rent was shared and benefited the vast majority of them. The key period was that of the post-war boom, during which social protection systems became stronger, providing citizens with an enhanced set of social rights. Finally, if the imperialist rent was shared in a 'democratic' way within the triad, it was also because of the pressure created by the communist alternative. Indeed, workers in the triad nations had a counter-project to available in case liberal systems were not willing to reform so as to better meet their interests.

Today, in the era described as neoliberalism, the first and last conditions are increasingly undermined. First of all, so-called 'emerging' nations increasingly tend to challenge Western domination. Thus, a growing share of the global economic surplus tends to fall beyond its grasp; this continues to adversely affect the living standards of their workers, which has steadily declined over the last three decades. Secondly, with the fading communist alternative and the triumph of the TINA ideology (There is no alternative), power relations have been reversed in favour of capital, which no longer hesitates, as in the days of the 'Fordist compromise', to sacrifice national interest for the sake of its irrepressible desire to accumulate for the sake of accumulation. As a result, the 'social benefits' previously gained by triad workers start being re-commodified. Without the pressure exerted by an alternative societal project, 'liberal democracy' has all but lost any emancipating potential under the onslaught of contemporary challenges.

It is in light of these elements that the difficulties linked to importing 'liberal democracy' in Africa should be assessed: how to ensure that liberal (and therefore non-democratic) regimes achieve a good democratic performance in countries lying at the periphery of the capitalist system? It is also in light of the contradictions arising from this project - consolidating democracy through liberalism - that the 'return' of social movements in Africa should be analysed. The latter is the outcome of the profound discontent felt by African people vis-à-vis liberalism: what political liberalism promises without being able to fulfil it, economic liberalism ('neoliberalism') systematically and relentlessly precludes.

In the wake of the 'Arab spring', many wondered whether sub-Saharan Africa was going to experience similar uprisings. In the case of West Africa, the context seems to differ on a crucial aspect related to the temporality of the protest cycle, so to speak. In North Africa and the Middle East, the 'street' rose up to demand the departure of tyrants that had been strongly holding on to power for several decades and who were to some extent the pillars of the neo-colonial order. In West Africa, this tyrant hunt prevails in a very small number of countries (Burkina Faso with Blaise Compaore, the Gambia with Yahya Jammeh or even Togo with Faure Gnassingbe). It is not however the main driver of the many forms of protest punctuating the political landscape of the region. Nowadays, social movements in this part of the continent do not mobilise so much to demand the advent of 'liberal democracy', but rather to denounce its limits and to deepen it in a more democratic way. They take place in a context where the hope initially generated by the 'democracy of the ballot box' has faded. From a qualitative point of view, this cycle of protest is different from the former. While these struggles hold much promise, they nevertheless contain numerous ambiguities.

Political liberalisation without constitutional performance

In West Africa, there is a long tradition of resistance and popular struggles against the colonial order. As Ibrahim Abdullah points out in the case of Sierra Leone, Freetown has been a hotbed of intensive associative life since the 19th century. Liberia formally gained its independence as early as 1847 and also has a rich history of resistance by indigenous populations to the American version of neo-colonialism. In most other West African countries, numerous associations and social movements emerged in the framework of national liberation and independence struggles. Examples are given here, whether in the case of Nigeria with the Zikist movement, Mali under the leadership of Modibo Keita or Cabo Verde and Guinea Bissau under the leadership of Amilcar Cabral.

In the post-colonial era, the literature on social movements and democratic struggles in Africa identifies two milestones. The first dates back to the 1980s with massive protests against structural adjustment programmes, sometimes leading to military coups and political changeovers. The second milestone occurred at the beginning of the 1990s and extended the previous wave of protest: everywhere African populations rose to demand a regime change and broaden democracy in the political sphere (Dwyer and Zeilig 2012).

In countries such as Benin, this process led to the organisation of national conferences, whereas in others, such as Mali, the help of the military was deemed necessary. Twenty years before the 'Out with Moubarak!' slogan of the Egyptian youth, the Ivorians were already chanting 'Out with Houphouët!' The contribution of African peoples to the onset of the multi-party system should therefore not be overlooked, as argued by Issa N'Diaye, who takes a stance against what he refers to as the 'La Baule theory'. According to this theory, it was the speech made by François Mitterrand in 1990 at a France-Africa summit that alone triggered the movement for the elimination of one-party regimes on the continent. In fact, the La Baule speech was given birth by the popular struggles observed in many countries for a genuine independence and democracy.

Initially, the liberalisation of political regimes that started at the beginning of the 90s had generated much hope. Indeed, this development led to the opening up of the public space, which the previous single-party regimes had long attempted to restrict. With the generalisation of the multi-party system, previously clandestine political parties were able to take part in elections and an oppositional dynamic was more less institutionalised in the parliamentary interplay. The private media also took part in this political liberalisation process. From independence until the beginning of the 1990s, we may recall that countries such as Togo and Benin only had a single newspaper, a single television station or a single radio station, all under state control (Faye 2014). The opening up of public space proved beneficial to trade unions and civil society organisations. In the latter case, increased public presence also reflected the new policies of donors and rich nations. In the context of de-legitimation of the state and a narrowing of its role in the economic sphere, their logic was henceforth to work more closely with civil society organisations on developmental issues, for which the state had previously been the privileged partner. Since then, the reasoning is that a 'vibrant' civil society is a pillar for democracy and 'good governance'. Finally, everywhere in Africa, ordinary citizens wholeheartedly welcomed such liberalisation of the public space through the possibility of voting for their representatives and through various means of expression and protest.

The contributions contained in this volume unanimously acknowledge the fact that the liberalisation of the public space, which started in the 1990s for most African countries (for a country like Senegal, this process started as early as the mid-70s) produced a strengthened culture of public protest. Mobilisation, demonstration or protest was no longer as difficult as previously, even though protest activities continued in some contexts to include major risks. Citizens became increasingly aware of their 'rights' and no longer hesitated to claim them openly by resorting to various collective actions and by making the most of the possibilities offered by information and communication technologies.

However, liberalisation does not imply democratisation. Short of recognising such a distinction, one might fall into the trap of making teleological/ ethnocentric analyses that tend to be based on the implicit assumption that political trajectories in Africa should follow the Western model once the institutions of 'democracy' have taken root there. The concept of 'democratic transition' is typical of this point of view in so far as it tends to model the experience of African countries against that of Western countries, and narrows down the democratic issue to its formal political aspects. In the political sphere, liberalisation essentially implies the implementation of an institutional framework that holds an ongoing competition for political power and provides for the possibility to oppose the decisions and practices of powers. As a formal process, it renders the issue of the balance of power empirical.

In the case of West Africa, just like elsewhere on the continent, the liberalisation of political systems, with the gradual transition from so-called 'dictatorial' regimes to multi-party systems, did not lead to the constitutional performance and to the socio-economic performance expected by the people. In other words, in spite of the discourse on 'popular sovereignty', the people are not necessarily better governed than before and their material living conditions have not always improved. This is a major lesson to be drawn from this volume. In fact, in countries such as Guinea, a debate rages on between those who think that the current economic and political situation is worse now than it was before the advent of the multi-party system, and those who argue to the contrary.

After two decades of political liberalisation, the West African public space remains relatively unreceptive to the concerns of ordinary citizens. Even exemplary countries such as Cabo Verde only consider the political participation of citizens from an electoral perspective. Regarding the reason why the adoption of the multi-party system failed to hold its promise to substantially involve ordinary citizens and civil society, one must argue that ethnocentric theses that present 'democracy' as a privilege of given cultures, as well as 'elitist' theories that place the responsibility of the current political deadlock with rulers and the elite, seem to overlook the most crucial aspect.

According to Oskar Negt (2007), the public space referred to by Habermas when speaking about 'liberal democracy' is in actual fact a 'bourgeois public space'. This is a space that is constructed on the basis of bourgeois parameters and only allows for the forms of publicity compatible with the reproduction of the capitalist economic system. The bourgeois public space is based on the political exclusion of the masses, especially the working class, and is programmed to operate under a private mode. In other words, the bourgeois take advantage of political power and of the state apparatus to strengthen their private interests, namely their economic position. This explains why the bourgeois public space does not allow for the vast majority of men and women to 'politically express their interests and existential aspirations' (Negt 2007:38). The main stake in the bourgeois public space, in Africa just like everywhere else, is generally to determine which fractions of the bourgeoisie shall have a private monopoly on the state for a given period of time.

In the case of African countries, aside from the low level of economic development, their specificity resides in the avatars of the construction of the nation state. The post-colonial state inherited despotic and oppressing traits from the colonial administration, namely its tendency to manipulate membership identities in order to preserve its power and the privileges therein. As a result, ethnic, religious and community lines continue to shape the definition of citizenship and the running of contemporary political systems, as many contributions to this volume underscore. In states where the nation has not yet become an empirical reality, political liberalisation has often revived, or created, tensions along identity lines. This has been tragically epitomised by the issue of 'ivoirité'.

If political liberalisation has been disappointing in Africa, it is essentially because the public space that it has contributed to broadening quickly shrivelled up along partisan and electoral considerations, thus depriving citizens of any major political involvement. Instead of strengthening popular sovereignty, it has rather asphyxiated it and denied it any autonomous political expression.

The oligarchic domestication of universal suffrage shows first and foremost through electoral exclusion. In West Africa, millions of citizens of voting age are prevented from exercising their voting right simply because they are not registered in the electoral database. In relative terms, Burkina Faso, Côte d'Ivoire and Mauritania are the three champions of electoral exclusion. To mention only the case of Burkina Faso, around four million out of a total of eight million potential voters were in this situation during the 2013 legislative elections.[6] The first consequence is that the rates of electoral participation

---

6 On African electoral statistics, see the website of the African elections database as well as electionguide.org

are often overestimated in countries where electoral exclusion reaches significant proportions. The second is that the regimes that are leaders in terms of electoral exclusion generally need a limited number of votes to achieve the majority required to stay in power.[7]

Alongside electoral exclusion (exclusion of a quantitative nature), programmatic exclusion (exclusion of a qualitative nature) is the other major form of oligarchic domestication of universal suffrage.[8] In multi-party systems, the political offer - in terms of political programmes or even societal projects - is de facto the monopoly of political parties. However, given that the capitalist commodification logic nowhere spared the political sphere, it turned the latter into a somewhat competitive market where privileges, money, positions and honours are handed out and turn political parties into 'businesses' more concerned with conquering power and receiving prebends than by the willingness to build decent societies. In most African countries, the 'success' of the multi-party system was such that it is not rare to note the existence of more than 100 political parties, each aspiring to receive its slice of the cake. Political parties are as quick to readily merge into heterogeneous coalitions and unholy alliances as they are to split and give birth to new and smaller parties. Generally managed by all-powerful monarchs, most political parties hardly ever manage to survive their leaders or the internal conflicts that divide them.

This is how the 'privatisation' of the public space and its corollary of political dispossession of citizens starts within political parties and is enhanced by the configuration within which they operate as de facto patronage structures,

---

7   During the 2013 legislative elections in Mauritania, the regime in place only needed to collect 127,000 votes out of a voter base estimated at 1.8 million voters in order to ensure a parliamentary majority. In addition to electoral exclusion, it appeared that nearly one third of polling cards were void in the first round (see electionguide.org). As usual, France lauded the 'strong participation' of voters (*Le Monde* (2013) 'En Mauritanie, l'opposition exige de nouvelles élections', 24 December).
8   Among the many means of domesticating popular sovereignty, we can mention (i) electoral boycott strategies by opposition political parties, which constrains voter choices, as well as the (ii) *sine die* adjournment of elections scheduled in the electoral calendar, which occurs when political actors fail to agree on the electoral process (after the 2002 legislative elections, Guineans had to wait until 2013 before the next ones were organised). These two techniques are more frequent with multi-party systems 'in transition'.

though enjoying constitutional legitimacy. It eventually reaches a point where the vast majority of citizens do not feel 'represented' by political parties, which tend to consider them as 'electoral fodder'.[9]

As is the case nowadays in Western 'democracies', the oligarchic domestication of universal suffrage increasingly manifests itself in West Africa through the absence of a democratic political offer; in other words, a political offer that reflects the concerns of the people and reinforces their political prerogatives. This situation has been described in many different ways: 'choiceless democracies' (Mkandawire 1999), 'low-intensity democracies' (Amin 2004, 2011), or 'pluralist single-party systems' (Issa N'Diaye in this volume). Often in de facto two-party systems, the dominant feeling is that 'all are the same'. As a result, in such circumstances, voting generally takes on a tie-breaking function between two oligarchic options (and that of oligarchic redistribution of power and related privileges) rather than a function allowing the majority to express its preferences. The manipulation of ethnic identity is all the more tempting that the oligarchic competition is tight and uncertain.

Scandals of corruption, suspicious wealth acquisition, political U-turns, unholy alliances, the lack of ethical principles, etc are as many illustrations of the consequences of the 'privatisation' of the public space. This process induced a growing dislike of 'politicking' as well as a search for alternative modes of expression and political participation. This assessment is unanimously shared by authors of this volume:

- Representative democracy can no longer deceive the masses; it has failed to honour its promise of benefitting the people (Lila Chouli).

- [In Cabo Verde], we thus have a democracy of political parties rather than a democracy of citizens (Claudio Furtado).

---

9   It would seem that this phrase ('bétail electoral') was coined by the Malian writer Aminata Traore.

- It is now probably safe to say that the masses have concluded that the political class is of a single breed and that there is no difference between the two dominant electoral machines: The Sierra Leone Peoples Party and the All Peoples Congress (Ibrahim Abdullah).

Economic liberalisation without socio-economic performance

In West Africa, like elsewhere on the continent, the liberalisation of political systems occurred simultaneously with the liberalisation of the economic sphere. While it was vigorously proclaimed that the civic and political rights of all citizens would henceforth be better protected, a methodical elimination of the slightest social advances previously made by workers was carried out, as well as a privatisation of the social and economic functions thus far entrusted to the state. Started at the beginning of the 1980s with structural adjustment programmes, this economic liberalisation ought to be considered as a 'privatisation' process, not in the strict sense of transferring the ownership of public or parastatal assets to the private sector, but rather as a structural reorganisation of the economic system so that it meets first and foremost national and foreign private interests: politicians, local business people, clientelist networks, foreign investors, etc.

Such liberalisation/privatisation consists first of all in removing from the state the instruments that consolidated its sovereignty (Nubukpo 2013). Budgetary and monetary policies, if they ever existed at all, are bound by international financial institution requirements, whose consent is often compulsory for African countries wanting to contract loans on the markets or to receive grant pledges. Secondly, it translates into the gradual withdrawal of the state from the strategic sectors of sovereignty at the basis of the production fabric, such as agriculture, the manufacturing sector, extractive industries, the banking sector, the energy sector and the telecommunication sector. This usually takes several forms, such as the removal of subsidies and trade protection (such as in the agricultural and manufacturing sectors), the sale of state and parastatal assets and the turning to foreign assets. Thirdly, economic liberalisation manifests itself by a reduction of the state's social functions. As employer, and therefore income provider, its role has been streamlined by the need to reduce the weight of the wage bill in the budget - although this is not incompatible with the creation of budget-consuming institutions and prebends to fit the client base. Its role as provider of basic goods, services and infrastructures is also restricted by the need to balance the budget and resort to market mechanisms to provide the elements needed for the survival of popular classes. Finally, such liberalisation affects what we now commonly refer to as 'the business environment regulatory framework'.

This does not consist of merely removing the administrative and regulatory barriers that hamper the fast creation of a business and the diligent resolution of trade disputes. It also entails making taxation simpler and more attractive, especially for foreign investors, introducing more flexibility in the labour market by gradually dismantling the protection granted to workers, and facilitating access to natural resources (land, water, mineral resources, etc) for investors. The liberalisation of the mining sector (with the rewriting of mining codes) and the massive land-grabbing phenomenon, two policies often backed by the World Bank, contribute to this dynamic of 'accumulation through dispossession', a concept used by the geographer David Harvey to refer to the contemporary forms of 'primitive accumulation' (Harvey 2003, 2005).

The transition towards multi-party systems did not fundamentally challenge the subjection of African economies to the interests of international capital. To some extent, this process even contributed to undermining further the 'sovereignty' of states on their economies and on economic policies. For most regimes considered as 'democracies', the reality behind labels and speeches is that sovereignty is but a word, and furthermore, one that has lost any meaning. In Africa, the concept of sovereignty no longer implies effective state control over a given territory and its resources. In the neoliberal era, it has come to mean 'the ability to provide contractual legal authority that can legitimate the extractive work of transnational firms' (Ferguson 2006:207). One of the effects of neoliberalism was therefore to turn African states into 'non-governmental' institutions. Kojo Opoku Aidoo gives a telling example here: a mere phone call from the International Monetary Fund resident representative was enough to repel a law that had previously been passed by the Ghanaian Parliament. The law sought to protect local farmers against foreign competition.

Thirty years of neoliberal policies failed to pull most African economies out of under-development and reliance on public development assistance, which is becoming scarce and is increasingly targeted at 'civil society'. Although the countries with the fastest growing economies in the world over the last few years are to be found on the continent, this has not yet translated into structural economic transformation. Catching up in many cases on the previously 'lost' decades, such economic growth is often driven by extractive industries. It has seldom been driven by the manufacturing sector. To achieve growth, an unprecedented increase in net income transfers to the rest of the world was required. During the last decade, the continent allocated on average five per cent of its GDP to the remuneration of foreign factors of production. In most cases, these income transfers took the form of profit remittances from foreign direct investment. Between 2000 and 2010, the rate of profit generated in Africa by foreign direct investment has almost doubled. Whereas it amounts on average to close to four per cent in developed nations, it can reach more than 100 per cent in some years for some countries of the continent. During this period, the inflows of foreign direct investment received by the continent are similar in value to the profits transferred outside the continent by foreign direct investment (Sylla 2014c).

The private nature of this growth, and therefore its limited social utility, is revealed in its inability to create decent jobs. This jobless growth results in massive unemployment, especially among the youth, and in the growing informal nature of employment and working conditions. Another outcome is the worsening of social inequalities, since employment plays a crucial distributive role in societies where social protection mechanisms are not well developed.

The disconnect between the economic system and priority social needs ('social demand') is all the more difficult to contend with for populations since the liberalisation of political regimes was expected to put an end to it. The so-called 'dividends of democracy', when they exist, fall for the most part into the pockets of the smallest number. For a model of political stability such as Senegal, it even seems that judging by the evolution of the GDP per capita, populations are on average as poor today as they were 50 years ago.

In West Africa, the people struggle because of their discontent with liberalism: they fight against the destructive effects of an economic system that benefits only a minority and put pressure on a 'representative democracy' that does not represent them and does not uphold the principles that it proclaims on a daily basis. 'Build a party that stands for Millions, not for billionaires', displayed a poster during a march by Nigerian motorbike drivers (Bosah 2012). This slogan is one of the most synthetic and expressive formulations of the contemporary demands in the region.

In spite of its ambiguities and limitations, the fight waged by social movements currently seeks to remove this double disconnect: that between the civic and the political, between citizens and the 'representatives'; and that between the economy and society, between what capital wants and what the people aspire to.

Social movements and protest logics

In the literature on this subject, the concept of 'social movement' is defined as collective protest action targeting a given adversary. The three important elements of this definition are the intentional nature of the collective action (the intention to act together in order to achieve a result), the protest dimension (defending a material interest or a cause) and the identification of an adversary (Neveu 2011:9-10).

In the context of this volume, it is interesting to note that the definition used for the concept of social movement is not always the same. A source of divergence relates to the issue of the type of adversary against which social movements are meant to fight. Building on the work of Alain Touraine, Modou Diome, for instance, defines social movements as collective actions targeting the state. Yet, many cases analysed here have targets other than the state, such as economic power, for example. Another source of discrepancy relates, so to speak, to the revolutionary nature of the struggle. Ibrahim Abdullah argues that social movements are yet to emerge in Sierra Leone because from his point of view, social movements are collective actions linked to a radical social transformation agenda. Inversely, Fernando Cardoso and Fodé Mané consider as social movement, regardless of the scale of its ambition, any protest activity emanating from outside of the formal sphere of the state and political parties.[10]

While these conceptual differences are probably linked to the diversity of the intellectual backgrounds of their authors, they also express various presuppositions on the nature of social movements and the roles they should play. At the same time, they reveal a paradox: while we all have a reasonably clear idea of what a social movement is, we nevertheless have tremendous difficulties providing a clear definition of it that is likely to garner unanimity. Should social movements be restricted to protest activities targeting the state or should the range of targets be broadened?[11] Is the revolutionary attitude a relevant feature in the definition of social movements? These are certainly

10   In South Africa, as underlined by Dwyer and Zeilig (2012:273), the term 'social movement' is used to refer to community organisations that are independent from the African National Congress government and its allies, and which tend to express a critical opinion towards their policies and practices.
11   For example, one might wonder whether the 'sex strike' launched at the end of August 2012 by Togolese women as a form of protest against their president is a social movement, in so far as it only exerted direct pressure on their companions (Bonal 2012).

crucial questions that need to be asked. While a strict definitional approach presents the advantage of making it possible to identify empirical criteria that delineate the object under study, it can also have the drawback of lacking analytical flexibility by setting rigid boundaries between related phenomena or by not paying sufficient attention to the evolutionary nature of the phenomena under study; hence the need for a methodological approach with a certain amount of pragmatism.

This is the approach suggested for instance by Francis Akindès, Moussa Fofana and Séverin Yao Kouamé, who refer more to 'mobilisation' than to 'social movements'. The issue they are concerned with is why and how people mobilise in Côte d'Ivoire? In other words, why do social groups decide at one point to protest publicly and how do they go about it? A narrow and too 'westernised' definition of social movements would probably not have allowed for analysing the forms of mobilisation they described, which involved civilians, the military and demobilised ex-combatants. In West Africa, a more contextualised conceptual approach is required in light of the importance of the military[12] and the religious phenomenon when it comes to political and social mobilisation. From a methodological point of view, the authors of this volume combined two types of approaches:

- an 'organisational' approach, in which the concept of social movement refers to the sector of organisations (such as trade unions, civil society organisations, human rights organisations, etc) that are meant to be different from the state structures (government and related services, public administration, etc) and from partisan entities (namely political parties), structures towards which they are supposed to target their actions in a logic of counter-balance;

---

12 West Africa is the leading region on the continent in terms of the occurrence of coups: since 1960, there have been 104 coup attempts, which amounts to half of those on the whole continent. Between 1990 and 2010, in the so-called 'democratic transition' era, 36 military coup attempts took place. Given the recent successful coups in Mauritania, Niger, Mali and Guinea Bissau, some authors have referred to a 'resurgence' of military coups in West Africa (Ben Barka and Ncube 2012).

- an 'event-based' approach in which the concept of social movement refers to collective protest activities observed in a given historical context. Whereas the 'organisational' approach highlights the structured, methodical and functional nature of protest activities by groups that somewhat enjoy institutional recognition, the 'event-based' approach has the advantage of introducing a notion of contingency - of unpredictability, of randomness, of suddenness - which an analysis focused on organisational dynamics would tend to overlook. The 'event-based' approach also side-steps the question of collective protest as the privilege of social groups and organisations that have been defined a priori.

Who protests and why in West Africa? The social movements observed over the last few years cannot be dissociated from the contexts within which they occurred. In a certain way, they take advantage of the breaches and opportunities provided by the existing political, economic and cultural systems at the same time as they react to the absences, excesses and tensions that they generate. Upon reading the chapters of this volume, and on the basis of the types of demand vis-à-vis the liberal-capitalist system, it seems heuristic to distinguish five main protest logics. These are the liberal, republican, partisan, corporatist and proletarian logics (see table1).

In addition to allowing the identification of the principles that structure specific forms of protest, reasoning in terms of protest logic (one could also speak of public presence logic) presents four analytical advantages. First of all, it helps to not consider all protest activities as being outright of the main logic supposed to be followed by organisations and social groups which lead them. For example, organisations of a corporatist type, such as trade unions, can in some circumstances express demands of a proletarian nature. Likewise, struggles previously guided by republican principles can turn into partisan struggles. Secondly, this type of reasoning protects against the temptation of assuming a total overlap between those who are fighting and the main beneficiaries of the outcomes of the struggle. In other words, the various protest logics can be expressed by social groups or organisations that do not expect a priori any material, political or symbolic benefit themselves. Thus one can fight for proletarian causes without being a proletarian, just like one can fight against specific forms of discrimination without being victim of these. Thirdly, this form of reasoning helps to 'resolve' the issue of the 'representivity', or of the 'legitimacy' of social movements, through a recognition of the fact that social movements are not necessarily led by popular classes and are sometimes motivated by corporatist or partisan considerations. Finally, it helps us realise that social movements do not have the same potential in terms of social transformation: some of them may fit within the logic of the liberal-capitalist system, while others are more able to overcome it or subvert it.[13]

Liberal struggles

From a liberal standpoint, protest activities can be justified by the concern of protecting the individual against the 'despotism of the majority'. As Tocqueville wrote: 'In our time, freedom of association has become a necessary guarantee against the tyranny of the majority' (*Democracy in America*, volume 2, Chapter IV). In so far as the electoral system is meant to reflect the preferences of the majority, the representatives of the people may tend to only listen to the concerns of the groups that make up the majority of voters. In so far as they represent a sort of counter-power, civil society organisations can in such cases exert pressure on the government in order for the rights of 'minorities' to be taken into account, in other words groups that are marginalised by the existing political order and/or which are perceived as victims of institutionalised forms of 'discrimination'. Protest that fits within a liberal logic is motivated by the desire to protect the interests of social groups considered as 'minorities'. The nature of public demand generally consists in claiming

---

13 The case of social movements that follow a "partisan" logic is discussed in the section on the civil society.

Table 2: Protest logics

	Nature of the public demand	Mobilisation themes	Type of actors	Interests taken into account
Liberal	Protecting and strengthening the rights of minorities. Equal protection from the law for specific social groups.	Discrimination, rights of women, gays, migrants, the disabled, refugees, etc.	Feminist movements, international and local NGOs specialised in the defence of human rights, etc.	Interests of groups perceived as minority or victims of discrimination.
Republican	Ensuring that existing political regimes (democratic or not) comply with the principles of liberal democracy.	Transparency of public processes and policies. Rule of Law and good governance. Upholding the constitution. Separation of powers. Participatory democracy.	Intellectuals, journalists, 'civil society' actors, citizen movements, etc.	Public interest (of the community of citizens).
Partisan	Conquering power, preserving it or gaining weight within the political game.	Denunciation of injustices, the partisan nature and the incompetence of adversaries, etc.	Political parties, religious organisations, ethnic-based political groups, etc.	Partisan interests (party, ethnic group, religion, community, etc.)
Corporatist	Protecting the material and moral interests of members of the corporation.	Working conditions, protecting social rights, etc.	Trade unions, student organisations, etc.	Interests of the members of the corporation.
Proletarian	Resisting the deterioration of the living conditions of the majority.	Socio-economic inequalities, access to basic social services, high cost of living, economic marginalisation and dispossession, etc.	Ordinary citizens, community-based associations, popular classes, etc.	Interests of society (popular and middle classes, etc.)

equal protection from the law and the consolidation of 'minority' rights. Generally led by international civil society organisations, or by their local relays and partners, liberal struggles are not the dominant form of struggle in West Africa. They nevertheless generate growing interest among governments and the general public. This is evidenced by the fast penetration of the 'rights-based discourse' into the language of ordinary citizens, social movements, the media and public authorities.

In spite of the unifying theme of human rights, the object of major demands tends to vary from one country to the next. In Sierra Leone, liberal struggles are led by organisations that protect the interests of the disabled and by those actively in favour of the rights of LGBTI communities. In Guinea, they are more focused on the issue of torture and that of detainee rights. In Guinea Bissau, among the most active civil society organisations are associations that fight against female genital mutilations and child trafficking. In Nigeria, in the recent period, liberal demands were mostly led by organisations fighting for gender equality, just like the Gender and Constitution Reform Network (GECORN), a network of more than 200 NGOs and community-based organisations that seek to remove any sexist language from the Nigerian constitution as well as to advance women's political rights (Olayode 2014). Liberal demands may sometimes generate counter-movements. In Ghana, this was the case of the protest organised in June 2010 by religious authorities in reaction to demands made by LGBTI communities.

Republican struggles

The logic of republican protest refers to the forms of protest that are aimed to ensure that those vested with public authority comply with a given conception of common good and public morality. In the republican theory, for example in Machiavelli, popular vigilance is what preserves freedom, understood as a condition of non-subjection. As the Nobles (the holders of knowledge, wealth and power) are unable to show virtue and only seek to oppress the people, the latter needs to rumble from time to time in order to make its voice heard and bring the Nobles to order. 'Where the people is not corrupted,' Machiavelli writes, 'tumults and other troubles do no harm' (Discourses, Book 1, chap. 17). Indeed, when the people is not corrupted, it struggles in principle against two things: the servitude the Nobles want to impose on them; and the threat of dissolution of the republic created by the excessive ambition of the Nobles and their rivalries.

As the liberalisation of African political regimes has not yet delivered on promises in terms of improving material living conditions and in terms of 'governance', not surprisingly, many ongoing struggles in most countries in the region focus on republican claims. What is at stake is to ensure that 'liberal democracy' delivers on its promise and complies with principles enshrined in the various constitutions. Since 'liberal democracy' appears presently as the political model that best embodies public good, or at least the default political model, the republican claims are more about deepening it than getting out of this framework. Given also the importance of the 'language of rights' in republican claims, it is not surprising that they maintain some closeness with liberal struggles.

The fight against corruption, for public transparency and accountability is one of the most recurrent themes. In Nigeria, civil society organisations often mobilise against corruption, a practice that leaves out no sphere of society, and primarily targets public bodies. Some activists even advocated the death penalty for those who are suspected of corruption (Baiyewu and Attah 2012). Since June 2012, the 'End Impunity Now' campaign was launched on the initiative of the Anti-Corruption Network, to demand that the federal government takes strong measures against this scourge and in particular that economic crimes be severely punished. Sometimes, the subject of the demands was the resignation of public authorities suspected of corruption. This type of campaign can be seen in Sierra Leone too, where the Budget

Accountancy Network is being mobilised to demand greater transparency in budgetary procedures and better allocation of public resources.

A second major theme is the fight against cases of murder that remain unpunished. This is a structural theme in countries that are politically unstable or affected by violent conflicts. In Guinea Bissau and Guinea, for example, the fight against impunity gathers together the relatives of victims of murders who demand that light be shed on these murders and that justice be rendered. In Burkina Faso, since the assassination in 1998 of the journalist Norbert Zongo, there were regular uprisings of the populations demanding impartial justice in the face of excesses by those in power and abuses by law enforcement officials. In February 2011, for example, the death of a young college student had triggered a spiral of violent protests which, combined with other events, led to a change of government. Under pressure from the street, the Burkina judiciary, contrary to its habits in this kind of case, quickly investigated the case, which led to the trial of the police officers held responsible for his death.

A third type of struggle revolves around challenging the public agenda and the (non)-decisions of the government and its branches. In Guinea Bissau and Ghana, the local populations have often protested against the decision of some municipalities to establish a garbage dump near their area of residence. Kojo Aidoo quotes a traditional leader whose words need not be commented on: 'We are not vultures to be kept on a refuse dump [...] It is therefore surprising that after voting [the government] to power, they are compensating us with waste.' In Burkina Faso, in late June 2013, a national protest gathering together trade unions, opposition parties, most civil society organisations and ordinary citizens was organised in order to challenge the appropriateness and legitimacy of establishing a senate, a measure wanted by Blaise Compaore's regime. One month later, on the very day of the senatorial elections, thousands took to the streets to express their disagreement with the government's political priorities: 'No to the Senate, we want jobs', 'No to 89 vampires in the Senate, we are tired and have no blood left for them', 'Better a lecture hall than a Senate', one could read on their placards.

A fourth type of struggle is about the defence of the constitution. In West Africa, citizens are increasingly less tolerant of the 'Bonapartist' temptation, in other words heads of state who want to remain in power beyond their constitutional mandate. Mamadou Tandja in Niger and Abdoulaye Wade in Senegal have paid the price for this. The former was deposed in a military coup, while the latter, after his candidacy was validated by the Constitutional Council, was finally defeated in the elections. Similarly, in Burkina Faso the enlargement of the 'oppositional public space' is not unrelated to Blaise Compaore's alleged Bonapartist tendencies.

Corporatist struggles

The logic of corporatist struggle refers to the forms of protests aimed at defending the material and moral interests of organised socio-professional groups that usually have significant resources and experience in political mobilisation.

In the recent period, corporatist struggles were the most recurrent type of struggles in West Africa. They were mostly led by student movements, public sector trade-unions, informal sector workers, etc. Despite the unflattering picture suggested by the adjective 'corporatist', there should be no mistaking the meaning of this type of struggle. In the current period, although they often articulate narrow and sector-wide prospects, corporatist struggles are part of society's self-defence, to use the language of Karl Polanyi (1944). Although their leaders may often be co-opted or corrupted by established powers, their struggle increasingly consists in stopping the deployment of neoliberal management principles in their usual spheres of action and claiming a state which assumes its social functions.

Students are generally part of all struggles. They are the protest group par excellence. In the past, they often stood up to the colonial regime and the single-party regimes. In the recent period, in most countries in West Africa, they participated in the major protests, albeit not always in unity (as in the case of Niger). It is however interesting to note that they often mobilised against the deterioration of the education system and the trend toward privatisation. In the paradigmatic case of Burkina Faso, in addition to repression when the regime in place seeks to distract public attention, the students frequently denounce the significant deficiencies in university infrastructure, the deterioration of the student condition and public policies towards universities. Within the student community, a new actor is emerging, raising the issue of the transition from the education sphere to the labour market. These are the young unemployed graduates. Faced with unemployment and limited employment opportunities, they are beginning to organise themselves in order to demand solutions from public authorities. This is the case in particular in Cabo Verde, Senegal and Sierra Leone.

In recent years, corporatist struggles have generally concerned the world of work as a whole. Thus, we can talk about a resurgence. In the face of the rapid dispossession of subaltern workers of the smallest social gains they have acquired in the past, a development facilitated by policies aimed at making the 'business environment' more attractive, and in the face also of the deterioration of social infrastructures, most sectors of activity in most countries are punctuated by strikes and protest movements. In the public sector, strikes are regularly organised by teachers and health agents in almost all the countries in the region. These two social categories, in comparison to others, have great capacity for mobilisation - owing to their important numbers and the congruence of their interests - and negotiation, in particular the major damages incurred by the community in case of prolonged interruption of their services. Their mobilisation also symbolises the failure of states that are no longer able to provide basic social services and properly deal with the staff assigned to these public service missions. In Liberia, as stressed by George Klay Kieh Jr., teachers and health workers grouped around Monrovia Consolidated School System Teachers Association (MCSSTA) and Liberia Health System Workers Association (LIHWA), respectively, have been the two most important social movements of the last few years. Apart from the corporatist struggles, they increasingly play the role of counter-power in the face of the excesses of Ellen Johnson Sirleaf's regime.

The struggles and resistances conducted in the mining sector are often much less visible than those of public sector unions. This is not a surprise, as in Africa, this is the sector of economic life most resistant to any form of publicity, and to any form of collective and democratic concern for the interests of those who are involved in them (workers in particular) and those whom they affect (local communities, local economies, the taxpayer, etc). As an area usually submitted to the law of international capital, which acts like a 'state within the state' in enclaves (often rural territories), many conflicts occur off the radar of trade unions and 'representative democracy' institutions, as emphasised by Alpha Barry in the case of Guinea. Sometimes, when the presence of the state is felt, it is to demonstrate its solidarity with capital: to be the one with the arms and stand apart from the one doing the robbery.[14] The Marikana phenomenon does not exist only in South Africa (Alexander 2013, Alexander et al 2013). In West Africa, the mining sector is the theatre for mini-Marikana, or even quasi-Marikana that occurs in the most silent way. In August 2013, during a protest against the conditions of employment of the Brazilian multinational company Vale, police forces fired on Guinean workers, killing 30 people. In Sierra Leone, as Ibrahim Abdullah reminds us, four workers were assassinated in 2012 following strikes to demand better working conditions. In Burkina Faso, in August 2012, 27 mine workers were dismissed and two others laid off because they wanted the 30-minute legal break provided for in a continuous 10-hour working day to be applied. This case of 'disobedience' to the employer's private regulation

---

14 This metaphor is borrowed from John Holloway. The peculiarity of capitalism as a system of exploitation, according to him, is that the person with the arms stands apart from the person doing the robbery; the latter (the state) merely supervising that the robbery conforms with the law (Holloway 2010a:32).

was handled with support from law enforcement, as reported by Lila Chouli. Job precariousness, denial of union rights, sexual harassment against women, racism, etc are practices against which workers in the mining sector rise up against on a daily basis.

In the transport sector, many protests have been identified, from those by informal sector workers to challenges to pricing policies in the hydrocarbons sector (Niger), repressive policies that target transport motorcycle drivers (Nigeria) and the lack of adequate infrastructure (Guinea-Bissau).

Apart from the economic sector, other types of corporatist struggles are noted which are illustrative of the failure of state structures in West Africa. In 2011, Burkina Faso experienced waves of military mutinies. Blaise Compaore, whose guard itself was in mutiny, nearly lost his throne. In Mali, the 22 March 2012 coup that deposed Amadou Toumani Touré was preceded by many forerunning events such as the 20-21 March mutiny of young soldiers as well as the protests of the wives of soldiers killed by the rebel forces in Northern Mali under the passive or even complicit gaze of the Malian state. In both cases, the mutiny focused on the alleged failures of the state in the management of the public good. In Côte d'Ivoire, the 'ex-combattants mal démobilisés' (ex-combatants whose demobilisation was poorly handled) were one of the most active social movements of the last few years. They regularly took to the street, demanding for the state to keep its promise: facilitate their social and professional reintegration in exchange for the laying down of arms.

Proletarian struggles

The logic of proletarian protest refers to the forms of protests relating to material claims whose satisfaction should benefit the vast majority of the population and not specific sectors or social groups. It is generally about struggles that are expected to generate positive impacts for popular and middle classes and groups perceived as excluded or marginalised by the economic system. The contributions in this volume have pinpointed three types of proletarian struggles that are illustrative of the forms of resistance deployed by the popular classes against the neoliberal practices of accumulation by dispossession and their consequences.

The fight against the high cost of living is the first example of proletarian struggle. The topic of the high cost of living raises the question of financial access of the lower classes to goods and services essential to their survival. As was found in several places in the global South, a wave of protests against the increased cost of living was also noted in many countries in West Africa (Burkina Faso, Côte d'Ivoire, Ghana, Mauritania, Niger, Nigeria, Senegal, and Sierra Leone).

In Burkina Faso, the protests began in 2007-2008. Initially, they were of a spontaneous nature. Subsequently, under the coordination of the General Confederation of Labour of Burkina (CGT-B), the movement was carried out by the Coalition Against the High Cost of Living (CCVC). As in many countries that did not succeed in achieving food sovereignty following trade liberalisation policies, the Burkinabe are import-dependent for most basic products. This dependency makes them vulnerable to the rising prices of imported goods. However, in the late 2000s, owing to financial speculation on agricultural products and the increase in the demand by giants such as China and India, the poorest countries in the world have seen a dramatic increase in their import bill (FAO 2009, UNCTAD 2010). In a country like Burkina Faso, the neoliberal management mode did not make it possible to absorb this shock. On the contrary, Claus-Dieter König stresses, the government has even increased consumption taxes, thus severely hitting the lower classes. Yet, this a priori absurd measure has a logical explanation: given that trade liberalisation tends to dry up customs revenues, the Burkina government had no other alternative but to increase consumption taxes in order to make up for this shortfall.

In Nigeria, in early January 2012, a protest movement, apparently the most important seen over the last 20 years, gathered virtually all social strata and all social movement actors in Nigeria: trade unions, civil society organisations, opposition political parties, ordinary citizens, religious authorities, etc. It stemmed from the federal government's decision to withdraw fuel subsidies. This decision resulted in the doubling of the fuel price which in turn led to an increase in the price of other basic goods and services. This was the last straw. Besides its disastrous impact on the living conditions of the population, this measure was unpopular for three other reasons. First, it was perceived as a betrayal by the federal government which did not comply with agreements previously entered into with trade unions and civil society. Second, it symbolised the corruption and neglect of Nigerian elites. Although Nigeria is an oil producing country, it is a net oil importer, since it is unable to refine the crude oil it produces. The main resource for which Nigerians rightly expected to have positive returns has therefore been a curse: it has served to enrich a minority, much to the dismay of the great majority, not to mention the lack of transparency surrounding the management of the oil 'windfall'. Last, the Nigerians felt that the federal government was simply following the dictates of the Bretton Woods institutions which, as usual, are always pressing for the withdrawal of state subsidies to basic goods and services. All these reasons fuelled the anger of Nigerians, who came out in massive numbers to protest in most capital cities. The impact of this event was amplified by the nation-wide general strikes initiated by major trade unions.

'Occupy Nigeria', the name given to this social movement in reference to the movement of the indignant falls within the global anti-capitalist struggle. It had an international influence through the leverage offered by social networks and support from the Nigerian diaspora. Social networks in particular made it possible to circumvent the media censorship orchestrated by the government and to counter its propaganda aimed at spreading the belief that the removal of the subsidies was a popular measure (Olayode 2014).

The second form of proletarian struggle concerns the provisioning of basic social infrastructure and services. Kojo Aidoo has analysed in this volume the case of the violent protest of June 2013 in Ashaiman. The youth in this shanty town in Tema rose up to denounce the delay noted in the delivery of a road by a private company. Their uprising was a way to express the frustrations accumulated by an extremely poor community feeling marginalised by the Ghanaian state. In Senegal, between September and October 2013, people have talked about the 'thirst and water riots', following three weeks of uninterrupted water cuts suffered by the households of the Dakar region.

Resistance to land grabbing, protection of natural resources and food sovereignty were the third major type of proletarian struggle observed in West Africa. In a context of the resurgence of rural movements (Moyo and Yeros 2005), it is not only the peasants as a social group who are mobilising against the current process of dispossession of their lands. Their struggle concerns rural communities as a whole, since the predatory practices in the land sector tend to affect the socio-ecological equilibrium of the areas in which they occur. It even happens, sometimes (like in Mali and Senegal), that the areas granted are larger than the area of the communities concerned. Not to mention the socio-cultural heritages destroyed, the land-grabbing process tends to generate an eviction dynamic of an economic nature (activities such as agriculture and stock farming are often jeopardised), and a geographic nature (populations are often illegally chased away from their normal place of residence). The forms of resistance against this practice have been not described under the related issue, of food sovereignty in the case of Mali, Senegal and Sierra Leone.

Cross-cutting struggles

Social movements do not always follow a single protest logic. Some have a multidimensional nature. This is the case, for example, of the Haratine movement in Mauritania. Haratines are people of servile origin. They belong to the majority ethnic component called 'Arab-Berber'. Since the late 1970s, they organised themselves to fight against slavery and its consequences. Their claims are of a liberal nature, insofar as they demand equal protection of the law for the Haratines and an end to the 'discrimination' against them as an identity group in all spheres of society. They are also of a republican nature, since the Haratines are not only fighting against their political exclusion. They also mobilise for the eradication of slavery in Mauritania, and for slavery cases to be brought to justice and punished. Zekeria Ahmed Salem stresses that it was in 2011 that the Mauritanian justice system, for the first time, condemned someone for slavery-like practices, despite the prevalence of the phenomenon.[15] This was an important victory for the anti-slavery organisations. Despite the identity aspect of their movement, the Haratines' struggles also have a proletarian dimension. From a demographic point of view, the Haratines reportedly make up nearly half the Mauritanian population. Better still, they are the most important section of the lower classes. They are those who perform strenuous and unskilled labour. It is the social group most vulnerable to poverty.

According to Zekeria Ahmed Salem, it is this 'proletarian' character that enabled the Haratine movement to reap the benefits of what has been improperly termed the 'Mauritanian Spring'. By denouncing the high cost of living and the poor working conditions that affect the lower classes, the movement could benefit from sympathy from the latter and from some resonance in the media. In 2012, a national agency to combat the consequences of slavery and fight poverty, a more than 40-year old claim, was thus born.

Another example of cross-cutting struggles is provided by the large-scale protests that occurred in Nigeria in 2013 against a constitutional reform project legalising underage marriage without explicitly stating it (Olayode 2014). The 'republican' character given to the claims has allowed massive

---

15   This issue affects other countries in the region, like Niger and Mali (see Abdelkader 2004 and Keita 2012).

mobilisation around a struggle that is fundamentally liberal. Thus, the organisations specialising in liberal claims could benefit from the support of ordinary citizens and public opinion in general.

Political systems and the transformative potential of struggles

In West Africa, the last three years have been rich with protest movements, even though the latter did not have the politico-media scale of the 'Arab Spring'. In many capitals in West Africa, places symbolising the resistance and the challenge of the existing socio-political order appeared (the so-called Place des 'Blocs' in Nouakchott, the Place de l'Obélisque in Dakar). Similarly, dates were recorded in the annals of popular protests. Sometimes, they serve as identity cards to some movements (the June 23rd Movement - Mouvement du 23 Juin - in Dakar, the February 25th Movement - Mouvement du 25 Février - in Nouakchott, the January Protests in Nigeria). In other circumstances, what is being claimed serves as an identity card to the movement (in Burkina Faso, this is the case of the Coalition Against the High Cost of Living and the Movement Against the Revision of article 37, called M37). In terms of results, the social movements have sometimes secured significant concessions from public authorities (introduction of matters of public interest in public debate, maintaining free healthcare programmes for children and breastfeeding women, removal of some harsh anti-poor taxes, reduction in the price of basic goods, compensation for peasant communities wounded by investments, resignation of officials, etc). Better still, social movements have sometimes succeeded in 'setting a precedent'. Some protests, though symbolic and ad-hoc, are warnings sent out to the authorities: there are decisions and practices that will no longer be tolerated. One can think in particular of the protests against the unilateral increases in the prices of basic foodstuffs, and the preventive protests against certain attempts at constitutional manipulation.

Although we can talk about a resurgence of social movements in West Africa, the dynamism differed across countries, and for a given country things may have been different from one year to another. This is to say that certain contexts and certain types of claims are more able to generate a sustained mobilisation.

The influence of the political context over the dynamic of social movements and the nature of their claims is perfectly illustrated by the case of Côte d'Ivoire, analysed by Akindès, Fofana and Kouamé. In the early 1990s, the adoption of a multiparty regime had freed up a space for mobilisation that was quickly conquered by a partisan logic which put up with violence and military interference. Since then, the weight of the partisan logic was such that it has made impossible the emergence of an autonomous national social movement. Civil society organisations had to make their choice according to the partisan menu presented to them. In these conditions, the mobilisations mainly concerned topics of partisan politics: national identity on the one hand, political legitimacy on the other hand. Other types of claims, whatever their legitimacy, which may have been over the deteriorating socio-economic conditions of households, for example, had no say. This is the case, for example, of the protests against the high cost of living. In Côte d'Ivoire, unlike in other countries of the region, there was not much success in terms of mobilisation and media coverage. Although the Ivorian housewives chanted 'Gbagbo, we are hungry, Soro, we are hungry' and demanded an autonomous public space vis-à-vis partisan quarrels, they could not be heard. Their claim was rapidly dealt with first by repression and afterwards with price cuts. In this hyper-partisan context, any protests were interpreted as an agitation orchestrated by one of the two parties. So, not surprisingly, one of the rare social movements that managed to carve out a place in the public space stemmed from the partisan struggle itself: the ex-combatants who were not properly demobilised.

Regardless of the influence of the political context, it must be stressed that the potential in terms of mobilisation and destabilisation of the regimes in place varies according to the type of claims. Because they are supposed to raise questions of public interest, the proletarian struggles (for example, Occupy Nigeria) and the fights against the Bonapartist procedures (for example, the fight against a new term for Compaore in Burkina Faso) have been the most sustained struggles, the ones that most attracted public attention in West Africa over the last few years. Corporatist struggles and liberal struggles can mobilise massively, and become events only when they take 'republican' and/or 'proletarian' forms. As regards the proletarian struggles, they are also scaled up by the involvement of corporatist organisations like trade unions, which have significant assets when it comes to mobilising their members and putting pressure on public authorities.

While we may talk about the resurgence of social movements in West Africa, it should be emphasised that contemporary social movements do not yet articulate a radical social transformation agenda. This is where they differ, for instance, with those of the colonial period. Social movements are mostly caught between sector-wide claims (liberal, corporatist) and ad-hoc claims. If, as indicated by many authors in this volume, social movement claims are increasingly about socioeconomic issues, they do not fall within a more global project aimed at addressing, and going beyond the root causes of the disconnects created by the existing politico-economic order. In the case of 'post-conflict' countries in particular, the 'revolutionary' feeling seems to have been weakened by the fresh memory of a painful past. In these circumstances, the priority is to return quickly to 'constitutional normality'.

While social movements are not necessarily popular movements, they do not have the same potential either, in terms of social transformation. The struggles to guarantee the rights of the 'minorities' (women, LGBTI, persons with disabilities, etc) and the struggles for better 'governance' (respect of the constitution, fight against corruption, etc), while important, do not fundamentally allow changing the existing system, a system whose logic they are deepening. In these two types of cases, what is at stake is less the nature of existing constitutional arrangements than their limited performance; it is less the assumptions of 'liberal democracy' than the fact that it has not kept its promise. Similarly, corporatist struggles, whether by trade unions, students, teachers, health workers, etc, will not be able to provide an alternative project as long as they remain narrow and confined within a sector-wide perspective. Finally, even if proletarian struggles have great potential in terms of social transformation and have often led to significant short-term gains, they will have limited effects as long as they are not articulated with a long-term social transformation project.

As can be noted in reading the chapters in this volume, social movements in West Africa are in a paradoxical situation: they must daily resist the damages of economic liberalism while at the same time put pressure on a weakened, 'nongovernmental' state - whose role is increasingly reduced to 'improving the business climate' - for it to put into effect the promise of political liberalism (that of guaranteeing permanently the rights of each individual). Unfortunately, the disconnects induced by the liberal-capitalist system tend to be reproduced in the structuring of social movements. In other words, social movements fighting to democratise existing political regimes tend to ignore the economic aspect of the problem, whereas those that resist the many forms of socio-economic dispossessions induced by the neoliberal model of accumulation tend to seek solutions that leave untouched - or do not question - the existing political systems.

The lack of a popular-based counter-project that articulates the economic and political dimensions explains the lack of radicalism of social movements as well as the uncertain and precarious nature of the democratic 'gains' for which they continue to fight. It condemns them more or less to one-time gains and to institutional advances that do not fundamentally transform the existing politico-economic order.

The cases of Senegal and Burkina Faso provide an illustration of the limits of social movements when they have no credible alternative, an alternative that can really challenge the existing order. In the first case, the massive mobilisation to oust Wade in 2012 was basically aimed at seeking the lesser of two evils. Wade was replaced by one of the former strongmen of his regime who became one of his main opponents. During the presidential election, Macky Sall the 'liberal' received support from the entire nation's 'living forces' and the political parties considered as leftists. In Burkina Faso, in the present context of the fight to prevent Blaise Compaore from having his brother succeed him or from seeking a third term in office, which is not allowed by the Burkinabe constitution, the same scenario is apparently unfolding, it is apparently the same scenario is unfolding. Zéphirin Diabré, the new leader of the Burkinabe opposition, is presently best placed candidate to succeed Blaise Compaore during the presidential elections planned in 2015. This former Mister Africa of AREVA was until recently a close collaborator of Compaore. Stating loud and clear his neoliberal convictions, he banks on the 'Macky Sall formula'. This concept made in Burkina Faso, refers to popular mobilisation in view of the 'alternation', that is to say, the rotation of political power within the neoliberal oligarchy. In the absence of a counter-project, this seems to be the final political outcome of social movement efforts.

Civil society's ambiguities

It is usually difficult to talk about social movements without talking about civil society. Among other reasons, this is because civil society is conceived as the natural habitat of social movements. This volume provides lessons that urge for a more critical look at the concept of civil society and the role it plays as an institutional reality in African political systems. On this point, some historical reminders will allow things to be put into perspective, and point to the limits of the current ahistorical and atheoretical approaches in examining the relationship between civil society and the state.

The distinction between civil society and state stems from liberal thinking. It is the very foundation of liberalism. With the concepts of 'representation' and 'human rights', it completes the intellectual structure of liberalism (Manent 1996). This distinction was unknown to ancient Greeks. In Aristotle for example, the citizen is a member of political society. As such, he/she takes an active part in the city's government: he/she can be a judge in the courts or a member of the people's assembly. 'He is a citizen in the highest sense who shares in the honors of the state' (Politics, Book III, 5.9). He who is excluded from the honours of the state, continues Aristotle, is no better than an alien.

After Hegel, Karl Marx too had well seen that the separation between civil and politic, between citizen and man, was a novelty introduced by bourgeois society. Under the feudal regime, political society overlapped with civil society. The operating scission did not oppose the 'civilian' to the 'political'. According to Marx, it rather opposed the 'socio-political' to the 'religious'; that is to say the subject to the believer, the temporal to the spiritual. While feudal society was organised by the religious vision of the world, bourgeois society was organised by what Engels calls the 'legal vision of the world'. While religion regulated social relationships in the feudal system, in the case of the bourgeois society, this is the role of the 'right', an impersonal legal mechanism of coordination of the movement of the different individuals or associations of individuals. In the Marxist sense therefore, 'right' only exists in the bourgeois society because it is the product of the scission between the civilian and the political. Equality in the bourgeois society is essentially of civilian nature (equality of all before the law). It is not of political nature (equal right to political participation).

Thus, for Marx, the man referred to in 'human rights' hides the member of the bourgeois civil society. This is why, in opposition to an erroneous interpretation of his thinking, it should be specified that 'what Marx reproaches Human rights is not that they are *formal* rights, it is that they are *rights*' (Binoche and Cléro 2007:217). From his point of view, the distinction between civil society and the state had to be transcended, in the same way as the bourgeois society was able to transcend the division between the political and the religious. In Marx's thinking, 'it is not about overcoming the tensions of civil society in the state as much as it is about subordinating the state to civil society, it is about [...] achieving political universality in civil society' (Binoche and Cléro 2007:210).

Regarding Africa, and using the words of Marx, we can say that there was a shift from a Hegelian phase (in which the issue was to overcome the tensions of civil society via the state), to a neoliberal phase (in which the issue is to subordinate the state to civil society). After independence until the late 1980s, the dominant approach was that the state should focus on bringing order to civil society, at the time characterised as archaic, traditional and the enemy of progress. It was an obstacle to overcome on the clear way ahead to 'modernisation'. To tackle the issue of national construction, the state had to urbanise, educate, secularise and de-ethnicise civil society. In this regard, the strengthening of civil society's political participation could be seen as an obstacle to the advent of democracy, since democracy was conceived as a product of economic development. This is what has been termed the 'Lipset Hypothesis', named after the American political scientist who had put forward this hypothesis in a landmark article (Lipset 1959). The state should have every latitude to create the bourgeois society and the type of individual that goes with it. This was the recommendation of the political 'science' of that time: 'political participation [of citizens] must be held down, at least temporarily, in order to promote economic development', wrote Samuel Huntington, the famous author of *The Clash of Civilisations* (Huntington and Nelson 1976, quoted by Przeworski and Limongi 1997).

As from the 1990s, after witnessing the role played by 'civil society' in the liquidation of the last vestiges of communism in Eastern Europe,[16] the

16 The political role played by civil society in the collapse of communism has often been celebrated and raised to the level of paradigm. However, the imperialist ramifications that have made possible such an outcome are rarely put to the fore. Countries in Eastern Europe, through the 'coloured revolutions' they experienced, have given the American strategists an opportunity to test in practice their theories on 'civil disobedience' and the regime changes made by

polarities have started to be reversed. As emphasised by James Ferguson (2006), the modernising properties have since then been allocated to civil society, while the state was depicted as an oppressive and sprawling structure that destroys the latter's potential. Described now as a counter-power and an indispensible pillar of democracy, civil society became a conceptual category that made it possible to account for the varied fortunes of the different political regimes across the world. Political regimes that are unstable, non-democratic, corrupt and find it difficult to come out of underdevelopment are those that do not have a 'vibrant' civil society, and vice-versa. This was the new axiom of the political 'science' that was deployed by 'Africanist' studies with ethnocentric hints that were severely criticised (Mamdani 1995, Comaroff and Comaroff 2000, McSween 2010).

In this process of political and theoretical rehabilitation of civil society, a new development occurred, the importance of which seems to have gone unnoticed by many. It is the emergence of the concept of 'governance'. A French term that appeared in the 13th Century, 'governance' was initially synonymous with 'government'. After being left in oblivion for centuries, it was reintroduced in contemporary political vocabulary as a managerial concept by Margaret Thatcher and her advisors in the early 1980s (Deneault 2013). In this context where the weight of the state had to be reduced in all spheres of life, the notion of 'governance' appeared to illustrate the fact that government activity per se was no longer the monopoly of the government, and that states had now to be managed like private businesses. Despite its analytical limits as a political concept, the term 'governance' has had the merit of showing in the era of neoliberalism that governments no longer govern in the traditional sense of the term. NGOs, civil society, donors, supranational political institutions, etc have each become 'governance' actors. Similarly, every sphere of life is now conceived as having its own 'governance'. That's

civilians. What the Central Intelligence Agency previously did secretly could now be 'outsourced' to 'civil society' organisations that had logistical support and were equipped with a new sort of Bible: the rhetoric of 'democracy' and 'human rights' (Engdahl 2011).

how we talk about corporate governance but also the governance of water, the mining sector, health, agricultural value chains, etc.

In the case of Africa, the concept of governance has a specific analytical function: it makes it possible to explain the failure of neoliberal policies and at the same time justify their desirability. Faced with the overwhelming failure of structural adjustment policies, the justification was to point to the inadequate attention paid to the weaknesses in the 'institutional framework' (for example, the administrations have refused to execute to the letter the SAPs, corruption has reduced the effectiveness of official development aid, etc). In the political area, the concept of 'governance' was also used to explain phenomena such as corruption and the socioeconomic inequalities that persist in countries that formally became 'democracies'. In this type of case, the 'governance' concept has offered an interesting subterfuge: 'democracy' alone is not enough; it must be completed by 'good governance'. Hence the emergence of strange formulas such as 'democracy and good governance'. The 'and' implies that it is possible in principle that some 'democracies' perform bad 'governance'. But, one might ask, as 'good governance' is not an intrinsic property of 'democracy', what prevents, for example, the use of an expression like 'authoritarianism and good governance', knowing that many so-called authoritarian regimes have better 'governance' indicators than many so-called democratic regimes? It is against this backdrop of conceptual confusions and ad hoc theorisation that the relationship between civil society and the state is usually addressed.

In the literature on Africa, the concept of 'civil society' refers to a space with no clearly defined boundaries, occupied by organisations that are between the state and the private space (the family in particular) (Brandes and Engels 2011). In these conditions, defining empirically the boundaries of civil society is undoubtedly a challenge. Ultimately, all we can say is that there are organisations that now claim to belong to 'civil society', although they differ from one another in many ways (from the point of view of their legal nature, their target goals, the funding mechanisms, the claimed ideologies, the geographical coverage of the activities carried out, etc). In Guinea for example, trade unions do not conceive of themselves as civil society organisations and, what is more, they prefer to keep their distance.

In West Africa, organisations that claim to belong to civil society, the 'official' civil society, are more specialised in liberal and republican causes. 'Human rights' and 'good governance' are generally their privileged field of action. They play an important part when it comes to documenting and giving visibility to human rights violations and to the many abuses of authorities. They are often those who disclose - through their publications, the media, social networks, etc - information that the political power and the economic power in particular tend to hide from citizens and the press. Similarly, it is often through their actions that certain topics of public interest are introduced in the public debate and that the authorities are presented with the demands of citizens. In times of tension, such as electoral periods, they try to spread a discourse of appeasement, to ensure the regularity of elections, and to encourage citizen mobilisation. Alongside the postures that tend to strengthen the republican principles, civil society organisations may also show less glorious features that tend to undermine the basis of genuine democratic politics.

Organisations that claim to belong to civil society are not always autonomous vis-à-vis the partisan logics in each society. This lack of autonomy takes many forms. First, the fact is that civil society is not a self-constitutive space. As much as the influence of international NGOs on the 'emergence' of civil society in Africa has been regularly stressed, the share of the regimes in place in the 'production' of civil society is often overlooked. In regimes with low popularity or legitimacy, it is often tempting to increase the size of the existing civil society by creating new organisations or 'citizen movements' aimed at defending the regime in place in arenas where the latter is not supposed to be active. In Mauritania, faced with youth movements challenging his power, Ould Abdel Aziz had to create counter-movements of youth, which contributed to the fragmentation of the protest movement. In Nigeria, faced with the unforeseen scale of the January 2012 Occupy Movement, the regime of Goodluck Jonathan succeeded in finding counter-movements which proclaimed loud and clear their happiness to see the price of oil double. In Côte d'Ivoire, at the height of the crisis, the area controlled by the rebels had 'its' civil society, which was organised through the Cabinet Civil, a sort of 'participatory democracy' body.

Second, instead of making public interest prevail, civil society organisations can at times encourage the expression of partisan claims of a religious, ethnic, regionalist, etc nature. In Cabo Verde, the Movement for Regionalisation is one of the rare social movements to have left its mark on the public debate. And yet, its project currently consists in demanding that the island of São Vicente recovers the prestige and centrality it has lost. Starting from the conclusion that the independence of Cabo Verde was 'bad news' for São Vincente, it articulates regionalist claims which, although imprecise, are potentially dangerous for the national unity of the archipelago. In Guinea, there is a similar logic with the 'regional coordination units'. They are associations based on ethnic and geographic ties that appeared between 1944 and 1956. After being stifled under the single party regime, they reappeared with the country's political liberalisation. Now, they mean to be heard and get their share of the pie. At times, they have threatened not to recognise the results of the vote, should they not be favourable to their preferred candidate. According to Alpha Barry, this 'community-based civil society', an expression he uses in a deliberately provoking manner, is a major obstacle to a genuine democratisation of the Guinean political regime:

> The most significant impact of the regional coordination units on political life is the fact that no reform is possible in Guinea. Indeed, all the reforms contemplated are hampered by all those who can rely on their coordination units to maintain the status

quo. The state is losing its substance and citizens are turning to their community.

Third, as a space of distribution and conversion of natural and symbolic resources, civil society nurtures opportunistic behaviours that are not necessarily inconsistent with its supposed role of counter-power. Some actors 'enter' civil society either to make up some material or symbolic deficits, or to leverage resources they would not be able to secure elsewhere. As shown by Souley Adji, Modou Diome, Claudio Furtado and Alpha Barry, this type of opportunistic behaviour concerns a range of profiles from idle retirees to artists lacking fame, politicians seeking to clean up their image, employers in conflict with the state, academics seeking prebends, etc. In Cabo Verde, as noted by Claudio Furtado, most so-called independent candidacies either come from mainstream political parties, or are supported by one of them: 'Many of the citizen movements which ran in the municipal elections were not actual offshoots of organised civil society; they were rather citizens who had not found a space in their respective political parties, or were a political ploy by parties who had lost all clout amongst their constituents.' In Niger, as Souley Adji explains, in the context of the struggle against 'neo-Bonapartism', many trade unionists and academics have found it profitable to be involved with civil society. Through their struggle for 'democracy', they were able to win some symbolic 'capital' which earned them 'lucrative' positions in government and public institutions. Souley Adji ironically talks about the 'Palace University', to emphasise the significant numbers of teachers of the University of Niamey who have been appointed as advisors to the president of the republic. Similarly, in Senegal, the leading figures of the struggle against a third term for Wade were co-opted by his successor, Macky Sall.

As the peoples are not always fooled, these opportunistic behaviours often contribute to undermining the credibility and legitimacy of organisations that claim to belong to civil society. As soon as they note that a civil society member has received his 'reward', his words barely count in their eyes.

Any public declaration he makes is then interpreted as being motivated by partisan, even personal considerations. When a great majority has been co-opted, civil society in their eyes no longer differs from political society. This loss of credibility can be seen in the context of transition governments in which civil society has received its quota of government positions (the case of Guinea and Niger) and in the context of regimes that won the elections through a large coalition of social forces including civil society (the case of Senegal).

In addition to the difficulties encountered by 'official' civil society organisations to become autonomous vis-à-vis the partisan logics and to resist opportunistic strategies, there is another more worrying issue, namely their tendency to be disconnected from the proletarian agenda. In Senegal, in early 2012, during the pre-election protests for the removal of Wade's candidacy, one could see through the slogans two perspectives confronting each other. On the one hand, there were the protesters, most of whom were close to 'official' civil society organisations. Their placards read: 'Touche pas à ma Constitution' (Don't touch my Constitution). On the other hand, there were workers in the informal sector in Dakar, in particular street vendors. Their placards read 'Touche pas à ma table' (Don't touch my table). The lack of solidarity of informal workers was due to the fact that the protesters had a tendency to destroy their work tools and, therefore, what constituted their 'property'. Besides, the material gains from defending the Senegalese constitution were all the less obvious to perceive than the constitution, which had been amended more than ten times since 2000 by the regime in place. Because of their perception that the law is rarely on their side, the 'bourgeois' themes, or themes with no direct link with their daily material existence, may not mobilise them. This kind of corporatist spirit can also be strengthened by the perception that the protests in which their involvement is sought are oligarchic struggles that have little to do with the interest of the many.

Last, it may happen that the problem is no longer the lack of autonomy of civil society organisations, but rather their 'excess' of autonomy. Sometimes, 'official' civil society has felt so strong and so sure of its legitimacy that it may have thought that it was a state within the state, meaning that it had a tendency to step outside of its role of counter-power and turn into some sort of government body. This is, for example, the scenario that was noted in Senegal just before the 2012 presidential poll. Faced with the growing popularity of Wade, the mainstream civil society organisations thought that the people they allegedly represented had given them a particular mission. Some even claimed that the Senegalese people were not ready to go to the polls and that the presidential election should be postponed, to give Wade time to finalise some projects that were dear to his heart. Yet, the presidential election was held in peace and without major problems. In the analysis of Modou Diome, this was the response of the silent majority to those who pretended to represent its interests.

In sum, contrary to the rosy picture of 'civil society' serving as a counter-power to an authoritarian and oppressive state, many contributions in this volume have shown that the so-called 'civil society' organisations are not always working for the strengthening of democracy and national unity. More often than not, 'civil society' is an arena in which the partisan struggles are displaced. When 'civil society' actors are not co-opted by the regimes in place, they can at times be used to provide a voice to regionalist, ethnic or religious claims. Not to mention that their agenda, although legitimate, is not always coherent with the priorities and daily struggles of the lower classes. In other words, the 'official' and mediatised civil society, the one that is recognised by the powers that be and by the 'international community', is not always a 'proletarian' civil society. Yet, this is apparently the challenge: to work to the establishment of a 'proletarian public space' (Negt 2007).

Future research avenues

The various contributions in this volume have tried to lay some groundwork by outlining the map of the mainstream social movements observed over the last few years in 12 countries in West Africa. They stressed on the one hand the relationship between the crisis of political 'representation' and the resurgence of social movements, and on the other hand, the latter's potential for social transformation. In the presentation below, the contributions were grouped according to the analytical importance given to the following three themes: social movements in the face of liberalism; social movements and the challenge of autonomy', and the ambiguities of civil society.

Based on this surveying exercise, some future research avenues can be identified. A first research theme focuses on the relationship between the media and social movements. The media are particularly influential in the making of an event, through the amplifying or atrophic effect they may have. In this vein, it could be interesting to study the ins and outs of the editorial strategies of the media in times of mass protests. In Nigeria, during the protests against the removal of the oil subsidies, most media aligned themselves with the federal government's propaganda. Contrariwise, in Senegal, during the pre-election mobilisations to oust Wade, the media were mostly on the side of the protesters and the opposition.

A second research theme concerns the role of transnational solidarity networks in the formation and dynamics of social movements. Beyond their material and financial support, transnational solidarity networks make it possible to massify the struggles and shift them to levels where they are more likely to achieve the desired results. The pressure they can put to bear on states, the 'international community' and public opinion in general is often important. However, there is a downside: it is the 'commodification of resistance' (Dwyer and Zeilig 2012). This was an issue briefly addressed by Claus-Dieter König: does the struggle for social transformation tend to be perverted by the support that activist organisations receive from their foreign donors?

The contributions in this volume have mainly dealt with social movements in a national perspective. It would be interesting to see whether social movements with a regional dimension are beginning to emerge. Ibrahim Abdullah, Claus-Dieter König and George Kieh have given some indications on the opportunities for alliances between social movements at the national and regional levels. It would also be interesting to see why some themes with a regional dimension have not led to sustained mobilisation. We can think, for example, of the issue of the CFA franc - a currency most African economists consider as a colonial relic - and to the Economic Partnership Agreements which are being negotiated with the European Union.

The study of the 'cracks', in the words of John Holloway (2010b), is another promising research theme. This term refers to alternative practices and models ordinary people experiment with in order to resist the capitalist order, but also to go beyond. These 'cracks' map the horizon of a possible world that is of greater quality than the capitalist-liberal civilisation.

Finally, it would be important to reflect upon how the specificities of the African context can make it possible to renew the important theoretical corpus which already exists in the analysis of social movements.

References

Abdelkader, G.K. (2004) *L'esclavage au Niger. Aspects historiques, juridiques, dénombrements statistiques*, Londres et Niamey, Anti-Slavery International & Association Timidria

Alexander, P. (2013) 'Marikana Massacre: A Turning Point in South African History?' *CODESRIA Bulletin* 1&2, 36-40

Alexander, P., Legkowa, T., Mmope B., Sinwell, L., Xezwi, B. (2013) *Marikana. Voices from South Africa's mining Massacre*, Athens, Ohio University Press

Amin, S. (2004) *The Liberal Virus: Permanent War and the Americanization of the World*, New York, Monthly Review Press

Amin, S. (2010) *The law of worldwide value*, second edition, New York, Monthly Review Press

Amin, S. (2011) 'The democratic fraud and the universalist alternative', *Monthly Review Press*, 63(5), https://monthlyreview.org/2011/10/01/the-democratic-fraud-and-the-universalist-alternative, accessed March 2014

Aristotle, *Politics*, http://classics.mit.edu/Aristotle/politics.3.three.html, accessed March 2014

Bayart, J.-F., Mbembe, A., Toulabor, C. (1992) *Le politique par le bas en Afrique noire. Contributions à une problématique de la démocratie*, Paris, Karthala

Baiyewu L., Attah, D. (2012) 'Capital punishment for corruption good because the elites fear death – Arewa Constitutional Forum', *Punch*, 2 December

Ben Barka, H., Ncube, M. (2012) 'Political Fragility in Africa: Are military coups d'État a never-ending phenomenon?', EconomicBrief, AfricanDevelopmentBank, September, http://www.afdb.org, accessed March 2014

Binoche, B., Cléro, J.-P. (2007) *Bentham contre les droits de l'homme*, Paris, Presses Universitaires de France

Bonal, C. (2012) Au Togo, une grève de sexe très politique, *Libération*, 28 August; http://www.liberation.fr/monde/2012/08/28/au-togo-une-greve-du-sexe-tres-politique_842391, accessed March 2014

Bosah, C. (2012) 'Okada riders protest ban and victimization', 11 December, http://www.socialistnigeria.org/print.php?text=2084, accessed March 2014

Brandes, N., Engels, B. (2011) 'Social Movements in Africa', *Vienna Journal of African Studies*, 20(11):1-15

Canfora, L. (2006) Democracy in Europe: *A History of an ideology*, New York, Wiley-Blackwell

Comaroff J. L., Comaroff, J. (2000) (eds) *Civil Society and the Political Imagination in Africa: Critical perspectives*, Chicago, University of Chicago Press

Dembélé, D.M. (2011) *Samir Amin. Intellectuel organique au service de l'émancipation du Sud*, Dakar, CODESRIA

Deneault, A. (2013) *Gouvernance. Le management totalitaire*, Québec, Lux éditeur

Dunn, J. (2010) *Setting the people free. The story of democracy*, London, Atlantic Books

Diouf, M. (1997) 'Mouvements sociaux et démocratie, perspectives africaines', in GEMDEV (dir) *Les avatars de l'État en Afrique*, Paris, Karthala

Dupuis-Déri, F. (2013) *Démocratie. Histoire politique d'un mot aux États-Unis et en France*, Québec, Lux éditeur

Dwyer, P., Zeilig L. (2012) *African Struggles Today. Social Movements since Independence*, Illinois, Haymarket Books

Economist Intelligence Unit (2011) *Democracy Index 2011: Democracy under Stress*, http://www.eiu.com, accessed March 2014

Ellis, S., van Kessel, I. (2009) *Movers and Shakers. Social Movements in Africa*, Koninklijke Brill NV, Leiden, The Netherlands

Ellul, J. (1972) *The Political illusion*, UK, Vintage Books

Engdahl, F. W. (2011) *Full Spectrum Dominance. Totalitarian Democracy in the New World Order*, third edition, California, Progressive Publishers

FAO (2009) *The State of Agricultural Commodity Markets 2009: High food prices and the Food crises - Experiences and Lessons learned*, Rome, FAO

Faye, M. (2014) 'Private media and social change in Africa: achievements, limitations and prospects', in N.S. Sylla (ed), *Rethinking Development*, Dakar, Rosa Luxemburg Foundation, 155-166

Ferguson, J. (2006) *Global Shadows. Africa in the neoliberal world order*, Durham and London, Duke University Press

Fillieule, O., Mathieu, L., Péchu, C. (2009) (eds), *Dictionnaire des mouvements sociaux*, Paris, Presses de Sciences Po.

Fillieule, O., Agrikoliansky E., Sommier, I. (2010) (eds) *Penser les mouvements sociaux*, Paris, la Découverte

Fini, M. (2013) *La démocratie et ses sujets*, translated from Italian, Paris, Le retour aux sources

Gills, B. (2001) (ed) *Globalization and the Politics of Resistance*, New York, Palgrave

Goodwin, J., Jasper, J. M. (2009) *The Social Movements Reader. Cases and Concepts*, second edition, Massachusetts, Oxford, Wiley-Blackwell

Harvey, D. (2003) *The New Imperialism*, new print, Oxford University Press, United Kingdom, 2013

Harvey, D. (2005) *A brief history of Neoliberalism*, New York, Oxford, University Press

Harrison, G. (2002) *Issues in the contemporary politics of Sub-Saharan Africa: the dynamics of Struggle and Resistance*, Palgrave School, UK

Holloway, J. (2010a) *Change the world without taking power. The meaning of revolution today*, new edition, London, Pluto Press

Holloway, J. (2010b) *Crack capitalism*, London, Pluto Press

Huntington, S. P. (2007) *The Clash of Civilizations and the Remaking of World Order*, reprint, New York, Simon and Schuster

Huntington, S.P. and Nelson, J. M. (1976) *No Easy Choice: Political Participation in Developing Countries*, Cambridge, Harvard University Press

Keita, N. (2012) (dir) *L'esclavage au Mali*, Paris, L'Harmattan

Larmer, M. (2010) 'Social movement struggles in Africa', *Review of African Political Economy*, 37(125):251-262

Lipset, S. M. (1959) 'Some Social Requisites of Democracy: Economic Development and Political Legitimacy', *American Political Science Review 53*

Losurdo, D. (2014) *Liberalism: A Counter-History*, translated from Italian, London and New York, Verso

Machiavelli, N. (1531) *Discourses on the first ten books of Titus Livius*, http://www.constitution.org/mac/disclivy_.htm, accessed March 2014

Mamdani, M., Wamba-dia-Wamba, (eds). (1995) (eds) *African Studies in Social Movements and Democracy*, Dakar, Codesria

Mamdani, M. (1995) 'A critique of the State and Civil Society Paradigm in Africanist Studies', in M. Mamdani and E. Wamba-dia-Wamba(eds) *African Studies in Social Movements and Democracy*, Dakar, Codesria

Manent, P. (1996) *An Intellectual History of Liberalism*, Princeton, Princeton University Press

Manent, P. (2009) « Grandeur et misère du libéralisme », Conference at the French institute, in Prague, 2 March ; http://www.philolog. fr/grandeur-et-misere-du-liberalisme-pierre-manent/ (accessed March 2014).

Manin, B. (2002) *The Principles of Representative Government*, Cambridge, Cambridge University Press

Manji, F., Ekine, S. (2011) (eds) *African Awakening. The Emerging Revolutions*, Cape Town, Dakar, Nairobi and Oxford, Pambazuka Press

McSween, N. (2010) *Repenser l'analyse des mouvements sociaux africains*, Québec, l'Alliance de recherche université-communauté/Innovation sociale et développement des communautés (ARUC/ISDC), Chaire de recherche en développement des collectivités (CRDC), Série: Recherches, no.32

Michéa, J.-C. (2009) *Realm of Lesser Evil*, Cambridge, Malden, Polity

Mills, C.W. (1997) *The Racial Contract*, Ithaca and London, Cornell University Press

Mkandawire, T. (1999) 'Crisis management and the making of "choiceless democracies" in Africa', in R. Joseph (ed) *The State, Conflict and Democracy in Africa*, Boulder, Colorado, Lynne Rienner, 119-136

Mo Ibrahim Foundation (2011) *2011 Ibrahim Index of African Gouvernance*, Mo Ibrahim Foundation, http://www.moibrahimfoundation.org, accessed March 2014

Motta, S., Nilsen, A.G. (2011) (eds) *Social Movements in the Global South: Dispossession, Development and Resistance*, Palgrave Mcmillan

Moyo, S., Yeros, P. (2005) (eds) *Reclaiming the Land. The resurgence of rural movements in Africa, Asia and Latin America*, London and New York, Zed Books

Negt, O. (2007) *L'Espace public oppositionnel*, (translated from German by Alex Neumann), Paris, Payot & Rivages

Neveu, E. (2011) *Sociologie des mouvements sociaux*, fifth edition, Paris, La Découverte

Nubukpo, K. (2013) 'L'Afrique doit se réapproprier les outils de sa souveraineté économique', in *Le retour de la question politique: crise de la représentation et luttes démocratiques en Afrique*, Actes du quatrième colloque international de Dakar, 22-24 May 2013, Paris, Gabriel Péri Foundation

Olayode, K. (2014) *The Dynamism and Contradictions of Social Movements in Nigeria*, working paper, Dakar, Rosa Luxemburg Foundation

Polanyi, K. (1944) *The Great Transformation: The Political and Economic Origins of our time*, second edition, Boston, Beacon Press, 2001

Prempeh, E. O. K. (2006) *Against Global Capitalism: African social movements confront neoliberal globalization*, UK and the United States, Ashgate

Przeworski, A., Limongi, F. (1997) 'Modernization: Theories and Facts', *World Politics*, 49(2):155-183

Skinner, Q. (1998) *Liberty before liberalism*, Cambridge, Cambridge University Press, Canto Classic edition 2012

Sylla, N.S. (2014a) 'Casting Democracy aside or Deconstructing the democratic discourse? On the need to theorize and practice politics differently', in N.S. Sylla (ed), *Rethinking Developement*, Dakar, Rosa Luxemburg Foundation, 1-27

Sylla, N.S. (2014b) 'Y a-t-il une relation entre démocratie et développement?', in D.M. Dembélé, N.S. Sylla et H. Faye, *Déconstruire le discours néolibéral. Volume 1 des 'Samedis de l'économie'*, ARCADE et Fondation Rosa Luxemburg, Dakar, Sénégal

Sylla, N.S. (2014c) *De l'Afrique marginalisée à l'Afrique émergente: critique de deux mythes contemporains*, document de travail

Tilly, C., Wood, L.J. (2012) *Social Movements 1768-2012*, third edition, Boulder, Colorado, Paradigm Publishers

Tocqueville, A. (1835) *Democracy in America*, volume 2, http://oll.libertyfund. org/titles/tocqueville-democracy-in-america-historical-critical-edition-4-vols-lf-ed-2010, accessed March 2014

United Nations Conference on Trade and Development (2010) 'The Least Developed Countries 2010. Towards a New International Development Architecture for LDCs', New York and Geneva, United Nations

United Nations Development Programme (2013) *Human Development Report 2013. The Rise of the South. Human Progress in a diverse World*, New York, UNDP

Wallerstein, I. (2001) 'Democracy, Capitalism and Transformation', Lecture at Documenta 11, Vienna, 16 March 2001, in Sessions on *Demokratie als unvollendeter Prozess: Alternativen, Grenzen und Neue Horizonte*, http://www2.binghamton.edu/fbc/archive/iw-vien2.htm, accessed March 2014

Wignarajan, P. (1993) (ed) *New Social Movements in the South: Empowering the People*, London, Zed Books

PART: 1

THE FAILED PROMISE
OF LIBERALISM

CHAPTER: 1

TOWARDS AN UNDERSTANDING

OF SOCIAL MOVEMENTS

IN CONTEMPORARY SIERRA LEONE

Ibrahim Abdullah[1]

This study examines the current socio-political landscape in Sierra Leone to investigate the existence of claim-making movements that appeared on the political radar between 2011 and 2013. It discusses the theoretical implications of importing social movement theory (SMT) and suggests a narrative that privileges the specificities of the African and Sierra Leonean situation. The study then identifies claim-making movements that belong to the 'new' social movements, as opposed to the 'traditional' movements wedded to organised labour. These 'new' movements fall into two broad categories: identity claim-making movements and economic/resource management claim-making movements. The former are deemed incapable of transforming themselves into social movements precisely because they are group-based and lack worthiness, unity, numbers, and commitment (WUNC). The economic and resource management movements, on the other hand, are seemingly well organised with a clear cut agenda, and capacity, to sustain their claim-making activities in furtherance of

1   I would like to acknowledge Abdul Karim Bah for his comments on an earlier draft of the paper

contentious demands. The study concludes with suggestions on coalition building and mass recruitment towards the goal of a full-fledged social movement articulating a counter project.

Introduction: theorising social movements

The literature on social movements or Social Movement Theory (SMT) is heavily skewed in favour of movements in the industrialised West. Partly because social movements originated in the West at the dawn of industrial capitalism in the late 18th century, most of the theorising has been Western-specific, concentrating predominantly on what appeared on the political radar in industrialised societies as claim-making organisations. The reproduction of capitalism as a global system of production and appropriation ensured that capitalist relations of production became dominant and hegemonic in non-Western societies. And like in the West, these claim-making institutions spurned by global capitalism emerged and became locked in contentious politics that are arguably claim-making in being driven in their collective attempts to expand the democratic space. The latter, claim-making as a distinctive feature of 'pursuing public politics', is central to understanding the emergence of social movements as a mode of politics specific to capitalism (Tilly 2004:7).

Charles Tilly, the acknowledged father of SMT, has argued that 'social movements emerged from an innovative, consequential synthesis of three elements': campaign; social movement repertoire; and WUNC displays (Tilly 2004:3-4). Campaign, he argues, involved 'sustained, organized public effort making collective claims on target authorities' while social movement repertoire constitutes the 'creation of special-purpose associations and coalitions, public meetings, solemn processions, vigils, rallies, demonstrations, petition drives, statements to and in public media, and pamphleteering' (Tilly 2004:3). The third element, WUNC displays - worthiness, unity, numbers, and commitment - takes the form of catchy slogans or labels that represent what the movement in question stands for. Such badges of identity not only help to publicise the movement as a recognisable brand to its constituents, but also aid in the recruitment of members.

What Tilly and his co-theorists in Europe and North America fingered as the fundaments of SMT – campaign, social movement repertoire and WUNC display - are in reality the matured operational architecture of claim-making institutions. To historicise the evolution of these institutions is precisely to reveal how and why they acquired these operational architecture in particular historical situations and not in others. Thus activists within social movements have not only taken exception to this kind of theorising about 'them', but have joined the conversation, proffering alternative frames of understanding about what they do from within and why they do what they do in particular ways.

But Tilly and his co-theorists have not actually elaborated a blue print for social movements everywhere. What they have done is to specifically map out the trajectory of contentious politics as exemplified by social movements as they evolved historically in Europe and North America. The challenge is not to reproduce what Tilly and others have identified as the important markers of social movements. Rather, it is to examine the possibilities of their emergence elsewhere in not too dissimilar circumstances. As Joel Beinin and Frederic Vairel cautioned in their study of social movements in the Middle East and North Africa: 'The historical specificities that inform any situation are never entirely reproducible' (Beinin and Vairel 2011:7). Thus Asef Bayat deploys the 'descriptive and prescriptive' concept of 'non social movement' in his study of contentious politics in the Middle East to capture the complex and fragmentary struggles by subalterns that might suggest the possibilities of a post-Islamic future (Bayat 2010:26).

This overarching relevance of historical specificity in understanding a universal aspect of modernity - the emergence of claim-making institutions - animates the study of social movements in Africa. The concern of scholars in

Africa has therefore not been in search of how to apply the fundamentals of SMT, but to examine the concrete conditions under which such movements emerge and flourish together with the attendant contradictions inherent in their operations (Mamdani and Wamba-dia-Wamba 1995, Cheru 1997, Nasong'o 2007). Historically, claim-making movements appeared under colonialism as a coalition of social groups - peasants, workers, intelligentsia and minority nationalities - demanding a stake in colonial political economy. This quest for a stake in racial colonial capitalism pitted the dominated against the state in both its settler and non-settler forms. The struggle against the colonial state by claim-making groups continued in the post-colonial period amidst deteriorating living conditions and authoritarianism (Mamdani and Wamba-dia-Wamba 1995, Dwyer and Zeilig 2012).

It is not coincidental that the first major anthology that specifically addressed the phenomena of social movements in Africa not only framed the issue in terms of 'social movements and democracy' but more importantly as 'the crystallization of group activity autonomous of the state'(Mamdani and Wamba-dia-Wamba 1995:7). Such framing skirts the division between social and popular movements; between 'new' community and identity-based movements and 'old' class-based movements; and between social and political movements, that is, the plethora of non-governmental organisations (NGOs) that now dot the African political landscape. How do voluntary professional and community organisations that are autonomous of state structures operate within a dependent capitalist society is the central question that Africanists/African scholars have set out to answer. Are these organisations constituted as democratic alternatives to the status quo that could deepen the struggle for democracy in Africa? Or are they a humbug on the process of democratisation from below because they tend to reproduce the very backward culture inimical to a people-centred transformative project? Answers to these questions dominate the conversation on social movements in the African context.

Historically, the major problem has been how to locate and galvanise those 'social forces' - workers, peasants, women, minorities, unemployed youth and middle class intelligentsia - that might provide the objective basis for the emergence of a progressive 'social movement' committed to a transformative project. Old and traditional class-based social movements like trade unions or peasant associations are fragmented on ethnic and regional lines; their leadership occasionally compromised and unreliable, while voluntary associational forms remain elitist and far removed from popular struggles (Larmer 2010). This search for social forces to construct a social movement anchored on popular claim-making has been fraught with multiple and contradictory processes as competing actors from all sectors of society deploy the very tactics that characterise politics in the wider society. The result has been mass fragmentation not only within the old and traditional class-based social movements, but also within the ubiquitous NGO universe that now dominates that sacred and contested space between the 'public' and the 'private' realm in most African societies (Dwyer and Zeilig 2012).

Fragmentation and mass coalition building occurred in a context of deepening crisis occasioned by the fall in commodity prices, the double hike in oil prices globally, the inauguration of the International Monetary Fund (IMF) induced structural adjustment policies (SAP), and the struggle for multi-party democracy. This period was marked by the proliferation of NGO's masquerading as civil society. At the forefront of this struggle for multi-party democracy were civil society activists with their defiant and popular call for 'change'/'changement politique'. In Sierra Leone this struggle for change was aborted by an armed 'revolution' from below and a subaltern coup that rocked the country for almost a decade (Abdullah 1998, Abdullah and Muana 1998).

The Sierra Leonean context: status quo and the struggle for democracy

Africa is witnessing a very significant period in its post-colonial history comparable to the anti-colonial struggles that swept the continent in the post-1945 period. In Egypt one of the most powerful Western-backed dictators was booted out of power by a mass uprising spearheaded by subalterns. Before him, Ben Ali, another darling of the West, was also forced out through mass action and pressure from below. Elsewhere on the continent, 2011 and 2012 witnessed popular uprisings and demands for change, as in Nigeria by a broad section of the labouring population after fuel subsidies were removed, triggering phenomenal price hikes. Burkina Faso, Malawi, Uganda, Swaziland, Botswana, Algeria, Gabon and Senegal saw similar street riots either for better living conditions, meaningful employment, or for freedom and a congenial democratic space. In South Africa, over 40 workers were gunned down by police in the Marikana mine massacre and a legislation drafted under Apartheid invoked against strikers for causing their own deaths!

Sierra Leone did not exactly escape this continental whirlwind. Strikes by university lecturers in public institutions of higher learning have been frequent in the past two years. In Kono and Bumbuna, the heart of the new mineral Eldorado, at least four workers were gunned down in 2012 following strikes for better conditions and a living wage. Musu Conteh, a 20-year old female worker hired by African Minerals, a giant mining conglomerate with 99-year leases to mine minerals, was among those killed. These rumblings from below and the counter-measures from above are arguably the beginnings of a process that could lead to a qualitative transformation in the continent's quest for a second independence - a process that started in the early 1990s with the return to multiparty politics and the democracy of the ballot box.

President Ernest Bai Koroma's All Peoples Congress (APC) - whose main campaign promise in 2007 was to run the country like a business - has failed to register any significant change in the living conditions of the majority of ordinary people. A 2012 Food and Agricultural Organisation (FAO) report concluded that over 80 per cent of Sierra Leoneans are still not eating adequately and not getting the required minimum nutrients necessary for healthy living (FAO 2012). Other studies have recorded a constant 70 per cent poverty rate, a figure that has painfully persisted since the end of hostilities in 2002. To crown it all, youth unemployment hovers at around 65 per cent. What then is the problem?

Sierra Leoneans are not only hungry; they are also, arguably, angry, impoverished and disease stricken. The general condition of the majority of rural and urban folks is characterised by a life of drudgery and indignity; a sub-human state in which those afflicted are ashamed of their enervating poverty even as they lack a coherent channel to galvanise their collective energy for real social and material change. The hope and expectations that heralded Koroma's 2007 electoral victory have fizzled out, consumed by the collective despair of a rootless population steeped in age-old poverty. The collective aspirations of marginalised and mainstream youths for a new dawn has uncovered a sombre reflection of how 'yesterday better pass tiday'.[2] And it is now probably safe to say that the masses have concluded that the political class is of a single breed and that there is no difference between the two dominant electoral machines: The Sierra Leone Peoples Party (SLPP) and the APC.

The February 2013 inauguration ceremony heralding President Koroma's second term in office managed to attract a few party faithful, swelled by a rented crowd of sycophants, less enthusiastic and less hopeful for the much trumpeted prosperity that he has promised the nation. From running the nation as a business enterprise to the much publicised *Agenda For Prosperity* conjuring a middle income future for the toiling masses, the claims of the political class remain hollow to a general populace faced with the grim reality

---

2 'Yesterday betteh pass tiday' translates to 'yesterday was far better than what we experience today'.

of increased cost of living, erratic power supply for those who can afford it, mass unemployment, and a rudderless ship of state.

The burden of the past

Like the Bourbon monarchy long before them, the Sierra Leone political class has learnt nothing and forgotten nothing. Even lessons from a recent civil war, fuelled in part by bad governance and widespread corruption, have gone unheeded as the political class set about doing business as usual. There are several instances of collective failure on the part of the APC-SLPP regimes in post-war Sierra Leone: the slow pace of devolution of power to local authorities; the palpable inability to enforce labour regulations to protect workers; the lack of any concrete direction on higher education; the inadequacies of health care services amidst a program of free health care for the needy; the chronic lack of social housing; the non-existence of a mass transit network for the urban poor and labouring population; and the continued delay in reviewing the 1991 constitution.[3] Trapped in a past it is unable to transcend, the political class could do no better than to reproduce the mistakes of that ignoble past.

Thus Sierra Leoneans still continue to chant 'high we exalt thee/realm of the free' even as they neglect their pan-African roots and the heroic resistance to slavery and colonialism that shaped the history and cultures of the people in Sierra Leone.[4] The offensive images on national television about an explorer named Pedro Da Cintra - a hired pirate in the pay of feudal mercantile interests in his native Portugal - who supposedly discovered Sierra Leone is a painful reminder that you do not build a nation by unveiling inflated infrastructural projects that are not aligned to any national plan. While such projects might be useful in cementing economic and social linkages within

---

3 A constitutional review committee was recently formed but the sticky problem of funding still remains.
4 These are the first and second stanzas of the national anthem.

the economy and society, they do not by themselves create the conditions for the flowering of a national consciousness that would free the collective energies of the people to register advances in the realm of science and technology.

National consciousness - the nuts and bolts of nation-making - is the raw stuff of history and culture. No nation can develop economically if it neglects or subverts its history and culture. No nation can invent a future without a solid knowledge of its collective past(s). In this enterprise, decadent colonial institutions have to be re-thought, if not discarded, in the light of current concerns. Sierra Leoneans want to move away from touting the institution of chieftaincy - that classic divide and rule structure - as a cultural heritage and begin to see it as a cog in the wheel of a democratic future; from seeing one group of Sierra Leoneans as subjects and another as citizens; from talking about a mythical 'Athens of West Africa' to a real knowledge-based society rooted in modern science and technology. Such seismic shifts would not only open their collective minds to a liberating future but also guarantee their collective identity as people.

Ethnicity and Corruption

Ethnicity and corruption constitute the two major internal stumbling blocks to a national regeneration project. The two, like twins, are linked in a complex web that guarantees their mutual reproduction and continued existence. If ethnicity is grounded in mobilising political support based on kinship ties - similar to language, culture and social origin - corruption is subverting established public institutions in furtherance of personal objectives and in pursuit of private gain. Unlike corruption which is criminalised, ethnicity is acceptable not only in everyday life in terms of one's association with his/her kinship group but more so in politics as a support network. Political mobilisation via ethnicity creates a rewarding system that promotes mediocrity and even sanctions corruption. Kinship connection can also serve as an insurance against possible prosecution in case of corruption charges. The dialectic between corruption and ethnicity runs through the history of post-colonial Sierra Leone.

The twin cancer of ethnicity and corruption have not only de-valorised national politics - all politicians are thieves, the masses seem to be saying - it has also meant that every potential candidate for election has to be identified or associated with a particular ethnic group. Once an individual declares his/her intention to run for public office the question of his/her ethnicity becomes the yardstick with which to judge his/her chances of succeeding. To ask about one's political support based on ethnic calculation underlines the salience of ethnicity in post-colonial politics. Politics, the game of eating - the politics of the belly - is not anchored on ethics or morality or even issues related to the interest of a particular community but one's primordial group. The 2012 election result revealed the pattern of ethnic voting that has characterised national elections since 1967.

The major challenge now is how to 'de-ethnicise' politics; how to re-centre the conversation on quotidian issues; on the multiple and collective challenges confronting the nation, and the provision of basic and meaningful social services. How to bring back morality and ethics to determine people's choices in their candidates and party preferences constitutes a major challenge in remaking the political. Sierra Leoneans need to think through the twin issues of ethnicity and corruption and devise appropriate strategies to engage the populace. The next elections will either be an affirmation of the cancerous ethnic divide that is threatening to tear the nation apart or an outright rejection of that historic fault line.

Arguably, the most defining feature of post-colonial Sierra Leone is the marginalisation of the majority of its citizens in the sphere of politics. Side-lined and boxed into a corner, the masses only become seemingly relevant during election time when their votes are solicited or when the big man is visiting to make the usual promises and commissions of a white elephant project. But this marginalisation or side-lining of the masses has a history rooted in the way political parties are formed, the rules and regulations governing their operation and the role of the masses between elections. Rather than serve the interest of the people who are members/supporters of political parties, these parties come to serve only the interests of a few at the top who shamelessly claim it as theirs. The dominance of elite interests in party formation and the lack of structures to guarantee recall or popular intervention have meant that the two dominant parties - SLPP and the APC - rooted as they are in the ethnic are the 'natural' representatives of the people. Rethinking the rules of the game might begin to open up popular discussions about issues regarding the control of party machines and the roles of specific groups within party structures. How to ensure popular participation during and after elections and how to guarantee accountability in all spheres of state-society relations are key questions in this regard. Popular participation might subvert ethnic chauvinism and hegemonic tendencies by opening the doors to issue-based conversations centred on the state of the nation. Exploring constitutional provisions in this regard might also be a good starting point.

Labour and unemployment

Trickling employment in a context of mass unemployment provides the background for the labour question in contemporary Sierra Leone. But the chronic lack of reliable data and statistics compounds the problem: we do not know how many people are available for employment on a monthly basis nor do we know the total number of those who are unemployed. Official estimates however put the figure of youth unemployment at around 65 per cent. Agriculture continues to soak up the majority of the labour force (more than 70 per cent nationally) followed by the service sector (15 per cent) and then industry, government and community.[5] Historically, organised labour has been active in mining, the civil service, railway, maritime/ports, and the

---

5   See Agenda For Change (2009): Second Poverty Reduction Strategy, 2009-2012; Agenda For Prosperity (2013): Road to Middle Income Status: Sierra Leone's Third Generation Poverty Reduction Strategy Paper, 2013-2018; Sierra Leone Youth Report (2012): Youth Development, 2012

service sector. Individual unions existed in most of these sectors even when there were major disagreements amongst and between unions affiliated to the umbrella Sierra Leone Labour Congress (SLLC). The centralisation of power under the APC one-party dictatorship in the 1970s and 80s and the emasculation of organised labour after the abortive 1981 strike dealt a mortal blow to organised labour from which it has still not recovered. The current challenge is how to revive and organise labour to build a credible labour movement around the moribund SLLC.

Strikes at Koidu in the diamond mines, rolling disturbances amongst workers at African Minerals, strikes at institutions of higher learning and the everyday dismissal and refusal to pay benefits to workers interpellates the state in its failure to guarantee what is due to labour as of right and by law.[6] There is growing and incontrovertible evidence that workers have been denied the right to organise - which right is enshrined in the constitution - and threatened with dismissal by mining companies. Allegations of racial discrimination have been levied against management in some mining companies and unfair labour practices such as casualisation have been used by management to slash wages paid to workers. The general working conditions in most foreign mining companies violate national laws as well as international standards. Officials in the ministry of labour are constrained - in part by human resource issues and in part by the high handedness of company officials - in enforcing the rules and regulations governing industrial relations in the mines.

Whilst the majority of working people are suffering degrading conditions in factories and mines, the worst hit categories are security personnel (those employed in private security firms) and domestic and casual labour. Security workers suffer long hours in hazardous conditions for low pay without transport allowance, protective weather clothing and health benefits, while their female counterparts suffer from constant abuse and discrimination.

6 See the following: Mining Watch, May 2012; Mining Watch, December 2012-May 2013; Network Movement for Justice and Development (2013), Ending Impunity in the Mining Sector in Sierra Leone: The Koidu Holding Case, July 2013.

Similarly, domestic workers work long hours for paltry wages, without leave or overtime, and are subject to multiple abuses, from physical to sexual abuse. Most of these workers are hired by foreign nationals and businesses. Security and domestic workers are mostly young women and men who are amongst the most marginalised and exploited.

A social movement rooted in organised labour will have to address working conditions as opposed to the profiteering interests of bosses and managers. Decent pay and decent working conditions with modern safety mechanisms should be addressed as well as working hours, the rights of workers against unfair dismissals, sexual abuse by employers, and the casualisation of work. The concerns of women workers are also critical. There is no movement around a national minimum wage. Above all workers, representation and participation - social, economic and political - that affects them must be taken with all seriousness if a social movement is to emerge from within organised labour.

Economic system: same, same

The reigning mantra in the sphere of the economy continues to be the TINA (There Is No Alternative) doctrine. In this context the dominant thinking that has prevailed in post-colonial Sierra Leone remains unchanged: the desire to attract foreign capital at all cost to develop mineral and agricultural resources. Yet after more than 50 years of trying to attract the much needed capital Sierra Leone still remains at the bottom of development rankings. Even so, successive regimes have doggedly refused to rethink the developmental path or explore other viable alternatives. Sierra Leone has staggered from the dream of a Singapore of West Africa envisaged by President Ahmad Tejan Kabbah to the unimaginable middle income status proffered by President Ernest Bai Koroma's *Agenda for Prosperity*. How this dream is to be realised within the framework of a discredited neo-liberal agenda remains the unanswered trillion dollar question. The promise made by the minister of agriculture in 2010 that Sierra Leone will cease importation of rice, the staple food, by 2012 still remains that: an empty promise premised on wining votes.

Meanwhile the economy is still characterised by its mercantilist beginning: an import-export enclave dominated by a Lebanese comprador merchant class. The revival of large scale mining after the cessation of hostilities in 2002 and the concession-cum-monopoly granted to African Minerals has unarguably taken the nation back to the kind of colonial era policies of 99-year leases with nothing concrete in return. The much touted growth in the mining sector which observers have translated into outrageous claims about Sierra Leone being the fastest growing economy in the world only amplifies the general misery and environmental degradation that characterises the lot of the citizenry in the mining enclaves.[7] The continued dominance of foreign interest in this sector will ensure that the much needed revenue that politicians crave will forever be siphoned off to distant lands to fatten the already fat cats who claim to be investing in Sierra Leone to alleviate poverty. Unscrupulous mining magnates, bio-fuel capitalists, and the local elites are locked in a threesome that continues to denude whatever independence Sierra Leone had over control of its resources.[8]

In these dire circumstances the issue of who controls what and who gets how much and why has to be tabled before the general citizenry. If national resources are expended in a particular manner citizens need to be part of the discussions to decide who gets what and why.[9] Such demands are consistent with the spirit and letter of the constitution. This spirit informs the dogged voluntarism of certain social groups to participate in a national conversation centred on management of economic resources. For it is only when such issues are tabled for discussion and excluded social groups invited to participate can Sierra Leoneans begin to talk of deepening democracy in the sense of inclusivity in determining their collective national destiny.

---

7 See *Mining Watch*.
8 On mining, see *Mining Watch*; on bio-fuel capitalists, visit: www.silnorf.org or www.greenscenery.org.
9 See section on social movements.

Social movements in action or social movements in the making?

Sierra Leone has a long history of voluntary associations in the city of Freetown dating back to the 19th century. These civil organisations flourished under colonial rule and during the first decade of independence before they were emasculated under the APC one-party dictatorship that lasted until war broke out in 1991 (Abdullah 1998). These voluntary associations of professionals, civil society activists and women were to spring up during the war years to demand an end to hostilities and a return to multi-party democracy. By the time war ended in 2002 Sierra Leone was awash with countless number of NGOs and civil society groups mostly involved in advocacy and some form of service delivery in place of a state that had practically ceased to exist. The gradual reestablishment of state structures throughout the country and the consolidation of peace underlined by the holding of three successive elections - 2002, 2007, and 2013 - witnessed a shift in their traditional areas of operation from advocacy to monitoring and participating in the business of governance. The current challenge is how to really build a social movement from the plethora of organisations and overlapping networks that now dot the sacred realm between the public and the private.

A recent study commissioned by the Network for Justice and Development (NMJD), one of the most vibrant civil society organisations in Sierra Leone, as part of a project - Initiative to Build Social Movements in Sierra Leone - funded by the United Nations Democracy Fund (UNDEF) identified the problem as 'the seemingly lack of visionary and dynamic leadership in social movements; and the aversion among civil society groups to work together in a more cohesive and coordinated way'(Report of a Study of Social Movements in Sierra Leone 2013: 4).[10]

---

10   This report suffers from serious conceptual flaws: from failing to provide an operational definition of social movements/civil society to conflating civil society organisations with broad coalitions involving multiple groups. It also lacks depth.

The report concluded by advocating for 'remedial interventions to re-engineer CSO platforms and social movements that are visionary, dynamic, more cohesive and well-coordinated' (Ibid.). How you re-engineer social movements when they are non-existent or in the making remains the most daunting challenge that the report failed to consider. The question therefore is not how to 're-engineer' social movements - 're-engineering' implies that these movements already exist and only need some gingering or shoring up to make them perform as social movements. Rather, it is how to 'invent' social movements in a way that would serve the collective interests of the excluded majority through the development of a 'formidable counterproject' (Cheru 1997: 164).

The most enduring feature of post-war Sierra Leone has been the enormous impact of rights-based notions on virtually everything that has to do with life. Demands on the state and state officials for the provision of energy, water and good roads are framed in terms of rights; a demonstration by polio victims/disabled citizens after eviction from city premises becomes a violation of their collective right to housing and decent living; and school children confronted with corporal punishment in schools respond by invoking their rights.

The pervasiveness of rights-based discourse partly fuelled by the injustice that propelled and sustained the brutal civil war is an integral part of the architecture of claim-making in contemporary Sierra Leone. A cursory examination of claim-making in this context underlines the popularity of rights-based discourse as the discourse of empowerment. Below are some of the most visible claim-making organisations that have enlivened the discourse on social movements in Sierra Leone in the period under review, 2011-2013.

Dignity Association and Pride Equality (LGBTI community)

Dignity Association and Pride Equality are two organisations that were formed in 2003 and 2007 respectively to defend and advance the rights of the lesbian, gay, bisexual, trans-gender and intersex (LGBTI) community in Sierra Leone. Considering the stigma attached to same-sex relations and the cultural and religious capital often mobilised on moral grounds to demonise such practices, their debut in post war Sierra Leone undoubtedly signalled a new dawn in terms of rights discourse and claim-making. The brutal 2004 rape and murder of Fanny Ann Edie, the founder of Dignity Association, did not deter others from joining the campaign for gay and lesbian rights. Pride Equality, formed three years after Edie's murder, recently published a book on gay and lesbian issues and the right to health services.[11] Both organisations are currently at the centre of campaigns to repeal laws specifically criminalising same-sex relations. The burning issues confronting these organisations are twofold: everyday discriminatory practices and the criminalisation of their sexual mores which carries the force of law and a penalty.

The community is seemingly under siege from fellow citizens (family members, friends, co-workers, landlords) state officials, medical practitioners, health workers, and law officials. A recent study captures the various kinds of physical and psychological violence, often exacerbated by the fear of victims to report crimes and the lack of legislative protections against offenses committed on the basis of sexual orientation and gender identity (Discrimination on the Basis of Sexual Orientation and Gender Identity 2013).

Members of this besieged community are excluded from accessing health care services on the grounds that they are sexually different even though such practices violate a national health policy that unambiguously affirms health services as a basic human right to be made available, accessible and affordable to all people without discrimination. The claims that this community is making

11 The title of the book is *Tearing Down Walls, Building Hope*. Pride Equality, formerly whycantwegetmarried.com, is slightly to the left of Dignity Association.

against tremendous odds raises fundamental questions about constitutional practice, the right of the individual and the rule of law - all central tenets of modern democratic practice.

The very Sierra Leonean constitution that guarantees equality and non-discrimination in the enjoyment of fundamental human rights and freedom criminalises same-sex relations. That is to say, it does not protect same sex activities. Section 61 and 62 of the Offences Against Person Act 1861 criminalises 'buggery' and 'attempted buggery', defined as male same-sex sexual activity (Discrimination on the Basis of Sexual Orientation and Gender Identity 2013). The Human Rights Commission of Sierra Leone (HRCSL), an independent human rights institution accredited since 2011 with an 'A' status to the International Coordinating Committee of National Institutions for the Promotion and Protection of Human Rights (ICC) has refused to enter the legal fray, arguing that 'the law of Sierra Leone does not give the commission the mandate to advocate and support LGBT human rights' (Ibid:8). The official reluctance to adopt and adapt the national law in line with Sierra Leone's international obligations in the numerous UN protocols raises fundamental questions about the law and the failure to protect minority rights.

The major question that the existence of this community poses with regards to its claim-making is the extent to which the apparatus of state is used to deny them their individual and collective rights, which constitutes a violation of the constitution. These are some of the issues which the recently constituted Constitutional Review Commission should address in the interest of democracy and social justice. The visibility of this minority community and their strident advocacy since 2011, together with the interest that the issue has generated internationally, demands that we pay close attention to how this community is continually side-lined and boxed out, and the possible repercussions.

Sierra Leone Union on Disability Issues (SLUDI)

People with disabilities suffer chronic exclusion in the public and private sphere in Sierra Leone. From the visually impaired to the physically challenged polio victim, the hearing and verbally impaired to the destitute amputee, it is a painful reminder of the excesses of the brutal civil war that engulfed the nation for a decade. The Sierra Leone Union on Disability Issues (SLUDI) is a voluntary association of persons with disability that emerged after the war to coordinate their respective activities in accessing and allocating needed resources. Its claim-making is in the sphere of rights and welfare of associated groups and they target state officials, NGOs and other donors for resources.

The organisation has been instrumental in accessing the public sphere through strident advocacy in wanting to 'tell their own story'. This has yielded tremendous gains: from representation at major policy events to undisputed recognition as the authentic voice of the disabled community. Their major victory during the period under review was the successful passage of long-delayed legislation: the Persons with Disability Act, 2011. Led by a lawyer, himself physically challenged, then a member of parliament, the organisation tirelessly lobbied parliamentarians across party lines to push through the bill. The organisation is currently working on the establishment of a Commission on Disability to compliment the 2011 Act, which guarantees their individual and collective rights as enshrined in the constitution.

Its links with international networks, most notably Handicap International, has guaranteed continuous support to keep the secretariat functioning in the four regional zones of the country together with its more than 80 affiliated organisations. And it usually takes the lead in celebrating World Disability Day. Their story presents a marked contrast to the LGBTI community.

National Youth Coalition

The National Youth Coalition (NYC) is an advocacy organisation that deals with the concerns of a specific category of Sierra Leoneans. It emerged in post-war Sierra Leone immediately after the 2002 elections when a Ministry of Youth and Sports was established to address what was then dubbed the 'youth question'. The organisational structure allows for individual as well as group membership, totalling some 25,000 in all. Its mode of operation is seemingly limited to raising issues of national concern that directly affect the welfare of youth. It does this through periodic press statements and workshops.

However, the activities of this coalition have been seemingly hampered by the creation of the National Youth Commission (NAYCOM) by an Act of Parliament in 2009 and the establishment of a new ministry - the Ministry of Youth and Employment and Sports - in 2012. The commission, directly under the supervision of the ministry, recently unveiled a National Youth Employment Action Plan (NYEAP) (Sierra Leone Youth Report 2012).Youth, defined as those aged between15-35, constitute 35 per cent of the population, or 1,799,601 people (Ibid:2). The majority are poor and unemployment hovers at around the 60 per cent mark. 'Within the West African region, Sierra Leone has one of the highest rates of underemployment amongst the youth, with the total number of young workers living on less than US$ one per day constantly increasing both before and after the post-conflict period' (Ibid:13).

The plight of Sierra Leonean youth is clearly beyond the capacity of an advocacy group that sits in the capital and occasionally issues press statements on matters concerning youth. The coalition has not undertaken any major research or published any reports on matters affecting youth. Its contribution has been marked by its inability to proffer a way forward with regards to tackling the 'youth question' in what is undoubtedly a national emergency.

Alliance for Land Accountability and Transparency (ALART)

ALART is a coalition of civil society groups and grassroots community based organisations that emerged as a result of global and local concern over the unchecked activities of bio-fuel capitalists in Africa and elsewhere in the so-called Third World. The world-wide demand and acquisition of arable land in Africa for the production of bio-fuel has been welcomed by many governments, with the view that this policy orientation would provide the much-needed investment to generate growth and provide employment and other ancillary benefits. But such optimism has dwarfed local concern over the possible environmental impact and loss of livelihoods. The counter-argument from above that investment would benefit the local population has thrown up stout opposition and resistance from below. ALART is a product of this resistance.

At the centre of the coalition's activities is Green Scenery - an environmental organisation that is anti-big business, pro-peasant and community-centred. It seeks to protect peasant rights to land and livelihoods against aggressive bio-fuel capitalists. Since its inception in 2010 the coalition has engaged in militant lobbying and advocacy, awareness-raising in affected communities, organising of dispossessed peasants and provision of an outlet for collective voices to be heard. Its central and unwavering demands have been for a halt to the large scale acquisition of land (land grabbing) by bio-fuel capitalists, a revisiting of the terms and conditions of land already acquired and a re-negotiation or annulment of agreements that are not in the best interests of the community and nation.

ALART's strident advocacy is backed by ground-breaking research on land holdings and availability of arable land, the possible impact of large scale alienation of land in a situation of shifting cultivation and the potential impact of large-scale land alienation on food production. The possible link between bio-fuel land alienation and generalised hunger has already attracted other civil society groups who are demanding an investigation into possible linkages (*Awoko* Newspaper, 3 September 2013). The most recent Global Hunger Index (2013) ranks Sierra Leone 66th out of a total of 78 countries (Welthungerhilfe et al 2013). The linkage between large-scale alienation of arable land and hunger is a real one.

Sierra Leone Network on the Right to Food (SiLNORF)

The Sierra Leone Network on the Right to Food (SiLNORF) was constituted in 2008 'as a national coalition of civil society organizations promoting the right to food by advocating against land grabbing in Northern Sierra Leone'.[12] Like ALART, SiLNORF is a movement from below in response to the large-scale activities of bio-fuel capitalists land grabbing in the Bombali District. Headquartered in Makeni, Bombali District, the coalition consists of 28 organisations ranging from grassroots collectives to NGOs and media outfits.

Its activities are centred on the operations of Addax Bioenergy, a Swiss multi-national corporation that had leased a hefty 50,000 hectares of arable land to produce ethanol for export to Europe.

SiLNORF's activities include organising briefings on the activities of Addax Bioenergy, assisting dispossessed peasants in articulating their individual and collective claims and providing needed support to victims of land alienation now organised as the Affected Land Users Association (AFLUA). The right to food is central to the organisation's work.

Their 2012 report was categorical about the threat posed to access to food and livelihoods by the Addax Bioenergy project in Bombali and Magbass Sugar Complex in nearby Tonkolili District. (Annual Monitoring Report on the Operations of Addax Bioenergy 2011-2012).[13]

---

12 See www.silnorf.org
13 Studies conducted by SiLNORF and others relevant to their mission are available on their website.

National Resources and Governance and Economic Justice Network (NaRGEJ)

NaRGEJ is a broad coalition of NGOs and CSOs concerned with the state of natural resources and their exploitation by multi-national corporations in alliance with the state. Its interest therefore goes beyond the traditional NGO/CSO concern with civic rights, political rights and advocacy. Informed by the history of neglect, extreme poverty and environmental degradation that has characterised communities were precious minerals are mined, NaRGEJ's *raison d'être* is how to ensure that the nation's natural resources - land, precious minerals, petroleum and aquatic resources - are owned by, and exploited for, the general benefit of the nation. To fulfill this mission the coalition has brought together journalists, environmentalists and social scientists whose work ranges from governance and management issues to monitoring and militant advocacy.

The Network Movement for Justice and Development (NMJD) serves as the hub of the coalition. Its key partner, the Association of Journalists on Mining and Extractives (AJME) publishes a magazine, *Mining Watch*, which covers every aspect of mining in Sierra Leone. In 2012 the coalition was invited to participate in a state-sponsored policy dialogue - the National Conference on Development and Transformation.

Their strident advocacy was instrumental in the inclusion of natural resources management as a central pillar in the *Agenda for Prosperity: Poverty Reduction Strategy Paper Three*. Advocating for citizen involvement in the management of public resources is a leap forward in holding public officials accountable for the utilisation of natural resources.

Budget Advocacy Network (BAN)

The Budget Advocacy Network (BAN) was constituted in 2005 as a coalition of local and international NGOs to combat government's excessive secrecy in budget finance and preparation. Its central concern - 'promoting participation, transparency and accountability in both the national and local budget processes' - is indicative of the new consciousness in contemporary Sierra Leone that citizens have for every aspect of governance relevant to resource mobilisation and expenditure.[14] Its web page declares: 'Sierra Leone provides minimal information to the public in its budget and financial activities.' To remedy this, BAN has engaged in strident advocacy and lobbying of politicians.

The coalition consists of seven CSOs and networks as members, together with a string of donors as partners: the British Department for International Development (DFID), United Nations Development Program (UNDP) and the Ministry of Finance and Economic Development (MoFED). For the 2012 general elections - presidential, parliamentary, local government and municipal - BAN designed a manifesto on the health sector with the active participation of six political parties.

Aspects of this manifesto were subsequently adopted by the six parties that participated in the exercise. Its greatest achievement so far has been to help sustain the free health care scheme for lactating mothers and under five children inaugurated in 2009. When the government slashed the budget allocation for health in 2011 - from 11 per cent to 7.4 per cent in 2012 - BAN went on the offensive to mobilise public opinion and lobby for an increase. The government had to back down by upping the said allocation to 10.5 per cent of the 2013 national budget. Its advocacy in the health sector is fuelled in part by the determination to reduce infant mortality - Sierra Leone has one of the highest rates of infant mortality in the world - by guaranteeing funding for the free health care scheme.

14   See www.bansl.org

BAN's concern with the 'health' of national and local budget processes has moved beyond its original involvement with budget tracking and analysis. The network is currently examining the loss of revenue as a result of the numerous concessions, waivers and tax holidays granted to bio-fuel capitalists, mining conglomerates and others on the exemption list. The National Revenue Authority (NRA), the body responsible for tax collection, recently revealed a colossal loss of Le 247 billion for the first six months of the year.[15]

The seven coalitions and networks discussed above belong to the 'new' social movements that evolved outside the 'traditional' movements of organised labour. Three of them are identity-centred and claim-making groups, whereas the remaining four are centred on bread-and-butter issues that impinge on economic survival and development. Put together, the activities of the latter group resonate with the collective aspirations of Sierra Leoneans - a key determinant in the evolution and success of any social movement - in their desire to actively participate in governance and by so doing experience real change in their material conditions. And such resonance has considerable implications with regards to recruitment of potential members, national support, relevance and resource mobilisation. The identity-centred, claim-making groups active in the public sphere will remain peripheral in the national psyche precisely because they are group based.[16] The claim-making of the LGBTI community is a real one in so far as it raises fundamental constitutional issues that border on the infringement of the rights of a minority group which the state is supposed to guarantee and protect. Their courage in 'outing' themselves and to openly organise in a decidedly homophobic context has met with stiff opposition from religious orders. The disabled community might survive as a group in alliance with larger groups, but the LGBTI community might be hard pressed to secure allies. Similarly, the youth coalition's inability to

---

15 *Standard Times* (2013) 'Govt. loses Le 247 billion', 23 August.
16 'Group based' simply means here that the claims are specific to a particular social group and therefore fail to gain traction nationally or appeal to others.

function in the interest of the group will be superseded with the emergence of an alternative forum or their absorption in a larger coalition. The point here is that none of these identity claim-making groups has a future as a social movement as presently constituted.

Large-scale land alienation and mineral exploitation: possibilities of a social movement?

What then are the possibilities for these networks and coalitions dealing with land, food, the environment and economic management of natural resources becoming the nucleus of a vanguard social movement? Do they have the resources to transform themselves into full-fledged social movements with a national scope and operational base complete with all the paraphernalia of performances that are characteristic of social movements? Put differently, what are the possibilities for such an epochal transformation given the context in which they currently operate?

Here again we turn back to Tilly for some guidance and direction. 'A social movement,' Tilly argues, 'consists of a sustained challenge to powerholders in the name of a population living under the jurisdiction of those powerholders by means of repeated public displays of that population's numbers, commitment, unity, and worthiness' (Tilly 1994:7).

Such a movement 'embodies contentious interaction' and involves a 'mutual claim-making between challengers and powerholders' (Ibid.). The coalitions identified as claim-making organisations that might constitute the nucleus of a vanguard social movement do possess an objective basis to mount a sustained challenge to the status quo by mobilising across the nation to present their demands on behalf of that very nation. The question of resonance - the unquestionable relevance of revenue generation and resource allocation - highlighted above can prove to be a powerful mobilising tool to galvanise participants in an enterprise that is increasingly holding out to be the only solution to their current misery and deprivation. The popular view that politicians, irrespective of party affiliations, have vested interests might just tilt the balance in favour of a social movement anchored in social justice via the redistribution of the national cake - natural resources.

To put forward such an argument is to imply that the coalitions in question are capable and equipped to carry out such a transformative agenda. Here the evidence might appear contradictory but on second reading lend itself in favour of the possibility of such a transformation. Sierra Leone is currently experiencing an investment flow that it has not seen since the halcyon days of the first decade of independence. And that investment flow is bunched in the extractive sectors: mining and agriculture. The large-scale alienation of land by bio-fuel capitalists together with the hydra-headed monster in the form of mining capital have created the conditions for the emergence of organisations from below that seek to champion the collective interest of the people. SiLNORF and Green Scenery have already demonstrated their willingness to pull together in the face of a common enemy - biofuel capitalists and large-scale land grabbing - by organising a national forum for land owners to discuss the implications of their activities on their collective livelihoods.

Since 2011 Green Scenery has single-handedly covered the activities of Socfin Agricultural Company Sierra Leone in Sahr Malen Chiefdom, Pujehun District, where the company has acquired a 50-year lease of some 16,000 acres of prime farmland with 'high level government support'.[17] In a series of press statements the organisation catalogued the 'secretive deals' that led to the land purchase and the 'tension amongst families, political representatives, and in affected communities' that it caused. It details the resistance mounted by locals who were against the land deal, which was signed in the presence of the minister of agriculture. It also covered the protests by workers hired by the company, the arrest of '30 peaceful protestors including their spokesperson',

---

17   Green Scenery (2011), Press Statement, 18 April 2011, www.greenscenery.org

their appearance in court for 'unlawful assembly, riotous conduct and threatening language' and the formation of a grassroots organisation - Malen Land Owners Association(MALOA) - in defence of their right to ownership of their land.[18]

The activities of SiLNORF in Bombali and Tonkolili Districts and that of Green Scenery in Pujehun District are matched by the activities of NMJD in the mining sector. NMJD is the hub that pulls together all popular and anti-business activities in the mining sector. The *Mining Watch* magazine, which debuted in 2011, is produced by AJME, an autonomous network within NMJD. AJME consists of 45 print and electronic media practitioners across the nation dedicated towards 'turning our resources from a curse into a blessing'. The organisation was a product of the collective desire 'to bolster the advocacy machinery of the Campaign for Just Mining and other partners including the Movement for Justice and Development (NMJD)' (*Mining Watch* 2012: 21). The magazine regularly covers all aspects of mining activities: from strikes to general labour conditions; from management's refusal to allow labour to organise to tension in the mining communities; from environmental degradation to the racist practices of white expatriates in the mining camps.

Indeed there are possibilities here for a social movement to emerge based on claim-making in the agricultural and mining sectors. The activities of SiLNORF, ALART, and NaRGEJ, with their grassroots organising and publicising, are suggestive of such a possibility. And the direction already charted by these groups does make room for a possible alliance with BAN - whose interest is in revenue and budget flow - as they collectively seek to track how resources are generated, disbursed and re/distributed/appropriated.

This seismic shift from traditional CSO concerns with civil and political rights to bread-and-butter issues anchored on resources are a concrete reflection of

---

18 These press statements are available on their website.

contemporary concern with resource allocation and development in terms of material benefit. How this alliance might pan out remains to be seen.

Conclusion: Can social movements widen the democratic space?

Social movements are historical formations that are peculiar to capitalism as a system of production/reproduction. They emerged at the dawn of capitalism, first in Britain, then Europe and America; and later in Latin America, Asia and Africa. Their performances are therefore rooted in and a product of capitalist production irrespective of their specificities. Historically, social movements have existed side by side with democracy and democratisation in Euro-America. They've also played the same historic role in Africa, first in the struggle against colonialism, and subsequently in the so-called struggle for second independence in the early 1990s.

That they played this historic role is suggestive of context, and in no way implies that social movements are by nature democratic. As a product of capitalism their claim-making exists, and is shaped, within the context of rules and regulations that govern their performances. This underlines their historic limitations: they agitate and get their members and numbers out as a show of force but in the final analysis 'they organize around the demand that powerholders recognize, protect, endorse, forward, or even impose a given program' (Tilly 1994:7). What this means is that whatever democratic leverage they possess is circumscribed by the inherent structural limitations imposed on how the business of democracy should be conducted. To surmount this constricting external barricade to their claim-making, social movements would have to develop a counter project to confront and eventually subvert the status quo.[19]

---

19   It is only when they develop such a counter project that social movements become revolutionary.

But such a radical option, though feasible elsewhere on the continent, remains a dim prospect in the Sierra Leonean context.[20] The most urgent challenges facing activists in Sierra Leone committed to building social movements is how to pull their collective resources together, network aggressively, develop and strengthen their claim-making apparatus nationally, seek alternative sources of resource mobilisation and funding to ensure autonomy from potential donors, expand their grassroot support base by recruiting more members and last but not least establish a solid network of seasoned researchers with a clear agenda and focus on national and international issues of concern to the nation. The above would help create the ideal conditions for the emergence and development of a network around land alienation and mineral exploitation - arguably the most important issues impinging on the collective livelihood of the citizenry. The collaboration between and amongst the different coalitions is a move in the right direction.

The shift in CSO agitation and advocacy from concern with civic and political rights to the current concern and obsession with economic rights and livelihoods is symptomatic of the changing times. The national resonance of the economic as against the civic and political is in line with the best tradition of democratic demands.

This begins to not only link the political and the economic and, by so doing, widen the democratic space and the arena of claim-making beyond the civic and the political. It also provides the context within which issues around social justice and social citizenship begin to take shape as part of everyday discourse.

---

20   The ten-year civil war has put paid to any talk about revolution/revolutionary transformation in contemporary Sierra Leone.

References

Abdullah, I. (1998) 'Bush path to Destruction: The Origin and Character of the Revolutionary United Front (RUF/SL)' *Journal of Modern African Studies*, 36(2): 203-235

Abdullah, I. and Muana, P. (1998) 'The Revolutionary United Front of Sierra Leone: A Revolt of the Lumpen Proletariat', in C. Clapham (ed) *African Guerrillas*, Oxford, James Currey, 172 –193

Bayat, A. (2010) *Life as Politics: How Ordinary People Change the Middle East*, first edition, Stanford, Stanford University Press

Beinin, J. and Vairel, F. (2011) (eds) *Social Movements, Mobilization, and Contestation in the Middle East and North Africa*, Stanford, Stanford University Press

Bevington, D. and Dixon, C. (2005) 'Movement-relevant Theory: Rethinking Social Movement Scholarship and Activism', *Social Movement Studies: Journal of Social, Cultural and Political Protest*, 4(3): 185-208

Cheru, F. (1997) 'New Social Movements: Democratic Struggles and Human Rights in Africa' in J. H. Mittleman (ed) *Globalisation: Critical Reflections*, Boulder, Lynne Rienner

Dwyer, P. and Zeilig, L. (2012) *African Struggles Today: Social Movements Since Independence*, Chicago, Haymarket Books

FAO (2012) 'FAO Country Programming Framework 2012-2016', http://coin.fao.org/coin-static/cms/media/12/13636074556260/country_programming_framework.pdf, accessed March 2014

Frost, D. (2012) *From the Pit to the Market: Politics and the Diamond Economy in Sierra Leone*, Oxford, James Currey

Larmer, M. (2010) 'Social Movement Struggles in Africa', *Review of African Political Economy*, 37 (125):251-262

Mamdani, M. and Wamba-dia-Wamba, E. (1995) (eds) *African Studies in Social Movements and Democracy*, Dakar, CODESRIA

Nasong'o, S.W. (2007) 'Negotiating New Rules of the Game: Social Movements, Civil Society and the Kenyan Transition' in Murunga, G. R. and Nasong'o, S.W. (eds) *Kenya: The Struggle for Democracy*, London/Dakar, Zed Books and CODESRIA

Press, R. (2010) 'Peaceful Resistance in Contemporary Africa: Non-Violent Social Movements in Kenya, Sierra Leone and Liberia', Paper Presented at the Annual Meeting of the American Political Science Association, Washington D.C., 2-5 September

Tilly, C. (1994) 'Social Movements as historically specific clusters of political performances', *Berkeley Journal of Sociology*, 38:1-30

Tilly, C. (2004) *Social Movements, 1768-2004*, Boulder/London, Paradigm Publishers

Welthungerhilfe, International Food Policy Research Institute, Concern Worldwide (2013) *Global Hunger Index: The Challenge of Hunger: Building Resilience to Achieve Food and Nutrition Security*, Bonn, Washington DC, Dublin, http://www.ifpri.org/sites/default/files/publications/ghi13.pdf, accessed March 2014

CHAPTER: 2

COLLECTIVE MOBILISATION AND THE RESURGENCE OF THE SLAVERY ISSUE IN MAURITANIA

Zekeria ould Ahmed Salem

Mauritania is a country that has been marked, in recent years, by instability of state power, palace revolutions and attempts at top-down 'democratisation'. At the same time, and since 2007, Mauritania is experiencing various social protests involving nearly all social categories. What has been improperly called the "Mauritanian spring' has been triggered by social discontent. This discontent expressed the refusal by popular classes and the youth to accept an increase of extreme poverty, social decay and, even more, lack of prospects. The dividends of these protests have accrued to the haratine movement which fights since the end of the 1970s to end slavery practices and its legacies.

The period of significant social and political changes Mauritania has been experiencing for over a decade was particularly marked by an upsurge in various forms of social protest. The expansion and simultaneousness of social movements in recent years has been remarkable. Since 2007 in particular, protests have been expanding and increasing horizontally to include a growing number of social sectors and categories. The various collective mobilisations have in common, among other factors: a remarkable sociological diversity of the dissatisfied, a national scope and collective action repertoires that are both classic (sit-ins, strikes, marches, demonstrations) and original in that, for example, social movements have literally invaded the state and its administrative buildings. It has become routine practice for groups ranging from public sector 'temporary' workers to unemployed graduates, people who have been dismissed from public and private enterprises, landless or homeless citizens, women, disabled people, retired people and Imams to camp for days in areas around administrative buildings (or within the walls of a courthouse, or even in front of the presidency).

The claims of the various groups concerned have been only partially articulated in terms of demands for radical change in the regime or in questioning the global socio-political order. Yet the demonstrators were calling for the resignation of the government, the cancellation of questionable public procurements and better sharing of national resources for the poorest and marginalised segments of society, including unemployed youth. But, up to and including 2011, what was improperly called the 'Mauritanian Spring' did not turn into a generalised revolt. It benefited not opposition parties and political forces, but rather pre-existing and well established organisations and social movements which were key actors in the process. This applies in particular to the movements that preceded and partly inspired the recent protests due to their national dimension, their militant experience and the historical, political and symbolic weight of the cause they champion. Likewise, the economic and social dimensions have become predominant in the claims expressed, because they appear to adapt to the concerns most widely shared by all actors, beyond their differences or political affiliations. This is even more obvious for the organisations and groups whose central claims relate to economic exclusion, downward social mobility or 'administrative' marginalisation.

We have witnessed, for example, the resurgence of claims for national inclusion by Negro-Mauritanian groups originating from the River Senegal Region (in particular the Peul or Halpular ethnic groups). For example, a new social movement led by youth from this ethnic group, known as *Touche pas à ma nationalité*[11] (TPMN) emerged in 2011. Its leaders took over the already old nationalist claims by Negro-Mauritanians calling to end political exclusion. TPMN protested in particular against the blockages which the 'Afro-Mauritanians' would face during the 'barometric census', underway in the country since 2010. But in this situation, what was even more remarkable was the revival of the social movements created and led by people of servile origin (*Haratine*) and members of the majority ethnic component called 'Arab-Berber'. Yet, since most of the popular and poor classes in Mauritania are precisely of *Haratine* origin, the resurgence of the issue of the legacy of slavery and its economic and social aftermath appeared to be fully in line with the privileged themes of the recent socio-economic mobilisations. As such, it deserves special attention, due to its central and exemplary character in these ongoing dynamics. In what follows, I will first revisit the events that led to the protests recently observed in Mauritania, focussing on the turn taken as of January 2011. Next, I will review the government's reaction and response to the intensifying protests and strikes as well as the effects of protests on the political scene. Lastly, I will explore the forms in which the so-called issue of 'slavery' and the marginalisation of the *Haratine* were expressed on this occasion. To do so, I will dwell on the actions led by the *Haratine* movements in general and, in particular, by a non-authorised organisation called *Initiative de Résurgence du Mouvement Abolitionniste*[2] (IRA-Mauritania). This focus is all the more interesting given that, throughout the actual period of protest, this organisation carried out actions showing that denouncing the status of the *Haratine* had to be paired with special attention to the dimensions of economic empowerment and liberation from exploitative labour.

---

1   Don't touch my nationality
2   Initiative for the Resurgence of the Abolitionist Movement

A protest fever or a 'pseudo-spring'?

Initiated in early 2011, the protests against deteriorating economic conditions, the high cost of living or social injustices rapidly reached several big cities in the country, affecting most sectors in society. The first large-scale public demonstration took place on 13 January 2011 in Nouakchott, gathering thousands of people who denounced the 'rising prices', unemployment and the 'economic crisis'. Certainly, when Yacoub Ould Dahoud, a man in his forties, set himself on fire in front of the Presidential Palace on 17 January, one would have expected increased tension. But things did not turn out the way it had been expected after this spectacular event. However, in the following days, hundreds of people organised protests in the streets of Nouakchott, often in a dispersed manner. Other protests took place simultaneously inside the country, mainly in the mining area in the north, in Zouerate and even in medium-sized cities like Atar, in the centre, or in Nema, in the far east.

This protest fever was not really new. Since at least the September 2007 riots in which one person was killed in Bassiknou, near the border with Mali, various social movements had begun consistently deploring the worsening living conditions and the inability of the state to support the population in a context of inflation and increasing unemployment. The discontent expressed the refusal to accept an increase of extreme poverty, social decay and, even more, lack of prospects.

Since then, the protest movement appeared to expand and reach more big cities. In the capital city Nouakchott, the so-called '25 February' youth movement, using Internet-based mobilisation, became increasingly famous, showing similarities to the Arab model. Its leaders were trying to establish permanent protests, especially starting from March where organised outings were held on a bi-weekly basis on Tuesdays and Fridays. But what was striking was the will to hold these protests in one geographic place, based on the Egyptian model. In this case, the so-called Place 'des blocs', a public place in the centre of Nouakchott granted to people close to the regime under conditions deemed to lack transparency, was erected as a major gathering place and a symbol of the refusal of a return to 'clientelist practices' (see below). The protesters often expressed a refusal of clientelist or clan-based domination at the highest levels of government. However, upon taking office in 2008, President Ould Abdel Aziz had promised to dismantle a well-established clientelist system, a promise which was made with a force proportionate to the disappointment expressed among the working class and the middle class. The austerity and rigour advocated by the government appeared to affect mainly the middle and working classes. That's why the anger of large categories of the Nouakchott population was triggered by the increasing scarcity of the manna of government grants. Not satisfied with 'turning off social taps', as the expression was sometimes heard in the streets, the new regime had also put an end to the privileges of civil servants (housing, cars, fuel, etc) which were in fact for many 'indirect social safety nets'. The government was then accused of excluding the middle and working classes without being irreproachable in its management of public goods. But it is true that most of the claims concerned the rising prices and lack of employment. Although they were rarely massive and most often divided, the numerous demonstrations only led to moderate clashes between demonstrators and police forces. While the reunification of the collective actions in question did not appear at any time to be a common goal of the groups engaged in the movements, few social or professional sectors escaped the temptation to take to the streets. Yet, it was visibly as if all the groups mobilised were wary of political exploitation, wherever it may come from, and focused more on issues relating to purchasing power, working conditions and the economic situation. For all that, as I will demonstrate, it is clear that all the claims and criticisms of the movements engaged in the protest were underpinned by a feeling of anger at an unstable political order and a political regime which, although recent (President Ould Abdel Aziz came to power on 6

August 2008), was largely perceived as being as illegitimate and unfair as its predecessors.

A favourable political context?

The major recent demonstrations concerned the high cost of living, social injustices and the 'return' of corruption. But, in some aspects, they were closely linked to the institutional blockages and the political and economic instability that had been affecting the country since at least 2005. We need to revisit this short-term trajectory to understand the political background of the most recent social movements.

Indeed, since the fall in August 2005 of the regime of Maaôuya Ould Taya (who had been in power since 1984), the country was wide open to legal protests and authorised demonstrations. Likewise, the democratic transition conducted at that time led to a satisfactory electoral process from the point of view of political actors, civil society and the international community. At that time, observers of the country commended the 'Mauritanian democratisation' which was even touted as an 'example for the Arab world'. It is true that at the time, the *Comité Militaire pour la Justice et la Démocratie*[3] led by Colonel Ely Ould Mohamed Vall, had organised a democratic transition that enabled the establishment of an elected civil regime under the direction of President Sidi Ould Cheikh Abdallah. However, with the rapid crisis that occurred with his parliamentary majority underhandedly supported by the army, 'the first democratically elected President of the country' was overthrown by General Mohamed Ould Abdel Aziz on 6 August 2008. The coup de force, which was rejected by the international community and the opposition organised within a *Front National de Défense de la Démocratie*/National Front for the Defence of Democracy (FNDD), was an opportunity for Mauritanian political forces to use protest and occupy the streets to challenge the military regime. It is not by chance that this FNDD activism embodied the refusal of

---

3 Military Council for Justice and Democracy

coups in general and thus symbolised the acute political crisis that would last a year before the Dakar Agreement signed on June 2009 between FNDD and the junta led by Aziz made it possible to organise presidential elections, still won by Aziz in July 2009.

The increased demonstrations during the following years were, therefore, an extension of an existing movement. If the regime succeeded in stabilising the institutional field as of July 2009, despite protests by the opposition crying electoral fraud, it was at the cost of the accumulation of popular expectations of a head of state that did not cut corners on promises to improve economic and social conditions. Indeed, during the whole year in which the regime of Aziz was not yet 'legitimate' (between August 2008 and July 2009), he lavishly distributed 'gifts' to vulnerable populations, planned roads in peripheral areas, distributed food, recruited dozens of unemployed youth and imprisoned civil servants charged with embezzlement of public funds, etc. The candidate Aziz had, besides, adopted the slogan of a 'president of the poor' engaged in bringing about a 'New Mauritania'.

Furthermore, after he was elected, the new head of state had additional political resources following his recognition by the international community. Supported now by Western powers led by France and the United States, he appeared very soon as a guarantor of regional security in the face of terrorism in northern Mali. He had thus the wherewithal to deal with popular pressures internally. This was all the more possible since the opposition was, at the time, brought down by the failure of the famous Dakar Agreement and its electoral consequences. But in early 2011, the global political situation of the country seemed again somewhat confused. Wild rumours of embezzlement, nepotism and personal enrichment were increasing the disillusionment relative to the advent of a 'New Mauritania', as promised by Aziz as an election candidate. In a context where he had much room for manoeuvre, the president was increasingly accused of exercising personal domination while using well-meaning rhetoric (such as the 'fight against profligate waste'), without succeeding in improving the living conditions of the population. The Internet fora close to the opposition even accused the head of state of selling at cut-price the mining and/or fisheries resources of the country to the profit of foreign and/or local capitalist interests. The storming of the public space of Nouakchott by hundreds of protesters is therefore to be understood in relation to these alleged excesses. However, the sole real attempt at federating the protests around prevarication and economic mismanagement as central themes came from the *Mouvement du 25 février*.[4] After hesitating for some time to negotiate with the authorities, the movement finally officially handed over a platform of demands to the Ministry of the Interior. The treatment of the demands of one of the main social movements by the government is illustrative of the global reaction of the authorities towards the whole wave of protests.

Between exploitation and ad hoc responses

In Mauritanian opinion, the spectre of the wave of revolts in the Arab world was omnipresent. But the local situation bore little resemblance in terms of scale with what was occurring in Tunisia or Egypt. It is true however that the masses of young people occupying the Mauritanian streets were clearly in line with what was termed the 'Arab Spring'. But, in addition to the fact that the comparison was, objectively, quite excessive, it is obvious that the newness of the regime had granted it considerable leeway, compared with the contexts of the 'Arab Springs', where the populations demanded the removal of corrupt powers established for decades. Aziz himself kept repeating that he did not have enough years of service to arouse a revolution. Thus, he did everything to give credence to the idea that the structural crisis affecting the population was the result of an accumulation of problems attributable to previous regimes.

---

4 February 25th Movement

The authorities conducted a large campaign to explain that the regime in place could not be accountable for the existing injustices and the economic mismanagement that had ruined the country in previous years. It was all the easier to pursue this rhetoric in that Aziz had led an anti-corruption policy and made numerous pledges to that end. Intensifying the campaign for the control of public management since 2009, he had committed to arresting and imprisoning the perpetrators of corrupt practices, not hesitating, as soon as he was elected, to put in jail many public enterprise or development project leaders whenever they were suspected of embezzlement. He had also arrested some of the major businessmen close to the former president, Ould Taya, and forced them to repay several billion ouguiyas which they had allegedly received from the former regime.

On the street, the scale and violence of the demonstrations and marches did not reach uncontrollable proportions. The protest fever was, besides, controlled by the authorities. The latter had skilfully decided to trivialise the expression of vested interests in the public space. Faced with protests, the government did not provide an unequivocal response. It appears indeed that its global strategy to prevent any unification of the protesters bore fruit. The calls for dialogue were also repeated over and over again by the representatives of the state. However, these calls were not rapidly heard by protest organisations.

While the government was demanding to meet with the protest representatives, its efforts had remained unsuccessful for some weeks. The February 25th movement, for example, refused the proposal by the Ministry of the Interior for dialogue and claimed that the government should satisfy the movement's demands without prior negotiations 'in view of the obvious timeliness of the claims'. It would therefore take a few months to dissipate the mistrust, which only disappeared as the wave of protests faded away. Nevertheless, when Aziz received a delegation of the 25 February movement leaders in June 2011, he tried to convince them that he himself was a 'young man in rebellion' against the establishment and the classic conception of public management. He even argued that he came to power precisely to end clientelism and mismanagement, to combat extreme poverty and lack of employment for the youth, and to promote the redistribution of national resources. In these circumstances, in parallel with the protests, the head of state and his government set themselves up as indirect members of the movement for denouncing and reviewing the economic and political practices that had prevailed in the country over the past 50 years. In a special live broadcast on national television in July 2011, Aziz even claimed that the demands of the youth were also his own, and justified his seizure of power by force in 2008.

In any case, it was from this moment that a change could be seen in the interactions between the actors of the ongoing social conflict. All claim-making groups had rapidly decided to ignore government bodies (prime minister, minister of the interior, etc) and to speak directly to the head of state. In actual fact, their marches had already been converging on the presidency. Many of them demanded to be received by Aziz. The latter quite regularly responded positively to their demands, which somewhat held back the unrest. But when this dynamic was initiated, the general protest movement had already begun to lose its intensity.

In the social field, public authorities also hurried to defuse the protests by dealing with the most pressing issues; that is to say by putting in place social measures intended to nip in the bud any attempt of reunification or scaling up of the protest dynamics. Following the mass demonstration that took place in Nouakchott on 13 January 2011, for example, the first large-scale response was a nine-billion ouguiya[5] social plan, making it possible to lower by 30 per cent the price of basic foodstuffs in a network of specialised shops. Intended to make basic essentials available at affordable prices, this so-called *Emel* (Hope) operation helped keep down the level of discontent of some vulnerable categories of the population, regardless of the substantive and

5   1 US dollar = 300 ouguiyas

procedural controversies aroused by this classic initiative led by authorities in this type of situation. Other measures to ease the political climate were subsequently announced or initiated. In June 2011, a decree on the decriminalisation of press offenses was adopted while agricultural plots in the Senegal River Valley in Mauritania were allocated to young graduates within the framework of the crop year that was starting.

On the political front, the authorities deliberately isolated the national political elites, including within the dominant party *Union pour la République*[6] in order to reach out to the 'youth'. That's how the head of state had triggered, much to the dismay of his political friends, the creation of a 'party of the youth' which was said in official circles to be 'forbidden to people under 40'. It appeared that this party, called *al-hîrak al-shababi, or* The Youth Movement, was meant to be an attempt to get back part of the protesters, well beyond the 25 February movement. The move was all the more successful as it not only eventually marginalised the 25 February movement itself, but also diverted many of its supporters from the street protests.

Displeased with the 'youthist excess', some allies of the regime who had been supporting it since 2009 slammed the door on the 'enlarged presidential majority'. This was the case of the Arab nationalist party HATEM, and of the Islamist party TAWASSOUL. Since then, the latter has even expressed that it has no hope that the current regime will improve in the short term. More broadly, for all parliamentary opposition parties, the state of permanent demonstration during this period was a sign of blockage and anomie which the head of state refused to take seriously or to address. The democratic opposition leader Ahmed Ould Daddah, president of the Rassemblement des Forces Démocratiques[7] (RFD), the main parliamentary opposition party, even went so far as to say that the country suffered from a 'vacancy of power'. But in fact, the opposition, which is significantly weakened, exhausted, defeated and strongly divided, was itself in full generational transition. For example,

6   Union for the Republic
7   Rally of Democratic Forces

its aging leaders were cut off from their cadres and their constituencies. They no longer managed to attract the Mauritanian population, most of whom (over 65 per cent) are under 30 years of age. Therefore, the discontent did not profit the opposition, despite its eagerness to support it. It even proved unable to exploit a protest movement that was diffused, fragmented and resistant to political exploitation. This weakness of the opposition in embodying an alternative project or instrumentalising the discontent was the main asset of the government in power. But above all, the discontent enabled already existing organisations to thrive on sectional, ethnic or social class claims. It is within this framework that organisations advocating for some special interest groups increased their activism. In this regard, advocacy groups for the Arabic-speaking populations of slave descent (*Haratines*) appear to have been better able to effectively use the protest environment of recent years. Their experience therefore deserves a detailed analysis.

The 'Haratine' movements and the denunciation of 'slavery-like governance'

The political handling of the 'crisis' clearly showed that the protest situation had contributed to the return in force of ethnic issues. Thus, when the government called for inclusive dialogue, only some parties responded to this initiative. The decisive presence of two opposition parties led by *Haratines*, namely *Alliance Populaire Progressiste*/People's Progressive Alliance (APP) of Messaoud Ould Boulkheir and *al-Wiam* of Boydiel Ould Houmeid, was notable. Thus, in September 2011, a new national conference (*assises*) was finally officially launched under the gaze of the media and public opinion, leading to reforms on: national unity and social cohesion, the strengthening of democracy and justice, audio-visual reform, the status of the opposition, the electoral code, the alternation of power, the place and role of the army, governance, the administration and, finally, security challenges and the fight against terrorism. In any case, this dialogue had been perceived by the authorities as the ultimate means to appease the political and social arena. The list of announced reforms was intended not only to give back the initiative to the institutional policy framework, but also to give tokens of goodwill to each social group in the country. The dialogue was an objective in itself and certainly appeased part of the social arena. Above all, it was obvious that regardless of the immediate effectiveness of the ad hoc measures taken by public authorities, the claims perceived by the government as most threatening and serious appeared less likely to be effectively dealt with in the short term. This was the case for the far more complex ethnic issues which were reflected in broader and more open claims expressed during the sporadic demonstrations, be they under cover of particular economic or administrative issues. This was especially the case for the issue of the eradication of slavery and its economic and social legacies. Indeed, this was the very reason why the national dialogue resulted, in among other things, the decision to include in the constitution currently under reform a provision to foster the implementation of laws criminalising slavery and slavery-like practices. However, this was only one political measure in a long list of measures starting with the July 1981 law abolishing slavery and the September 2007 law criminalising slavery. Beyond all this, at stake were the issues of the *Haratine* and slavery, which had re-emerged at the heart of the recent protests. But in order to better understand this dimension, which we are going to explore in depth, we should briefly go over the origin and evolution of the *Haratine* social movement.

Since March 1978 and the creation of the *Mouvement de libération et d'émancipation des Haratines*[8] *(El Hor:* 'free man' in Arabic*)*, the *Haratine* aimed to eradicate slavery and its legacy in Mauritania. But they also aimed to establish a policy to address the promotion and economic empowerment of a population of servile origin often estimated (in the absence of official figures) by activists at slightly less than half of the population. But these recurrent claims have in recent years taken on a dual feature focused on economic equality on the one hand, and identity-related aspects on the

---

8   Movement for the Liberation and Emancipation of the Haratine

other. We are going to use two examples to illustrate: the short-lived *Front Uni pour l'Action des Haratines*/Haratine United Front for Action (FUAH), and IRA Mauritania. The latter is now closely related to one of the most important social movements in Mauritania that goes beyond its category or ethnic nature.

In fact, while organisations stemming from *El-Hor* have increased since the mid-1990s as part of the 'democratisation' of civil society, some initiatives have stood out. In particular, this is the case with *SOS-Esclaves,* which has received sustained national and international attention since 1995. Its actions were mainly geared to denouncing cases of 'servile work' and traditional slavery. It also meant to bear witness to the suffering of the victims and help them recover their rights. But in the early 2000s, we saw the emergence of various movements clearly geared towards the claim for economic equality and the sharing of economic and political resources. Thus, in 2008, we witnessed the creation of FUAH, which stood out with the publication of a paper entitled *'Bilan : 50 ans d'exclusion et de marginalisation systématiques des Haratines'.*[9] The purpose was to document 'with figures to support it', the exclusion of this category of the population from administrative, economic and military positions. This study articulated in a detailed manner the claim by the *Haratine* of their prior settlement in Mauritanian territory and their dispossession by 'Arab-Berber invaders'. According to the document, there is a relationship between the lack of schooling of the *Haratine* and their subsequent reduced access to public service, deliberately orchestrated by both colonisation and the postcolonial power. However, according to FUAH, the exclusion of the *Haratine* was a well-considered postcolonial plan to keep them away from the economic resources of the country to which they would have priority entitlement as a 'demographic majority'. All the successive regimes since then have sanctioned this policy, regrets FUAH. The document provides a comprehensive analysis of what it qualifies as a deliberate policy of

---

9   The document has been largely released on the Internet, mainly on www.cridem.mr and www.haratines.com

instrumentation of the economic reforms in view of excluding the *Haratine* group, while at the same time strengthening the Arab-Berber group.

According to the organisation, the systematic exclusion of the *Haratine* from land ownership is exemplified by the policy of a state refusing in practice (and despite the existing laws) to implement the individuation of land ownership. By continuing to recognise in practice the tribal ownership of the lands farmed by the *Haratine*, the state prevents the latter from access to land ownership and forces them into sharecropping. And that is how, in rural areas, the *Haratine* are doomed to remain relegated to 'menial works in which they are exposed to new forms of slavery-like practices'.

But it is when the document addresses the high cost of living that it somehow heralds the issues raised during recent protests, in particular by *Haratine* organisations. The high cost of living, according to FUAH, affects the *Haratine* first, because 'the continued surge in the prices of basic necessities (rice, oil, wheat, sugar, etc), butane gas bottles and building materials, to name but a few, adversely affect the living conditions of Mauritanians, and the *Haratine* are mostly affected by extreme poverty. In these circumstances, the document denounces a genuine 'policy of economic strangulation'.

It is indisputable that in terms of social subordination and obvious economic exclusion, the *Haratine* are in an incomparable situation. This is probably the reason why the current resurgence of the movement for the defence of these groups sometimes privileges campaigns aimed at fighting enslavement in the current economy which is even, as will now be seen, a focus of the denunciation of slavery and its legacy. That's why recent social movements gave it a prominent place and offered the *Haratine* activists an opportunity to be more active.

In relation to the degrading working conditions of most of their community members, the message of *Haratine* activists has been simple: slavery ends where depersonalised and non-domestic paid work begins. This would be the main thrust of the arguments and mobilisation of the IRA, when the circumstances appeared to be most favourable. Two examples illustrate this point. The first example is that of dock workers (mostly of *Haratine* origin) in the ports and markets of Mauritania. The second example is the even more sensitive issue of domestic workers of servile origin who remain employed by their 'former masters' under conditions that IRA consider to be slave-like. Later, the Mauritanian state and justice system would be compelled, under increased pressure during the 'Mauritanian Spring', to consider these conditions in the same light.

The porters

In early May 2010, hundreds of black men working as dock workers/ porters blocked the entrance to the central market of Nouakchott to protest against their working conditions and demand a wage increase. For most knowledgeable Mauritanians, this was not a trivial social conflict. Most of the striking workers were *Haratine,* probably the only people in the country to do menial work in the most strenuous and least paid professions such as domestic workers, car washers, porters, butchers' shop assistants, shepherds, farmers, sharecroppers, watchmen and unskilled workers. This particular protest of the dock workers, therefore, referred to one of the most important political challenges in the country. In this case, the issue of work and its forms holds pride of place alongside identity and political issues.

After several strongly repressed demonstrations, the conflict was finally settled through the classic political method of combining promises to improve conditions with subtle threats. But, for unions specialising in the defence of the *Haratine,* such as the *Confédération Libre des Employeurs de Mauritanie* (CLTM), this was only part of the just fight of former slaves for the whole *Haratine* community to have access to a decent economic life and to the fruits of the equitable distribution of national resources. For other human rights organisations such as IRA, this revolt had an even broader meaning. According to its charismatic president Birame

Ould Abeid, there was a whole political economy of slavery. In a text entitled *'Le fardeau de l'homme haratine ou la gouvernance esclavagiste'*,[10] he summarises how the *Haratine* protest should be understood:

> Every time we pretend to chase away the obstinate and daily reality of slavery, it comes back quickly. Current developments speak for themselves in this respect. It is rare indeed for a social conflict to be as emblematic as that of the dockers' conflict.

> While some persist to see in it a simple union or corporatist struggle for minor one-off benefits, it is obviously a further and undoubtedly indicative demonstration of a process of perpetuation of a dual regime of domination and exploitation, all the more violent that it is institutionalised. The very fact that dockers in Mauritania are exclusively *Haratine* should convince the sceptical - real or feigned - that the 'liberation' of slaves always comes through... slavery. It is as if the political economy of inequality at birth is strengthened in this country by sustainable, deeply rooted and implacable mechanisms.

> From whatever angle it is addressed, the issue of slaves and the *Haratine* leads to the same finding: the country's majority community stay under domination and bent under the throes of exclusion. But above all, it is denied the right to complain or to lament its own submission. The prevailing opinion, another reflection of the hegemony, finds it perfectly normal and even natural that a human group of such importance in the Mauritanian historicity and reality be methodically despised and kept away from the minimum conditions for survival. It is a fortiori kept away from power positions and condemned to hold the smaller portion of power. The community hardly

---

10 The burden of the Haratine man: slavery-like governance

accepts to leave to it the spat-out crumbs and the leftovers of its feasts, exactly like in the good old days of feudality. The whole society gladly wipes its feet on the social mat that these authentic wretched of the Earth represent. He who believes, by chance, in such a severe statement is very naive. (…) The freedom of the *Haratine* who are generously called the 'former slaves' has no value in the absence of minimum guarantees of survival. This freedom granted to a few is all the more false that it comes with total deprivation nurtured by perfectly functional mechanisms.[11]

The years 2011-2013 were therefore marked in a sensational way by the mobilisations of IRA around these themes. In the midst of the period of January - July 2011, the anti-slavery organisation appeared to focus the interest of the press to the detriment of movements such as 25th February, who were thus doomed to show solidarity with the *Haratine* activists in order to remain part of the social protest.

Speaking out against servile work

The movement against servile work lent a unique characteristic to the overall protest movement and gave *Haratine* activists a leading role in the social equality movement. Relegation of people descended from slaves to menial work was condemned because it both symbolised and perpetuated the apparent subordination and the manifest exploitation of the *Haratine*. The protest against domestic labour by the *Haratine* in the homes of their former masters took aim at the supposed reincarnation of the master-slave relationship. In this relationship, the *Haratine* appeared to be chained to their masters through domestic labour in a way that strikingly mirrored the illegitimate slavery relationship. In order to understand the logic behind this

---

11 Birame Ould Abeid « Le fardeau de l'Homme haratine ou la gouvernance esclavagiste », document published on www.cridem.org and subsequently by the French-speaking press in May 2010. The text can be consulted on the following site: http://haratine.blogspot.com/2010/06/le-fardeau-de-lhomme-haratin-ou-la.html

reasoning, which was omnipresent in the protests that anti-slavery activists organised as of late 2010, a certain number of facts should be recalled.

In the traditional slavery situation, which continues to exist in certain forms in the country, slave labour is alienated in the framework of a 'family' relationship that is all the more fictional since it is established that the slave and his or her offspring 'belong' to the family. Slaves belong to a family, but they also identify themselves as belonging to the tribes of their masters, to which they indeed belong as 'second class' members. This distinction is important in a country where tribal background is still a highly meaningful component of an individual's social identity. Even when they have been freed, the *Haratine* sometimes remain emotionally and even physically attached to these networks, even though their status continues to be that of a servant. That is why movements such as *El-Hor* focus above all on economic emancipation through salaried employment. And it is doubtless also one of the reasons why an organisation such as *SOS-Esclaves* developed an argument in the late 1990s according to which freeing slaves was still a means of keeping them in servitude as long as the community did not bring to bear the necessary resources to ensure true economic, social and psychological emancipation for the *Haratine* people. One of the most spectacular manifestations of this situation is the fact that some former slaves continue to do domestic work in the homes of their former masters under conditions condemned by organisations such as IRA. In recent times, the organisation even managed to bring court cases against former masters whose former slaves performed servile work for them with no formal contract or salary. The purpose of those complaints was to obtain what all *Haratine* activists had been seeking for the last 30 years, to wit for the Mauritanian justice system to condemn perpetrators and accomplices of slavery-like practices. As we shall see, this goal, which until recently appeared to be out of reach, was only achieved after the violent *Haratine* protests of 2011, in the midst of the Arab spring.

In December 2010, just weeks before the dawning of what would be known as the 'Maghreb Spring', clashes between demonstrators and police officers took place in front of a police station in Arafat, a densely-populated neighbourhood on the outskirts of Nouakchott. The immediate cause of the skirmish, which nearly developed into a riot, was a demonstration organised by IRA. Members of the organisation, who were all descendants of slaves (*Haratine*), were protesting against the dismissal of a 'case of slavery in flagrante delicto' which they claimed to have brought to light. They particularly condemned the impunity enjoyed by the woman who employed two young 'slave' girls without payment. Invoking the seriousness of a crime duly punished by the law of 2007 on the criminalisation of slavery and slavery-like practices, the activists moved closer towards violence on that day, breaking with the peaceful tradition of anti-slavery movements in Mauritania. The confrontation culminated in the collective arrest of the organisation's leadership. However, only its president, Birame Ould Abeid, stayed in prison for several weeks. In January 2011, a Nouakchott court condemned Oumou Mint Bakar Vall, whom IRA accused of slavery, to six months in prison without parole. She was the first person in the history of the country to have been condemned for slavery, but only spent a few days in prison before being released.

Subsequently, Birame Ould Abeid stood trial along with other members of his organisation. The group was sentenced to six months in prison for having 'participated in an unauthorised demonstration'. The verdict handed down against Ould Abeid and his companions was based on accusations of 'assembly and disruption of the public peace, and use of violence against police officers'. Ould Abeid related the incident in court, stating that what had happened was part of an attempt to frame IRA members. According to the president of IRA, they did not conduct an assembly, but had gone to see the administrative authorities, as was the usual practice for most activists faced with cases involving slavery. They were then physically attacked by police and had no other choice but to defend themselves. They claimed that the police threw teargas bombs at them and beat up their leader. During the trial, Ould Abeid questioned the hidden motives of the security forces. In any case, he refuted the idea that his organisation was a proponent of violence. The convicted activists were eventually released in late February 2011 after they were granted a presidential pardon.

In late March 2011, a similar case involving exploitation of a minor girl, described by activists as slavery, was also brought to court. IRA was involved in the process with support from another, older association known as *SOS-Esclaves*. They were also joined by the *Association des femmes chefs de ménage*,[12] one of the rare anti-slavery organisations headed by a person who is not a slave descendant. Due to fears that the justice system would once again dismiss the case with no further action, the leaders of all three associations (Birame Ould Dah, Boubacar Ould Messaoud and Fatimettou Mint El Mokhtar) camped within the walls of the Nouakchott courthouse and undertook a hunger strike that lasted three days. This event, which was without precedent in the history of Mauritanian protest movements, was followed by the media with considerable interest. Opposition MPs visited the activists, the authorities sent envoys, the government actively sought to reach a bargain with the hunger strikers, and sympathisers organised nightly vigils in front of the Nouakchott courthouse. The situation continued until the people accused of slavery were arrested a few days later. At that time, it became clear that the fight against slavery represented, more than ever, the key demand of the underprivileged social classes.

This was particularly true to the extent that, following that case, President Ould Abdel Aziz urged the government to reactivate the legal arsenal aimed at combating slavery and its most far-reaching consequences, described by the report on the proceedings of the Council of Ministers as 'new practices within social relations that need to be reviewed and corrected in order to bring them into line with the standards characterising the rule of law,

---

12   Association of Women Heads of Families

which are equality and justice for all citizens.' Aziz asked the government, accordingly, to produce a strategy to be implemented as quickly as possible, particularly in relation to domestic labour, with a view to enshrining the rights and duties of both parties. In that framework, the ministry in charge of labour promptly published an order regulating domestic labour. In social terms, Moorish families were panic-stricken and for some time refused to hire servants 'belonging to their tribes' for fear of becoming embroiled in one of the many judicial proceedings systematically launched by IRA in such cases.

At the same time, state television organised a debate on the issue of slavery and child labour with the notable participation of all of the stakeholders involved in this highly sensitive social issue. Participants included the president of the National Human Rights Commission, MPs, representatives of the police and human rights advocates.

Finally, in an atmosphere of widespread protest, social movements focusing on the issue of slavery and the condemnation of slave labour often monopolised media attention in a context marked by expressions of discontent in the streets and around public buildings. This forced the other sectorial movements to include the claims of the anti-slavery organisations in their mobilisation mechanisms, thereby granting the re-emergence of the slavery issue and the marginalisation of groups of people descended from slaves a starring role in the protest movement that swept the country at that time. From this standpoint, the cause of the *Haratine* people ultimately seems to have benefitted more from the 'Mauritanian Spring' than the *ad hoc* groups created for the protest movement. This is probably why one of the cases taken to court on that occasion, involving a 13-year-old child, Said, employed by a family in the Brakna region, came to a successful conclusion in December 2011.

And yet does this truly spell the end of the euphemistic treatment of the subject (exploitation of isolated minors, etc) and systematic dismissal of cases of this kind? It is difficult to answer this question, as it is difficult to know what economic opportunities will arise from the strong mobilisation of *Haratine* activists who, thanks to the pseudo Mauritanian spring, have certainly been able to reach an audience well beyond the circle of their usual sympathisers. One thing, however, is sure: the government has been obliged to undertake significant political actions in this regard. In 2012, it set up a national agency to combat the consequences of slavery and fight poverty (*Agence Nationale de Lutte contre les Séquelles de l'Esclavage et pour la Lutte contre la Pauvreté*). However, this was a demand that had been repeatedly put forward by *Haratine* social movements since at least the late 1970s.

Conclusion

Beyond the mobilisation witnessed in recent times, the modes of governance at play in social movements in Mauritania are hardly a recent phenomenon. After all, Mauritania is a country that has been marked, in recent years, by instability of state power, palace revolutions and attempts at top-down 'democratisation'. But Mauritania is also a country where generational changes and changes in political personnel affect the political economy of a national entity faced with growing economic and social issues against a backdrop of major social transformations. In this framework, challenges can be identified such as demographic transition, the evolution of traditional social structures and ethnic tensions. The role of economic change should also be stressed, with the growing interest in extractive industries, and the persistent crisis in the agro-pastoral sector against the backdrop of the changing role of the state in the economy. In a North African regional environment subject to spectacular political change, Mauritania, with its Arabic-speaking majority, is also exposed to external political events. Numerous protest groups draw their inspiration from the ideologies and movements of Arab youths revolting against their governments. However, internal dynamics seem to dominate in the current mobilisations, which is the reason why protests always focus on strictly local issues.

This is exemplified by the way the issues surrounding the fate of the *Haratine* people dominated the recent protest movements. *Haratine* activism was prepared to play a leading role in the protest campaign, including by capitalising on its increasingly recognised image as almost the sole defender of a category of the population that is *the* symbol of social exclusion, economic exploitation, marginalisation and poverty. The discourse of the *Haratine* militants no longer focuses solely on the abolition of slavery, or on the integration of *Haratine* elites. Militants increasingly raise issues such as resource sharing, social justice and economic equity. This shift was notable during the recent protests, which were furthermore in phase with those of other social strata such as Negro-Africans, the unemployed, and youths. Beyond the episodic discontent, it should be noted that the consequences of ongoing social changes will depend on the way social injustices and issues of marginalisation and economic justice are handled in the context of a multi-ethnic, post-slavery society, which remains politically unstable.

References

Ciavolella, R. and Fresia, M. (2009) « Mauritanie : la démocratie au coup par coup », *Politique africaine* n°114, juin Paris, Karthala

Ould Ahmed Salem, Z. (2013) *Prêcher dans le désert. Islam politique et changement social en Mauritanie*, Paris, Karthala

Ould Ahmed Salem, Z. (2005) 'Mauritania: A Saharan frontier-state', *The Journal of North African Studies*, 10(3/4): 491–506

Ould Ahmed Salem, Z. (2010) 'Militants aux pieds nus: transformations du mouvement social des Haratines de Mauritanie', *Canadian Journal of African Studies*, 44(2): 283-316

Ruf, U. P. (2001) 'Ending Slavery. Hierarchy, Dependency, and Gender in Central Mauritania', New Brunswick, NJ, Transaction Publishers

CHAPTER 3

SOCIAL MOVEMENTS AND DEMOCRATIC STRUGGLES IN LIBERIA, 2011-2013

George Klay Kieh, Jr.[1]

The study of social movements has attracted considerable scholarly interest over the years, as reflected in the burgeoning literature. However, the bulk of studies have focused on the industrialised liberal democracies - the United States and European states. Consequently, there is a paucity of literature on the developing world, including Africa. This adversely affects the development of theoretical frameworks that are both generalisable and parsimonious. In this vein, there is a need for scholarly attention to be paid to the countries in the developing world, including African ones, as a central focus of the theory-building project in social movement studies. Like the other developing countries, the literature on social movements in Liberia is extremely limited. In fact, the study of social movements in the country is usually problematically treated as an adjunct to other overarching research.

1   I would like to thank Ndongo Samba Sylla, and Bruno Sonko of the Rosa Luxemburg Foundation for their encouragement. Also, my thanks and appreciation go to Richard Yidana, associate professor of sociology and African and African-American studies at Grand Valley State University, Michigan, and my dear brother, friend and colleague, for his immense contributions to my education about social movements in Africa. However, I alone assume full responsibility for the contents of this chapter.

For example, references have been made to social movements in broader studies about the military coup, the two civil wars, democratisation, ethnic relations, and human rights, among others. Accordingly, there is the need to give attention to social movements as the primary focus of research projects. It is in this vein that this study on social movements in Liberia was conducted. Overall, contemporary social movements in Liberia have become sectoralised—labour, students, etc.—thereby lacking the cohesion that was characteristic of the 1970s.

Introduction

The trilogy of state formation, state expansion and state consolidation in Liberia has been characterised by contradictions, crises and conflicts. In fact, some of the conflicts assumed violent complexion at various historical junctures in the country's history (Leavitt 2005, Kieh 2008, 2012). More recently, the country was plagued by two civil wars: the first one from 1989-1997, and the second from 1999-2003 (Sawyer 1992, Adebayo 2002, Dolo 2007, Kieh 2008, 2012). C.E. Zamba Liberty, one of Liberia's most respected historians, provides the following poignant summation of the problematic nature of the Liberian state-building project: 'It may be accurately said that Liberia was conceived in controversy and developed in controversy. Today, it still seems to be engulfed in controversy, (Liberty 2002: VI).

Over the years, Liberia's problematic state-building trajectory has engendered multifaceted crises of underdevelopment - cultural, economic, political, security and social (Liebenow 1970, 1987, Lowenkopf 1976, Wreh 1976, Mayson and Sawyer 1979, David 1984, Kieh 2008, 2012). For example, in the political sphere, the core crises have been the emergence of an apartheid-like liberal democratic political system from 1847-1947 that was pivoted on the exclusion of the members of the indigenous ethnic groups, the majority of the population, and an authoritarian governance architecture from 1955-2003 (Liebenow 1970, Lowenkopf 1976, Sawyer 1992, Dolo 1996, Kieh 2008,

2012). Since 2006, a hybrid political system (the combination of liberal democratic and authoritarian elements) has emerged (Kieh 2012, Freedom House 2013). In the economic realm, the country's peripheral capitalist political economy has generated inequalities and inequities in wealth and income (Mayson and Sawyer 1979, Davis 1984, Kieh 2008, 2012). This has resulted in a dialectical tension between a higher standard of living for the members of the ruling class (state managers, relatively wealthy local business people, resident foreign merchants, and the metropolitan-based owners of multinational corporations like Firestone), and a life of mass and abject poverty and deprivation for the members of the subaltern classes (workers, peasants, the unemployed and *hoi polloi*).

Significantly, the travails of the Liberian state-building project have led to the emergence of social movements at various historical points. In other words, the contradictions, crises and the resulting adverse effects on the various subaltern classes have led to the rise of social movements as the *deus ex machina*[2] for waging democratic struggles against the ruling class and its regimes. Characteristically, the various ruling class-based regimes have uniformly employed the full battery of the state's repressive machinery—military, police and security organisations—as the dominant mode for counter-resistance and suppression. On balance, in some cases, the resistance-counter-resistance dynamic has helped advance the democratic struggles, while in other cases, it has stymied them.

Against this background, this chapter will seek to address several interrelated questions. First, what is the rationale of the various socio-political struggles that have been taking place in Liberia since 2011? Second, what forms have these struggles taken? Third, what has been the political impact of these struggles? Fourth, do these struggles represent a viable response to the 'crisis' of so-called 'representative democracy?' Fifth, has the declining legitimacy of the governing elites opened the path to alternative forms of democratic

---

2 'God from the machinery'

expression and participation? Sixth, what challenges do they bring? Seventh, how have the Liberian elites responded to these challenges? Eighth, what are the limitations of these social movements?

The travails of state-building in Liberia: the crucible

The state-building project in Liberia has evolved in three major phases: the pre-settler state phase (prior to 1820), the settler state phase (1820-1926) and the peripheral capitalist state phase (1926-present). Although each phase was shaped and conditioned by various forces and factors, cumulatively and ultimately they produced the current portrait of the Liberian state in terms of its nature, character, mission and political economy. The state-building project is critical because, among other things, it provides the crucible in which social movements have waged democratic struggles for human rights and the advancement of the material well-being of the majority of Liberians.

The pre-settler state phase

Prior to the arrival of the manumitted Africans from the United States beginning in 1820, the area now called Liberia was known as the Grain Coast (Beyan 1991, Sawyer 1992, Kieh 2008, 2012). It was inhabited by various ethnic groups —the Bassa, Belle, Dei, Gbandi, Gio, Gola, Grebo, Kissi, Kpelle, Krahn, Kru, Lorma, Mandingo, Vai—that had migrated there from various parts of Africa (Beyan 1991, Sawyer 1992, Kieh 2008, 2012). Each ethnic group had various polities replete with their own cultural, economic, political and social systems (Sawyer 1992, Kieh 2008, 2012). These polities interacted with one another through various channels and modes, including diplomacy, trade and war.

Importantly, the intervention of the repatriates from the United States under the tutelage of the American Colonisation Society (ACS) aborted these indigenous state-building projects in two major ways. The ACS, backed by American military might, sought to dislodge the various indigenous ethnic groups from their land (Movement for Justice in Africa 1980, Kieh 2008, 2012). The resulting military 'tugs and pulls' diverted the attention of indigenous ethnic groups from state-building. That is, occupied by the imperative of survival, the various indigenous ethnic groups shifted their resources from the building of their respective states to their defence. In addition, the military intervention of the US on behalf of the ACS created instability that militated against continual indigenous state-building efforts. Another negative effect of the American military intervention was that it enabled the ACS and the repatriates to impose their version of the American cultural system on these indigenous polities (Kieh 2008, 2012).

The settler state phase

The settler phase of the Liberian state-building project was conditioned and shaped by the repatriation of freed Africans from the US to the Grain Coast (now Liberia), beginning in 1820. With the disintegration of the slave-based economy in the American South, the American ruling class was faced with the problem of addressing the challenges posed by a relatively large pool of freed Africans (Smith 1972). As Smith (1972:3) aptly observes: 'The United States Government believed that the "subsequent" emancipation and education of blacks coupled with their fast birth rate would in due course enable them to dominate the U.S.' Having examined various options, the American ruling class and its government made the determination that one of the solutions to the US's racial problem was the repatriation of the freed Africans back to Africa, their ancestral homeland.

Consequently, the ACS, which was organised in 1816 by some of the leading members of the American ruling class such as Henry Clay, who served as speaker of the house of representatives, Associate Justice Bushrod Washington, and General Andrew Jackson, were given the responsibility by the American government to organise and execute the repatriation project (Beyan 1991, Kieh 2008, 2012). Accordingly, the US government gave the ACS the amount of US$100,000 plus a military escort (Kieh 2008, 2012). Subsequently, the ACS undertook an exploratory mission for the ostensible purpose of finding a place in Africa to which the freed Africans could be repatriated (Beyan 1991, Kieh 2008, 2012). Initially, the ACS chose Sierra Leone in West Africa, and repatriated some of the freed Africans to this area. However, after the outbreak of malaria, and the resulting deaths of several of the repatriates, the settlement was moved to the Grain Coast (now Liberia). Interestingly, neither the American government nor its surrogate the ACS consulted with the peoples of Sierra Leone and the Grain Coast about the desirability of the repatriation project. Instead, as a reflection of American hubris, the repatriation project was foisted on these areas. In short, the American ruling class viewed both Sierra Leone and the Grain Coast simply as a vehicle for addressing an 'American problem, without regards for the views of the inhabitants of the areas' (Kieh 2012:5).

Regrettably, the repatriates, who were victims of American hubris and discrimination, brought these vices with them to the Grain Coast. That is, with what Brown (1941:10) poignantly refers to as the 'slave psychology', the settlers had the illusion that they were superior to their African kin, who they met on the Grain Coast, simply because they had lived in the US, howbeit as slaves. Cassell (1970:18) captures the tenor thus: '[Africa] was a grim land cursed with a burning sun and torturing insects. [And] the [American Government's] plan was [designed] to dump free Negros into the savage wilds of Africa as a circuit route back to bondage.'

The resulting 'clash of civilisations'(Huntington 2007, Kieh 2008, 2012) witnessed the concerted and sustained efforts of the repatriates to impose their parody of American civilisation on the various indigenous Liberian polities, and the determination of the indigenes to resist. Ultimately, backed by American military power, the repatriates were able to impose their imitation of American civilisation on the various indigenous polities that were in proximity to the evolving settler state. This included the imposition of the so-called American version of Christianity, American names, American architecture reminiscent of the South, and the replication of various American symbols.

Backed by American military power, the repatriates were also able to take land from the various indigenous polities, mainly through the use of force. Even when the ACS engaged in land negotiations with the various indigenous polities on behalf of the repatriates, the threat of the use of force always served as the anchor. For example, during a 'land purchase', 'American Navy Lieutenant Robert Stockton placed a loaded pistol on the ear of King Peter and forced him to sign the deed giving away Cape Mesurado to the settlers' (Movement for Justice in Africa 1980:3).

The settler phase of the state-building project was constructed in three major stages. The first stage, the colonial period (1822-1839), was characterised by the control of the ACS, which acted as a classical colonial power (Beyan 1991, Kieh 2008, 2012). And this was clearly reflected in the design and operation of the Liberian colonial state. For example, an agent of the ACS, who was akin to a colonial governor-general, administered the colony as a super-dictator, as reflected in his performance of executive, legislative and judicial functions (Beyan 1991, Kieh 2008, 2012). The agent's decisions could only be vetoed by the board of directors of the ACS (Kieh 2008, 2012). Also, the governance tapestry was anchored on a battery of repressive laws such as the Respect for Authority Law (Kieh 2008, 2012). The contradictions produced by the dynamics of the operation of the colonial phase found expression in various struggles (Kieh 2008, 2012). One form pitted the agent and other functionaries of the ACS against the light-skinned segment of the settler stock (the repatriates). The crux of the conflict was over the light-skinned settlers' demand to be given positions in the colonial bureaucracy, howbeit, as junior managers (Kieh 2008, 2012). The other conflict involved the ACS's functionaries and the light-skinned settlers, on the one hand, versus the dark-skinned settlers. The centrepiece of the conflict was the dark-skinned settlers' contention that the agent and other functionaries of the ACS privileged the members of the light-skinned section. Also, there was a conflict between the functionaries of the ACS and the various indigenous polities over various issues, including land. Similarly, various conflicts pitted indigenous polities against the settlers or the repatriates (the combined light-skinned and dark-skinned sections) over a host of issues, including land, culture, political repression and economic exploitation.

The commonwealth period (1839-1847) witnessed the transfer of the routine administrative functions of the Liberian colony to the light-skinned wing of the settler stock by the ACS (Burrowes 1982, Kieh, 2008, 2012). However, the ACS retained control over judicial matters and foreign relations. Like all other colonial situations, the ACS's decision was shaped by the cumulative effects of the various struggles against it by sectors of the colonised population—both the settlers and the indigenes. The relinquishing of control over the routine administrative functions of the colony helped reduce the personnel cost of the ACS. Notwithstanding, by retaining a veto power over the decisions of state managers, the ACS was still in control.

Enthused by the perks of state power, the light-skinned settlers declared Liberia an independent state on 26 July 1847, over the opposition of both the dark-skinned settlers and the ACS. The dark-skinned settlers' opposition was based on their view that the time was not propitious for declaring independence (Kieh 2008, 2012). This was because it would favour their light-skinned kin (Kieh 2008, 2012). Nonetheless, the light-skinned settlers pressed on with the formulation of the modalities for the new state. For example, the process of designing the constitution was exclusionary in that only representatives of the settler stock were allowed to participate. The resultant constitution denied citizenship to people of indigenous background (this was changed in 1947). The national symbols—seal, motto and flag—

reflected the historical-cultural experiences of only the settler stock (Kieh 2008, 2012).

The incipient political economy was based on several major elements. The political system was based on apartheid-like liberal democracy in which only the settlers enjoyed political rights and civil liberties, among other things. However, the indigenes were required to pay taxes to the settler state, and to perform a series of civic and other functions reflective of 'taxation without representation'. In essence, politics was a contest between and among various factions of the settler stock, who occupied the upper and middle tiers of the class structure (Burrowes 1982, Kieh 2008, 2012). The mode of production was embryonic capitalism, with agriculture as the mainstay of the economy. Later, the economy developed shipping and commercial sectors. The dominant development paradigm was autonomous capitalist development: the members of the ruling class were wedded to the idea that Liberia would develop based on the so-called ingenuity of the local capitalists. The resulting political, economic and social conflicts pitted the ruling class against various sections of the subaltern classes.

Interestingly, by 1869, the local capitalists began to face strong competition from European-based capitalists, whose businesses were relatively more capitalised and benefitted from the technology introduced by the Industrial Revolution. Unable to compete with the European capitalists, the various businesses that were owned by the local Liberian capitalists collapsed and along with this the process of autonomous capitalist development. Faced with the resulting economic hardship, the erstwhile local capitalists sought employment in the state bureaucracy (Kieh 2008, 2012). This subsequently led to state managers using the state as an instrument for the primitive accumulation of capital. As well, this set into motion the practice of expanding the bureaucracy to accommodate those with connections to the faction of the local ruling class that controlled the machinery of the state at a particular historical juncture.

Amid the growing economic problems and the lack of a development strategy, the state managers sought solutions from the suzerains of the world capitalist system. In 1870, the Liberian government borrowed US$0.5 million from the British government (Kieh 2012).

Again, in 1901, another loan of US$0.5 million was contracted from a consortium of British capitalists (Kieh 2012). Five years later, another loan of US$1.7 million was contracted from an amalgam of American, British, French and German capitalist interests (Kieh 2012). Similarly, in 1926, Liberia was forced to contract a loan of US$5 million from the US-based Finance Corporation as part of the American government's imposition of Firestone.

The peripheral capitalist state phase

The penetration of foreign capital, beginning in 1926 with the American-based Firestone Plantations Company, heralded the birth of the peripheral capitalist phase of the Liberian state-building project. And this was reflected in several ways. The process of incorporating Liberia into the world capitalist system, which commenced in 1869, was completed. Also, the locus of the class structure shifted from ethno-communal considerations to the individual's relationship to the means of production. This was shaped by the introduction of wage labour. The differentiations in income and wealth provided the basis for the construction of a class system. Importantly, the Liberian political economy became an appendage of the world capitalist system, as well as the system's handmaid in the Liberian social formation. As David (1984: 58) observes, '[The Liberian domestic political economy] should be seen as straddling not one but two levels of articulation: between the world capitalist economic system and the peripheral social formation as a whole, and within the social formation'. By 1955, the Tubman regime introduced a *de facto* one-party state with the True Whig Party (TWP). Central to the process was the harassment and imprisonment of opposition leaders and other critics of the regime, as well as the banning of opposition political parties (Liebenow 1970, Lowenkopf 1976, Wreh 1976, Sawyer 1992, Kieh 2008, 2012). Similarly, the Tubman regime suppressed the political rights and civil liberties of Liberians.

To make matters worse, in spite of the influx of foreign investments under the regime's 'Open Door Policy', the material conditions of the subaltern classes did not improve. This led Clower et al (1966) to refer to the phenomenon as 'growth without development'. Tubman ruled with an 'iron hand' for 27 years, until his death in 1971.

When Tolbert, who served as Tubman's vice president for 19 years, ascended to the presidency in 1971, he made some effort to introduce liberal political reforms such as freedom of association, of the press, and of speech (Kieh 2008, 2012). This was in recognition of the fact that the majority of Liberians were weary of the Tubman years of political repression. Significantly, Tolbert's decision to liberalise the political space led to the formation of three major national social movements—the All People's Freedom Alliance (APFA), the Movement for Justice in Africa (MOJA), and the Progressive Alliance of Liberia (PAL)—as well as the emergence of the labour and student movements as major political forces in the Liberian polity. However, pressured by the conservatives in the local ruling class and the ruling TWP, Tolbert took steps to close the political space. Two major steps were the revival of the Emergency Power Act under which the national legislature illegally gave the president of Liberia expansive powers to crack down on dissent, among other things, and the passage of the revised Sedition Law, which criminalised criticism of the Liberian government (Kieh 2008, 2012). Exasperated by the Tolbert regime's resort to authoritarianism, the national social movements in collaboration with the student movement organised a massive anti-government demonstration on 14 April 1979 (Kieh 2008, 2012). The Liberian government responded to the demonstration with force.

For example, under the 'shoot to kill orders', security forces killed and wounded scores of people, including by-standers (Cordor 1979, Kieh 2008, 2012).

A year later, the Tolbert regime and the ruling TWP were overthrown in a military coup organised by the American government (Dunn and Tarr 1988, Tolbert 1996). The US government organised the coup for two major reasons. It believed that Tolbert was no longer a reliable neo-colonial client because his regime had established diplomatic relations with the Soviet Union, China and other then socialist states in central and Eastern Europe. The other reason was that the US was worried that Tolbert had given the so-called communists in the national social movements and student movements the opportunity to capture state power, and turn Liberia into a Soviet satellite in Africa.

The 12 April 1980 military coup brought Samuel Doe and the People's Redemption Council (PRC) to power. Interestingly, some of the leaders of MOJA and PAL, the two prominent national social movements, were appointed to various positions in the military junta. However, after a little over a year, Doe became threatened by Major-General Thomas Weh Syen, his deputy, who, based on the framing by the US, he portrayed as an ally of the Soviet Union and other socialist countries. Subsequently, Weh Syen and the progressive members of the PRC were executed in 1981 after a kangaroo trial by a military tribunal (Sawyer 1987, 1992). Also, Doe used the opportunity to purge some of the members of the two national social movements who were serving in the government by linking them to Weh Syen and the so-called 'socialist plot' to overthrow his government (Sawyer 1987, 1992). Having eliminated his major opponents in the ruling military junta, Doe then turned his attention to the execution of his plan to transition to a civilian president. The plan included the selection of an election commission that was subservient to his presidential ambition, as well as the banning of the Liberian People's Party (borne out of MOJA), and the United People's Party (the political vehicle of PAL) (Sawyer 1987, 1992). Using fraudulent means, the election commission declared Doe the winner of the 1985 presidential election (Seyon 1988). However, as 'civilian president', Doe continued his reign of terror, as well as the neglect of the material conditions of the subalterns (Sawyer 1987, 1992, Kieh 2008, 2012). These provided the proximate causes for the first Liberian civil war, which commenced on 24 December 1989, when the Taylor-led National Patriotic Front of Liberia (NPFL) attacked Liberia from neighbouring Cote d'Ivoire (Adebajo 2002, Kieh 2008, 2012). About a year into the first civil war, Doe was captured and killed by the Prince Johnson-headed Independent National Patriotic Front of Liberia (INPFL) (Kieh 2008).

After a seemingly endless cycle of peace-making along with peacekeeping led by the Economic Community of West African States (ECOWAS), the first Liberian civil war ended in July 1997. A month later, a presidential election was held and Charles Taylor, the leader of the NPFL and presidential candidate of the National Patriotic Party (NPP), won a landslide victory with over 75 per cent of the votes (Lyons 1998, Kieh 2011). Taylor won because, among other things, Liberians were fearful that he would resume the war, if he had lost (Lyons 1998, Kieh 2011). Having fulfilled his presidential ambition, Taylor established a repressive governance architecture that suppressed political rights and civil liberties, including muzzling the press, among others. As well, the Taylor regime refused to address the material conditions of ordinary Liberians. Instead, Taylor and his government officials continued the policy of plundering and pillaging the country's natural resources for their personal gain (Kieh 2012). The horrendous performance of the Taylor regime provided the *terra firma* for the second Liberian civil war (from 1999-2003). Eventually, an ECOWAS brokered agreement led to the resignation of Taylor in August 2003, after the expiration of his term of office and his departure from the country for Nigeria, where he was granted asylum (Kieh 2012). This then paved the way for an ECOWAS-mediated Comprehensive Peace Agreement that ended the war (Kieh 2012).

After a two year transitional period (October 2003 - October 2005), presidential and legislative elections were held in October 2005. After two rounds, Ellen Johnson Sirleaf was declared the winner of the presidential race (Harris 2006, Sawyer 2008, Kieh 2013). Sirleaf was a member of the old ruling class, whose horrendous performance led to the first civil war. Also, she had held several positions in the TWP-led government of Tolbert, as well as at the World Bank, the United Nations, and with the institutions of international finance capital. Based on her background, Sirleaf designed a neo-liberal development strategy for Liberia that has led to the deterioration of the material conditions of the majority of the subalterns (Kieh 2013). In addition, her government has been the most corrupt in the history of Liberia (Transparency International 2013). However, using the power of incumbency, Sirleaf won a second term of office, following two rounds of the presidential race in 2011. In fact, the election was marked with violence and the boycotting of the second round of the presidential race by the Congress for Democratic Change (CDC), the runner-up (BBC News 2011). Importantly, the re-election of Sirleaf has not led to an improvement in the well-being of ordinary Liberians, as reflected in the burgeoning rate of mass abject poverty and deprivation (Kieh 2012). Also, while the subalterns are living dangerously on the margins, the functionaries of the Sirleaf regime and their relations are continuing the practice of the primitive accumulation of wealth through various corrupt means, ranging from the stealing of the state's money to the receipt of bribes from multinational corporations and other businesses that are interested in exploiting Liberia's vast natural resources (Transparency International 2013).

The portrait of the Liberian state

The Liberian state-building project has produced a portrait of the state in terms of its nature, character, mission and political economy that provides the political and socio-economic context in which social movements have waged, and continue to wage, democratic struggle. By its nature, the Liberian state is an alien construct that does not represent the historical-cultural experiences of both the majority of Liberians (the indigenous ethnic groups), as well as all Liberians (Kieh 2008, 2012). Instead, it represents the experiences of the Africans who were repatriated from the US, as well as a parody of the American cultural and political systems.

The Liberian state has a multidimensional character that has been described variously as 'criminalized', 'exclusionary', 'exploitative', 'negligent', 'neopatrimonial', and 'prebendal', among others (Agbese 2007, Kieh 2008, 2012). Historically, one of these dimensions of the state's character has been ascendant at particular historical junctures (Agbese 2007, Kieh 2008, 2012). However, under those circumstances, the other dimensions have been present, but latent (Agbese 2007).

In terms of its mission, the Liberian state has two major functions. It provides propitious conditions for the metropolitan-based owners of multinational corporations and other businesses to accumulate capital by exploiting the country's vast natural resources and labour, and destroying the environment through various forms of pollution (Kieh 2008, 2012). The other is that the state enables the members of the faction of the local wing of the Liberian ruling class that controls state power at particular historical moments to engage in the primitive accumulation of wealth by using their political offices and connections to engage in sundry illegal acts, such as the stealing of public funds, and the extortion of money from foreign investors and others.

The resulting political economy is anchored on a class structure that consists of three major clusters: ruling, *petit bourgeois* and subaltern. The ruling class has two wings: local and external. The local wing is comprised of state managers, relatively well-off local business people, and resident foreign merchants such as the Lebanese. The external wing is occupied by the owners of foreign-based multinational corporations such as Firestone. The *petit bourgeois* class comprises the intellectuals, artists and other entertainers. The subaltern classes embody the working class, the peasantry, the unemployed, and the *hoi polloi*. The central conflict has, and continues to be, between the ruling class and various sections of the subaltern and *petit bourgeois* classes over the vitriolic violation of political human rights, socio-economic inequalities, inequities, and the broader gamut of social injustice. In other words, the Liberian state is 'akin to a buffet service in which the faction or fraction of the local wing of the ruling class which controls state power at a particular historical juncture and their relations eat all they can eat' (Kieh 2009:10). This means that the members of the local wing of the ruling class use the instrument of the state to provide for their material well-being, while neglecting the basic human needs of the subalterns and the *petit bourgeoisie*.

The major political and economic developments in Liberia, 2011-2013

The major political developments

The 2011 national referendum

A national referendum was held on 23 August 2011 with four proposed constitutional amendments on the ballot:

1. Amendment to Article 52(c) to change the residency requirement of a presidential candidate from 10 to five years (Constitution of Liberia 1986, National Election Commission of Liberia 2011a). The proposed amendment had two underlying political objectives. The major one was to allow the incumbent (Sirleaf) to seek a second term of office since she did not meet the constitutionally prescribed 10 year residency requirement (she re-established residency in Liberia in 2003). The other objective was to use the requirement to prevent some of the major presidential candidates like Winston Tubman of the Congress for Democratic Change (CDC) from contesting the election, since they would not have fulfilled the five year requirement.

2. Amendment to Article 72(b) to change the retirement age of the chief justice and associate justices of the Supreme Court and judges of subordinate courts from 70 years to 75 years (Constitution of Liberia 1986, National Election Commission of Liberia 2011a). The ostensible political goal on the part of the Sirleaf regime was to allow then Chief Justice Johnny Lewis to remain in office for the duration of Sirleaf's second term. This was because Lewis had been quite instrumental in serving Sirleaf's political agenda. For example, he cast the decisive tie vote in the 3-2 Supreme Court decision that expanded presidential appointive powers to include the mayors of cities (Boweh 2008).

3. Amendment to Article 83(a) to change the date for the holding of the elections for the president, vice president, members of the senate and members of the house of representatives from the second Tuesday in October to December (Constitution of Liberia 1986, National Elections Commission of Liberia 2011a). Clearly, this proposed constitutional amendment was beneficial to all those who were seeking any of the aforementioned offices in 2011 and beyond. This is because the elections for these offices are held during the rainy season, when travel for campaigning, given the poor conditions of the roads in the country, becomes extremely difficult.

4. Amendment to article 83(b) to change the threshold for determining the elections of public officers from an absolute majority to a plurality (Constitution of Liberia 1986, National Elections Commission of Liberia 2011a). This amendment had two potential benefits. The key one was that it would have served the re-election purpose of Sirleaf, who had made the determination that it was not possible for her to garner the constitutionally-required '50 per cent plus 1' in the first round, in order to avoid a run-off. This was because Sirleaf was cognisant of the dissatisfaction of the majority of the voters with the poor performance of her regime, especially in the areas of human welfare. The other benefit was that it would have help eliminate the cost, among others, that is associated with holding run-off elections.

Unsurprisingly, only 34.2 per cent of the registered voters participated in the referendum (The National Elections Commission of Liberia 2011a). Two major factors accounted for this. The horrendous state of the material conditions of the majority of Liberians as a result of the poor performance of the Sirleaf regime made them determine that the referendum would not help change their terrible social and economic conditions. The other reason was that the majority of the voters made the decision that the proposed amendments were designed to serve the second term agenda of Sirleaf. In the end, all four of the proposed constitutional amendments were rejected, as evidenced by the fact that none of them received the constitutionally required 67 per cent of the votes (Constitution of Liberia 1986).

The 2011 Nobel Peace Prize

Sirleaf and peace activist Leymah Gbowee were awarded the Nobel Peace Prize in early October 2011(Cowell et al 2011). The selection of Gbowee came as no surprise, because of her exemplary leadership in the Liberian Women's Peace Movement, and the resulting impact in helping to end the country's second civil war in 2003. Specifically, the Liberian Women's Peace Movement undertook several activities, including the offering of daily prayers and the holding of vigils for peace at the Springs Payne Airfield junction in Monrovia, the capital city. Also, the movement played a pivotal mediatory role in encouraging the warring factions to end the conflict.

However, the selection of Sirleaf for the prize came as a great surprise to those familiar with her record of helping to foment war in the country (Truth and Reconciliation Commission of Liberia 2009). For example, Sirleaf was a major supporter of the November 1985 abortive coup led by General Thomas Quiwonkpa, one of the leaders of the 12 April 1980 coup that brought Master-Sergeant Samuel Doe and the PRC to power (Truth and Reconciliation Commission of Liberia 2009). Also, she was one of the principal architects of the Charles Taylor-led insurgency that culminated in the first Liberian civil war in 1989 (Truth and Reconciliation Commission of Liberia 2009). Against this backdrop, the Truth and Reconciliation Commission of Liberia accused Sirleaf of being responsible for aiding and abetting the commission of war crimes and crimes against humanity during the first Liberian civil war (Truth and Reconciliation Commission of Liberia 2009). Thus, it was shocking that the Nobel Peace Prize committee would have disregarded Sirleaf's anti-peace record, and awarded her the Nobel Peace Prize. Winston Tubman, the presidential candidate of the Congress for Democratic Change (CDC), during the 2011 presidential election, put the case this way: '[President Sirleaf] does not deserve [the Nobel Peace Prize]. She is a warmonger. She brought war on our country and spoiled the country.' (Reuters 2011:1).

Gbowee resigns from National Reconciliation Commission

In October 2012, Nobel Laureate Leymah Gbowee, a strong supporter of Sirleaf, resigned her post as chair of the National Reconciliation Commission, a government body that was established by the Sirleaf regime to help promote post-conflict national reconciliation in Liberia (Pesta 2012). According to Gbowee, she resigned because the Sirleaf regime had failed to improve the material conditions of ordinary Liberians, and had been engaged in the practice of nepotism. Gbowee asserted that:

> I have been through a process of really thinking and reflecting and saying to myself, you're as bad as being an accomplice for things that are happening in the country if you don't speak out...
> It is wrong, and I think it is time for [President Sirleaf] to put [her son Robert Sirleaf] aside. He's senior economic advisor, and that's well and good, but to chair the oil company board - I think it's time he steps aside (Pesta 2012:1).

The Monrovian mayor saga

Mary Broh, the former mayor of Monrovia, and a confidante of Sirleaf, gained notoriety for allegedly recurrently violating the law during her tenure. For example, in February 2013, the former mayor was accused of leading a group of women to prevent the imprisonment of then Montserrado county superintendent Grace Kpaan, who was ordered jailed by the house of representatives for contempt (*The Analyst* 2013).Thereafter, Sirleaf suspended Broh for time indefinite (*The Analyst* 2013). However, Broh subsequently resigned.

Interestingly, in March 2013, Sirleaf appointed the former mayor as head of the project implementation unit for the Omega Village in Paynesville (allAfrica.com 2013). Then, strangely, in July 2013, Sirleaf re-nominated Broh as the mayor of Monrovia (Wolokolie 2013). After weeks of the Sirleaf regime engaging in 'political wheeling and dealing' with the Liberian senate, the senate surprisingly refused to confirm Broh for the position (Johnson 2013). Stunned by this major political defeat, Sirleaf withdrew the nomination.

Sirleaf's handling of the Broh case is symptomatic of the crisis of leadership that is bedevilling Liberia as a result, among other things, of Sirleaf's tendency of not matching her pro-democratic governance rhetoric and its associated tenet of the rule of law with practice. In addition, it is a reflection of Sirleaf's recurrent demonstration of a lack of political will to hold her confidantes, friends and relatives accountable for their actions, ranging from dealing with them over accusations of corruption to the violation of the law.

National chair of ruling party criticises government performance

H. Varney Sherman, the national chair of the ruling Unity Party (UP), criticised the performance of his party-led government in the national oration commemorating Liberia's 166th Independence Day anniversary. For example, he observed:

> Madam President and Members of the leadership of our country
> we all know that the large majority of our people do not have
> pipe-born water and human waste disposal facilities, even
> though these are an absolute necessity for their health and well-
> being…Our country cannot be transformed when public service
> is evaluated by the Liberian people as the place where corruption
> exists, persists, and is practiced as a matter of course and with
> impunity (Front PageAfrica 2013:1).

Sherman and Sirleaf were bitter rivals during the 2005 Liberian presidential election. Sherman was the candidate for the Coalition for the Transformation of Liberia (COTOL), an alliance of the Liberian Action Party (LAP), which Sirleaf helped to organise in the mid-1980s, and the Liberian Unification Party (LUP). However, Sirleaf resigned from LAP in 1997, when the party nominated Cletus Wotorson as its presidential candidate in the July 1997 special presidential election. In her bid to also contest the presidency in 1997, Sirleaf joined UP. However, surprisingly, in April 2009, LAP and LUP merged with UP. As part of the political deal, Sherman was elected national chairman of the expanded UP.

The 2011 national elections

The presidential election

On 11 October 2011, the first round of the presidential election was held with 16 candidates, including Sirleaf, the incumbent, who was seeking a second term (National Elections Commission of Liberia 2011b). According to the results of the first round, Sirleaf, the standard bearer of UP, received 43.9 per cent of the votes, while Winston Tubman, the flag bearer of the CDC, garnered 32.7 per cent (National Elections Commission of Liberia 2011c).

The other 14 candidates shared between 0.2 per cent to 11.6 per cent of the vote (National Elections Commission of Liberia 2011c).

Since no candidate received the constitutionally-required absolute majority, a run-off election was held on 7 November 2011 between the two top vote getters - Sirleaf of UP and Winston Tubman of CDC. However, CDC boycotted the second round claiming that it was cheated during the first round. Nonetheless, Tubman was placed on the ballot. According to the results, Sirleaf received 90.7 per cent of the votes to 9.3 per cent for Tubman (National Election Commission of Liberia 2011d). The results were exaggerated due to the boycott, as well as the fact that Sirleaf really only received an additional 77,598 votes: she received a total of 530, 020 votes in the first round and 607, 618 votes in the second round (National Election Commission of Liberia 2011c, 2011d).

Also, prior to the holding of the run-off election, there was post-election violence when a CDC organised demonstration turned bloody (BBC News 2011). In addition, on 7 November 2011, the Sirleaf regime closed down three media outlets - Kings FM radio station and Clar TV, Love FM and TV, and Shiata Power FM and TV (Committee to Protect Journalists 2011). The Sirleaf regime justified its action by claiming that the three media outlets were 'broadcasting hate messages against the government and deliberately spreading misinformation and messages of violence and instigating the people to rise up and take to the streets, (Committee to Protect Journalists 2011:1). In response, CDC rejected the electoral outcome, and vowed not to recognise Sirleaf as the legitimate president of Liberia. But after negotiations, CDC renounced its claim and vow (Fofana 2012). Thus, Sirleaf was inaugurated for a second six-year term on 16 January 2012 (Fofana 2012).

The legislative election

The election for the National Legislature—the entire house of representatives and half (15) of the senate—was held simultaneously with the presidential election on 11 October 2011. In the senatorial election, 99 candidates representing political parties and independent candidacies contested for the 15 seats (National Elections Commission of Liberia 2011e). According to the results, the ruling UP and the National Patriotic Party (NPP) won four seats each (National Elections Commission of Liberia 2011f). The CDC, the main opposition party, won two seats (National Elections Commission of Liberia 2011f). Overall, the ruling party now has 10 seats in the senate, a net loss of one seat. Although this gives the ruling party the plurality of votes, it does not have a majority in the upper legislative chamber.

For the house of representatives, 662 candidates, also representing various political parties and independent candidacies, contested for the 73 seats (National Elections Commission of Liberia 2011g). The results were as follows: the ruling UP won 24 seats and the CDC, the principal opposition party, garnered 11 seats (National Elections Commission of Liberia 2011h). Again, the results indicate that while the ruling party has the plurality of seats, it does not have a majority.

Major forthcoming events

Two major events are forthcoming. The first is the senatorial election, which is scheduled to be held in October 2014. Half of the 15 seats will be up for grabs. These are the seats that are occupied by the senior senators, as per the staggering process that was implemented in 2006. Under the process, of the two senators per county, the one who received the lesser amount of votes during the 2005 election was classified as a junior senator, and served for six years rather than the constitutionally stipulated nine years. The National Elections Commission has already promulgated the timetable for the election

(National Elections Commission of Liberia 2013). Under the calendar, the electoral activities will begin on 15 September 2014 with the publication of the voters' roll update regulations, and end on 14 October 2014 with voting (National Elections Commission of Liberia 2013).

The second major event is the 2017 presidential and legislative election. For the presidential race, there will be no incumbent since Sirleaf is barred by the constitution from seeking a third consecutive term of office (Constitution of Liberia 1986). This could create the space for several candidates to compete for the office. Also, elections will be held for all 73 seats in the house of representatives, and half (15) of the seats in the senate.

Major economic developments, 2011-2013

Land and multinational corporations

The Sirleaf regime has undertaken a systematic campaign of mortgaging Liberia's land to multinational corporations. The campaign is conditioned by two major currents. The Sirleaf regime is determined to broaden the sources from which they can engage in the primitive accumulation of capital through the instrumentality of the state. The other reason is that as a fervent champion of neo-liberal development dogma, Sirleaf has the illusion that foreign investment can promote socio-economic development in Liberia.

Some of the notable land cases have included the leasing of additional land to Sime Darby and Golden Veloreum in 2012. The former is owned by the Malaysian-based multinational Sime Darby (Ford 2012). Sime Darby has signed a 63-year agreement with the Liberian government to develop 220,000 acres of land for palm oil (Ford 2012). Golden Veloreum is an oil palm company owned by American and Indonesian capitalists. It has signed a 65-year agreement with the Liberian government for 865,000 acres of land (Baron 2012). In some cases, the Sirleaf regime has moved farmers from their land in order to lease the land to these foreign multinational corporations (Ford 2012). One of the adverse consequences of the mortgaging of the country's land is the contribution of this process to food insecurity. That is, by forcing farmers off their land in some cases, the Sirleaf regime is making it difficult for food to be produced locally, thereby contributing to the increase in mass hunger, under-nourishment and malnutrition.

Interestingly, the Sirleaf regime has made the claim that the Liberian government owns all land—both public and private. Hence, this provides the so-called legal basis for the regime's ongoing mortgaging of the country's land. In addition, amid the avalanche of criticisms from communities, whose lands have been mortgaged to multinational corporations, Sirleaf offered this very strange response:

> When your government and the representatives sign any paper with a foreign country the communities can't change it…You are trying to undermine your own government. You can't do that. If you do so, all the foreign investors coming to Liberia will close their businesses and leave; then Liberia will go back to the old days (Sirleaf 2011:1).

Individuals and communities that have been victimised are mounting strong resistance. For example, in February 2012, several communities in Grand Cape Mount County protested the seizure of their land and its subsequent leasing to Sime Darby Plantations (IRIN 2012). In addition, various Liberian civil society organisations have strongly criticised the Sirleaf regime for its land scheme. As Sawyer (2009:3) observes, 'Land questions are explosive.' In fact, many Liberians are boldly declaring, 'The next war will be about land' (Sawyer 2009:3).

Fearing the dire consequences of the seizure of their land by the Sirleaf regime, and its subsequent leasing to Sime Darby Plantations, several farmers in the Grand Cape Mount County have expressed their unequivocal opposition to the land grab scheme. This has taken the form of using various media outlets to convey their sentiments to the larger Liberian population. In addition, some of the farmers have demanded direct meetings with Sirleaf, in order to express their consternation to her. Besides the very important issue of land ownership, the land grab scheme has potentially catastrophic consequences for food security in Liberia.

The allocation of oil wells

One of the major economic developments over the past two years has been the allocation of oil wells, as Liberia has joined the 'club' of oil endowed states. The wells have been allocated by the Sirleaf regime through the National Oil Company (NOCOL), which was chaired by Robert Sirleaf, President Sirleaf's son (Global Witness 2011). The oil wells have been allocated to mainly metropolitan-based corporations like Chevron-USA (Global Witness 2011).

The process of allocation has been fraught with the engagement in various acts of corruption by various officials of the Sirleaf regime, who are using their respective offices to receive bribes from various oil companies seeking leases. For example, 'NOCOL paid U.S. $120,400 in what it referred to as "lobbying fees" to the Liberian legislature, so that oil contracts would be passed. But, the stated position of the Liberian Auditing Commission is that the "lobbying fees" are bribes (Global Witness 2011:6).

The exploitation of forest resources

In 2012, it was discovered that several logging companies operating in Liberia were exploiting the country's forest resources by circumventing the forest laws, as well as the Community Forest Management Agreements (CFMAS) (Global Witness 2013). The CFMAS were designed to ensure that communities with forests were involved in the proper governance and management of the resource (Global Witness 2013).

In the report issued by the special independent investigating board that was appointed by Sirleaf, there was the cataloguing of specific instances of abuse, including suspicious payments to officials, the widespread use of forged documents and a network of linked companies that together had obtained private users permits (PUPs) covering 1.6 million acres of forest (Global Witness 2013:2). This network includes Forest Ventures, Nature Oriented and Timber, Atlantic Resources and Southeastern Resources, which is connected with the notorious Malaysian logging giant Samling (Global Witness 2013:12).

The major scandals

There were several major scandals, mainly involving cases of corruption, from 2011-2013. Three of these cases are noteworthy. The Roberts International Airport corruption saga involved the managing director being charged with stealing over US$300,000 of public funds (Sungbeh 2013). The saga unleashed a whirlwind of accusations and counter-accusations involving the managing director, her boyfriend, who is being accused as her accomplice, the chair of the board of directors of the Roberts International Airport, the minister of finance and several other officials of the Sirleaf regime. The former managing director has been indicted, but she has left Liberia for the US. Hence, the Sirleaf regime would have to seek her extradition.

The other case involves alleged acts of rampant corruption in the Liberian police. In a major study, 'No Money, No Justice: Police Corruption and Abuse in Liberia', conducted by Human Rights Watch, sundry acts of corruption were catalogued, including police officers engaging in 'shakedowns'(Human Rights Watch 2013:2). These entail police officers following 'local residents and under the pretext of searching them for contraband items or weapons, demanded money, sometimes using threats or violence. Motorcycle taxis, street vendors, and taxi drivers are particularly vulnerable to extortion and theft by the police' (Human Rights Watch 2013:5).

Put into context, the alleged acts of corruption in the police can be attributed to several major factors, including the prevalence of corruption in the Sirleaf regime, the culture of impunity, low salaries, the lack of a culture of professionalism, and poor vetting during the recruitment process.

The European Union's health improvement aid drama was another major scandal. The Sirleaf regime used US$13 million in aid within four months, without the money ever being used for its intended purpose, which was to help improve health care in Liberia (Liberia Corruption Watch 2013). Interestingly, the ministry of finance has had difficulty explaining the way the aid was used, as evidenced by its failure to demonstrate that the aid was used in the country's health sector.

The issue of corruption has been a vexatious issue in the Sirleaf regime. Particularly, her consistent lack of political will to bring those accused of engaging in corruption to justice has reinforced the culture of impunity. For example, Willis Knuckles, the former minister of state for presidential affairs and a confidante of the president, was accused of engaging in influence peddling, but was never brought to justice. In fact, Sirleaf has failed to act on the report of her own commission, which she appointed to investigate the matter (*Star Newspaper* 2008). In 2013, Transparency International (TI) ranked Liberia as the most corrupt country, in the world (Transparency International 2013). TI asserted that 'the vast majority of Liberians surveyed said they believe the country (Liberia) is run either largely or entirely by few entities acting in their own selfish interests' (Hess and Sauter 2013:1). Sungbeh (2013:1) provides an excellent summation of the corruption epidemic in the Sirleaf regime:

> Vacancy: Positions available in the Ellen Johnson Sirleaf administration. Candidates must be ready to go to Liberia (not to

do actual work to change lives and rebuild crumbling institutions) but to steal from government and get rich quick. No prosecution or confiscation of stolen wealth, but reappointment to another influential and lucrative position. Qualification: Be a presidential friend, or a presidential sycophant. Corruption is running wild like fire and out of control in Ellen's Liberia. It is like a pandemic.

Social movements and democratic struggles

Social movements in Liberia have evolved against the backdrop of what McAdams (2004:203) generally refers to as 'political opportunities and constraints'. Social movements have emerged in these two contexts, especially in the case of constraints propelled by an increased performance deficit of the various regimes, political repression and socio-economic malaise, among others. In essence, the combination of authoritarianism and material deprivation have compelled Liberians from the *petit bourgeois* and subaltern classes to organise various social movements as the *deus ex machina* for waging democratic struggles. Dolo (2007:59) lays out the texture of the socio-economic and political environment in which social movements in Liberia have evolved:

> With a landscape dominated by authoritarian rulers, Liberians were enmeshed in powerful political, social and economic systems that were impervious to change. Leaders held no regard for the welfare of citizens or their participation in the nation's politics. Citizens bore their suffering and discrimination and nervously awaited change.

Several major cycles can be discerned in the development of social movements in Liberia. Cycle one (1847-1973) was marked by the rise of various single issue-based ethnic movements with limited scope. Cycle two (1973-1980) was characterised by the inception of national social movements such as the Movement for Justice in Africa (MOJA) and the Progressive Alliance of Liberia (PAL) with agendas that were multi-purpose, and whose scope was broad - the support base covered the totality of the country, and encompassed various sectors. Cycle three (1980-present) has witnessed the decline of national social movements, and the re-emergence of single issue and sectorally-based social movements with limited support bases. In this vein, in order to examine the travails of social movements during the period 2011-2013, it is important to first interrogate or generally map out the rise and fall of the two national social movements—MOJA and PAL.

A general mapping of social movements

The Movement for Justice in Africa (MOJA)

MOJA was founded in 1973 by Liberian intellectuals, who had returned home from their academic studies in the US (Dolo 2007, Moran 2008, Press 2009, Sherman 2011). The core of MOJA's base consisted of intellectuals, students, workers and farmers. The initial thrust of the organisation was the promotion of pan-Africanism and this found expression in the mobilisation of support for the various liberation struggles in South Africa, Namibia, Angola, Mozambique, Guinea-Bissau and Cape Verde. As *Perspective Magazine* (2003:1-2) notes, 'MOJA was born in Liberia out of the realization that justice is the indispensable ingredient for peace, democracy and progress world-wide.' Central to this initial orientation was the organisation of chapters in the Gambia and Ghana. Later, MOJA was transformed into a national social movement with a populist ideology. The emergent thrust was on political and socio-economic reforms in the Liberian polity.

MOJA used three major forms of democratic struggle. The key one was its collaboration with PAL in organising the 14 April 1979 mass demonstration against the political and socio-economic excesses of the ruling class. Another method was the regular issuance of position papers on various domestic and foreign policy issues. Also, MOJA used its collaborative work with the Liberian American Swedish Mining Company (LAMCO) and Bong Mining Company's workers' union that involved the negotiation of labour agreements as a form of democratic struggle.

The various forms of struggle used by MOJA made a political impact on three levels. At the level of the state, MOJA's various forms of struggle as well as its political conscientisation activities—mass monthly meetings, cadre training classes, newsletter, etc.—played a pivotal role in the development of mass political awareness. Also, the 14 April 1979 mass demonstration forced the government to abandon its plan to increase the price of rice, the country's staple food. The negotiation assistance rendered to the workers helped to position them to extract relatively greater benefits from LAMCO and the Bong Mining Company.

MOJA's democratic struggles were in response to the broader and multidimensional crises of underdevelopment in Liberia, and the failure of the Tolbert government and the ruling class to address these issues. For example, although the Tolbert regime initially showed an inclination to tackle the political aspects of the crises of underdevelopment, it subsequently chose not to do so. The major reason was the fear by members of the ruling class that addressing the crises of underdevelopment, especially political liberalisation, would have posed a threat to their privileged position, including their stranglehold on political power.

The ruling class and its regime responded to MOJA in various ways: surveillance of the organisation's leaders and key members, intimidation, harassment, arrest, imprisonment and dismissals from positions even in the private sector and educational institutions like the University of Liberia and Cuttington University. The apex of the repressive responses was the arrest and imprisonment of several leaders and key members of MOJA after the 14 April 1979 mass demonstration.

As a national social movement, MOJA had several limitations. A central one was the inadequacy of financial and material resources. Also, MOJA lacked an alternative and comprehensive 'blueprint' for building democracy and promoting human-centred development in Liberia. Another shortcoming was that MOJA failed to properly analyse the 12 April 1980 coup. This was demonstrated by the fact that the organisation viewed the coup as a 'revolution'. Consequently, several members of MOJA were quick to accept various positions in the military regime. Significantly, MOJA totally abandoned its activities, the ban on politics notwithstanding. So, since 1980, MOJA has not been able to resume its activities, and to regain its erstwhile status as the pre-eminent champion of the subaltern classes in Liberia.

The Progressive Alliance of Liberia (PAL)

PAL was established in 1975 by some diaspora Liberians who were studying and working in the US (Dolo 2007, Moran 2008, Press 2009, Sherman 2011). Three years later, PAL transferred its operations to Liberia. The base of PAL's support consisted of a small core of intellectuals, students, workers and the *hoi polloi*. Driven by a populist ideology, PAL's major thrust was the acquisition of state power. In this vein, in 1980, PAL was transformed into the Progressive People's Party (PPP) and subsequently registered as the first legal opposition party in the country since 1955 (Sawyer 1992, Kieh 2008, 2012).

The major form of struggle used by PAL was demonstration. For example, PAL played a pivotal role in organising the 14 April 1979 mass uprising in collaboration with MOJA. Also, in March 1980, the Progressive People's Party (PPP), the political arm of PAL, organised a demonstration against the ruling class and its government.

Like MOJA, PAL's democratic struggles were waged against the backdrop of the failure of the Tolbert regime to address the country's burgeoning economic, political and social problems. As has been discussed, although the Tolbert regime initially showed signs that it was willing to negotiate a *modus vivendi* with the national social movements as the foundation for addressing the country's major challenges, the regime subsequently backtracked under an avalanche of pressure from the far right-wing faction of the local ruling class.

Characteristically, the ruling class and its government responded to PAL's pro-democracy struggles with surveillance of leaders and key members, intimidation, harassment, dismissals and imprisonment. For example, in response to the 1980 demonstration that was organised by PPP, the party was subsequently banned by the national legislature, and several leaders and members of the party were charged with treason and imprisoned.

Social movements, 2011-2013

As discussed, since 1980, Liberia has returned to the era of the sectorally-based and mainly single issue social movements. That is, there are no longer national social movements with broad agendas and a national base. What factors accounted for the shift? When the military coup occurred on 12 April 1980, it was fully embraced by MOJA and PAL. This was reflected in the fact that several of the leaders and members of the two movements took up various positions in the military regime. Importantly, the two groups essentially folded their activities. This meant that MOJA and PAL effectively became dormant. Even after the relationship with the military junta collapsed, the two organisations did not resume their activities.

The other factor was the increased repression by the military regime. In turn, this instilled fear in the populace to the extent that people refrained from even entertaining the idea of organising national social movements. The resulting vacuum was filled by the student movements both at the level of the Liberian National Students Union (LINSU) and the University of

Liberia Students Union, as well as student governing bodies at other tertiary and secondary institutions. Thus, students assumed the national mantle for leading the resistance against the military regime.

The Monrovia Consolidated School System Teachers' Association and the Liberian Health Workers' Association were chosen as the case studies, because they were the only two movements that were actively engaged in resisting the Sirleaf regime's neo-liberal governance approach and its attendant creation of propitious conditions for the predatory accumulation of capital by metropolitan-based multinational corporations and other businesses from the 'global North' during the period 2011-2013.

Monrovia Consolidated School System Teachers' Association (MCSSTA)

The MCSSTA was organised in the late 1970s as the vehicle for promoting and articulating the collective interests of teachers in the largest public school system in the country. The organisation was formed during the waning days of the Tolbert regime. During the Doe and Taylor regimes, the organisation operated quietly, in view of the super-repressive proclivities of the two regimes.

The organisation's central instrument for the waging of democratic struggles has been strike action. For example, on 15 October 2012, the association engaged in a strike to protest the very low salaries of public school teachers. Benedict Wisseh, the president of the association, provided the following rationale for the strike action: '...the teachers [were] demanding salary increases, transportation allowances and scholarships' (Butty 2012:1). By the time of the strike, teacher salaries at MCSS ranged from US$140 to US$500 per month depending on their level of education (Butty 2012).The strike affected over 20,000 public school students (West African Democracy Radio 2012). It had minimal political impact, because it did not generate support nationally. The only base of support was provided by the students of MCSS, who staged a demonstration near Sirleaf's office on 22 October 2012 to insist that the demands of their striking teachers be met (Hanson 2012). Hence, the required mass support that was imperative for pressuring the Sirleaf regime into addressing the vexatious issue of low salaries was lacking.

However, the strike action was a reflection of the crisis of Liberia's emergent hybrid political system under the Sirleaf regime, the combination of democratic and authoritarian tendencies, and especially the poor performance of the government in terms of addressing basic human needs. However, the strike action did not pose any serious challenge to the local ruling class. This was because, as has been discussed, it did not generate widespread support.

The Sirleaf regime responded by making two promises. The first was to appoint a commission to examine the teachers' grievances. The other was to take action to address the grievance about low salaries. It will be interesting to see if Sirleaf fulfils these promises, especially the recommendations that her commission might come up with. This is because since her tenure she has appointed several commissions in similar circumstances, but has usually failed to act on their recommendations.

The association has several potentials, which if fully harnessed could help advance the democratic struggle in Liberia. MCSSTA could play a pivotal role in the building of linkages among teachers throughout the country. In turn, these relationships could be used to establish a national association. Such a movement would have great leverage because it would be a major anchor in a critical sector of the country. Another benefit would be the fact that such a national movement would have a large and diverse membership base that covers the entire country. These advantages would then position the teachers well to both negotiate for better working conditions for their members, as well as to advance the broader national democratic agenda of genuine political human rights and the advancement of the material conditions of ordinary Liberians.

On the other hand, the association has several limitations. Its current membership base is small. Hence, it does not command a large base that could engage the Sirleaf regime in a struggle for a better education system and improved working conditions for teachers throughout the country.

The association has a limited resource base in terms of personnel, finance, equipment and logistics. That is, the movement does not have a full-time secretariat to run the day-to-day affairs of the movement. To make matters worse, the association does not have the requisite financial and material resources that would enable it to implement its activities effectively and efficiently.

Also, the low salaries of teachers coupled with the general state of abject poverty in Liberia make the leaders of the association vulnerable to co-optation through the offering of positions in the state bureaucracy to some of the members of the national leadership and/or the offering of bribes by the Sirleaf regime. The capitulation of the association to any of these inducements would undermine its integrity and adversely affect its activities.

The Liberian Health Workers' Association (LIHWA)

The Liberian Health Workers' Association is a fairly new social movement that was formed to advocate for the welfare of health workers in the country's public health system. Although it is sectorally-based, its membership base spans the 15 counties of the country. This therefore gives the movement an advantageous bargaining position.

Like the MCSSTA, LIHWA's principal vehicle for waging its democratic struggle is through strike action. For example, on 21 July 2013, about 20,000 health workers went on strike (Lazuta 2013). The strike action began as a 'go-slow', and cumulatively, it paralysed the operations of various public hospitals throughout the country (Lomax 2013). The major demand was for a salary increase from the then minimum of US$150 per month to US$200 per month (Lomax 2013). The strike lasted for two weeks, and ended after the Sirleaf regime promised to address the health workers' concerns. However, realising that the Sirleaf regime does not always keep its promises, George Williams, the secretary-general of LIHWA, warned that, 'members were prepared to take further industrial action, if the government goes back on assurances given to the union' (Gordon 2013:1).

In terms of political impact, given the importance of the health sector, and its country-wide scope, the strike action had an appreciable political impact. This was reflected in the fact that citizens throughout the country were complaining about the various adverse consequences of the strike action for their personal well-being and that of their relatives. Clearly, the burgeoning complaints were pivotal to pressuring the Sirleaf government to make the promise to address the grievances.

Overall, LIHWA has great potential for becoming a viable social movement. For example, the scope of its membership gives it an important presence throughout the country. LIHWA could use this position as leverage in negotiating with the Sirleaf regime on behalf of its members, as well as in helping to advance democratic struggles in the country by advocating policies and programs that help advance the material conditions of all Liberians, especially the subalterns. Also, LIHWA and MCSSTA could develop a partnership, which they could subsequently use to help establish a broad—based national social movement.

However, LIHWA is hamstrung by the same obstacles as MCSSTA. For example, LIHWA does not have the requisite human, financial and logistical resources that a national movement requires to establish an effective presence, as well as to implement its policies and programs effectively and efficiently. In addition, like the MCSSTA, the leaders of LIHWA are also vulnerable to the bribery epidemic, given the sordid state of the standard of living in the country.

Conclusion

The dominant genre of social movements in Liberia is that they are sectorally-based—education, health care, etc. That is, social movements in the country tend to operate in silos, in contradistinction to the 1970s, when there were two national social movements—MOJA and PAL— that sought to co-ordinate collective action. Thus, this is the overarching framework through which social movements waged democratic struggles during the period 2011-2013.

Importantly, the democratic struggles of the various social movements during this period were a clear reflection of the crisis of the quasi-liberal democratic political system evolving under the Sirleaf regime. Particularly, the struggles are direct responses to the failure of the Sirleaf regime to address the material conditions and the associated well-being of the majority of the Liberian people. Although there have been some improvements in the political domain in terms of political rights and civil liberties, the Sirleaf regime's performance in the social and economic spheres has been horrendous. This is reflected in abject mass poverty and deprivation, the lack of adequate educational and health services, clean drinking water and sanitation, and the increasing levels of food insecurity. The material deprivation that has been visited upon the subalterns by the Sirleaf regime has provided the context for the democratic struggles that are being waged by the various sectoral-based social movements, as well as others.

Overall, social movements in Liberia have several major limitations. The first limitation is that they lack a national base. Second, the single movement approach to waging democratic struggles has tended to militate against the political impact of these struggles. One of the major reasons is that it is easier for the government to deal with social movements on an individual basis. Third, there is an inadequacy of financial, material and human resources to effectively carry out their various activities. Fourth, the strangulating effects of poverty have made the leaders and key members of social movements vulnerable to co-optation and bribes from the Sirleaf regime. Fifth, the various struggles lack a transformative orientation. That is, they seem not to be designed to ultimately press for the fundamental transformation of Liberia's peripheral capitalist political economy.

Although Liberia lacks national social movements, the sectoral-based ones have demonstrated their capacity to challenge and struggle against the excesses of neo-liberal governance in the country. This has been evidenced by the various actions that groups such as MCSSTA and LIHWA have taken. In other words, the various actions that have been taken by these two movements and other groups in the country have helped expose the venal underbelly of the neo-liberal governance model and its visitation of mass abject poverty and social malaise on the Liberian subalterns. If their potentials are fully and properly utilised, both organisations could become influential players in Liberian politics. In addition, they could play lead roles in the formation of a national social movement.

Finally, several areas have emerged that deserve further research. A major one concerns the need to conduct comprehensive studies of the various national movements, such as MCSSTA, LIHWA and others. Another area could be the prospects for the revival of MOJA and PAL. A third area could be the possibilities for forming new national social movements and the major obstacles that would be faced by these formations.

References

Adebajo, A. (2002) *Liberia's Civil War: Nigeria, ECOMOG and Regional Security in West Africa*, Boulder, Colorado, Lynne Rienner Publishers

Agbese, P. O. (2007) 'The Political Economy of the African State' in G.K. Kieh (ed), *Beyond State Failure and Collapse: Making the State Relevant in Africa*, Lanham, MD, Lexington Books *allAfrica.com* (2009) 'Liberia: UP-LAP-LUP Celebrate Historic Merger', 2 April, http;//www.allafrica.com/stories/200904020991.html, accessed 16 June 2013

allAfrica.com (2013) 'Liberia: Statement by H.E. President Ellen Johnson Sirleaf on Services Rendered by Former Acting Mayor Broh', 5 March 2013

Baron, E. (2012) 'Palm Oil Industry Accused of Land Grabs in Liberia', *Global Post Rights*, 27 December

BBC News (2011) 'Liberia Election: CDC Monrovia Protest Turns Deadly', 7 November, www.bbc.com/news/world-africa-1562417, accessed 20 June 2013

Beyan, A. J. (1991) *The American Colonization Society and the Creation of the Liberian State: An Historical Perspective, 1822-1900*, Lanham, MD, University Press of America

Boweh, B. (2008) 'No Municipal Elections: Supreme Court Recognizes President Sirleaf's Appointment of City Mayors', *Star Radio*, 11 January

Brown, G. W. (1941) *The Economic History of Liberia*, Washington D.C., Associated Publishers

Burrowes, C. P. (1982) 'The Settler Ruling Class Thesis in Liberia: A Reconsideration', Occasional Paper, Chicago

Butty, J. (2012) 'Liberian Teachers Enter Second Week of Strike', *Voice of America*, 22 October

Cassell, C. A. (1970) *Liberia: History of the First African Republic*, New York, Fountainhead Publishers

Clower, R. W., Dalton G., Harwitz, M., Walters A.A. (1966) *Liberia: Growth Without Development*, Evanston, Illinois, Northwestern University Press

Committee to Protect Journalists (2011) 'Liberian Government Silences Three Broadcasters', 8 November

Constitution of Liberia (1986) Monrovia, Government Printing

Cordor, S. H. (1979) 'The April 14 Crisis in Liberia', Occasional Paper, Monrovia, Liberia

Cowell, A., Kasinof, L., Nossiter, A. (2011) 'Nobel Peace Prize Awarded to Three Activist Women', *The New York Times*, 7 October

David, M. (1984) 'The Love of Liberty Brought Us Here: An Analysis of the Development of the Settler State in 19th Century Liberia', *Review of African Political Economy*, 11(31):57-70

Dolo, E.T. (1996) *Democracy versus Dictatorship: The Quest for Freedom and Justice in Africa's Oldest Republic-Liberia*, Lanham, MD: University Press of America.

Dolo, E.T. (2007) *Ethnic Tensions in Liberia's National Identity Crisis: Problems and Possibilities*, Cherry Hill, NJ: Africana Homestead Legacy Publishers.

Dunn, D. E., Tarr, B.S. (1988) *Liberia: A National Polity in Transition*, Metuchen, NJ: Scarecrow Press.

Fofana, B. (2012) 'Liberia: Monrovia Inauguration Marks Political Détente', *allAfrica.com.* 16 January

Ford, T. (2012) 'Liberia Land deal With Foreign Firms "Could Sow Seeds of Conflict"', *The Guardian (UK)*, 29 February

Freedom House (2013) *Freedom in the World: Comparative and Historical Data, 1972-2012*, Washington D.C., Freedom House

Front Page Africa (2013) 'Tomorrow is Not an Option: Text of Sherman's 166th Liberian Independence Day Speech', 29 July

Global Witness (2011) *Curse or Cure? How Oil Can Boost or Break Liberia's Post-War Recovery*, London, Global Witness

Global Witness (2013) *Avoiding the Riptide: Liberia Must Enforce Its Forest Laws to Prevent a New Wave of Illegal and Destructive Logging Contracts*, London, Global Witness

Gordon, G. (2013) 'Liberian Health Workers to End Two Week Strike', *AFP*, 9 August

Hanson, V. (2012) 'Liberia: As Teachers Continue Strike Action - MCSS Students Demonstrate', *The Inquirer Newspaper*, 23 October

Harris, D. (2006) 'Liberia 2005: An Unusual African Post-Conflict Election', *Journal of Modern African Studies* 44(3):375-395

Hess, A.E.M. and Sauter, M.B. (2013) 'The Most Corrupt Countries in the World', *Wall Street Journal*, 14 July

Human Rights Watch (2013) *No Money, No Justice: Police Corruption and Abuse in Liberia*, New York, Human Rights Watch

Huntington, S. P. (2007) *The Clash of Civilizations and the Remaking of World Order*, New York, Simon and Schuster

IRIN (2012) 'Liberia: Land Grab or Development Opportunity?', 17 February

Johnson, O. (2013) 'Senate Finally Rejects "General Broh"', *Heritage Newspaper*, 7 August

Johnson-Sirleaf, E. (2011) Remarks delivered to rural community members affected by the operations of Sime Darby, a multinational oil producer, 6 December

Kieh, G. K. (2008) *The First Liberian Civil War: The Crises of Underdevelopment*, New York, Peter Lang Publishing

Kieh, G. K. (2009) 'The State and Political Instability in Africa', *Journal of Developing Societies*, 25(1):1-25

Kieh, G. K. (2011) 'Warlords, Politicians and Liberia's Post-First Conflict Election', *African and Asian Studies*, 10(2/3):83-99

Kieh, G. K. (2012) *Liberia's State Failure. Collapse and Reconstitution*, Cherry Hill, NJ, Africana Homestead Legacy Publishers

Kieh, G. K. (2013) 'Liberia's Second Post-Conflict Presidential Election', *Journal of International Studies and Development*, 3(1):123-141

Lazuta, J. (2013) 'Liberian Government Talks with Striking Health Workers', *Voice of America*, 1 August

Leavitt, J. (2005) *The Evolution of Deadly Conflict: from 'Paternaltarianism' to State Collapse in Liberia*, Durham, NC, Carolina Academic Press

Liberia Corruption Watch (2013) http://www.liberiacorruptionwatch.org/ (accessed July 2013)

Liberty, C. E. Z. (2002) *Growth of the Liberian State: An Analysis of Its Historiography*, Northridge, CA, The New World African Press

Liebenow, J. G. (1970) *Liberia: The Evolution of Privilege*, Ithaca, New York, Cornell University Press

Liebenow, J. G. (1987) *Liberia: The Quest for Democracy*, Bloomington, Indiana University Press

Lomax, S. (2013) 'Liberia: Health Care on Hold: Liberia Hospitals Turn to Ghost Town after Go-Slow by Doctors', *FrontPage Africa*, 23 July

Lowenkopf, M. (1976) *Politics in Liberia: The Conservative Road to Development*, Stanford, CA: Hoover Institution

Lyons, T. (1998) *Voting for Peace in Liberia: Post-conflict elections in Liberia*, Washington D.C., The Brookings Institution Press

Mayson, D. T-W. and Sawyer, A. (1979) 'Capitalism and the Struggle of the Working Class in Liberia,*Review of Black Political Economy*,9(2):140-158

McAdam, D. (2004) 'Revisiting the U.S. Civil Rights Movement: Toward a More Synthetic Understanding of the Origins of Contention' in J. Goodwin and J. M. Jasper (eds) *Rethinking Social Movements: Structure, Meaning and Emotion*, Lanham, MD, Rowan and Littlefield

Moran, M. H. (2008) *Liberia: The Violence of Democracy*, Philadelphia, PA, University of Pennsylvania Press

Movement for Justice in Africa (1980) *The Situation in Our Country: MOJA's Proposal for Change*, Monrovia, MOJA

National Elections Commission of Liberia (2011a) National Referendum on Proposed Constitutional Amendments, Monrovia

National Elections Commission of Liberia (2011b) The List of Candidates for the 2011 Presidential Election, Monrovia

National Elections Commission of Liberia (2011c) The Results of the 2011 Presidential Election, Monrovia

National Elections Commission of Liberia (2011d) The Results of the Second Round of the 2011 Presidential Election, Monrovia

National Elections Commission of Liberia (2011e) The List of Candidates for the Senatorial Election, Monrovia

National Elections Commission of Liberia (2011f) The Results of the 2011 Senatorial Election, Monrovia

National Elections Commission of Liberia (2011g) The List of the Candidates for the 2011 House of Representatives Election, Monrovia

National Elections Commission of Liberia (2011h) The Results of the 2011 House of Representatives Election, Monrovia

National Elections Commission of Liberia (2013) The Calendar of Events for the 2014 Senatorial Election, Monrovia

Perspective Magazine (2003) 'MOJA Celebrates 30th Anniversary, Archbishop Michael Francis Honored', 24 March

Pesta, A. (2012) 'A Nobel Smack down in Liberia: Leymah Gbowee vs. Ellen Johnson Sirleaf', *The Daily Beast*, 10 October

Press, R. M. (2009) 'Candles in the Wind: Resisting Repression in Liberia (1979-2003)', *Africa Today*, 55(3):3-22

Reuters (2011) 'Sirleaf Does Not Deserve Nobel Prize, Say Weah, Tubman', 7 October

Sawyer, A. (1987) *Effective Immediately: Dictatorship in Liberia, 1980-1986 - A Personal Perspective*, Liberia Working Group Paper No. 5, Bremen, Germany, Liberia Working Group

Sawyer, A. (1992) *The Emergence of Autocracy in Liberia: Tragedy and Challenge*, San Francisco, Institute for Contemporary Studies Press

Sawyer, A. (2005) *Beyond Plunder: Toward Democratic Governance in Liberia*, Boulder, Colorado, Lynne Rienner Publishers

Sawyer, A. (2008) 'Emerging Patterns in Liberia's Post-Conflict Politics: Observation from the 2005 Elections', *African Affairs*, 107(427):177-199

Sawyer, A. (2009) 'Land Governance Challenges: The Case of Liberia', presentation at ARD Week 2009, World Bank, Washington D.C., 2 March

Seyon, P.L.N. (1988) 'The Results of the 1985 Liberian Elections', *Liberian Studies Journal*, 13(2):220-239

Sieh, R.D. (2013) 'U.S. $13 Million Diversion in Liberia: What Went Wrong with European Union Money?' *FrontpageAfrica*, 27 June

Sherman, F. (2011) *Liberia: The Land, Its People, History and Culture*, Dar es Salaam, Tanzania: New African Press

Smith, R. (1972) *American Policy in Liberia: 1822-1971*, Monrovia, Liberia, Providence Publications

Star Newspaper (2008) 'Dr. Dunn Named Head of Ad Hoc Group to Investigate Knuckles-Gate II', 13 September

Sungbeh, T-W. (2013) 'RIA Saga Reinforces Sirleaf Administration's Image as Corrupt', *The Liberian Dialogue*, 17 March

The Analyst (2013) 'President Sirleaf Wheels into Prison Brouhaha - Suspends Fugitive Kpaan, Bravado Broh - Will That Pacify the House? 25 February

Tolbert, V. (1996) *Lifted Up: The Victoria Tolbert Story*, St. Paul, MN, Macalester Park Publishing

Transparency International (2013) *Global Corruption Barometer 2013*, Berlin, Transparency International

Truth and Reconciliation Commission of Liberia (2009) *The Final Report of the Truth and Reconciliation Commission*, Monrovia: Truth and Reconciliation Commission

West Africa Democracy Radio (2012) 'Liberia: Teachers' Strike Affects Over 20,000 Public School Pupils', 18 October

Wolokolie, A. (2013) 'Liberia: Ellen Re-Appoints Mary Broh', The *Inquirer Newspaper*, 10 July

Wreh, Tuan (1976) *The Love of Liberty: the rule of President W.V.S. Tubman in Liberia, 1944-1971*, London: C. Hurst and Co

CHAPTER: 4

NEOLIBERAL GLOBALISATION AND SOCIAL MOVEMENTS IN GHANA: THE CASE OF ASHAIMAN

Kojo Opoku Aidoo[1]

Ghana's slum community of Ashaiman is notorious for violent protests, the most serious of which took place in 2013. While the protests appear to be motivated primarily by immediate economic concerns, they can be linked to the neoliberal policies implemented in Ghana over the last 20 years. These policies have led to economic deprivation and marginalisation, but have also generated a social movement which could in time challenge the balance of power.

Introduction

Two mega trends of contemporary capitalism are globalisation and neo-liberalism. This is a study about social movements and the struggles for

1 First, I would like to acknowledge the Rosa Luxemburg Foundation for generously providing the funding for this research work. Second, I am also thankful to Kafui and Collins Brobbey, post-graduate students at the Institute of African Studies, University of Ghana, for assisting with the fieldwork and searching for critical information for me. However, the views expressed in this report are those of the author.

social justice in an era of neoliberal globalisation. It is an explanation of how the devastating impacts of neoliberal policies, in combination with social and economic exclusion, generated a social movement in a Ghanaian slum community, Ashaiman, which has seen a miscellany of social protests culminating in the violent youth protests of June 2013.

The connectedness of neo-liberal globalisation, displacement, urbanisation and social protest has not been well interrogated even though the current literature on neoliberal globalisation reveals that it has its most profound effect, and triggers the most resistance, in urban slums that are the destination of a massive influx of displaced rural dwellers. It therefore becomes important to rectify that anomaly, that lacuna, via thorough analysis of the 'complexities of local political struggles as they are both [globalisation and neoliberalism] shaped and constrained by disjunctures in global regimes of accumulation and continuities in the nature and uneven dispersal of political power' (Chollett 2013). In other words, a historically informed comprehension of how people contest their material, cultural, and political dispossession in an increasingly liberalising and globalising environment becomes compelling.

As recent empirical studies show, the process of displacement and the associated problems of 'slumization' invariably generate resistance and struggle (Zeilig 2009). During such resistance and struggle, the oppressed or the 'wretched of the earth' (Fanon 1965) demonstrate a capacity to act independently of the structures of domination. This chapter analyses the context and texture of social protest in contemporary Ghana, with Ashaiman as a case study.

In 2013, the slum community of Ashaiman exploded. The Ashaiman protest was an instance of the masses acting autonomously of the structures of domination, but also forging coalitions with community-based organisations in a slum community in order to construct a non-institutional space in which activists could contest the legitimacy of state power and fight against the effects of neoliberal globalisation. More than that, the protest was spontaneous rather than planned. And, spontaneity tended to obfuscate the class content and direction. It suggests that the working class in Ashaiman is a class-in-itself, but not yet a class-for-itself.

The Ashaiman protests of 2013 demonstrate the potential for profound economic, social and political transformation from below. They demonstrated, even if momentarily, the capacity of the masses to intrude onto the stage of history as central actors in the production of their own emancipation. Basically, this chapter interrogates the processes of displacement, disempowerment and communal resistance in Ashaiman, a sprawling slum community within Tema Metropolis of Ghana.

On 24 June 2013, a violent demonstration by drivers and a section of the youth of Ashaiman in protest against poor social conditions in the municipality turned bloody. 'As early as 5am that day, the rampaging youth blocked all the roads leading to the town by burning lorry tyres on the roads. The rowdy demonstrators accused their Member of Parliament (MP), Mr Alfred Agbesi, and Municipal Chief Executive Numo Adinortey Addison of neglecting their social and economic needs, especially the rehabilitation of road networks' (Darko 2013).

Ashaiman gives credence to the view that social movements are not timeless. They tend to have a life-cycle in that they are created, they grow, they achieve successes or failures and, eventually, they dissolve and cease to exist. Ashaiman is thus utilised here as a quintessential demonstration of the emergence, subsistence and declivity of social movements in contemporary Ghana. Because social movements are often shaped and structured by context, it is pertinent to set the tone and background by delving into the Ghanaian political system and political economy. It is important to look at the existing literature to see what it says about social movements in contemporary Ghana.

A brief review of the literature

Much pessimism informs the writings about social movements in contemporary Ghana. Langdon (2010) asserts that despite claims that Ghana is now receiving the 'dividends of democracy', the country's current form of democracy has favoured outside investors and side-lined the average Ghanaian. Using Ferguson's (2006) notion of 'topographies of power', Langdon explores the dominance of neo-liberal forms of transnational governmentality in Ghana and the emerging forms of struggle that combine Ghanaian social movements with transnational solidarity networks. He reveals how this type of struggle also 'constructs a parallel topography of power where transnational solidarity networks turn local struggle into episodes deracinated from the location of struggle'. Thus in Langdon's scheme of things the emerging forms of struggle by social movements in contemporary Ghana, being deracinated, are displaced from contesting the power, authority and legitimacy of the central state. What is more, Taylor (2002) points to the fact that the new mediation role of the 'state under the liberalized governance mantra of "steering" rather than running the economy is in fact a pretext for maintaining stability in a nation's citizenry in an effort to facilitate capital accumulation and extraction.' The presumption here is that the Ghanaian state effectively serves the interests of metropolitan capitalism.

Granted these arguments, two important facts are logically deducible from Langdon and Taylor: the Ghanaian state serves the interests of capital as against the interests of citizens; and the ensuing episodes of struggles are deracinated from the location or root of struggle. Langdon and Taylor are unable to explain why and how struggles like the Ashaiman protest remained localised and outside the purview of transnational solidarity networks. It is important to examine the nature, genesis, rationale and tactical dynamics of protests that are the direct outcome of marginalisation and neglect by the neo-colonial state, but which do not benefit from transnational solidarity networks.

Generally, the neo-liberal framework and the World Bank and International Monetary Fund (IMF) have contributed immensely to shaping Ghana's transition to democracy. Boafo-Arthur (2007) notes the peaceful transfer of power between the two main political parties in Ghana that occurred in 2000 and 2008, a sign that potential conflicts can increasingly be resolved through the ballot box. That notwithstanding, he also concedes that the steady implementation of structural adjustment programmes that deregulate the market have depressingly impacted on the vulnerable in society. Consequently, Langdon (2010) argues that Ghana's democratic dividend is not only 'under pressure conceptually, where its meaning is linked to improving conditions for foreign capital rather than the livelihoods of average Ghanaians, it is also under pressure from Ghanaian social movements that have developed new strategies for contesting the truth claims of the dividends of Ghana's democracy'.

The Ashaiman social protests are to be comprehended in this context. By and large, Ghanaian social movements, such as coalitions of farmers' associations and collectives of communities affected by mining, are extensively contesting the reconfiguration of Ghana's democratic government into a mechanism of management, stabilisation, and privatised control coercion in the service of foreign capital (Langdon 2010). Whilst it is the case, as Langdon (2010) and Taylor (2002) argue, that Ghanaian social movements link up with transnational networks of support, it is also the case that in slum communities, deprived of social amenities, the people without transnational solidarity networks are mobilising, often spontaneously, to contest their subjugation and deprivation.

The political system

Ghana is a country of 24 million people comprising over 60 ethnicities, 52 major languages and hundreds of dialects. It is located on the west coast of Africa, with the Ivory Coast to the west, Burkina Faso to the north and Togo to the east. It is a unitary state divided into ten political and administrative regions, with the capital at Accra. Ghana won political independence from British rule in 1957 and by 1981 had undergone eight major episodes of governmental changes via military putsch, evidence of consolidated political instability (Oquaye 2004). Each of these governmental alterations was followed by estrangement of the majority of the population. Each time, the new government, civilian or military, failed to stabilise the social and economic conditions of the country. During this era of political instability and uncertainties, civil society remained exceptionally weak and powerless until some form of political settlement was achieved in 1992. It has been observed that the frequent governmental changes sowed the seeds of confusion, fomented discord and nurtured disorientation among the Ghanaian population (Chazan 1983). The confusion, discord and disorientation in turn generated passivity and embedded political disinterest among the Ghanaian people.

Since the return to political democracy in 1992 Ghana is consistently and persistently presented as an example of the success of the dominant political and economic development paradigm. In what ways then has change in the political context affected social movement activism? In what follows an attempt is made to locate social movement activism within the political economy framework, emphasising the 'primacy of domestic politics' (Whitfield 2011, Mustapha and Whitfield 2009). In other words, an attempt is made to delve deeper into the emerging Ghanaian political economy and system in order to explain social protests in recent times. We try to establish the connection between the liberalised political environment and the upsurge in social protests.

The political settlement

In 1992 Ghana, after years of military rule, sustained a credibly successful re-democratisation wave with a conspicuous new 'political settlement' enshrined in a new constitution. The optimistic view that re-democratisation would engender reform of dysfunctional institutions has been contested by Whitfield (2011), who draws attention to the structural genesis of clientelism in Ghana. He argues that democratisation does not destabilise clientelist politics, 'because the organization of clientelist political coalitions is driven not by the absence of democracy but by the structural features of the economies in developing countries'. Neither does democratisation have much to do with accelerating economic transformation (Whitfield 2011).

If Ghana has two main and very cohesive political parties and enjoys a striking 'new political settlement', there is however an 'open access' deficit, as the political order is still not fully open, in that there are major barriers to entry to challenging the dominance of the two historic parties. The distribution of power within the political parties and the relationship between the parties and private domestic, state and foreign capital at different levels, and society in general, are crucial determinants of the dynamic of capitalist development that has emerged during the process of market liberalisation.

Ghana's fourth republic is supposed to foster a pluralistic and competitive multi-party democracy. Six general elections have been conducted during this period (1992, 1996, 2000, 2004, 2008 and 2012), with each election leading to improved party representation and participation as well as high levels of citizen participation. By and large, an institutionalised two-party system that is a variant of the Westminster political system is developing. The two main parties are the New Patriotic Party (NPP) and the National Democratic Congress (NDC).

The NPP represents a political faction which follows the Busia/Danquah political and ideological tradition.[2] Its political and ideological outlook can be described as conservative, liberal, urban, Asante-based, chief-allied, and linked with professionals (Agyeman-Duah 2003). Historically opposed to the Danquah tradition is the faction dating from Ghana's first president,

---

2 Busia /Danquah tradition refers to the right-wing and conservative political faction in Ghanaian politics.

Kwame Nkrumah, which is more populist, leftist, and entails a critique of foreign dependency. The NDC is characterised as 'a populist, working class and agrarian party heavily dependent on a rural constituency' (Lindberg and Morrison 2005). The divisions of course are not absolute, and do not always correspond to right/left ideologies, incorporating a large measure of pragmatism. Nonetheless, the dynamic between the factions is critical to understanding Ghana's politics (Nugent 1995).

Ghana has been identified as an important instance of democracy in Africa, yet the story of this democratic success overlooks the crucial role social movement activism has played in locally reconfiguring and deepening what democracy means. The pertinent questions addressed here are: when states fail, do mass-based social movements develop to address the ensuing social problems? To take the case of Ashaiman, what factors provoked the violent communal 'insurrection'? Which social forces were behind it? In what ways is the Ashaiman resistance likely to be replicated in Ashaiman itself or in similar slums? How did the Ghanaian state respond to the crisis, and its potential to generate nation-wide communal clashes? And, what lessons must be learnt? This chapter will interrogate these questions. The basic argument is that social movements such as the Ashaiman communal uprising are the product of the processes of displacement, which in themselves are part of the ongoing efforts to contest both local and global power relations.

General socio-political struggles: 2010-2013

Since 2010, the Ghanaian political scene has been a theatre of intense political struggle, sometimes class induced, sometimes ethnic in content.

Before addressing these recent developments, it is instructive to revisit an episode illustrative of the deficit of autonomy of even the best 'democracies' when faced with the dictates of the Bretton Woods institutions.

During the preparation of the 2003 budget, rice farmers appeared appeased. The NPP administration was willing for the first time to place the needs of the farmers, over and above the needs of transnational interests via the introduction of tariffs on rice importation. Nonetheless, this hope quickly fizzled out as the new tariffs for rice and poultry included in the budget were never enforced. According to Christian Aid (2003) a call from the local IMF representative led to the enforcement of the tariffs being suspended despite their having been approved by Ghana's legislature. The telephone call by the IMF was further reinforced by James Wolfensohn, president of the World Bank at the time, when he went out of his way at a conference in Greece to tell Ghana's government officials to 'scrap the higher import duties' (Christian Aid 2005: 34). Rice farmers and poultry farmers in Northern Ghana waged protracted struggles to have the tariff enforced. Eventually, the farmers successfully went to court to seek justice. The government was censored by the high court, which saw their action as a breach of the Ghanaian constitution (Christian Aid 2005). Unfortunately, within a few days the government convened an emergency session of parliament where the act containing the tariff was repealed. Christian Aid has maintained that excessive pressure by the IMF led to the scrapping of the tariffs. Since then, the arm-twisting tactics of the Bretton Woods institutions have set the Ghanaian state and farmers on a collision course, giving further credence to the view that the multilaterals dispossessed Ghana of the development policy agenda.

Ethnic conflicts are a part of the Ghanaian political scene. Talton (2009) utilises the Konkomba-Nanumba conflicts in Northern Ghana to encapsulate post-colonial socio-political struggles in Ghana. He shows the ways in which 'historically marginalized communities have defined and redefined themselves to protect their interests and compete with neighboring ethnic groups politically and economically'. He uses the Konkomba and their relationship with their historically dominant neighbours to show the ways in which local communities identify power, tradition and belonging. Through rich narrative and analysis, Talton challenges popular thinking on the construction of ethnicity, the basis for social and political conflict, and the legacy of European colonial rule in Africa. However, ethnic analysis has its own limitations, which is more than made up for by class analysis. Ethnic conflicts have taken place mostly in Northern Ghana. Yet, there has been extensive labour unrest and popular demonstrations in Ghana since 2010, which Talton's 'constructions of ethnicity' is unable to account for.

Outside ethnic conflicts, there are some protest movements led by religious groups. In June 2010, thousands of livid youth in the Sekondi Takoradi Metropolis 'staged a massive demonstration against reports of gay and lesbian parties in the oil city' (Sulemana 2010). The demonstration, on Friday 4 June, witnessed the first ever homophobic protests in Ghana. Over 1,000 protesters defied a downpour to register their displeasure as they went through the principal streets of the metropolis wielding placards. The demonstration was organised by the Muslim community in Takoradi, with support from other religious groups and concerned citizens.

In July 2010, people of Agyemankwata demonstrated over the Kwabenya landfill, which would be the nation's first sanitary refuse dump. They were concerned about the health impact of the landfill, its outdated construction plans and the possibility of displacement. During the protest, the town's traditional leader, Asafoatse Ayitey II, warned government officials about their obligations to voters. 'We are not vultures to be kept on a refuse dump,' he said, 'It is therefore surprising that after voting [the government] to power, they are compensating us with waste,' the chief argued (Bozo 2010).

Generally, Ghana's labour front has, for the past two years, been bedevilled with numerous unrest by workers who want higher salaries and better conditions of service. From the beginning of 2013, the Ghana Medical Association (GMA), the Ghana National Association of Teachers (GNAT), the National Association of Graduate Teachers (NAGRAT), the University Teachers Association of Ghana (UTAG), Polytechnic Teachers (POTAG), the Federation of Universities Senior Staff Association (FUSSAG) and pharmaceutical workers have gone on strike at different times. In March 2013, NAGRAT and GNAT both embarked on a nation-wide strike to back their demands for improved working conditions and salaries. In February 2013, the GMA withdrew out-patient services as it embarked on a nationwide strike over salary distortions. This was followed by strikes by UTAG and the Teachers and Educational Workers Union (TEWU) over non-payment of negotiated salaries.

In October 2013 the Trade Union Congress gave the Ghana government a 10-day ultimatum to reduce tariff increases on electricity and water by two-thirds and spread the remaining third over two years. Otherwise, the TUC would activate 'all forms of protestations'. This decision was reached by all of organised labour including the leadership of 18 labour unions, public sector groups like the GMA, nurses and workers in private sector unions. GNAT, a very prominent member of organised labour in Ghana, immediately declared its support for the TUC statement. Thanks to this pressure, the government decided to lower the prices of electricity and water (Asamoah 2013).

The strikes have moved beyond the urban labour front to engulf the rural setting. In October 2011:

> ...the youth of Aflao in the Ketu-South District went on a violent demonstration to protest against the deletion of Aflao from the list of newly-created municipalities in Ghana. The demonstrators, who started the street protest from the Ghana-Togo border in the early hours of the day, carried placards, some of which read, 'Enough is enough, Aflao needs a face lift'; 'We need municipality'; 'NDC Ketu-South will become a rural bank'; 'Aflao deserves better'; 'Eva Glo[3], NDC, do you want a change' and 'NDC please fulfill your promises to the people', among

---

3 Eva Glo is an expression which connotes that the Ewe ethnic group is supportive of the NDC.

others. The demonstration was the biggest ever in the history of the traditional area against a ruling of government and brought economic activities in the border community to a halt for hours, as many business people left their goods to join the large crowd [...] Over 300 police personnel from Ho, Anloga, Tongu and the Ketu North and South divisions were mobilised to supervise the demonstration (Agwebode 2012).

Basically, we can classify the pervasive labour agitations in contemporary Ghana into three categories, namely, political strikes, where people try to impress on the government to take a particular decision in their favour; negotiable labour agitation which has the National Labour Commission as the arbitrator[4] and lastly, negotiated wages but where the employer has no money to pay.[5] Whilst these socio-political struggles have confronted the Ghanaian state in various ways, they have mostly utilised institutional structures and operated within the legal framework to seek redress. However, there have been political struggles by social movements that have utilised unorthodox, non-institutionalised and violent methods of agitation. These agitations have been unpredictable, spontaneous and have confronted and challenged state power, authority and legitimacy. The Ashaiman social protests may be cast in this mould, as they did not resort to the use of legal or institutional channels to redress their grievances. Ashaiman presents an inimitable and instructive instance of spontaneous, violent social protest in a debilitating setting of neoliberal globalisation.

---

4 Negotiable labour agitation in the Ghanaian context refers to specific labour demands over which trade unions must negotiate with the Labour Commission, and the Labour Commission can seek a court injunction to declare a strike illegal.
5 This expression refers to a situation where the Labour Commission, Fair Wages Commission and trade unions reach an agreement about minimum wages, but where the Ghana Employers, Association or even the state is unable to raise the money to pay. This became a problem after the Single Spine Salary Structure (SSSS) was implemented.

The study site

According to Owusu (2004), Ashaiman is one of the oldest squatter settlements in Ghana. In 1960 it had only 624 people; it is now a municipality with over 200,000 people and several vicinities. The growth of Ashaiman coincided with the growth of the harbour city of Tema as harbour workers who could not afford to live in Tema settled in Ashaiman. As Owusu (2004) further observes, residents would, in the course of time, construct improvised houses with containers from the port. The town grew and became a bustling commercial centre. Ashaiman is organised along ethnic, religious and occupational identities and dominated by four ethnic groups comprising Ga-Dangbe, Ewes, Dagomba and Akan speaking people. There is also a large population of migrants from other West African countries such as Nigeria, Ivory Coast, Togo, Burkina Faso and Mali.

Owusu (2004) maintains that Ashaiman is largely underdeveloped compared to surrounding settlements such as Tema and Accra. It is a deprived and marginalised settlement, although it is reported to be a major source of revenue to the Tema Metropolitan Assembly. Generally, Ashaiman has serious social and economic problems as infrastructure and social amenities are lacking.

Local chiefs and opinion leaders hold authority in the neighbourhoods. Hometown associations, friend clubs, youth groups and mutual aid societies have been formed. Residents have built schools, churches and mosques. However, the level of economic development and public service delivery has not kept up with the rapid urbanisation of Ashaiman. Most development initiatives have been undertaken by the community themselves, with scanty state support. In the 1980s, the community came together to demand more services from the Tema Municipality, of which it was a part. This was followed by a struggle for more autonomy from Tema that lasted until 2007.

In 1989, Ashaiman was used as a pilot for the government's newly-implemented decentralisation plan. Local leaders who had already established authority and legitimacy stepped into formal positions of power. They served as assembly people in their respective communities. Local participation in politics was further bolstered with the support of Nimba Community Support Services and IBIS[6], two NGOs. In 2003, they established the Ashaiman Governance Forum. This forum brought together residents, leaders and the Ashaiman Municipal Assembly - which is the highest administrative and political decision-making body within the municipality - to discuss development and community issues. The forums were very vibrant and were used as a mechanism to hold leaders accountable. Leaders would be forced to explain their positions and their actions. After each forum, a task force would follow up on the most important issues which arose from the forum. It was from these forums - with support from other organised groups - that a movement emerged demanding municipal status for Ashaiman. After a long and protracted struggle, Ashaiman was granted municipal status in 2007. In a nutshell, Ashaiman fought and won important political representation.[7] Ashaiman has thus become one of the ten municipalities in the Greater Accra region of Ghana. Its capital is Ashaiman, which is situated about four kilometres to the north of the port city of Tema and about 30km.

The evidence suggests that Ashaiman slum dwellers are politically active and engage with the Ghanaian government in important ways. Slum communities have their own strategies of governance depending on their historical conditions and institutionalised state-society linkages.

And as the rate of urbanisation increased in Ashaiman, the dwellers continued to play a progressively important role in Ghanaian politics and in the deepening of its democracy.

6 IBIS is a Danish non-governmental organisation working at global, national and local levels for the empowerment of civil society and underprivileged communities with a focus on equal access to education, influence and resources. The name is a symbolic reference to the ibis bird flying from North to South and feeling at home in both hemispheres.
7 Under Ghana's decentralisation programme, there are district, municipal and metropolitan assemblies. Ashaiman moved from a district assembly to become a municipal assembly, which gives Ashaiman political autonomy.

The genesis of Ashaiman

A brief history of the origins of Ashaiman is in order. Oral history has it that:

> Nii Ashai founded the town in the 17th century after he moved
> from Tema. He named it Ashaiman meaning Ashai's town. His
> two brothers, Nii Amu and Nii Oko, settled in adjoining towns
> now called Mantseman and Moniomanye, respectively. Nii Tetteh
> Amui II is now the head of Ashaiman.

> Ashaiman grew as other migrants from the Dangme West
> District, precisely the Ada area, came to settle in the town and
> were followed subsequently by other ethnic groups including the
> Ewes and Northerners. As Ashaiman expanded, communities
> such as Lebanon, Middle East, Jericho and Bethlehem that derived
> their names because soldiers, who returned from peacekeeping
> duties in these countries, settled there, and Zongo Laka sprang
> up. The most prevalent ethnic groups found in the district are
> Ga-Dangbe, Ewes and Dagomba's (Nunoo 2008).

The Ashaiman municipality has an average household size of five. The main occupations in Ashaiman include farming, especially crop farming, livestock and poultry, as well as fishing, manufacturing, food processing, quarrying and construction, commerce and kente weaving.[8] Illiteracy is high in Ashaiman. Ashaiman has 17 public schools and 286 private schools consisting of nursery, primary and junior high schools.

Ashaiman Senior High School (SHS) is the only public secondary school. There are seven private secondary schools. It has only one public health centre, 14 private clinics and one private maternity home. Many residents depend on the services of traditional healers, and Ashaiman has a Traditional

---

8   Kente is a colourful cloth entirely hand-woven by Ghanaian weavers.

Healers Association with over 100 members, who treat various kinds of tropical diseases. These traditional healers sometimes worsen the health problems of the people (Nunoo 2008).

Periphery underdevelopment

Whilst the North-South development gap in Ghana is traceable to the concentration of resources in southern Ghana, the overwhelming underdevelopment in urban slum communities such as Ashaiman can only be explained by the displacement of rural populations, a displacement that is the direct outcome of peripheral capitalism. Neo-liberal capitalist penetration in the peripheries engenders a large reserve army of unemployed, which eventually migrate to the urban centres. They eventually become slum communities: deprived, dispossessed, alienated and disempowered. Ashaiman is a quintessential example of uneven development and extreme urban poverty. The majority of Ashaiman residents live below the national poverty line (King and Kumasi 2004) and live without water and sanitation or occupy jam-packed, dilapidated structures (Torresi 2012). Social infrastructure is collapsing or non-existent. It is these social conditions that define and shape Ashaiman's existence and engagements with the central state.

A history of protests

It is useful to start with the nature of the power structure and local politics in Ashaiman. Ashaiman, as indicated earlier, is a multi-ethnic, multi-national community that sprang up as a result of migration. It has formal and informal, elected and unelected leaders. Ashaiman has one elected member of parliament, a municipal assembly made up of elected and appointed assembly people and a municipal chief executive.[9] Besides these formal

---

9   The municipal chief executive is the highest political office within the municipality, appointed by the central government in consultation with traditional leaders.

political leaders, Ashaiman has many traditional, ethnic and religious leaders who wield enormous power and influence. There are also unionised leaders who frequently agitate for the welfare of members. Generally, the political class in Ashaiman is perceived as militant and radical. Since Ghana re-democratised in 1992, the social democratic NDC has dominated Ashaiman in general elections, with the more conservative, Akan-based NPP also having a fairly large number of votes, thus reflecting the ethnic and class mix of Ashaiman. Such is the radical informal power structure of Ashaiman that, in the face of ingrained marginalisation, residents have intermittently waged protests and contested their subjugation and deprivation.

Social exclusion is a catalyst for protest movements, as it is a critical underlying cause of conflict and fragility. Where societal groups are disempowered and socially excluded from the state or its key institutions, as is the case with Ashaiman, they may develop parallel political economies, but also seek to challenge the authority, autonomy, power and legitimacy of the state.

The state's failure or even refusal to handle such challenges through political negotiation or some form of consensus building may lead these groups to have recourse in violent opposition. Denials or violations of rights based on social exclusion and discrimination can therefore lead to state fragility. Ashaiman demonstrates a connectedness between social exclusion and violent protest. Generally, the people of Ashaiman are politically active and engage with the Ghanaian state in important ways. Ashaiman has been the scene of violent protests and threats of boycott in modern Ghana. And, even though the violent protests in Ashaiman are the direct by-product of neglect, social exclusion and disempowerment, interestingly the dominant narrative in the explanation of the uprisings in historical and political scholarship has been a-historical and a-political. These explanations see the protestors simply as 'troublemakers'.

In the narratives of the political class and aspects of the Ghanaian media, Ashaiman is a 'trouble-maker'. Such a-historical, a-political and a-theoretical rationalisation stems from discomfiture with class, ideological or even a political economy analysis. We may trace the genesis of such narratives to the inveterate violent protests that have emanated from Ashaiman since independence. The political class is certainly unhappy with a violent class next door. Ashaiman suffers the most scandalous form of horizontal inequalities. And, horizontal inequalities can be manipulated to engender political violence. Horizontal inequalities or forced inequalities existing between different subcultures in the same society can lead to resentment and tension, and may encourage group mobilisation. And the group mobilisation may be unstructured and aggressive.

There is a high sense of entitlement among the Ashaiman people. In April 2009, a group calling itself 'Ashaiman NDC Taskforce' emerged and seized a lorry park at Ashaiman from its legitimate operators. The group, whose membership was made up of NDC supporters, claimed the ruling party had promised them jobs, which it had failed to honour. Therefore, they seized the lorry park and operated it themselves to make money to cater for their families. The action of the group led to the firing of guns and resultant injuries. It took police reinforcements from Accra before the situation was brought under control (Daily Graphic 2009).

The employment of threats and actual use of force by Ashaiman residents have gone hand in hand with resort to orthodox means of seeking development. In July 2010, the Ashaiman Municipal Assembly and other stakeholders organised a development forum, aimed at finding lasting solutions to development problems facing the community. The forum, which was co-organised by three non-governmental organisations, Foundation of Sustainable Livelihood, Ulti-Trust Foundation and Urban Youth Show, was on the theme: 'Making Development a Reality in Ashaiman'.

The purpose of the event was to address pertinent issues affecting the socio-economic progress of the municipality. During the interactive session, residents expressed the need for by-laws to regulate the collection of refuse and advocated stiffer punishment for those who polluted the environment. During interviews with residents the author found that the by-laws were never passed, and that Ghanaian political leaders have only paid lip service to developing Ashaiman. There is environmental pollution and many buildings continue to be constructed on water ways, with the result that there are devastating floods whenever it rains in the area. This has engendered innate resentment among the Ashaiman people, and it was evident that the community had been sitting on a timebomb.

In June 2012, the chiefs and people of Ashaiman called on the Tema Development Corporation (TDC) to revert 21 parcels of land to the chiefs and Ashaiman Municipal Assembly for development projects. They threatened that anything short of this would result in a prolonged quarrel between the TDC and the people since they would not allow any structure to be erected on the said land by TDC. In a separate statement, they also called on the government to speed up the process of amending the legislative instrument that would make the said land a free zone area. They warned that if the government failed to intervene in the case, the people of Ashaiman would not vote in the then upcoming 7 December 2012 parliamentary and presidential elections. This statement was jointly signed by all the ethnic chiefs of Ashaiman Traditional Council led by Nii Anang Adjor (chief of Ashaiman), Nii Kormey (acting jasetse[10] of Ashaiman), Alhaji Masawudu Imoro (Beriberi chief of Ashaiman), Mr Emmanuel Nartey (stool elder of Ashaiman), Mr. C.O. Martei (stool elder), Naana Dugbakie Okor Dede I (Ada queenmother of Ashaiman), Mr Ali Sikatse Ayornu (proposed chairman for the community) (Adzigodi 2012).

---

10 Acting jasetse refers to the sub-divisional chief in charge of domestic affairs within the traditional governance system.

Alongside the economic demands, the Ashaiman people also made very political demands. In 2012 the electorate of Ashaiman threatened to boycott the 2012 general elections if the Mills administration failed to assist them in securing a parcel of land near Michel Camp, which was released to the Free Zones Board for the construction of staff bungalows (Ghana Daily Guide 2012).

Prior to the most recent riots in 2013, there had been previous bloody riots. On 3 June 2008 there was a violent clash between commercial drivers and the police at Ashaiman. The youth of Ashaiman had staged a demonstration in November 2007 to back their demand for Ashaiman to be made a municipality, an autonomous political district. The concern of the people of Ashaiman was that it had been alienated, neglected and marginalised in terms of development. A five-member committee of enquiry chaired by Justice Honyenuga, an appeals court judge, which investigated the incident, made a number of recommendations. These included the dismissal of the Ashaiman divisional commander of the Motor Traffic and Transport Unit of the police service (MTTU), assistant superintendent of police Timothy Dassah, in addition to the paying of monetary compensation to the families of Moses Kassim and Moses Ofori, the two who lost their lives during the violent riots (Nunoo 2008).

The 2013 riots were the most widespread, devastating and sustained in the history of Ashaiman. At dawn on 2013 the youth of Ashaiman and drivers of the local branch of the Ghana Private Road Transport Union (GPRTU) blocked the main Ashaiman-Tema Road in protest against delays by contractors in completing the project.

> As early as 5am, the rioting youth blocked all the roads leading to the town by burning lorry tyres on the roads [...] By 6am, the actions of the demonstrators had spilled over to the Tema motorway, where the demonstrators took control of the toll

booths and drove out the attendants, causing traffic jams on all roads towards the toll booth at the Tema end of the motorway and on the Aflao and Afienya roads. The protesters also vandalised every structure in their way. The youth fought street battles with the police for hours. Unable to contain the situation, the Tema and the Ashaiman police called for reinforcements (Darko 2013).

The protest became so violent and threatened to spill over to Tema City, to the extent that the Ashaiman district command announced the deployment of 200 military-cum-police personnel to patrol the municipality to maintain law and order. To reassure residents and commuters, deputy superintendent of police David Eklu told journalists that the team would offer 24-hour patrols (Darko 2013). At least one police officer suffered serious injury and was rushed to a nearby hospital for treatment. The Ashaiman community was rendered ungovernable. It took a combined team of police and the military several hours to bring sanity to the community.

Even though the protests lasted 24 hours it turned out to be costly in terms of looting, destruction of property and the working hours lost. As a result of the riots the Ghana government ordered an immediate resumption of construction work on Ashaiman roads.

Meanwhile, in July 2013 some workers of the Ashaiman municipal assembly protested the non-payment of their transportation allowance by turning up late for work. The workers said they had not been paid the transportation allowance due to them, thus resulting in their decision to protest (Darko 2013).

Conclusion

Ashaiman does not enjoy transnational solidarity networking. Neither are Ashaiman struggles deracinated from their roots. The connections between neo-liberalism, social exclusion, and social movements seem muted in the Ashaiman protests. Whilst the protests, on the surface of things, seemed to have been against the poor nature of infrastructure in Ashaiman, on a more basic and fundamental level the remote causes were the long pent-up feelings in the community resulting from decades of alienation, marginalisation, disempowerment and dispossession. Ashaiman offers a quintessential example of how the processes of globalisation engender displacement, urbanisation, resistance and protest.

The Ashaiman protests were the indirect outcome of the neo-colonial economic structure and neoliberal policies underway in Ghana since 1992, when the government implemented World Bank/IMF structural adjustment programmes. These policies have led to massive retrenchments, and the creation of a large class of 'lumpen proletariat' who have aggregated in slum communities, of which Ashaiman is one. Despite its economic deprivation, Ashaiman nonetheless has vibrant social institutions, welfare societies, churches and youth clubs and coalitions which supply a fundamental basis for civic order and social mobilisation in the development process of the settlement.

For now, Ashaiman appears generally sectorial in its demands and approach. Ashaiman struggles appear apolitical, and driven by economic concerns. With respect to prognostication, we can say that because Ashaiman is faced with a number of intractable challenges, which are structural in origin, the people will continue to challenge the authority, power and legitimacy of the Ghanaian state in significant ways. And, in the long run, sporadic, unorganised protests will give way to planned and conscious social and political action that may challenge the neocolonial mode of production.

References

Adzigodi, D.N. (2012) 'Revert Ashaiman Community 21 Lands to the Chiefs and Assembly', 16 March, http://www.ghanaweb.com/GhanaHomePage/regional/artikel.php?ID=232790, accessed March 2014

Agwebode, S. (2012) 'Massive demonstration turns violent at Aflao, 22 February, http://thechronicle.com.gh/massive-demonstration-turns-violent-at-aflao/, accessed March 2014

Agyeman-Duah, I. (2003) *Between Faith and History: A Biography of J.A. Kufuor*, Trenton, Africa World Press

Ake, C. (1995) 'Socio-political Approaches and Policies for Sustainable Development in Africa', Paper delivered at the annual meeting symposium of the African Development Bank, Abuja, 25 May

Asamoah, K. (2013) Press conference of Trade Union Congress on 10 November, Accra, Ghana

Bates, R.H. (1981) *Markets and States in Tropical Africa: The Political Basis of Agricultural Policies*, Los Angeles, California University Press

Bozo, P. (2010) 'A Landfill causes protests in Ghana', 22 July, http://www.worldpolicy.org/blog/landfill-causes-protests-ghana, accessed March 2014

Cabral, A. (1969) *Revolution in Guinea: Selected Texts*, New York, Monthly Review Press

Boafo-Arthur, K. (2007) (ed) *Ghana: One decade of the liberal state*, London, Zed Books

Chazan, N. (1983) *An Anatomy of Ghanaian Politics: Managing Political Recession (1969-1982)*, Boulder, Colorado, Westview Press

Chollett, D. L. (2013) *Neoliberalism, Social Exclusion, and Social Movements Resistance and Dissent in Mexico's Sugar Industry*, Lexington Books

Christian Aid (2003) *Struggling to be heard: Democratising the World Bank and IMF*, http://www.christianaid.org.uk/Images/struggling_to_ be_heard.pdf, accessed March 2014

Christian Aid (2005) *Damage Done. Aid, Death and Dogma*, http://www. christianaid.org.uk/images/damage_done.pdf, accessed March 2014

Darko, R.H. (2013) 'Mayhem at Ashaiman; Policemen, journalists flee for dear lives', 25 June, http://graphic.com.gh/archive/General-News/ mayhem-at-ashiaman-policemen-journalists-flee-for-dear-lives. html, accessed March 2014

Fanon, Frantz (1965) *The Wretched of the Earth*, Grove Press, Algiers, Algeria

Ferguson, J. (2006) *Global shadows: Africa in the neoliberal world order*, Durham, Duke University Press

Freire, P. (2000) *Pedagogy of the Oppressed-30th Anniversary Edition*, New York, London, Continuum International Publishing Group

King, R., Kumasi, K. (2004) 'Perceptions of the Residents of Ashaiman of Problems of Road Safety (Draft Report)' prepared for Global Road Safety Partnership, Accra, http://www.afd-ld.org/~handicap-csr/ pdf/sociological-survey/perceptions-of-problems-of-road-safety- grsp-2004.pdf , accessed March 2014

Langdon, J. (2010) 'Strategies of Social Movements in Ghana: Questioning the Dividends of Democracy and/or Being Embedded in New Topographies of Power', *Canadian Journal of Development Studies/ Revue canadienne d'études du développement* 29 (3-4):373-392

Lingberg, S., Morrison, M. K. C. (2005) 'Exploring voter alignments in Africa: core and swing voters in Ghana', *Journal of modern African Studies*, 43(4):1-22

Lipton, M. (1977) *Why poor people stay poor: urban bias in world development*, Cambridge: Harvard University Press

Malcolm X Grassroots Movement (MXGM) and the Jackson People's Assembly (2012) 'The Jackson Plan: A Struggle for Self-determination, Participatory Democracy and Economic Justice', http://mxgm.org/the-jackson-plan-a-struggle-for-self-determination-participatory-democracy-and-economic-justice/, accessed March 2014

Marx, K. (1852) *The Eighteenth Brumaire of Louis Bonaparte*, http://www.marxists.org/archive/marx works/1852/18th-brumaire/, accessed March 2014

Mustapha, A. R. and Whitfield, L. (2009) *Turning Points in African Democracy*, Woodbridge, James Currey

Nugent, P. (1995) *Big Men, Small Boys and Politics in Ghana: Power, Ideology and the Burden of History, 1982-1994*, London and New York, Pinter

Nunoo, L. (2008) 'Spotlight-on-Ashaiman', Ghana News Agency, 3 June

Oquaye, M. (2004) *Politics in Ghana: 1982-1992. Rawlings, Revolution and Populist Democracy*, Accra, Tornado Publications

Owusu, T. (2004) 'Urban migration and the growth of squatter settlements in African cities: Some theoretical and empirical observations', *National Social Science Journal*, 21(2):68-78

Ransby, B. (2003) *Ella Baker and the Black Freedom Movement: A Radical Democratic Vision*, Chapel Hill, University of North

Schmidt, M., van der Walt, L. (2009) *Black Flame: The Revolutionary Class Politics of Anarchism and Syndicalism*, Oakland, AK Press

Sulemana, A-R. (2010) 'Ghana is not a home for homosexuals', 21 June, http://abdulrahimsulemana.blogspot.com/2010/06/ghana-is-not-home-for-homosexuals.html, accessed March 2014

Talton, B. (2009) *Politics of Social Change in Ghana: The Konkomba Struggle for Political Equality*, New York, Palgrave Macmillan

Taylor, A. (2002) 'Governance' in G. Blakeley, and V. Bryson (eds) *Contemporary political concepts: A critical introduction*, London, Pluto Press

Torresi, B. (2012) 'Information is Power: Ashaiman Residents Drive Profiling in Greater Accra', http://www.sdinet.org/blog/2012/08/16/information-power-ashaiman-accra-residents-drive-p/, accessed March 2014

Whitfield, L. (2011) 'Ghana: Vicious Circle of Competitive Clientelism – Easy Financing and Weak Capitalists', paper presented at the Danish Institute for International Studies, Copenhagen

Zeilig, L. (2009) (ed) *Class Struggle and Resistance in Africa*, Chicago, Haymarket Books

CHAPTER: 5

THE WINDS OF CHANGE
IN WEST AFRICA: WHERE NEXT?

Claus-Dieter König

Looked at through the lens of regulation theory, what role will West African social movements play in the coming years? With a crisis in global capital accumulation and neoliberal modes of governance, alliances amongst social movements could herald louder calls for a national and regional economic policy that is geared towards domestic needs.

In the aftermath of the 'Arab Spring', the 'African Awakening' (Manji and Ekine 2011) became an issue. In fact, West Africa has no spring as a season per se; the pace of the seasons is determined by the direction of tropical and other winds. As a result, the protest spree that broke out in Nigeria in January 2012 was eventually dubbed by BBC News and the local media as the 'Nigerian Harmattan'.[1]

This chapter analyses social movements in West Africa in their social context, based on the concepts of the regulation school that analyses societies under the regime of accumulation, the mode of regulation and the hegemonic model.

---

1 Harmattan is a dry and hot wind blowing from Northern Africa.

In practice, social movements articulate their objectives based on, and in contradiction to, hegemonic positions. They seek to clarify and express their interests depending on the current regime of accumulation. Their strategies are developed in the political spectrum of the government and civil society, which is the mode of regulation per se. Social movements are important in the sense that they extend the individual's field of action through collective action. These social struggles, in a context marked by a feeling of powerlessness vis-à-vis predominant trends, help in gaining experiences that solidify them over time as counter-powers. Besides, social movements broaden the perception of economic and social conditions that determine the living situation.

Can the concept of regulation theory, as developed for the analyses of capitalist centres, be applied to Africa? To answer this question, it is necessary to define this concept more precisely. The concept of accumulation regime refers to the economic aspects of social reproduction. The stress is placed on the means of production characterising the society, their hierarchic interaction and their relations with the global economy.

> The focus is on (a) the type of production organization and the place of wage earners in this production process; (b) the time horizon of creation of capital and utilization of the capital; (c) the subdivision of the value produced in wage and profit; (d) the composition of the social demand, also in relation to the development of production capacities in the various segments of social production; (e) the mode of articulation with the non-capitalist forms that occupy a key place in the social formation under review (Boyer 1986: 47).

The concept of accumulation regime can thus be used where the capitalist means of production interact predominantly with non-capitalist means of production. This is the case in West Africa, even if the non-capitalist means of production play a dominant role.

In any case, accumulation should be considered as a global phenomenon. It would not have been possible in Europe without the contributions from Africa, as Walter Rodney (1972) pointed out when he analysed the history of capitalism in Europe.

The globalised regime of accumulation integrates West Africa and indeed each country or even various regions of the same country in a specific way. Elmar Altvater speaks of various forms of *Inwertsetzung* (valorisation) and the 'integration of a region in the functional framework of the global market economy' (Altvater 1987:94), which is characterised by the specific articulation of the capitalist mode of production with regional specificities including the natural conditions, the mode of regulation and the hegemonic model.

The regimes of accumulation in Africa are characterised by the predominance of non-capitalist modes of production and social relations. They are widespread and represent the basis for the survival of the population. They are not geared towards capitalist accumulation. Africa is primarily included in the global process of accumulation through the extraction of raw materials. The latter is capital-intensive and dominated by foreign capital. It is of an enclave nature, meaning that it generates few spin-offs for local economies that rather suffer the harmful effects on subsistence agriculture (this is the case for the Niger Delta with the damage caused by oil extraction) and the exploitation of subsistence economies through the provision of a cheap labour force. In fact, Africa is not integrated in a wider economic process in which a greater vertical integration operates via local processing industries which allow the creation of local capital (Goldberg 2008). In this sense, structural adjustment since the 1980s destroyed what had been achieved in the 'development decades' (the 1960s and 70s).

Africa, like all other peripheral regions, participates in the accumulation process, even while capital is accumulated outside Africa by a net transfer of resources to the countries of the capitalist centre.

If the creation of capital is not only viewed as an accumulation of means of production or money, but as a social relationship, this becomes more obvious. Neocolonial relations are part of the relational structures which, on the international scene, form the 'capital' itself. This particularity of capitalist accumulation structures the social conflicts in Africa and has, for example, triggered special forms of social struggles.

The mode of regulation represents all the institutional forms, the networks and explicit and implicit standards assuring the concordance of behaviours with the dynamic reproduction of social conditions beyond their conflicting particularities. The institutional forms are the ways of regulating behaviours, routine and coordination that govern social action, and provide the social system with relative sustainability (Lipietz 1985, Hirsch 1992, Hübner 1989).

The description of the specificity of the mode of regulation in Africa must take into account both the state and civil society. In Africa, states have a history and a character different from those in Europe. The state in Africa succeeds as 'a political reference, even when lack of legitimacy and the absence of social services reinforce special identities and loyalties, (Eckert 2011:57). 'Traditional leaders' and religious guides (such as the marabouts in Senegal) play an important role in regulation in the different states, and are often backed institutionally by the government, or via clientelist structures. Thus, they can either contribute to the legitimacy of the state or delegitimise the state through the escalation of ethnic or religious conflicts that call national cohesion into question (for example in Nigeria). Since the state, in the wake of structural adjustment programs, withdrew from its classical scope of action, a framework emerged whereby public service functions are occupied by non-state organisations. As part of their projects, several forms of participation and decision-making structures have been created along with the state and local government entities. Thus, at local level, many governance structures have surfaced as part of development projects (Bierschenk, de Sardan 2003).

Lastly, the concept of the hegemonic model widely fits the West African context. We have observed the appropriation, notably by city dwellers, of individualistic values. Here, the brainwashing operated by global neoliberalism has also spread to the point that it paradoxically strengthened reactionary waves in the area. On one side, there are evangelical and pentecostal churches that have lifted the degenerated form of individualism promoted by neoliberals to the rank of a religion; on the other side, there are Islamist groups claiming the obligation to oppose 'true faith' to Western individualism.

One of the major strengths of regulation theory lies in its analysis of crises. According to the theory, relatively stable formations follow unstable conflict-type formations and vice versa. In stable phases, the accumulation, the regulation and the hegemonic model operate together somewhat, such that economic growth is made possible through regulation institutions which, at the same time, are confirmed by the hegemonic mode, insofar as they enjoy a strong legitimacy in society. These stable formations dwindle, and phases of crisis follow that are also phases of a 'quest' for reconfigured modes of interaction between these three levels to re-establish their functional cohesion. Social movements emerge during such crises, mobilise, innovate and act like counter-powers. Eventually, as an element of finding a mode of regulation and a new hegemonic model, social movements become institutionalised and can be functionally integrated in the ensemble of social regulation.

Claus-Dieter König

State withdrawal and the narrowing of the political field

On the economic front, independent West African countries follow the development path of the post-war era (as from 1945). Based on an economy of agricultural exports with little diversification, African countries have tried to boost industrialisation by import substitution. Whatever the side on which the government was during the cold war, the state was a central player in economic development. From the agricultural surplus, savings were amassed to finance industrial development. This was possible through state-owned agencies in charge of the marketing of agricultural produce, notably those destined for the global market. The gap between the domestic purchasing price and the export sales price was generally used to finance investments. We can certainly not speak of an established hegemony, having seen the frequent military coups and the instability of many African states. We can, however, witness, upon formal independence, a first process of acquisition *(aneignung)* of state-owned structures by the population, notably the urban elite.

The point in this article is that as from the 1980s, we have witnessed a structural change of the regimes of accumulation and modes of regulation that have culminated in structural changes of the hegemonic model. This process led to a provisional result, in the 1990s, which caused the relative stability and the obvious weakening of social movements from this era to the end of the first decade of the 21st century.

The debt crisis of the 1980s marked the end of the 'developmental' state, as the IMF and World Bank funds were then hinged on a political precondition: structural adjustment. This constraint compelled governments to reduce vital services and to disengage from the economy. It materialised in the privatisation of state-owned companies. State-owned companies processing agricultural products (such as cotton) were then privatised and often closed thereafter, and this led to a decline in processing depth. Bretton Woods institutions and the World Trade Organisation (WTO) then came to impose the liberalisation of trade policy that eventually culminated in the rise in imports and the destruction of existing industries. The progressive withdrawal of the state from agricultural policy weakened this sector and ushered it into crisis. Today, agricultural products no longer dominate the export statistics of African countries, as they are increasingly replaced by the accelerated extraction of mineral resources.

These extractive industries continue to be like an economic enclave, a process stepped up by uniform legislation on mining extraction to the benefit of ore-mining companies.

On the political front, these developments coincided with the wind of change that swept through Africa in the 1990s, when elections and formal democratic systems started being the accepted standard. The liberation from autocratic and over-paternalistic systems was positively welcomed by populations and the youth in particular. Formal democratisation was a hoax behind which clientelism and corruption were still rife. The mining sector overtook agriculture in importance. However, mining did not integrate the larger population in a way family-run agriculture does, thus causing the comprador bourgeoisie[2] to distance itself from the people. The government no longer showed paternalistic behavior *vis-à-vis* the population; it simply ignored it. In ore-mining, a sector where profits must be guaranteed to foreign capital and the exploitation of resources rid of any risk, even the so-called model democratic states displayed unequalled suppression capacities (this is the case of Ghana, for example, according to War on Want, 2006).

The state has progressively withdrawn from public action. Neither the industrial sector, nor the state-run social security systems guarantee basic conditions of living to the people. This function is now attached to rural

---

2 Theories on the state (for example Nicos Poulantzas) and the theory of dependency refer to a bourgeoisie which, in economically-dependent states, serves as a lever to operations (particularly in trade) of external capital and that are subject to its interests.

and patriarchal subsistence farming and similar forms of informal urban economies, to the solidary structures of families and to rural networks based in urban areas. Yet, these solidarity networks should be taken with caution, as they partly rest on informal constraints.This interaction between the regime of accumulation, the mode of regulation and the hegemonic ideology, a result of the 1990s, now tends towards disintegration. It is against this backdrop that social movements emerge, taking root from the weaknesses and contradictions of the existing social formation. They surface to denounce the agricultural crisis and the high cost of living mostly affecting the urban population - a phenomenon described below through the cases of Senegal, Mali and Burkina Faso. A key element of the hegemonic model is the redirection of the movements of political opposition towards NGOs funded by donors that focus their action on themes related to human rights.

The contradictions of existing social formations appear in the loss of legitimacy of the African-type neoliberal state that surfaced in the 1990s:

> For people in West Africa, the State, which has been altered by the effect of structural adjustments and the neoliberal offensive, represents an alien entity, if not a potential enemy. Even in the traditional field of actions of the State, we have noticed a lack of efficient strategies. Instead, the State is privatized in a double movement. This privatization is 'double' because, on the one hand, many State-run services of general interest (water supply, agricultural policy, etc.) are privatized, and on the other hand, power elites in West Africa, generally concentrated around the President, use State resources for personal wealth creation or to tighten their grip on power. These elites even try, with more or less success, to establish real family dynasties handing over power from father to son.

Therefore, the State action often has the function of ridding societies of their land, water and other public assets of general interest or marketable resources with the view to amassing value towards a primitive accumulation of capital (…)

Furthermore, the State action is geared towards establishing clientelist networks and legitimating power which, on the whole, is concentrated around the president's office (König 2010: 2).

In this connection, Gero Erdmann (2003: 278) actually uses the concept of the neo-patrimonial state whereby he has, since the 1990s, diagnosed processes of state failure and decline.

Democratisation, in the framework of the liberal state, has lost its progressive character and resembles more an empty shell than anything else. Elections can indeed, in some particular conditions (like in Senegal in 2012) make a necessary regime change possible, but they are mostly cases of a costly process aimed at legitimising domination systems whereby democracy is more a mirage than a tangible reality. They often culminate in an ethnic polarisation (for example in Guinea and in Cote d'Ivoire). On the whole, voter turnout is so minimal that the winner of the elections is generally chosen by less than one quarter of the population.

Opposition parties rarely propose a real, relevant and differentiated program. During elections, they often present an alternative based on the person of the political leader and not on a program, and simply limit their campaign to criticising the incumbent. Electoral campaigns are also marked by a lack of real in-depth debates and a clear-cut discourse on strategic and political options. The rest of the democratic process is rid of any content worthy of the name.

Attempts at decentralising state competence end up ineffective. Though the decentralised administration entities acquire competence, they often do not secure any adequate financial and human resources. The result is the fragmentation and non-formalisation of political practices in place. Non-government organisations tend to substitute for state action, hence the strong dependency on external development programs (Bierschenk, de Sardan 2003).

In a nutshell, in the African mode of regulation, NGOs funded by foreign donors have retrieved many functions formerly devolved to the state, notably on the social front. This has led to the incorporation of social movements from the opposition side into the NGO business; which also tends to weaken the social movements. As from the 1990s, Nigeria has become an interesting example of the demobilising effect resulting therefrom.

Against the high cost of living

In West Africa, tendencies to dissolve a tottering social formation can be illustrated through the wave of protests against the food price hike, inflation of energy charges and the prices of other commodities of daily use.

In Burkina Faso in 2007/08, the price of staples skyrocketed in a fraction of time; the price of rice doubled in one year (FAO, undated). Subsequently, in 2008, new taxes, mainly affecting the poor, were introduced. This stirred a protest spree in Bobo Dioulasso, the second largest city in Burkina Faso, which later spread to other cities and to the capital, Ouagadougou.

The rise in the cost of living in West Africa finds its source in the dependency on imports of food staples. It is the offshoot of an extraverted regime of accumulation, the lack of food sovereignty, and thus the need to import food products and other basic commodities. The cost of living, the production conditions and salaries cannot be harmonised through an internal negotiation process (wage negotiations by labour organisations). The fight against the food price hike and the high cost of living actually denounces a price setting mechanism that happens abroad, a struggle almost impossible to wage locally.

Dependency on importations of critical staples has been introduced since the colonial era, strengthened by a farming policy centred on cash crops, and cemented through liberalisation as part of structural adjustment programs and the policy of the WTO. Such is the structural particularity of the regime of accumulation in West Africa that makes the region vulnerable to exogenous price hikes.

At first, it seems illogical in this price hike situation that the Burkina government chose to increase taxes, which eventually affected the poor in particular. Actually, this situation is the consequence of the liberalisation of foreign trade. Budget resources of West African states derive, for the most part, from customs duties. If the latter are abrogated, the state must then look for substitute revenue internally. Given the small size of the formal sector in the economy, which means that income and payroll tax is not sufficient to cover government spending, there only remains the option of creating tax on consumption. The result is an explosive mixture of a high cost of living and tax hikes, which cannot but fuel resistance.

In Burkina Faso, the first phase of this movement of resistance was marked by the absence of a central organisation. The protests of early 2008 in Burkina Faso broke out spontaneously. It was later that many confederations of trade unions held, under the leadership of *Confédération Générale du Travail du Burkina* (CGT-B), an awareness tour during which they called for action and informed the population nationwide on what they termed as the adverse result of anterior consultations with the government (Nacanabo 2011: 243; *Le Travail* 2008: 3, *Le Travail* 2011: 2).

As and when the protests spread, CGT-B took the initiative to set up an alliance grouping of trade unions and other types of labour organisations which eventually managed to achieve the greatest mobilisation around the issue. 2008 saw the creation, under its initiative, of the *Coalition Contre la Vie Chère la Corruption, la Fraude l'Impunité et les Libertés* (Coalition against the High Cost of Living, Corruption, Impunity and Liberties, *CCVC*). From this moment, CCVC coordinated strike actions and protests against the high cost of living. These continued up to May 2008 and still break out every year. CCVC actions reached their peak on 8 April 2011 as part of a wave of massive protest that broke out after the death of a young student, which was blamed on police abuse. School children and students protested all over the country.

Security forces then reacted with massive violence and killed several protesters. Traders and unionists came on board, and on 14 April, the presidential guard launched a mutiny (Jeune Afrique 2011, Marima 2011, Kéré 2011).

Engels (2012) explained the CCVC success by what she calls a 'successful framing' against the high cost of living that federated all the themes and actors of the protests (trade unions, students, school children, human rights movements). This framing made it possible to cast light on the daily consequences of extraverted accumulation and a state that contributed to compounding these daily problems by only seeking to resolve a fiscal crisis through suppression of the poor. If this framing was successful in terms of mass mobilisation, it was also because it revived critiques against the government generally anchored in the collective conscience: a state that is only democratic by name and which serves for the enrichment of a small group.

The CCVC platform insisted both on the economic context and on relating the price hike to structural adjustment programs (*Le Travail* 2008). Better still, CCVC focused, as a starting point, on the daily problems affecting the population and resolutely called out to local and national decision makers during demonstrations. Thus, the claims were not geared to abstract interlocutors (such as international financial investment) but were always related to feasible measures and concrete demands to institutions and stakeholders recognised by the population.

For an independent agriculture

The second example in connection with the rise in social movements touches on the peasant and farmer social movements. Two main objectives structure the claims of these movements: on one side, a reorientation of agriculture for the promotion of sustainable family-type farming methods, and on the other side the fight against the massive purchase, by foreign investors, of big plots of land, a trend that has been on the rise since 2007 (Goita 2011).

To understand agricultural policies, we should first look back to the colonial era. In West Africa, the colonial policy laid emphasis more on the export of cash crops, to the detriment of the subsistence crops. This experimental process, that lasted decades, thus increase dependency on foreign countries, both in terms of food and access to production inputs such as fertilisers and seeds. At the time, just like today, the bulk of producers were smallholders. They sold their products to middlemen that hold the monopoly on exports and, as from World War II, have controlled state marketing circuits. They were also frequently dependent on these middlemen or state-run entities when purchasing production inputs. Choices on the variety of crops, irrigation, stockpiling and marketing were mostly dictated from abroad rather than by farmers and their experiences and concerns. Smallholders have, since the colonial era, been deprived, in agricultural policies, of the knowledge related to autonomous production and the methods to enhance this. They just buy basic inputs (seeds and fertilisers) and care about putting these inputs into the soil and harvesting the products before selling them at preset prices (Bley 1984).

> Colonialism made the modern States in Africa to take action in agriculture without addressing farmers' interests. Thus, the relations between the Government and rural farmers is marked by an authoritarian trend. African agriculture is subject to the interest of State institutions, cities, industry, and over time, more to the interests of an upper urban and rural class. This actually

appears to be a problematic legacy, as farmers' resilience and the productive responses of the rural areas in the face of other forms of pressure rife at the colonial era, are weakened by the inequitable conditions of the global market and the increasing demographic pressure (Bley 1984: 34).

African agricultural policy has not radically changed since independence. It has remained centred on an export system with few incentives for farmers and widely geared towards smallholder farming which, both in terms of input and marketing, is dependent on state or private middlemen (Goita 2011). Basic conditions have declined, with the deterioration of the terms of trade, through the drop, on the global market, in the prices of many agricultural export products. With SAPs, many state-run marketing structures have disappeared, likewise the processing enterprises in the countries of origin. As from the mid-2000s, another issue has intensified, endangering the rural population: land grabs. Some foreign private entities and state investors buy and lease large areas of land for various reasons such as speculation, long-term food security for the population of the foreign investing country, and the rise in the production of biofuel.

Farmers' movements in Senegal and in Mali correlate resistance to land grabs with the commitment to production conditions that allow them to gain in sovereignty and access to seeds, fertilisers and the possibility of selling their products. They fight for a form of self-determined agriculture and insist on the fact that family-type cultivation has benefits in terms of efficiency comparable to industrialised agriculture. They bring forward this claim in the context of food sovereignty and the availability, at local level, of subsistence means of agriculture, challenging the notion of 'food security' that can be ensured through imports. This concept was discussed during a conference held in Mali in 2007 on the sidelines of a meeting that brought together 500 delegates representing farmers' organisations from 80 countries (Bernau 2012).

The economic future of African countries depends, among other factors, on their capacity to no longer import the most basic products for their populations. Only by doing so will they be able to selectively disconnect from the global market in a strategy to build and protect local industries.

In Mali, foreign investors are particularly interested in the land administered by the *Office du Niger* in and around the internal Niger Delta, because this area hosts relatively accessible irrigation methods and is fit for large-scale agriculture. The data on the land already sold, or already engaged in pre-contracts, varies. The Oakland Institute has provided a detailed list amounting to about 555,000 ha (Oakland Institute 2011). Local populations know nothing about these sales until they are evicted from their land. Since these areas are often not immediately used, this process can last years and even decades. Investors and the government allege that the investments are injected for the benefit of farmers. However, in the best cases, the latter become under-paid workers in plantations. In most cases, they are evicted from their land without, or with very little, compensation (oral contribution of farmers during constituent congress of their trade unions, Unions of Farmers of Mali, 'Land-Labour-Dignity'). The big plantations host large-scale irrigation systems that deprive neighbouring farms of water resources. In the Sahel, land grabs are still tantamount to a grab on water resources (Bernau 2012).

Resistance against land grabs has recorded its first case of success. In Northern Senegal, the population of the Fanaye Village has succeeded, after fierce struggles marked by the death of two people, in imposing the withdrawal from the area of the Senegalo-Italian Senthanol/Senhuile joint-venture that eventually established the project elsewhere (AFP 2012).

Some farmers' organisations, such as the National Council for Consultation and Cooperation of Rural Farmers (CNCR) in Senegal or the National Coordination of Farmers' Organisations (CNOP) in Mali, propose a form of family-type agriculture as an alternative agricultural policy. The aim is to achieve a qualitative change in the predominant form of farming in West Africa. This new model would ensure sovereignty for farmers on what and how they cultivate (Forum des exploitations familiales agricoles 2012).

In fact, farmers, both men and women and the urban movements fighting against the high cost of living, are combatting different aspects of the same problem: the economy is extremely dependent on exogenous factors, and the dynamics of internal development are paid little heed. Since SAPs wiped out the model of the 'developmental' state, extraverted accumulation has become the official doctrine. This is what potentially unites these movements. The social struggles already waged are likely to give rise to a convergence of movements that might have great mobilisation potential as far as the majority of the population in urban and rural areas is concerned.

I have highlighted here struggles against the high cost of living in Burkina Faso as well as struggles against land grabbing in Senegal and Mali. However, these forms of struggle prevail in all African countries.

Viewed from the perspective of the regime of accumulation, these struggles can converge towards a battle for the appropriation of the entire value chain of consumer products, notably subsistence crops. Without this reorientation, it would be difficult for these two movements to sustainably impose their claims. Remarkably, CCVC has succeeded in laying the emphasis on the responsibility of national policy. Yet, it might have a limited leeway if it does not propose structural reforms. Grants for staples bought at high prices cannot be a sustainable solution. All the states of the region lack adequate means. Without marketing of the agriculture produce in domestic markets, the reorientation of agriculture towards sustainable smallholder farming is doomed to failure. And yet, such is a key milestone in the path towards more economic integration and a dynamic of endogenous accumulation.

The taming of the shrew

The third example that I would like to give is the development of the democratic movement in Nigeria. In this connection, I would like to raise eyebrows on the process through which some organisations at the forefront of the protest movement have been integrated into regulation institutions; this has contributed to weakening them.

In Nigeria the SAPs and the military regime of Ibrahim Babangida were opposed by an important democratic movement. In spite of its vehement rejection by the majority of the population, the regime of Babangida decided in 1986 to adopt an austerity program, which offered the country the possibility of securing IMF funds (Olukoshi 1991). The wave of protests mobilised a large section of the population - students, school children, workers, women vendors, unemployed people and drivers of public transportation. All this started from demonstrations organised by the National Association of Nigerian Students (NANS) and human rights organisations. The anti-IMF demonstrations rocked the entire country in May 1989, before reaching the climax of the protest movement in 1992 (König 1994).

In November 1991, human rights organisations launched the Campaign for Democracy (CD). Its objective was to convene a sovereign national conference after a large-scale mobilisation of the population, as an alternative to the transition program towards a civilian government pledged by the Babangida regime, a program viewed as non-democratic. In one year, the CD campaign became the coordinating organisation spearheading the resistance against the military regime which, through repeated measures, derailed the much-heralded transition to a civilian government. In September 1992, the government decided to cancel the primaries for the presidential candidacy in the two parties it had created and which were the only ones authorised, as part of the transition program, to participate in the polls. The campaign then called for civil disobedience. A wave of demonstrations and bill-posting activities broke out in November. The activists rapidly faced massive state suppression. The presidential elections were eventually held in June 1993 due to pressure exerted by social movements under the CD campaign. The government later declared the poll results null and void and, subsequently, the CD-coordinated protests became the most intense since independence.

One of the general strikes was called by CD in the South-East from 12 -14 August 1993 and a few cities of the North followed (König 1994). In the face of this situation of tension, a small group of committed human rights activists moved to spearhead a national protest movement. Babangida later relinquished power to a government of transition that was charged with organising new elections. The transition government was rapidly wiped out by a military coup that took General Sani Abacha to the helm.

Abacha launched a wave of massive suppression against the democratic movements. A global wave of protests broke out in the wake of the execution of nine activists of the Movement for the Survival of the Ogoni People (MOSOP), including the famous scenarist and writer Ken Saro Wiwa.

Apart from the suppression, another process came to weaken the democratic movement: this was the propensity of leading organisations to work as human rights organisations and NGOs financed from abroad. The important role played by NGOs as an integral part of the institutional structure of social regulation is a characteristic of the mode of regulation in West Africa. One consequence of this 'NGOism' is the domestication and lack of firm-handedness of the key organisations and people on the forefront of the social movements, insofar as their actions are geared towards meeting the requirements of foreign donors in terms of conferences, reports and speeches on the human rights situation, instead of focusing on the organisation, political training and mobilisation of the population. Many actors of the social movements blamed this trend, dating back to the mid-1990s, for the continuous weakness of the movements engaged in the fight against structural adjustment programs (Social Action 2008).

Thus, activists of social movements were absorbed by the workload in NGOs and were no longer available for mobilisation and organisational actions.

In these times, when politically exposed people had to deal with suppression very likely to culminate in assassinations, the NGOs financed from abroad naturally offered much: personal security owing to their international contacts, a professional career, and better still, international recognition of their work and the results thereof, which compensated for the often frustrating experiences in terms of defeat and demobilisation that the leaders of social movements often encountered.

In Nigeria, this process started before the phase of strong mobilisation under the CD campaign. Back in 1989, a group within the biggest human rights organisation - the Civil Liberties Organisation (CLO) - provoked a split, putting forward the fact that a human rights organisation cannot be neutral politically. Though it did not adopt a neutral stance after that, CLO remained an important source of support for the CD campaign. It is important to note that the issue regarding political independence was discussed within human rights organisations. This actually meant that their capacity to build an alliance with politically committed social movements in Nigeria, like at the time of the National Association of Nigerian Students (NANS) or the Academic Staff Union of Universities (ASUU), was limited.

This is an example of a process of the institutionalisation of social movements that integrated them in a firm structure of social regulation. On this issue, there are similarities with the integration of the workers' movements through negotiations on the Collective Labour Agreement. In the Nigerian case, the question is to know how NGOs and human rights organisations can be considered as social regulation institutions. They act as such because they channel social conflicts and the fight for human rights towards an institutional settlement that departs from mobilisation for protests and for the awakening of the masses.

This process goes along with a transmutation of hegemonic ideas, basically amongst intellectuals. The years of struggle for independence, as well as the period following independence, were marked by ideas of social progress and national construction involving the populations. The strengthening, at global level, of individualistic ideas (which are not necessarily related to the development of an authentic individuality) has also marked the intellectual discourse in Nigeria since the 1980s, particularly within the universities.

Actors of the Nigerian social movement now see strong potential for the strengthening of their struggles. In early 2012, the elimination of the fuel price subsidy prompted a big protest movement that some people, such as the leaders of United Action for Democracy (UAD), qualified as the greatest mobilisation since the Campaign for Democracy, if not since independence. Even the partial reintroduction of the subsidies did not change much about the fact that the people's conscience had been rekindled. The experience that the protests can lead to partial successes will trigger new protests. The protests of January 2012 were coordinated by the Labour Civil Society Coalition. The weakness of this coalition was perceived when the trade unions stopped the strike after the partial reintroduction of the subsidies, without consulting the partners of the UAD coalition and the Joint Action Forum. One year after the successful protests, UAD wanted to test its capacity to be the nucleus of social mobilisation. During the first anniversary of the January 2012 protests, UAD called for a two-day wave of demonstrations all over the country, with a general strike, to demand the end of massive corruption within the state apparatus. In any case, we have noted that the leading actors of NGOs are now focusing more and more on the political training of the population, in a bid to raise public awareness of the national problems and step up the potential of the mobilisation of social movements (UAD 2012, Apampa 2012).

A resurgence of social movements?

In the upcoming years, we will see whether there will be a resurgence of social movements in West Africa which, beyond the call for good governance and transparent and fair elections, will bring social issues to the fore. My argument would be confirmed if these social movements, through their daily experiences, demand an economic reorientation. In the meantime, we have grounds to think that the functional cohesion of extraverted capitalist accumulation, regulation marked by an African mode of state neoliberalism, and the proliferation of NGOs as support for international cooperation, will increasingly dissolute and go into crisis. Other indications on this matter can be provided if alliances are formed amongst social movements for a family type of agriculture, against the high cost of living, against the expropriation of people's assets, against corruption, for a mining policy serving the national interest, and for a national or regional economic policy more geared towards domestic needs and enhancing existing or upcoming value chains. I do believe in that, and so do others (Manji and Ekine 2011).

References

AFP (2012) 'Senegalese villagers vow to fight biofuels project', http://phys. org/news/2012-08-senegalese-villagers-vow-biofuels.html, accessed 28 November 2012

Altvater, E. (1987) *Sachzwang Weltmarkt*, Hamburg, VSA

Apampa, S. (2012) *Occupy Nigeria – es geht um mehr als den Preis von Benzin,* https://www.boell.de/de/navigation/afrika-occupy-nigeria-proteste-benzinpreis-korruption-13844.html, accessed March 2014

Bernau, O. (2012) *Landgrabbing: Neokolonialer Landraub in Afrika. Der globale Widerstand wächst,* in Archipel 202, www.forumcivique.org

Bierschenk, T., de Sardan, J. (2003) 'Powers in the Village: Rural Benin between Democratisation and Decentralisation', *Africa* 73(2): 145-173

Bley, H. (1984) Problematisches Erbe. Kolonialismus und Landwirtschaft, *der überblick*, 20(1): 32-34

Boyer, R. (1986) *La Théorie de la Régulation. Une Analyse Critique*, Paris, La Découverte

Eckert, A. (2011) Nation, Staat und Ethnizität in Afrika im 20. Jahrhundert, in Sonderegger, A. Ingeborg, G. Birgit, E. (eds) *Afrika im 20. Jahrhundert. Geschichte und Gesellschaft*, Wien, Promedia: 40-59

Engels, B. (2012) Brot und Freiheit: Proteste, gegen das teure Leben' in Burkina Faso, *Sozial, Geschichte Online* 9/2012: 85-115

Erdmann, G. (2003) Apokalyptische Trias: Staatsversagen, Staatsverfall und Staatsverfall – strukturelle Probleme der Demokratie in Afrika, in Bendel, P., Croissant, A., Rüb, F. (eds) *Demokratie und Staatlichkeit, Systemwechsel zwischen Staatlichkeit und Staatskollaps*, Opladen, Leske und Budrich: 267-294

FAO (n.d.) 'Burkina Faso', http://www.fao.org/isfp/information-par-pays/burkina-faso/fr/, accessed 9 January 2012

Fondation Gabriel Péri (2011) *La crise globale et l'Afrique: quels changements? Actes du colloque de la Fondation Gabriel Péri, Dakar 18-19 mai 2010*, Paris, Fondation Gabriel Péri

Forum des Exploitations familiales agricoles (2012) *Communiqué*, Dakar

Goldberg, J. (2008) *Überleben im Goldland. Afrika im globalen Kapitalismus*, Köln, PapyRossa

Goita, M. (2011) La souveraineté alimentaire en Afrique de l'Ouest: la résistance des peuples contre les agressions du dedans et dehors, in *Fondation Gabriel Péri* (2011): 137-153

Hirsch, J. (1992) Regulation, Staat und Hegemonie, In Demirovic, A., Krebs, H-P., Sablowski, T. (eds), *Hegemonie und Staat. Kapitalistische Regulation als Projekt und Prozess*, Münster: westfälisches Dampfboot: 203-213

Hübner, K. (1989) *Theorie der Regulation. Eine kritische Rekonstruktion eines neuen Ansatzes der Politischen Ökonomie,* Berlin, edition sigma

Jeune Afrique (2011) 'La contestation gagne du terrain au Burkina Faso', 18 April

Kéré, P. (2011) 'Burkina Faso after the recent socio-political shocks', *Pambazuka News,* Issue 538, http://pambazuka.org/en/category/features/74704, accessed 9 January 2012

König, C. (1994) *Zivilgesellschaft und Demokratisierung in Nigeria*, Münster, Hamburg, Lit

König, C. (2010) *Westafrika: Wann werden die Schönen geboren?* Berlin, Rosa Luxemburg Stiftung

Lipietz, A. (1985) Akkumulation, Krisen und Auswege aus der Krise. Einige methodische Überlegungen zum Begriff, Regulation, *Prokla* 58: 109-138

Marima, T. (2011) 'Uprising in Burkina Faso: Why no cameras?', *Pambazuka News*, Issue 527, http://pambazuka.org/en/category/features/72927, accessed 24 January 2012

Manji, F., Ekine, S. (2011) *African Awakening: The Emerging Revolutions*, Pambazuka Press, Cape Town, Dakar, Nairobi, Oxford

Nacanabo, S. (2011) Des réponses syndicales à la crise : l'expérience du Burkina Faso, in Fondation Gabriel Péri (2011): 243-254

Olukoshi, A. (1991) *Crisis and Adjustment in the Nigerian Economy*, JAD Publishers, Lagos

Rodney, W. (1972) *How Europe Underdeveloped Africa*, London, Dar es Salaam : Bogle-L'ouverture

Siambo, E. (2011) La crise alimentaire et la situation actuelle au Burkina Faso, in Fondation Gabriel Péri (2011): 166-180

Social Action (2008) *Programme for Political Education and Mass Mobilisation in the Niger Delta and Nigeria, A Project Concept Note*, Port Harcourt

The Oakland Institute (2011) *Understanding land investment deals in Africa: Mali*, Oakland, Oakland Institute

Le Travail (2008) Organe D'information et de Formation de la CGT-B, Ouagadougou, n° 46, Octobre

Le Travail (2011) Organe D'information et de Formation de la CGT-B. Ouagadougou, n°50, mars

United Action for Democracy (UAD) (2012) *Towards the 1ˢᵗ Anniversary of the January Uprising*, Abuja, Port Harcourt

War on Want (2006) *Anglo American: The Alternative Report*, London, waronwant.org

PART: 2

SOCIAL MOVEMENTS
AND THE QUEST
FOR AUTONOMY

CHAPTER: 6

THE HOWS AND WHYS
OF MOBILISATION
IN CÔTE D'IVOIRE

Francis Akindès, Moussa Fofana and Séverin Yao Kouamé

The aim of this contribution is to provide a socio-historical review of the changes that have taken place within social movements from 2002 to the present day. With the outbreak of the armed rebellion in September 2002 and the occupation of the whole northern part of the country, Côte d'Ivoire experienced a political face-off between two movements (the 'Young Patriots' and the 'Patriotic Movement of Côte d'Ivoire', which was later renamed 'Forces Nouvelles' or the 'New Forces'). These two groups opposed each other over conflicting definitions of the notion of the fatherland. The first goal of this chapter will be to explain how the fatherland became the focus of polarised mobilisation from 2004 to 2010, what mobilisation organisations it gave rise to and what logic these organisations developed as justification. The end of eight years of politico-military crisis, whose bloody epilogue was the post-electoral conflict of October 2010, the arrest of the former president on 11 April 2011 and the inauguration of Alassane Ouattara in May of the same year, opened the door to new forms of social movements. As if there was a transmutation in methods of mobilisation, these new movements are led mainly by union activists voicing complaints over the high cost of living and by ex-combatants, who were not properly demobilised, calling for their promised socio-economic reintegration. The second goal will be to demonstrate how changes in the political sphere determine the nature and objectives of social mobilisation and how this mobilisation continues to be perceived as an outcome of political strategies.

At the beginning: politician-led mobilisations

The early years of Côte d'Ivoire's post-colonial history were marked by relative political and social stability, as well as by strong economic growth performances between 1960 and 1980. Although economic growth generated substantial investments during this prosperous period, its positive spinoff was invested in a clientelist system that helped stabilise the social and political front. At the time, a space of quasi-consensus was formed around the redistribution of the 'windfall'. From the arrangements developed under the 'Houphouetist compromise', a 'balanced' system emerged in which political support was maintained through opportunities for enrichment under the benevolent hand of the charismatic father figure, who also benefitted from the centrality of power under the single-party system. During that period, the foundations for a 'trade unionism based on participation and supervision' (Touré 1998) were laid across the different segments of society. Despite associations and movements such as the Students and Pupils Movement of Côte d'Ivoire (MEECI),[1] the Association of Ivoirian Women (AFI) or even the General Union of Workers of Côte d'Ivoire (UGTCI), the idea of a civil society that was not in the service of the single party, and even less that of protesting government measures in the street, was unimaginable at the time.

---

1   In terms of union representation, MEECI, which served as a tool to control young people in the nation's schools and universities, replaced previous associations that had been closed down. The National Union for Students of Côte d'Ivoire (UNECI) was founded in 1958 by Harris Mémel Fôté, who was arrested; in 1964, UNECI became the National Pupils and Students Union of Côte d'Ivoire (UNEECI) which, although it was instigated and shaped in its early days by state supervisory bodies, was subsequently dissolved by the political bureau of the Democratic Party of Côte d'Ivoire (PDCI) when it sought to gain independence and distanced itself from the party in 1967 (Amondji 1984, Proteau 1998).

The 1990-2000 period was preceded by economic hardship in the late 1980s. In the run up to this period, other than discontent among certain professional categories[2] and a few strike movements that were quickly stifled, the deterioration of the country's economic situation and the ensuing social tensions failed to give rise to any real social movements despite numerous causes for mobilisation.[3] The political and social stability that characterised the previous period broke down with the drop in prices of the cash crops which had formed the basis for the 'Ivoirian miracle' for nearly two decades. The accentuated and prolonged effects of the economic crisis of the late 1980s eroded the foundations of the 'Houphouetist compromise' stability pact and plunged the country into a 'post-miracle' period coinciding with a demand for democratic openness and the new terms and requirements of the global economy.

In 1990, what was still being described in government newspapers as a 'social stir' had become more organised in its expression through the effective mobilisation of pupils and students, fostered by members of the budding cells of the future political opposition parties. When the (re)establishment of a multiple party system became definite in April 1990, the newly democratised social and political space in Côte d'Ivoire experienced its first street demonstrations with the creation of numerous political opposition parties and a student union, the Student Federation of Côte d'Ivoire (FESCI). The motivations for the protest, which were both social and political, applied across all segments of society, from farmers to civil servants to youth. On 14-16 and 21 May 1990, scarcely a month after the reintroduction of political pluralism, the army and police respectively hit the streets of Abidjan in the midst of the protest. The 'uniformed corps' thereby showed that their loyalties could no longer be taken for granted by the authorities and that the government no longer controlled the levers that regulated society.

---

2   In February 1982 there were teacher strikes in higher education. In April 1983 teachers in the secondary school system went on strike.
3   The implementation of structural adjustment programmes (SAPs) led to higher prices for urban transport and rising prices for petrol, water, electricity, staple goods and foods. The price hike occurred at a time when the wages of civil servants were frozen and numerous public and private enterprises were closing.

As of this time in 1990, major mobilisations within Ivoirian society developed in the framework of political agendas and chiefly obeyed strategies linked to the vagaries of the power struggles and political issues of the moment. Indeed, one can readily recall the demonstration that drew some 20,000 people on 31 May 1991 in Abidjan were protesters chanted 'Houphouët, resign!' following a punitive raid by the military on the university campus of Yopougon on the night of 17 May 1991. Violent student demonstrations also took place on the campuses of Abidjan on 29 and 30 January 1992. These acts of mobilisation can be ascribed to the alliance between political players and a certain fringe of young people; a fact confirmed when the violent march of 18 February 1992 saw the arrest and imprisonment of political leaders, including Laurent Gbagbo and young trade unionists.

In short, a series of sometimes violent collective actions established mobilisation as both a hallmark of the allies of the political opposition and as a specific action in their pursuit of power. Social mobilisation remained in the service of political strategies. Setting aside such obvious and important societal issues as immigration, youth unemployment, the education crisis and privatisation, the political class focused its genius on the rules of accession to power and the terms and conditions of its exercise. The shifts in the balance of power in the new political arena notably gave rise to the Republican Front, an alliance between the Ivoirian Popular Front (FPI), led by Laurent Gbagbo, the Rally of the Republicans (RDR), led by Alassane Ouattara and the Union of Democratic Forces (UFD), an alliance of several small parties. This alliance launched an active boycott between September and October 1995, chiefly in protest of the provisions of the electoral code and for the establishment of an independent electoral commission. The boycott prolonged the violent mobilisations initiated in 1990. The streets, now recognised as a space where the Ivoirian political order could be regulated or deregulated, were once again occupied in December 1999 by young non-commissioned officers returning from a peacekeeping mission in Central Africa.

When their calls for the payment of their bonuses went unheard, they deposed President Henri Konan Bédié and put General Robert Guéï in power.

The national identity crisis and its political uses (December 1999 - October 2000)

The interlude of political transition under Guéï is a major focal point in analyses of the recent political history of Côte d'Ivoire for at least three reasons: (i) it corresponds to a time when the cards were being re-dealt and the players strategically repositioned; (ii) it clarified the discourse of the main political leaders and the nature of their support (popular, community, ethnic, religious, etc) around the essential issues of the Ivoirian crisis; and (iii) it ended with a violent confrontation of mobilised political and social forces and bequeathed on the FPI regime established at the end of the transition the seeds of politico-military instability which would sprout between October 2000 and September 2002.

In December 1999, the putsch that placed Guéï in power revealed the stifled discontent that had long been appeased under the lengthy reign of President Félix Houphouët-Boigny (1960-1993). The military coup shattered the strategy set in place by Bédié, the constitutional successor to Houphouët-Boigny, to lock down political power. As a result, the fall of Bédié was applauded by all of his political competitors. In the view of certain analysts, the public statements made by his opponents following the putsch contributed to the trivialisation of the use of armed violence in the arena of political competition (Le Pape 2003). The brief transition period led by Guéï was studded with bloody episodes. It was marked by several attempted coups followed by serious purges in the army.[4] The targets of the purges were soldiers and officers suspected of being close to or supporters of Ouattara, the former prime minister. Several were exiled to neighbouring Burkina

---

4   The mutinies and attempted coups occurred on 4 July 2000, 17-18 September 2000 and 7 January 2001.

Faso, where they later formed the main core of the Patriotic Movement of Côte d'Ivoire (MPCI) rebellion.

During the same period, confrontations were also witnessed between Ivoirians on the basis of their ethnic, regional, political and even religious affiliations. One of the high points of these confrontations occurred during the referendum for the new constitution in July 2000. During the popular consultation, public debate had focused on the conditions for eligibility to run for the office of president. For several months, the subject had inflamed public opinion in Côte d'Ivoire, revealing polarised positions[5] (Diabaté, Dembélé and Akindès 2005). The tensions between ethnic groups and party supporters came to a head with the violence that followed the presidential election of October 2000, when supporters of Gbagbo and the FPI fought supporters of Ouattara and the RDR. A mass grave containing 57 bodies of people purported to be natives of the North was discovered in the Yopougon neighbourhood of Abidjan. What was known as the Abidjan events of 24-26 October 2000 culminated in a total of 150 deaths, according to Human Rights Watch. At the outcome of this showdown, Gbagbo succeeded in imposing himself as president elect.

Armed insurrection as a cause for mobilisation (September 2002)

On 19 September 2002, Côte d'Ivoire experienced yet another armed conflict. Following an attack against the Gbagbo regime, the different armed forces formed a rebellious coalition that maintained control over the northern half of the country. The situation was unique, notably due to the civilian mobilisation witnessed in both the North and South alongside the belligerent armed forces.

5 This was known as the war of AND/OR. The formulation 'be of Ivorian origin, born of a father and a mother themselves of Ivorian origin' prevailed over the alternative formulation stating 'born of a father or a mother of Ivorian origin'. The result of the referendum was interpreted by partisans of the FPI and the PDCI as a victory over usurpers of Ivoirian nationality and their champion, Ouattara of the RDR. Although he claimed and proved his northern Ivoirian origins, the various successors to power have perpetuated doubts about his Ivoirian citizenship and that of his supporters.

The mobilisation was essentially led by young Ivoirians who chose to support one or the other of the parties by enrolling as combatants or activists in political organisations. The mobilisation of youths on both sides of the traditional dividing line between rebel forces and pro-government forces was facilitated by young leaders who became figureheads of a 'patriotic war', a reference to the rhetoric they developed around the concept of the fatherland. The most important figures were Guillaume Soro, who led a coalition of three armed groups known as the *Forces Nouvelles* (FN) in the North and South, and the young leaders of the counter-insurrectional movement: Charles Blé Goudé, who led the Alliance of Young Patriots for National Revival (AJPSN); Damana Adja Médard, who headed the National Coalition of Resistance of Côte d'Ivoire (CONARECI); and Eugène Djué, who led the Union for the Total Liberation of Côte d'Ivoire (UPLTCI). Their point in common was that they were all former leading members of FESCI. These young people had moved on from union mobilisation, the experience of which they had capitalised on, to political mobilisation with a view to exercising actual political functions in those troubled times.

Mobilisation structures differed in the North and the South. Initially, young people expressed their support for the rebellion essentially by joining the ranks of combatants in the occupied military barracks and camps. With only a little less than 800 members in September 2002, by early 2003 Soro's Armed Forces of the New Forces (*Forces Armées des Forces Nouvelles*, initially the MPCI) claimed a membership of more than 35,000 combatants and this subsequently reached 42,564 in 2006.[6] At the end of the post-electoral crisis in 2011, following the successive movements of demobilisation, ineffective reintegration, remobilisation and new enlistments, the actual number of ex-combatants in the rebellion, although growing, was hard to pinpoint.

The FN also benefitted from the support of young people mobilised in the economic and social spheres to assist the political leaders of the rebellion in

---

6 This figure was produced in April 2006 by the DDR (disarmament, demobilisation and reintegration) division of the United Nations Operation in Côte d'Ivoire (UNOCI).

the administration of the occupied zones. Thus, with the participation of a civil society in the service of the FN, structures and organisations were set up in the Centre-North-West (CNO) zone to take on roles in areas in which the military command was not involved. In the political and administrative sphere, young people joined the New Forces Youth (JFN) and participated in the running of the FN general secretariat or facilitated the interface between military authorities, local and international non-governmental organisations and civil organisations through the Civil Cabinet.[7] Certain young people with no organic ties to the rebellion set up a 'senate' in Bouaké, which organised public debates on a variety of topics. It should also be noted that another group of young people (mainly comprising former students) were co-opted to act as tax officials and administrators in the *Centrale économique*, a technical structure that gathered financial resources to allow the rebel organisation to support itself.

The picture of mobilisation is completed by the enlistment of young pupils and students in the maintenance and running of a semblance of an education system, particularly after the exodus of a sizeable population of civil servants - including teachers - who left for the government zone. Their mobilisation in support of schooling, although it was not initially supported by the FN, eventually became a significant part of support for the insurgents. The commitment of the 'volunteer teachers' who adopted the slogan 'no to intellectual genocide' gave rise to the Movement of Volunteer Teachers of Côte d'Ivoire (MEVCI), which would later be associated with the actions of the rebel group. In the zones under rebel control, numerous demonstrations of support were organised at different moments in the crisis through the combined action of organisations that explicitly espoused the cause and the discourse of Soro and his men.

---

7   The Civil Cabinet was an administrative body under the former rebellion. It was in charge of relations with civil society and political organisations in the occupied zones. The cabinet members, also known as delegates, formed a sort of interface between the military forces and the people. In practice, the Civil Cabinet of the New Forces governed the civilian sphere in the occupied zones with support from a constellation of organisations that, while they claimed to represent civil society, had, for the most part, openly sided with the rebellion.

At every rally in support of Gbagbo in the southern zone, the abovementioned organisations, in the framework of the coordination of civil society organisations in the CNO zones, were there to represent the opposite view and federate their actions in various areas.

The structure of mobilisation observed in the government zone was different, as it was organised in keeping with the style and charisma of the young protest leaders. In reaction to the insurrectional movement of the MPCI, the youth organisations aligned with the presidential movement mustered their forces and answered the call of Blé Goudé. On 2 October 2002, he was able to organise a massive demonstration attended by approximately a million people to show the support of the Ivoirian people for the regime.

Unable to deploy an effective army against the rebellion, the authorities set up a counter-insurrectional response in tandem with the patriotic youth organisations. This 'patriotic galaxy' was actually a heterogeneous collection of civilian and paramilitary organisations, headed by young political leaders in close relationships with the authorities. Their large numbers, their shifting strategic alliances that changed with the circumstances and the nature of their activities muddled the map one might otherwise have been able to draw of the constellation of 'Young Patriot' organisations. However, one constant emerged from their affirmation of their patriotic commitment: 'safeguarding the institutions of the Republic' and 'fighting neo-colonialism so that the country's resources stay in the hands of Ivoirians'. Every activist in the 'patriotic galaxy' had his or her own definition of the content of resistance, its forms and the actions deemed appropriate for the defence of the beleaguered fatherland. However, in the end, the real link between these numerous organisations was their sympathy for the political figure of Gbagbo (Akindès and Fofana 2010).

The Pan-African Congress of Young Patriots (COJEP), FESCI, the open-air forums and parliaments (including the celebrated 'Sorbonne' of the plateau) and a series of pro-government vigilante groups or militias - Wê People's Patriotic Alliance (APWê), Ivoirian Movement for the Liberation of the West of Côte d'Ivoire (MILOCI), Group of Patriots for Peace (GPP), etc - formed the complex structure of the patriotic movements on offer for young people in the government zone. Their funding was rooted in networks of relationships between their principal leaders and the regime in power. We will not enter into the internal tensions within the movements or the internecine power struggles between the young leaders that saw the emergence, for a time, of the term 'bread-and-butter patriot'[8] which highlighted the extraordinary mobilisation capacity of the 'Young Patriots'.

At the height of the Ivoirian crisis, the following events stand out among the exploits of the 'Young Patriots': demonstrations in support of Gbagbo and in protest against the Linas-Marcoussis Agreements[9] respectively on 18 January and 1 February 2003; the youth rally at the Champroux stadium on 26 April 2004 with the participation of the army chief of staff, the president of the National Assembly and first lady Simone Gbagbo; the June 2004 march followed by a sit-in in front of the 43rd French marine infantry battalion (BIMA) to call for the departure of the French army; the mobilisation on 6 and 7 November 2004 against French Licorne troops (the name of the French forces in Côte d'Ivoire) in response to the destruction of the air fleet of the defence and security forces and sporadic opposition to the operation to identify the population between July and October 2006. Ultimately, the support of the 'Young Patriots' was on the side of the presidential team and Gbagbo throughout the crisis and up until the violent outcome of the post-electoral crisis of 2010.

---

8 This expression refers to a category of young members or leaders of patriotic organisations whose chief motivation was the filling of their bellies.

9 These agreements were the product of talks held from 15 to 26 January 2003 in France, on the invitation of President Jacques Chirac, between the representatives of the party in power and its allies, opposition parties and the armed rebellion movements. Overall, the agreements maintained Gbagbo in power, and recommended the formation of a reconciliation government led by a prime minister who would remain in his position until the next election, the restructuring of the army and the revision of presidential eligibility criteria. The rebellion was also given the ministerial portfolios of defence and the interior within the reconciliation government. However, Gbagbo refused to apply this provision and used other players to mobilise young supporters in the street to protest.

Fatherland and nationality as causes for mobilisation

It should be recalled that, on the passing of Houphouët-Boigny, the emerging discourse in the political class, far from offering genuine solutions to actual development problems, was chiefly built around the issue of legitimacy to exercise power. This discourse was transferred to the social fabric through the channel of ideologies (cooked up in political laboratories) that reified as yet poorly defined notions, such as national identity, autochthony and the fatherland. The opposition born of the discordance in the political discourse gave rise to an active boycott in 1995 (on the subject of the electoral code); to the overthrow of the Bédié regime (which was applauded as bringing an end to 'Ivoirity', the restrictive concept of Ivoirian nationality); to the and/ or opposition surrounding the constitution of 2000 (finally adopted against a backdrop of the affirmation of a debatable autochthony); and to the crisis that began with the attempted coup of 2002 (which took up the grievances accrued during the political debate). This final crisis, which combined political and military elements, as we have seen, was also mirrored in social mobilisation. It reached its dénouement at the outcome of the most deadly post-electoral violence in the history of the country. From the denunciation of Ivoirity (under the Bédié regime) to the protest against the electoral list (under the Gbagbo regime), not forgetting the debate on the conditions of eligibility for the supreme office (under the military transition), it is clear that the battles mobilising and opposing Ivoirian political and social forces were played out against the backdrop of national identity, the right to vote and antagonistic conceptions of the fatherland.

The registers of justification of the engagements of the MPCI in the North and of the collection of organisations making up the 'galaxy of Young Patriots' in the South revealed these antagonistic concepts of the fatherland around which Ivoirians have mobilised in recent years. Indeed, the disqualification of presidential election candidates, young rebel soldiers in the North calling for ID papers so that they would be recognised as Ivoirians, the commitment of the 'Young Patriots' in the South to protect, in their words, the Ivoirian nation against foreign control of the national economy, were thinly veiled manifestations of conflicting conceptions of autochthony and the fatherland.

In sum, from one peace agreement to the next, the project for authentic autochthony can be formulated as follows: 'Only "real Ivoirians" should lead the country or have the right to elect its leaders.' But how can we recognise real Ivoirians? Although the residual goal of the successive peace agreements was to pave the way for credible and transparent elections, this issue was still the driving force behind the mobilisations observed.

Mobile courts and the violent July 2006 mobilisations

In a country divided, against a backdrop of mass violence, the consensus on the need to identify 'real Ivoirian citizens' took the form of a national identification campaign implemented through mobile courts (*audiences foraines*) in 2006-2007.[10] Based on the ideological rhetoric and partisan interpretations of citizenship that accompanied the mobile courts, we can analyse how the search for 'authentic Ivoirians' gave rise to numerous strategies and stratagems on the part of the political players, who were already aware that that dimension of the conflict was an opportunity for vote seeking.

Identifying citizens through mobile courts was a vital step towards settling the Ivoirian crisis. Indeed, during this operation, the supporters of the opposing sides that arose from the different political alliances[11] confronted each other directly for the first time.

---

10 The 'mobile courts' were public hearings that delivered auxiliary judgments to persons born in Côte d'Ivoire but who had not been reported to the civil state. Mobile teams composed of judges, clerks, prefects, sub-prefects, locally elected officials and doctors were sent to these hearings in order to examine the requests made by applicants and their accompanying witnesses. When an applicant obtained a court judgment, this entitled him to a certificate of nationality which granted him/her the right to vote. The important issue around public hearings for political parties resided in the enlargement of the electoral basis. The party in power feared that this could inflate the number of votes potentially acquired by the opposition.

11 These were the supporters of the FPI and all of the so-called 'patriotic movements' on the one hand and the supporters of the coalition of political parties united under the G7, which formed the opposition, on the other hand.

The operation took place against the backdrop of the adoption of a consensual method for identifying potential voters through the Pretoria Agreement[12] signed on 6 April 2005 under the auspices of African Union mediator Thabo Mbeki. Under the agreement, Gbagbo conceded the validation of the eligibility of all signatories of the Marcoussis Agreement, the broadening of the independent electoral commission to include representatives of certain technical ministries and institutions (this allowed for one representative each for the president of the Republic, the president of the National Assembly and the president of the Economic and Social Council), and the certification of the elections by the United Nations.

That same month, Ouattara and Bédié sealed their union in the RHDP (the Houphouetist orientated Rally for Democracy and Peace), on 18 May 2005. The Ivoirian political scene was rocked by this alliance, chiefly because the balance of power no longer favoured Gbagbo. Furthermore, the strategic battle fought by the different political movements did not hesitate to resort to violence because, as we will see, being Ivoirian, being registered on the voters' list and exercising one's right to vote was not self-evident.

From that moment on, the registration of the population towards their inclusion on the voters' list, the preparation of the electoral rolls, the chairmanship of the Independent Electoral Commission, etc would generate mobilisation and conflicts between RHDP members on the one hand and law enforcement and the 'Young Patriots' on the other. This episode is of interest, since it makes it possible to appreciate the stakes involved in autochthony, conflicting conceptions of the notion of the fatherland and above all the meaning that should be given to the fact of holding or not holding identity papers during the Ivoirian conflict.

---

12   The agreement was signed during the year in which elections were supposed to be organised to put an end to the crisis, at the end of Gbagbo's first mandate in October 2005. The Linas-Marcoussis and Accra (I, II and III) agreements no longer had a chance of bringing about peaceful elections since the signatories had entrenched themselves in their positions following the bloody repression of an opposition march in March 2004. The agreement was intended to clarify the political agenda in the run up to the elections and above all definitively designate the potential candidates for the presidential election.

It seems that, in Côte d'Ivoire, national identity or citizenship - defined as the legal bond between a person and a state - remained a basis for discord between Ivoirians, despite the amendments made to the law governing the issue.[13] Although it was a major focus of negotiations between Ivoirians at the roundtable in Marcoussis, the issue of nationality continued to give rise to entrenched and opposing positions on the part of political supporters through their opposing groups, notably when it came to the implementation of the Pretoria Agreement.

The goal of the mobile courts, intended to serve as the preliminary stage in the identification of the population, was to ensure the legal existence of a fraction of the population that lacked administrative documents. It targeted people over the age of 13 years, whatever their nationality, which were born on the national territory and had never been officially registered. On 16 July 2006, the day before the official launching of the operation, the president of the National Assembly, Koulibaly Mamadou, asked the JFPI to oppose the mobile courts. In his view, the UN Resolution no. 1633 (21 October 2005), the Pretoria Agreement and the other arrangements between the parties had established disarmament and the redeployment of the administration as a prior condition for the operation aimed at establishing the electoral rolls to ensure fair and transparent elections, but those prerequisites had yet to be made effective. His call to protest was supported by Affi N'Guessan, president of the FPI, who also called for the boycott of the mobile courts 'by every means'. The other organisations of the patriotic galaxy took action in the wake of those calls and disrupted the conduct of the identification phase in several locations in the zone under government control. On 19 July 2006, the Young Patriots paralysed all activities in the city of Abidjan. The implementation of the call for a boycott gave rise to confrontations between the Young Patriots and opposition party youth, leaving at least three dead and several wounded, and causing the destruction and pillage of public and

---

13   Law 61-415 of 14 December 1961, amended by laws 64-381 of 7 October 1964 and 72-852 of 21 December 1972 on the Nationality Code.

private property in Divo, Oumé and Grand-Bassam. The coordination of the women patriots led by Bro Grébé aligned with that position hostile to the identity operation on the pretext that 'the form of the mobile courts are not at all acceptable to the people, as it leads to violations of the laws in force'.[14]

Beyond the justifications each side advanced for the violence witnessed, there were important stakes surrounding this operation which paved the way for the upcoming electoral competitions. While the presidential alliance worried that 'an artificial modification of the electoral demographics'[15] might be created under its eyes and at its expense, the rebellion seized the opportunity to give substance to the effectiveness of the combat it intended to lead for the 'undocumented' and the RHDP mobilised to stimulate and probe its potential electorate. But what was the structure of the ideological foundation of these mobilisations for or against the mobile courts? Analysis of the discourse reveals the ideological foundations developed and shared by each political movement in relation to national identity and the notion of the fatherland and this provides real insights into the motivations for their respective mobilisations.

The 'patriots' on the side of the president were attached to the idea of defending the fatherland through various means of defence they had developed throughout the crisis and particularly during the mobile court operation, which they perceived as selling out Ivoirian nationality. This was apparent in the discourse of Miaka Ouréto, then secretary general of the FPI: 'They want to grant citizenship to Burkinabè, Malians, and Guineans. In the future, Côte d'Ivoire will have problems because we will have created an artificial population that is difficult to manage.' Similarly, 'young patriot' leader Dago Vincent asserted that the national identity was threatened:

---

14 Agence ivoirienne de presse, 22 July 2006, « La Coordination des femmes patriotes exige le désarmement avant les audiences foraines »
15 Ibid. Among other subjects of suspicion, the FPI accused Minister of Justice Koné Mamadou of wanting to 'organise an electoral fraud'. According to the presidential group, the minister from the rebel movement was about to grant Ivoirian nationality to 'three or four million fictional voters' (Le Figaro, 25 July 2006, 'Les audiences foraines embrasent la Côte d'Ivoire')

(...) beyond the economic reasons, one of the real reasons for this manoeuvre is a will to do away with Ivoirian identity. The approach of [Charles Konan] Banny[16] will take us straight to the situation in Kosovo where the Serbs who own the land are now in the minority. We will stand up and make a common front, Ivoirian citizenship will not be sold out and Ivoirians will not disappear. We are fighting a war for the total liberation of Côte d'Ivoire.[17]

The peril hanging over Ivoirian nationality, the need for patriots to protect it and above all the denunciation of the agreements binding Côte d'Ivoire to the former colonial power formed the foundations for the mobilisation of the presidential movement supported by the Young Patriots. The book by former First Lady Simone Gbagbo, entitled *Words of Honor* (*Paroles d'honneur*) provides a summary of the ideology mobilising the partisans of the presidential movement:

Côte d'Ivoire is our country. We are not here because we were posted here as civil servants. We are not here for a day or two, for a meeting. We are here because we were born here and we will be buried here. That is the difference between us and some people (Gbagbo 2007: 474, of the original French version, *our translation*)...

Fighting for our land is a legitimate combat. That is why we need to fight so that our country belongs to us and to get back all of our property, all of our wealth. At the same time, we need to review the outdated alliances that bind us to the former colonial power (Gbagbo 2007: 442, *our translation*)

---

16 Prime Minister in charge of the political transition after the resignation of Seydou Elimane Diarra, who was appointed during the Linas-Marcoussis Agreement negotiations, Banny, a former governor of the Central Bank of West African States (BCEAO), took office on 4 December 2005. Initially, he had some difficulties forming a government. The difficulty of collaborating with the main protagonists of the crisis and especially the presidential group, which refused to grant him full powers as expected, formed an obstacle to his mission. Banny's mandate ended with the signing of the Ouagadougou Agreement (March 2007). He was supposed to implement the technical aspects of preparations for the election and the disarmament of combatants. Under Ouattara in 2011, Banny was appointed chairman of the Dialogue, Truth and Reconciliation Commission (CDVR).

17 Notre voie (2006) 'Vincent Dago, Président du Congrès des toits rouges de Yopougon', No. 2442, 20 July

For the other side, this idea of national identity was an extension of xenophobic and even racist ideology. It was criticised by the rebellion and its political allies, along with the ideology of Ivoirity that tends to put Ivoirians into categories. The ideological construct they marshalled against this representation of national identity is outlined, in terms ringing with victimisation, in Guillaume Soro's autobiography:

> Laurent Gbagbo and his supporters decided to make the concept of 'Ivoirity', invented in 1993 by former President of the Republic of Côte d'Ivoire Henri Konan Bédié, their own. Ivoirity is a word whose true meaning is none other than: 'Côte d'Ivoire for the Ivoirians' or, plainly put, for those from the South, since northerners are considered strangers in their own country (Soro 2005: 20, of the French publication, *our translation*).

> ...the law on identification which obliges all citizens to identify themselves in relation to their village promotes patronymic discrimination, de facto. We feel that it is inacceptable to deprive Ivoirian politicians of their citizenship. We demand that the political arena be open to all without exclusion (Soro 2005: 58).

> The conflict is between Ivoirians. Some have taken up arms because they felt excluded and persecuted. Ivoirity was created to deny part of the Ivoirian population the right to breathe the air of their own country. Exiled or considered strangers in their own land, these Ivoirians have no right to speak. We are fighting against the concept of Ivoirity (Soro 2005: 142).

The issue of nationality, caught between the right of the soil and the right of blood, between the exclusive concepts of the 'patriotic resistance fighters' and the inclusive concepts of 'anti-Ivoirity', was a complex seedbed of mobilisation and counter-mobilisation in the political battles opened by the crisis of September 2002. Although no definitive response can be provided, the violent 'debate' between the conflicting concepts only managed to put off for a decade the issues relating to socioeconomic conditions or the future of young people. In their platforms, the candidates running in the presidential election of October 2010 naturally promised to deal with those challenges. In the aftermath of the post-electoral crisis, the issues became more acute, giving rise to another form of social mobilisation in which stakeholders' claims and demands were addressed to a feverish and hyper-vigilant regime.

In the wake of the antagonisms built around the divergent conceptions of the fatherland and Ivoirity, the crisis that followed the second round of presidential elections of 2010 also created a new space and new stakes for mobilisation. In fact, at the heart of this other mobilisation lay confrontations between equally antagonistic definitions of 'legitimacy' and 'legality'.

The post-electoral crisis of 2010-2011

According to the provisions contained in Article 36 of the Constitution of the Republic of Côte d'Ivoire, elections must be held in the month of October of the fifth year of the mandate of the president in office to ensure democratic change or continuity of government. Gbagbo debuted in late 2000 under conditions that he himself described as 'catastrophic'. However, in September 2002, an attempted coup tried to topple his regime. The coup, pitting itself against the last platoon still faithful to the incumbent regime defending the seat and institutions of power in Abidjan, developed into an armed rebellion that soon sought to take near-total control of the key cities in the northern part of the country, with the city of Bouaké as its headquarters. There then followed a series of summit meetings, mediations and political compromises that were unable to quell the rebellion. Quite the contrary, over several years, the de facto partitioning of the country enshrined the coexistence of two zones of military and politico-administrative influence: one under the authority of the regime in Abidjan known as the 'government zone' and the other, led by the armed rebellion and its political wing, known as the Centre, North and West zone (CNO).

Under those conditions, when the deadline was reached for the organisation of new presidential elections, Gbagbo was able to take advantage of the provisions of Article 38 of the constitution stipulating that, in case of particular circumstances or events adversely affecting territorial integrity or natural disasters preventing proper organisation of the ballot or announcement of the results, the head of state can remain in office. The next five years were marked by a particular focus on political compromise and joint management of state power between the presidential party (the FPI) on the one hand and the civil-political opposition on the other hand, led by parties such as the PDCI, the RDR, the Union for Democracy and Peace in Côte d'Ivoire (UDPCI), the Movement of Forces for the Future (MFA) and the armed rebellion. After five more deferrals, the elections were finally held on 28 October 2010 and their outcome, in November 2010, gave rise to another form of violent mobilisation. In fact, after a relatively peaceful first round, in which 14 candidates competed for the votes of the electorate in a relatively 'good-natured' atmosphere, the second round generated a highly polarised politico-military environment, in which the issues were crystallised around the legitimacy of the two personalities who both proclaimed themselves president.

After coming in first and second respectively at the outcome of the first round of the presidential election of 28 October 2010 with 38 and 32 per cent of the votes cast, Gbagbo and Ouattara faced off again in the second round. Theoretically benefitting from the call launched between the two rounds by Bédié, the PDCI candidate who came in third with 25 per cent of the ballot, for his supporters to transfer their votes to the RHDP coalition, Ouattara was on 2 December 2010 declared the winner by the Independent Electoral Commission (CEI) after a series of incidents at the body's headquarters, with 54.1 per cent of the vote against 45.9 per cent for the outgoing president. These results were immediately challenged by the Constitutional Council which, based on the invalidation of certain results on suspicion of fraud in certain constituencies in the North of the country, declared Gbagbo victorious with 51.45 per cent of the ballot the following day. The country therefore had two presidents, each claiming his legitimacy based, in the case of Gbagbo, on the decision of the Constitutional Council of the Republic of Côte d'Ivoire and, for Ouattara, on the certification of the results of the second round by the CEI and the international community. Both men were sworn in and both formed governments.

This nth political crisis, which could not be resolved by the different African mediation efforts, led to mobilisation and belligerent physical engagement in the politico-military arena to defend the varying ideas of legitimacy and its sources. When the outgoing president refused to yield to economic sanctions, a huge military offensive was led by pro-Ouattara military forces. Former armed rebellion members backed up by auxiliaries of all stripes including traditional *Dozo* hunters and semi-demobilised ex-combatants and young civilians enlisted in the midst of the conflict and descended on Abidjan to put Ouattara in office and confer full power upon him. On the opposing side, despite significant defections from their ranks, the last platoon remaining faithful to Gbagbo attempted to resist to 'uphold the constitutional authority' of their mentor, although they ultimately capitulated after the decisive intervention by the French army and United Nations Operation in Côte d'Ivoire (UNOCI) forces. As mentioned above, the registers of mobilisation built around the defence of the imperilled fatherland were frequently called upon by the Young Patriots close to the former head of state to justify their obstinacy not to surrender power to Ouattara unless they fell under a military defeat.

When the crisis ended with the arrest of Gbagbo and certain of his close collaborators on 11 April 2011, mobilisation frameworks changed very quickly in Côte d'Ivoire, and their polarisation around political issues was quick to subside. In defeat, the patriotic galaxy described above had no channel for mobilisation. Its leaders were in exile or under arrest, and the monopoly on violence (legitimate or not) was now held by the FRCI (the new name for the national army) of which the majority was now in favour of Ouattara. A new form of political mobilisation developed outside the country, in European or African capitals, calling for the liberation of Gbagbo. Within Côte d'Ivoire, the movements that backed the armed insurrection beginning in 2002, led by the supporters of partisans of the ex-rebellion against the counter-insurrectional mobilisation of the Young Patriots, were no longer relevant given the mono-polarisation of the political arena. Mobilisation focused instead on issues of socioeconomic survival for certain components of society, and was led by two groups of actors in particular: ex-combatants calling for socioeconomic reintegration and households suffering from the rising cost of living.

Demonstrations against the high cost of living

Borne by the dynamics of the hunger riots that rocked numerous countries around the world in 2008, the mobilisation against the high cost of living in Côte d'Ivoire took place as it had elsewhere, generating protest movements of variable scope. In close correlation with the mortgage crisis that rocked the United States beginning in mid-2007 and the rising price of oil, the price of numerous staple food items spiralled on the global market. The price rise was generated by market speculation and low quantities of products available for sale. Consequently, for a growing number of people belonging to the least privileged strata of the population, it was increasingly difficult to gain access to basic necessities. Hence the proliferation of violent movements intended to show their exasperation with the inertia of the government authorities.

Born in Mexico, the street protests spread to capital cities in numerous countries, including Côte d'Ivoire. Thus, in late March and early April 2008, when the people - mainly housewives - took to the streets of Abidjan chanting 'Gbagbo, we're hungry! Soro, we're hungry! We want to eat... Enough is enough! We can't buy anything, we're tired', the streets of many other capitals such as Cairo, Algiers, Douala, Bobo-dioulasso, Port-au-Prince, etc were also in turmoil for the same reasons.

However, in Côte d'Ivoire, the fact that this reaction took place in the context of a socio-political crisis completely cancelled out much of its attraction for certain categories of the population who would ordinarily have been involved. Obviously, with the price hikes that saw the prices of certain products spiral in the space of only three days, jumping from USD$1.68 to USD$2.16 per kilogram of beef and from USD$1.44 to USD$2.04 per litre of petrol, there was cause for discontent among the population, half of whom were believed to live below the poverty line. However, when the street protests began in 2008, Côte d'Ivoire was in the midst of its sixth year of politico-military crisis.

Faced with an armed rebellion that it had difficulty containing, the regime in power in Abidjan was obliged to strike a compromise. After experimenting with various inclusive government solutions[18] recommended to end the crisis and share power, the political agreement signed in Ouagadougou[19] entailed direct joint administration of state power with the former armed rebellion, and its secretary general, Guillaume Soro, was promoted as prime minister to Gbagbo. However, before the rapprochement between the two main protagonists in the political crisis, suspicions that street movements were used to undermine the authority of the head of state led to almost systematic repression of this type of demonstration.

Thus, in March 2004, an opposition march, calling for full application of the Marcoussis Agreements (signed under the auspices of the French government) and criticising the granting of the container contract for the Port of Abidjan to the French Bolloré group, was violently repressed. Certain sources say there were some 120 dead, although the authorities put the number at 37. In this context, even the work stoppages by certain trades such as carriers were

---

18   Led successively by Seydou Diarra and Charles Konan Banny
19   Signed on 4 March 2007 under the auspices of the Burkinabè facilitator, President Blaise Compaoré

seen in the light of a conspiracy against the Gbagbo regime. On the streets of Abidjan, the only entities that could organise such events were the Young Patriots and the patriotic galaxy who supported Gbagbo.

Under these conditions, for the households and civil society actors at the heart of the demonstrations against the high cost of living, even those not known for their sympathy for the Gbagbo regime, legitimate protest over a matter as banal as the difficulty households faced in feeding themselves decently involved a risk: that of providing or being perceived as an opportunity for the political and military opposition to decry and/or undermine the head of state. As noted by Nassa (2011: 30) in a research paper he wrote at that time on food security in the Centre-West of the country, many households who 'had a hard time putting food on the table every day' due to the rising cost of basic necessities felt extremely concerned by what was happening on the streets of Abidjan. However, they felt 'that the issues sparking the protests often strayed from the problem of food [...] in a conflictual national context by [going far beyond] the genuine nutritional problems faced by the urban population.' Thus, even as the spontaneous nature of the movement was emphasised, the slogans chanted by demonstrators always explicitly mentioned the two 'heads' of Côte d'Ivoire's executive branch: the head of state and the prime minister.

This approach did not prevent police repression, however, which was diversely perceived. On Tuesday 1 April 2008, there were at least two dead in Abidjan (one in the Port-Bouët neighbourhood in the southern part of the city and one in Yopougon in the north) following the repression of widespread protests against the high cost of living.[20] Indeed, in the view of some, the responsibility for the police intervention lay with the prime minister, suspected of having sought to use it as a means of discrediting the head of state. For others, quite to the contrary, Gbagbo was presented as

---

20 This figure was provided by Agence France Presse and reproduced by Radio Canada International. See for example: http://ici.radio-canada.ca/nouvelles/animations/2008/AFP/FoodPricesFR1104/index1.html. accessed March 2014

being inclined to disproportionate use of violence against any attempt to challenge his authority. However, the government did implement measures to appease the street movement. In an address to the nation dated 1 April 2008, the head of state promised to eliminate customs duties and reduce VAT on staple items such as rice, oil, milk and soap to nine per cent.

This battery of measures, whose chief merit was to give the impression that the government was listening to the people, was unable to check the price hikes. Several years later, in 2013, when political polarisation around the confrontation between the armed rebellion and the Gbagbo regime ended after Ouattara took office as head of state and Gbagbo was arrested and transferred to the ICC in The Hague following a long and violent post-electoral crisis, a Côte d'Ivoire branch of the Occupy Movement (*les Indignés*, in French) tried to mobilise households along the lines of what was being done in Europe. As in 2008, this attempt at mobilising protests around the issue of the high cost of living failed to generate popular enthusiasm. It drew little media attention and, although it took place in a relatively different socio-political context, it was equally risky in terms of street demonstrations. The country was progressively recovering from the post-electoral crisis. The divide had shrunk between the politico-military opposition fighting a regime whose legitimacy was significantly eroded by a decade of struggle against an insurrection it found difficult to quell.

However, although the streets were freed of the activism of the Young Patriots, they could not be occupied by others, since the fear of being branded as pro-Gbagbo and thus incurring the wrath of the new regime was still strong.

Although the social movements revolving around the high cost of living had little impact and garnered little social involvement in a national environment strongly crystallised around the political question and the struggle for power, the movement of the demobilised participants in the politico-military crisis had considerably greater impact. In fact, although it was announced at the time of the signing of the first political agreements meant to put an end to the military conflict, the process of demobilisation, disarmament and reintegration of ex-combatants in Côte d'Ivoire was undermined by the interplay of partisan interests at work at the highest levels of government. Under these conditions and several months after the official end of the armed crisis, violent reactions continued to take place, weakening the new institution in charge of the process. At the heart of the process, internecine power struggles finally gave way to socioeconomic survival demands formulated by socially excluded young people calling for integration and social rehabilitation.

Post-conflict mobilisation for the social reintegration of ex-combatants

The process of uniting, disarming and demobilising ex-combatants, combined with defence and security sector reform, was laid out in the framework of the Marcoussis political agreements as one of the ways of preparing Côte d'Ivoire for a progressive return to normal after the armed rebellion. However, during the decade-long politico-military crisis, these issues (disarmament, demobilisation and reintegration) constituted - along with the issue of the organisation of elections - the chief bones of contention between the parties to the conflict on the one hand and, on the other hand, between the beneficiaries of the proposed integration and the public authorities. The first point of friction, between the public authorities themselves, prevailed during the years of joint administration of the state between Gbagbo's FPI regime and the politico-military opposition essentially led by New Forces secretary general Guillaume Soro. Tensions were fuelled by obvious issues of strategic interest and political calculation.

The end of the 2011 post-electoral crisis revealed significant divergences between the viewpoints of the citizens and the public authorities, leading to violent forms of social mobilisation involving demobilised ex-combatants. Thus, when the issue of demobilisation and social reintegration of ex-combatants was raised in Côte d'Ivoire, the parties in conflict (the FPI regime which came to power after the elections of 2000 and its politico-military opposition led by the former armed rebellion embodied by the New Forces) were quick to oppose each other over its implementation, for a variety of strategic reasons.

The first of these reasons has to do with the will to control the process in order to harness the financial windfall involved. Because it is perceived by many donors as an essential step to ending the crisis and returning to peace in Côte d'Ivoire, the process of disarmament, demobilisation and reintegration (DDR) of ex-combatants very quickly enjoyed the financial attention of a good many of them. For instance, the World Bank announced support of CFA F40 billion for DDR implementation. The financial windfall generated by the international community's interest in the process led to special strategies on the part of the parties in conflict to ensure its control. The idea seemed to be to find a way, in the context of an armed conflict whose outcome was uncertain, to take advantage of the resources arising from the DDR operation in order to keep the auxiliary forces that made up most of the troops in the conflict on both sides on standby so that they could be remobilised if fighting broke out again.

In light of this, the strategies deployed included maintaining instability and setting up multiple organisations for the implementation of the process, with each organisation depending on different authorities close to either the prime minister's office or the office of the president of the republic. Thus, between 2003 and 2011, a dozen organisations shared responsibility for the reintegration of Côte d'Ivoire's ex-combatants. The first of those organisations, set up following the initial Marcoussis Agreements, was the National Disarmament, Demobilisation and Reintegration/Community Rehabilitation Programme (PNDDR/RC) which was replaced by two entities: the National Program of Reintegration and Community Rehabilitation (PNRRC) and the Integrated Command Centre (CCI). In the same activity niches covered by these organisations, a National Civic Service Programme

(PSCN) was set up in March 2008. There was also a National Committee for the Coordination of Activities for Reintegration of Ex-combatants and Community Rehabilitation (CNCA RE-RC) and a National Secretariat for Reconstruction and Reintegration (SNRR) established on 25 March 2010, which replaced the short-lived Ministry of Reconstruction and Reintegration. Later, in 2011, a ministerial department was created for ex-combatants and war victims. All of those structures were later dissolved, and those that still existed were replaced by the Authority for Disarmament, Demobilisation and Reintegration (ADDR). On the ground, in addition to these Ivoirian organisations, demobilised troops were also in contact with implementing agencies such as Care International, German Technical Cooperation (GTZ), the DDR division of the United Nations Operation in Côte d'Ivoire (UNOCI), the United Nations Development Programme (UNDP) Post-Crisis Unit, the World Bank's Post-Conflict Assistance Program (PAPC) and the African Development Bank's Post-Crisis Multi-Sector Institutional Support Project (PAIMSC), among others.

The other dimension of the opposition surrounding the process was more strategic in nature: it consisted of using the provision of reintegration services to ensure the loyalty of a 'clientele' of auxiliaries made up of young social outcasts who could easily be (re)mobilised if military hostilities resumed. These different elements weakened the process until the post-electoral crisis took place. With the reopening of the military front, a high proportion of ex-combatants who had not been properly demobilised were reenlisted in the conflict. Additional young people who had previously stayed on the side-lines of the conflict took advantage of the opportunity to join the remobilisation movement, with hopes of reaping benefits either through reintegration or more directly through the 'pay yourself' method. That is why there were some 60,000 young people waiting for reintegration at the end of the politico-military crisis that ceased in early 2011.

In order to find an efficient and sustainable solution to the issue of reintegrating that category of the population which posed a risk for the rest of society, the new Ivoirian authorities agreed to provide them with a single point of contact, the Authority for Disarmament, Demobilisation and Reintegration (ADDR). This organisation, under the supervision of the national security council, was henceforth in charge of implementing the vision of the Ivoirian public authorities with regards to DDR, in the overall framework of the national security sector reform policy. However, more than a year after its establishment, massive protest movements involving the intended beneficiaries of reintegration took place across the country. The principal towns and cities of the former CNO zone that were home to the majority of the auxiliary troops supporting the New Forces and subsequently the FRCI in their military struggle to overthrow the Gbagbo regime were subjected to the excesses of these young people. Through more or less structured actions of violent public disorder, these youths untiringly denounced the slowness and lack of transparency of the process. The reputation of certain national army officers was impugned by strong suspicions of favouritism, which were distilled and spread among the beneficiaries to sustain the revolt. In the space of six months, at least half a dozen protest movements paralysed socioeconomic activities in Man, Bouaké, Korhogo and Odienné in the northern part of the country, which had been formerly under the control of the armed rebellion. Most often led by protesters who set themselves apart from the official association of demobilised Ivoirians, the movement sought to make the public authorities aware of the discontent and need for social rehabilitation of a youthful population striving for social empowerment in an environment marked by a significant downturn in employment opportunities.

In order to find an efficient and sustainable solution to the issue of reintegrating that category of the population which posed a risk for the rest of society, the new Ivoirian authorities agreed to provide them with a single point of contact, the Authority for Disarmament, Demobilisation and Reintegration

(ADDR). This organisation, under the supervision of the national security council, was henceforth in charge of implementing the vision of the Ivoirian public authorities with regards to DDR, in the overall framework of the national security sector reform policy. However, more than a year after its establishment, massive protest movements involving the intended beneficiaries of reintegration took place across the country. The principal towns and cities of the former CNO zone that were home to the majority of the auxiliary troops supporting the New Forces and subsequently the FRCI in their military struggle to overthrow the Gbagbo regime were subjected to the excesses of these young people. Through more or less structured actions of violent public disorder, these youths untiringly denounced the slowness and lack of transparency of the process. The reputation of certain national army officers was impugned by strong suspicions of favouritism, which were distilled and spread among the beneficiaries to sustain the revolt. In the space of six months, at least half a dozen protest movements paralysed socioeconomic activities in Man, Bouaké, Korhogo and Odienné in the northern part of the country, which had been formerly under the control of the armed rebellion. Most often led by protesters who set themselves apart from the official association of demobilised Ivoirians, the movement sought to make the public authorities aware of the discontent and need for social rehabilitation of a youthful population striving for social empowerment in an environment marked by a significant downturn in employment opportunities.

Conclusion

In Côte d'Ivoire, the last decade has been marked by various protest movements. Noting that the previous decade (1990-2000) marked the apprenticeship of mass expression with street protests as an outlet for the social forces repressed under the single-party system, we have sought to analyse the players, their logic and the social issues that have marked the recent history of the Ivoirian people from 2002 to the present.

The education conducted by political entrepreneurs on mobilisation and collective action initially ignored subjects such as social integration, youth unemployment, the high cost of living, etc, which, although they affected the daily lives of ordinary citizens, were not the principal motivations for mobilisation. This period can be summed up by civil society mobilisation to implement the agenda of a political society suffering from a lack of standards and rules. Furthermore, in relation to the events we have described, the choice of violence as a means of collective action remained a strategic option used by all of the political entrepreneurs. We note that, initially, the economic contexts and the stakes of the political competition that determined both the form and the content of the project behind the collective action of the social movements was built around political questions such as political participation and the different conceptions of the fatherland and nationality.

Throughout the crisis, the expression of a social movement that was independent from the political movements was perceived as a utopia, particularly since the period was marked by an excessive or even an exclusive focus on politics in which Ivoirians were divided into 'us' and 'them'. As a consequence of this very 'black and white' way of interpreting the space of social mobilisation, all social initiatives or reactions to the economic crisis were stifled, even though they remained a constant despite the various forms of political change.

Due to its nature, the recent crisis has also marked the space of social movements in Côte d'Ivoire and dampened the potential participants. They seem to have deserted that space, which is often taken over by real activists focusing on themes with varying social stakes with a view to creating a debate or attracting the attention of national and international public opinion. At the same time, issues of national policy, public safety, community conflicts and tensions, schools and violence, corruption, economic governance, the high cost of living, etc are posed more acutely, and currently structure new spaces in which various players in the social movements are expected to take action, although paradoxically they have become more discrete.

While the current regime has called for and seems to have been granted a reprieve on the social front, latent tensions can be observed in the social fabric, manifested either by outbursts of anger or 'unexpected' manifestations of violence led by anonymous actors. It seems that, after the post-electoral crisis following the presidential election of October 2010, Ivoirian society, shaken to the core in social, political and economic terms, has undertaken a return to normal with little tolerance for contradictions and even less for independent social movements.

References

Akindès, F. and Fofana M. (2011) «Jeunesse, idéologisation de la notion de « patrie » et dynamique conflictuelle en Côte d'Ivoire», in F. Akindès (dir.) *Côte d'Ivoire, la réinvention de soi dans la violence*, Dakar, CODESRIA: 213-250

Amondji, M. (1984) Félix Houphouët et la Côte d'Ivoire: l'envers d'une légende, Paris, Karthala

Diabate, I., Dembele O. and Akindès F. (2005) (Ed.) *Intellectuels ivoiriens face à la crise*, Paris, Karthala

Gbagbo, S. E. (2007) *Paroles d'honneur*, Paris, Ed. Pharos/Jacques-Marie Laffont Editeur, Ed. Ramsay

Le Pape, M. (2003) «Les politiques d'affrontements en Côte d'Ivoire (1999-2003)», *Afrique Contemporaine* été 2003 (206): 29-39

Nassa, D.D.A. (2011) «Approvisionnement en produits vivriers d'une ville secondaire ivoirienne à l'ère de la mondialisation: l'exemple de Divo», in D.D.A. Nassa et C. Y. Koffie-Bikpo (dir.) *Production vivrière et sécurité alimentaire en Côte d'Ivoire,* Paris, L'Harmattan:26-31

Proteau, L. (1998) «La «reproduction » en question. Ecole, Université et mouvements sociaux en Côte-d'Ivoire», *in Questions sensibles,* Paris, PUF, coll. 'CURAPP': 359-375

Soro, G. (2005) *Pourquoi je suis devenu rebelle: La Côte d'Ivoire au bord du gouffre,* Paris, Hachette

Touré, I. (1998) «Ni meeting, ni défilé, le syndicalisme de participation en Côte d'Ivoire a-t-il vécu?», *Africa Development* vol. XXIII n°2 : 227-292

CHAPTER: 7

SOCIAL MOVEMENTS AND THE QUEST FOR ALTERNATIVES IN BURKINA FASO

Lila Chouli

Since the beginning of the post-colonial era, the presence of the social movement has been a constant in Burkina Faso's socio-political landscape. The strength of this movement has staved off the establishment of a monistic trade union system and of a single-party system, and has also initiated changes in the system of government. By the time the Fourth Republic was proclaimed in June 1991, the country had been through four constitutional systems and seven emergency governments. The social movement has been in the forefront since early 2011, with a number of labour conflicts in both urban and rural settings, and spontaneous revolts due to very concrete and localised hardships suffered by the people. We will focus on three of these: the struggle of miners to denounce their working conditions at gold mining sites held by international industrial groups, the mobilisation for peaceful change within the government and the response of students to the closure of student services in August 2013.

Introduction

In the first semester of 2011 (from February to June),[1] the government of Blaise Compaoré, which has been running Burkina Faso since 1987, was tottering. A popular movement, triggered by the death of a secondary school pupil from Koudougou (Centre-Ouest department) after multiple arrests by police and by the deadly repression of peaceful demonstrations calling for an investigation into the matter, placed the country in a situation that verged on insurrection. The popular movement was unexpectedly bolstered by a series of military rebellions (some eight waves of mutiny, each lasting several days and spreading across various garrisons in the space of less than two and a half months). At the time, numerous observers blamed the courtiers and entourage close to the president, saying that they had lied to him about the pulse of the nation and encouraged him to believe that all was well. Taking advantage of that premise, Compaoré decided to meet with various social constituencies (rank-and-file soldiers, tradespersons, justice staff, etc) in order to hear their concerns after the second wave of mutiny (in late March). The authority of Compaoré, which rested on the army—and especially the presidential guard, which also mutinied on 14 April 2011— was shaken. During this time, numerous demands by the different social constituencies were met and numerous promises were made, bringing about the 'normalisation' of the situation. But this return to normalcy was and is fragile; it was 'a social ceasefire, and not an end to hostilities' (Chouli 2012:297) and, since then, all eyes have been turned towards the next major socio-political crisis.

The president and the government, following the mutiny of the presidential guard, risked their all on an operation launched to disarm mutineers in Bobo-Dioulasso on 3 June 2011. This event marked a turning point, in that it displayed the strength and authority of the state. Members of the armed forces, some of whom had been implicated in previous mutinies, were placed

---

1   On the subject of 2011, see Chouli (2012)

in charge of the operation. It staged a sort of 'holy alliance' between the people[2] and the ruling class. Hundreds were dismissed from the army.[3] A conciliatory tone aimed at quelling the protest was applied across the board towards salaried employees who saw many of their demands met. Mutineers were listened to. The trial of the officers responsible for the death of Justin Zongo took place in August, with a speed uncommon in crimes involving defence or security forces.

As in the aftermath of the socio-political crisis following the death of journalist Norbert Zongo in 1998,[4] the regime once again proved its ability to bounce back. And yet the ills at the root of the biggest socio-political crisis the country had experienced in all of its post-colonial history were still there: social inequalities, high unemployment, limited prospects for young people in particular (some 67 per cent of the population under 25 years old), police violence, a climate of impunity, a political system that locked out the people, a bourgeoisie tied up with political and administrative mismanagement, the spiralling cost of living, longevity in power, etc.

The country, which is among the poorest in the world (183rd out of 187, according to the Human Development Index in 2012), shows strong growth rates (eight per cent in 2012). Wealth is concentrated in the hands of a minority close to the president (economic operators, officers, the armed forces, politicians, etc).[5]

Ten per cent of the Burkinabè population holds 50 per cent of the country's wealth (Conseil national de prospective et de planification stratégique 2005).

---

2 The foremost victims of the mutinies were the people who experienced pillaging, beatings, rapes and murder, even though the rebellions were directed at the government and the military command.

3 The situation in the army remains quite precarious. Hundreds of presumed mutineers have been incarcerated. Their brothers in arms have repeatedly expressed their discontentment. Furthermore, the government itself seems less self-assured, as does the military justice system. The question is how long they can maintain this *status quo*. In addition, the weapons stolen by the mutineers are still in circulation.

4 Norbert Zongo, editor of the weekly *L'Indépendant*, was assassinated on 13 December 1998. At the time, he was investigating the death of David Ouédraogo, driver of François Compaoré, the president's brother. This event marked a turning point in the mobilisation against impunity. The government, initially nonplussed by the popular reaction, was shaken. Strong mobilisation across the national territory, involving all of the different social constituencies, took place over more than two years against the backdrop of the most serious socio-political crisis of the Fourth Republic.

5 Since 2007, the country's economic growth has been 'above regional standards' at an average of 5.3 per cent (IMF 2013).

In 2003, the Burkinabè oligarchy held more than twice the annual national budget, safely tucked away in banks in rich countries.[6] Although some of the public opinion coups pulled off by the government during the crisis of 2011, such as the arrest of the director general of customs, Ousmane Guiro[7], and promises to take action against mismanagement of public funds made it appear that there was a genuine questioning of the practices of corruption and impunity, there has been no confirmation of a genuine change. On the contrary, Guiro, on provisional release for health reasons, ran in municipal elections. Joseph Paré, an ambassador in France who resigned in the wake of accusations of misappropriation, was discretely returned to his position before being eventually replaced.

Since the disarmament of Bobo-Dioulasso, the confidence of the presidential party and the political/economic/familial clan gravitating around Compaoré has been restored. It is significant, in this regard, that it was at that very time that the government abandoned the conciliatory tone - hardly typical of the Fourth Republic (dating back from 1991) - which it had adopted in relation to labour conflicts during the quasi-insurrectional phase: the first major strike following the disarmament (led by finance ministry workers) was put down. This was typical of the regime: with every major crisis, once order is restored, it returns to violence as a means of exercising its power.

In 2011, Compaoré heard the sound of marching boots and smelled the reek of smoke. The 'riot' phenomenon - complete with the burning of police stations and other symbols of power such as governors' offices, town halls, presidential party headquarters, etc - reached proportions never before equalled. Was it still possible to claim that his courtiers hid the truth from him?

---

6 *Le Pays* (2003) 'Droit dans les yeux : Banques suisses pour milliardaires burkinabè', 1 October
7 He was questioned and dismissed on 2 January 2012 following the seizure of nearly CFA two billion in the home of a relative.

Social mobilisation since the crisis of 2011

Since then, while social unrest has been less spectacular, it remains that major labour conflicts and social revolts have continued to take place. Furthermore, with the upcoming 2015 presidential election, a broader movement for peaceful political change seems to be developing. Institutional considerations have taken centre stage since the creation of the senate in May 2013. Obviously, we do not purport to separate the political sphere from the social sphere. However, the concrete problems faced by the citizens of Burkina Faso undoubtedly lie elsewhere: in the lack of access to water and healthcare, endemic unemployment, land expropriation and exploitation of miners and peasants.

In 2011, as in 1998, the fight against impunity included, from the very start, some very concrete demands regarding the day-to-day hardships experienced locally such as the high cost of living, poor management by local government, non-existent or dilapidated infrastructure, lack of employment, land access and water cuts. The 'categorical imperative' of 'Get out!' was proffered at all levels: to Compaoré, but also to mayors, law enforcement, military officials and employers. Social conflicts broke out in virtually every economic sector: bakeries, the hotel trade, the sugar industry, the fisheries, the craft industry, the rural agricultural sector, the mining sector, and the tertiary sector. The situation was favourable in terms of 'political opportunity structures' and the time was ripe to put demands, some of which had been ignored for years, back on the table. Certain conflicts were particularly noteworthy, such as the one involving the workers of the new Comoé sugar company, the largest private employer in the country, which extended beyond the framework of the factory. Women, children, young people, public and private sector workers and retirees demonstrated their solidarity with the struggle of the workers. Another important movement was the production boycott of cotton growers, which was particularly violent in places (causing injuries and deaths among both proponents and opponents of the boycott) and also spotlighted solidarity with the 'wretched of the earth' against their exploiters. Like the conflicts on mine sites (see below), these mobilisations were revelatory of the various forms of exploitation suffered by the people, particularly in rural environments.

Certain modes of action have aroused popular sympathy. For example, faced with the decision to grant provisional release to the five armed forces members sentenced on 22 March 2011, who were indirectly responsible for the first mutiny in 2011 (their brothers in arms had risen up against their condemnation), trade union organisations undertook an exceptional form of action inspired by justice personnel associations far beyond the borders of Burkina Faso. They called on justice system operators to 'uphold the principle of the equality of all citizens before the law by applying the benevolent jurisprudence of the Court of Appeal'.[8] In other words, not to sentence anyone to firm prison time and to grant provisional release to all those who requested it.

The meeting between the government and the labour unions was saluted by the latter in 2011. However, they deemed the 2013 meeting unsatisfactory, which is proof that the conciliatory tone of the authorities at the time was only aimed at reducing social tensions, whereas the balance of power - necessarily reversible - favoured the social forces. In 2012 and 2013, social conflicts affected various sectors of the economy such as bakeries, telecommunications, education and health.

Universities, spontaneous revolts and the question of violence

The academic world took centre stage, especially the University of Koudougou, the city described as a 'rebel city' where the social revolt began in 2011. On 3 October 2012, the administration imposed heavy sanctions on members of the National Association of Burkinabè Students (ANEB)[9] for

8 *L'Observateur Paalga* (2011) 'Suspension des activités juridictionnelles. La justice reprend du service', 11 April
9 ANEB is the national branch of UGEB, the General Union of Burkinabè Students, founded in 1960.

'disrupting classes and assaulting a teacher'[10] during a protest against the exam schedule.[11] Of the 16 students punished, two saw their trimester cancelled while the 14 others were slapped with sanctions ranging from temporary expulsion for one to five years to definitive exclusion from all public and private universities in the country. This was the case of Francis Nikiéma, then president of ANEB/Koudougou, who had been deeply involved in the movement against impunity the previous year. Decree No. 2012-646/PRES/PM/MESS of 24 July 2012, which served as the basis for the sanctions, was condemned by several organisations for being liberticidal and aiming to deprive students of their 'freedom to organise and protest'.[12] Many people saw a link between the adoption of the decree and the planned celebrations for 11 December (national Independence Day celebrations were to be hosted in the city in 2011 and were cancelled *de facto*).

Support was quickly offered by UGEB (which repeatedly came out in protest and called upon Burkinabè students abroad for support), the Coalition against the High Cost of Living (CCVC)[13], the Federation of National Teachers' and Researchers' Unions (F-SYNTER) and the Coordination of Pupils and Students of Burkina Faso (CEEB), amongst others. They all condemned the excessive sanctions and the appalling conditions at the public university.

This issue returned to the fore on the Ouagadougou campus during a visit by the prime minister on 18 March 2013. The visit was disturbed by students protesting their difficult studying conditions and the prime minister was obliged to flee.

The behaviour of students in particular and young people in general was singled out for its incivism. And yet, as demonstrated by the combined municipal and legislative elections of December 2012—which monopolised

---

10 *Le Stratège* (2012) 'Université de Koudougou: Ces sanctions sont inopportunes et excessives', 17 October
11 The facts that formed the basis for the sanctions were not clearly established.
12 Coordination of Pupils and Students of Burkina Faso (2012) Statement of the National Executive bureau in the context of the 14th anniversary of the drama of Sapouy (Burkina Faso), 15 December
13 The National Coalition against the High Cost of Living, Corruption, Fraud and Impunity and for Liberty (CCVC) was created in the wake of riots protesting the high cost of living in 2008. It brings together some 30 organisations.

the country's socio-political dynamics—violent action seems to have become the preferred method for making one's voice heard, including amongst the members and sympathisers of the Congress for Democracy and Progress (CDP). Riots occurred in several places. Non-conventional modes of action were also used by groups supporting the regime. This phenomenon of violent action was due in part to the relatively widespread conviction that only the language of force could make itself heard. This reflects the fact that, on the national scale, the authorities govern through force. It is also linked with the fact that certain politicians delegate violence during periods of tension: unemployed youths from the lumpen-proletariat or members of CDP are called upon to do things that the state does not wish to do openly. As Adorno writes (1951), 'The creation of barbarians through culture is however constantly deployed by this latter, in order to preserve its own barbaric essence. Domination delegates the physical violence, on which it rests, to the dominated.' Thus, the culture of violence is generated by the regime itself. Numerous spontaneous revolts have been sparked by the *hogra* (disdainful attitude) of the authorities, both local and central, which has caused a spectacular increase in radical opposition and protest actions aimed at the government and institutions.

Burkina Faso today is characterised by a series of street protests, extending largely beyond organised structures and which are not restricted to urban dwellers and/or 'intellectuals'. In both rural and urban areas, salient issues such as land access, evictions, agribusiness, land conflicts and corruption are the focus of spontaneous revolts.

In light of the lack of confidence in the authorities, notably at municipal levels, there is 'a tendency to set up parallel governance' (Sory 2013) to contest - or stimulate - municipal action. On the local scale, the people are increasingly able to impose their authority by superimposing their own agenda on that of the political authorities. Over the years, an 'oppositional public space' has developed in Burkina Faso, a concept which includes 'all rebellious human potential, seeking its own mode of expression', to quote Oskar Negt (2007).

Even though the experience of the struggle is not part of a strategy, it has allowed the people to progressively conquer a number of spaces, including institutional spaces.

This raises a crucial question for the government: how can it maintain its position in the face of the people, when they are organising and establishing their own authority? They no longer turn to the state for solutions to their problems. Indeed, the problem is the state, which is viewed by the majority as harmful and solely motivated by its own interests and those of its clients. Without hesitating to plunge workers and the people into anger and despair, the state's actions are superbly expressed by those living in the vicinity of the Essakane mine site:

> We no longer have authorities, we will resolve our problems with violence... What we're asking you, call Ouagadougou, tell them to send every last CRS officer [Compagnie républicaine de sécurité, the riot squad].

> Because we understand that our authorities' real expertise on the mine sites consists of using the CRS to crack down on the population; while the Ministers responsible for mining would rather dine with the mining companies but never have half an hour to talk with the surrounding populations. Let the CRS come. Some of us will fall. We want to see our police fire at us. But we also have faith in ourselves. We are sure that we will live to see the end of the Essakane Mine.[14] (*Our translation*)

---

14 Organisation for Community Capacity Building for Development (Organisation pour le renforcement des capacités de développement) (2011) Statements made by the population in front of police on the Essakane site

The curse of gold

In recent years, class struggles have increased in the mining sector around the world: the exploitation of miners (whatever the type of ore) has returned to the forefront of the news.[15] This does not mean that it was not already the norm, as proven by the example of Burkina Faso, but it remained unknown to most people outside the areas where the exploitation was taking place.

In the context of the economic crisis of capitalism, and its corollary global austerity, the African continent - among others - is increasingly targeted by imperialism, as well as the sub-imperialism of South African capital. However, the lives of the miners and the people who are ravaged remain revolting. They may even be at the forefront of a much broader movement avenging defeats such as those of the British miners. Indeed, the 51-week miners' strike in 1984-1985[16] 'symbolises [...] the defeat of the labour movement at the hands of the emerging neoliberal system.'[17] According to UNEP (2009), quoted by Cetri (2013), 'over the past 60 years, at least 40% of internal conflicts had a link to natural resources'.

In Burkina Faso, although cotton was considered the primary source of wealth in the country up until 2008, it has since been supplanted by gold. In recent years, the country has experienced a 'mining boom' benefitting international companies that rests on legal pillage and worker exploitation. 'Over the last fifteen years, Burkina Faso has experienced unparalleled economic growth in the mining sector, unparalleled in the world; it is the country that has progressed the most,'[18] according to the CEO of SEMAFO, Benoît La Salle.

---

15 For instance, in 2012, sizeable mobilisations took place on mine sites on every continent, sometimes tragically, as in South Africa, but also in Zimbabwe, Colombia, Chili, Spain, Mauritania, Zambia, Madagascar and Burma.

16 The closure of 20 'unprofitable' coal mines placed the most powerful union in the country, the National Union of Mineworkers, and the government of Margaret Thatcher, in opposition to each other. Over the course of a year, the strike involved more than 100,000 miners and prompted a wave of worker solidarity. Defeated by government repression and the determination of the government to establish a neoliberal order, the strikers obtained nothing. Unfortunately, the outcome of the strike considerably weakened union influence in the country.

17 *Our translation.* 'Et Margaret Thatcher brisa les syndicats', *L'Atlas histoire du Monde Diplomatique*, pp.88-89, 2011. Thatcher's method is in fact a textbook case in the literal sense: the volume published by Gouiffès (2007) on the subject has been presented in a review as a *vade mecum* that 'could serve as a lesson to our politicians in the event of a major crisis'. Le livre de la semaine (20 December 2007).

18 *Burkina 24* (2011) 'Industrie minière au Burkina (partie 1): Entrevue vidéo de Benoît La Salle, PDG de SEMAFO', 12 November

Gold production has grown significantly: from 754kg in 2007 it has risen to 30.2 tonnes in 2012, making Burkina Faso the fourth biggest producer in Africa in 2012, according to the International Monetary Fund (2013).

Presented as a source of wealth that would bring relief to rural people, it seems that gold has been more of a curse than a blessing.

Today, there are seven major gold mines in the country, most of which are majority-owned by multinationals (Canadian, Russian, British, etc), while the state owns an average of 10 per cent of the shares. In 2011, the mining sector witnessed a series of social conflicts over the working conditions of the workers but also over the living conditions of the populations surrounding the sites. The protest was sparked by a variety of factors, some of which are common to all industrial sites: These included:

- The working conditions of miners: the sector is characterised by tiny salaries, differences in treatment between national and expatriate workers and between miners and administrative staff in terms of wages and housing conditions, no employment contracts or pay slips, non-compliance with labour legislation, lack of security at facilities and accidents;

- The impact on the population surrounding the mine sites: this has included expropriation of peasant lands with paltry compensation, the increasing scarcity of water, the rising cost of living, the banning of gold washing (the main activity of the villagers), pollution, health issues, lack of employment for local youth and the disruption of local life;

- Violations of workers' rights through security measures set in place by mining companies: this involves the operation of private security companies, the establishment of gendarme stations on or near certain mine sites, video-surveillance in workers' 'homes', violations of union freedoms and arbitrary dismissals.

In 2011, traditional modes of action were used (work stoppages), but also non-conventional modes of action (sacking of facilities, confrontations between the populations and law enforcement, etc). In some cases, the events culminated in the flight of company officials. Above all, they revealed the collusion between the multinationals and the political authorities. 'The mining companies have set themselves up as powerful States within the State,' explained the Organisation for Community Capacity Building for Development (ORCADE).

At Taparko, where the first major gold mine has been mined commercially since 1999, the situation is still tense today. The capital of the company running the mines at Taparko (Somita SA), which entered into production in 2007, is divided between a Canadian company, High River Gold (90 per cent), and the state (10 per cent).

In August 2012, a new conflict broke out between the miners and the management: 27 workers were dismissed and two were laid off because they had decided in a union general assembly to take a 30-minute break during their continuous ten-hour shifts, as stipulated by their collective bargaining agreement. The workers were forcibly expelled, with the help of the CRS and gendarmes.[19] The dismissals took place while the regional labour board and the governor of the Centre-Nord region were mediating the conflict and conducting talks with workers. Somita asked the regional labour board for authorisation to dismiss an employee representative and a union representative on grounds that 'they had incited their colleagues to disobedience by encouraging them to refuse to submit to the work schedule established by the employer since 2007 and to carry out unauthorised work stoppages'. The labour board refused: no proof had been provided and it

---

19   Statement on the meeting of mine personnel and union representatives, CGT-B/SYNTRAGMIH, 13 September 2012

had reason 'to believe that the workers were solely targeted because of their positions as personnel representatives'. Somita went ahead anyway. The complaint against the company was not received until July, after repeated deferrals. ORCADE takes the view that the mine sites are 'a real time bomb' and has urged the state to 'significantly reduce the power currently held by the mining companies and to ensure compliance with the local authorities'.[20] However, the problem with the mining sector in Burkina Faso resides less in this power struggle than in the will of certain leaders to enrich themselves. Although the mining sector is above all a family affair (the president and his younger brother, François), there are numerous personalities gravitating around the sector: former ministers of mines, opposition leaders, former prime ministers and ministers (Tertius Zongo, Paramanga Ernest Yonli), the current prime minister, MPs, businessmen, etc (*Africa Mining Intelligence* 2013).

Certain organisations have addressed the issue of the mines alongside the mine workers' union (Syndicat des travailleurs de la géologie, des mines et des hydrocarbures), notably ORCADE and the Burkina Faso Movement for Human and People's Rights (MBDHP). The opposition parties, for their part, have yet to tackle the issue, as far as we know, although the personality of the leader of the new main opposition party (CFOP) brings it a certain amount of expertise in that area.[21] However, it should be noted that he is one of the personalities at the forefront of the movement against the creation of a senate.

Changes in the political landscape

Since the socio-political crisis of 2011, the political landscape in Burkina Faso has changed considerably. First, the internecine rivalries within the

20 Press conference of 5 November 2011
21 Zéphirin Diabré has been chairman of the AREVA group for Africa and the Middle East and international business advisor to the president of the group. The annual sales figure of AREVA is six times higher than the budget of the government of Burkina Faso.

presidential party, the Congress for Democracy and Progress (CDP), became increasingly visible with the 5th convention of the party in March 2012. The internal political crisis in the CDP dates back to even earlier times, as symbolised by the ousting in 2008 of one of the most faithful associates of Compaoré, Salif Diallo, who had denounced the failings of the institutions of the Fourth Republic and the patrimonialisation of power. Fedap-BC (Associative Federation for Peace and Progress with Blaise Compaoré), inspired by François Compaoré,[22] has become a driving force within the CDP. The aim of this 'apolitical association' is apparently to cripple the CDP by luring away its economic operators (a dozen members entered the executive secretariat) and cadres. However, the bigwigs of the CDP have held out, some of them perhaps expecting a reward for their loyalty when Compaoré leaves power. Unable to take over the CDP, Fedap-BC turned to a strategy of 'entryism' to establish itself as a party. François Compaoré - an MP since December 2012 - was appointed secretary in charge of the associative movement. Many believe that this strategy masks a will to establish a dynastic succession in his favour or to amend Article 37 of the constitution.[23] Today, Compaoré has reached an impasse, as the regime only remains in power due to his own personality. If he declares that he will not amend Article 37, the rivalry over his succession will come to light, further undermining the regime; if he does not, the resulting social agitation runs the risk of destabilising the country.[24]

The political opposition has also changed. During the legislative elections of December 2012, although the CDP won the majority of seats in the National Assembly (70 out of 127), the Union for Progress and Change (UPC) made

22 François Compaoré came to the forefront of the political stage after being in the shadows since 1989, first as special advisor to his brother, and then as economic advisor. He took the spotlight following the murder of Norbert Zongo.

23 The article establishing the restriction to two consecutive mandates was amended in 1997, but was reinstated in 2000 in the wake of the popular movement pursuant to the Norbert Zongo affair. At the time, some said that Blaise Compaoré could no longer run for president; others said that the law was not retroactive, and that he could therefore run in the next two elections (2005 and 2010). In 2005, the constitutional council decided in favour of the latter option. Thus, the term he won in November 2010 with 80 per cent of the vote (and a participation of only 1.7 million out of seven million potential voters) was supposed to be the last.

24 On 8 December 2013, in the international media (TFI, TV5, *Le Monde*), and then on 11 December during independence day celebrations in Dori, Blaise Compaoré explained that he did not exclude the possibility of running again in 2015, and that he might consult the people with a view to amending the constitution.

a striking entrance. The party, which was founded by Zéphirin Diabré in 2010, took 19 seats, making it the main opposition party (CFOP).[25] Diabré had been a minister in the government several times in the 1990s before pursuing his career abroad, notably in the UNDP, and then from 2006 to 2011 in the AREVA group.[26] He has a real international network at his disposal and seems to enjoy substantial means.

On 21 May 2013, the National Assembly voted for the creation of a senate, which was to comprise 89 members including 29 directly appointed by Compaoré. The idea of creating such a chamber dated back to 2010 and was subsequently taken up by the Consultative Council on Political Reform (Conseil consultatif sur les réformes politiques, CCRP), founded in 2011. Every period of tension since the beginning of the Fourth Republic has given rise to forums, conferences and consultations. In 2011, the authorities once again opened up an institutional solution aimed at bringing the situation back to normal. The official opposition and the coalition of civil society organisations for political and institutional reforms had rejected this council. At the time it was set up, it was agreed that no changes would be made regarding non-consensual issues, which is the case of the amendment of Article 37 of the constitution. The political opposition and a large section of the Burkinabè population saw the new chamber as an indication that Compaoré planned to amend Article 37 of the constitution, regarding which a referendum was envisaged. The senate would also allow Compaoré to broaden his clientelistic capacity. More generally, the chamber has been criticised for being a 'budget breaker' at a time of growing economic and social distress for the majority.

---

25 He replaced the former head of the opposition, Bénéwendé Sankara, president of the Union for Renaissance/Sankarist Movement.
26 For biographical information on Zéphirin Diabré, see *La Dépêche diplomatique*, 22 mars 2010, 'Zéphirin Diabré: Un parcours sinueux de l'économique au politique'; 23 mars 2010, 'Suite' on *lefaso.net*.

The fight against the creation of a senate

Diabré was one of the initiators of the mobilisation against the creation of the senate. For the first time in 20 years, a march was organised by the political opposition on 29 June 2013, marking a turning point. It was no longer the regime that determined the opposition's agenda, but the contrary, since the march against the creation of the senate and the amendment of Article 37 gave rise to a march by the CDP on 6 July.[27] Although through his initiative, Diabré seemed to have 'rallied the movement', this does not mean, however, that he or the opposition in general garners support in proportion with the political legitimacy of the call for a peaceful change of government.

The mobilisation should not be confused with party allegiance; in fact, for the time being, it cannot even be described as 'Caesarism', not even cynical Caesarism.

Since the combined elections in December 2012, the opposition has consolidated its unity around the UPC, the Sankarists and the Party for Democracy and Socialism, which came second in the presidential election of 2010. However, this unity is solely based on a change of government in 2015 and not on a political and social project. The opposition seems to focus solely on the succession of Compaoré. Furthermore, Diabré called on the president to declare 'publicly that he would not touch Article 37 and the debate is closed'.[28] The simple counterproposal of the 'anti' movement ('anti' or 'anyone but' Compaoré, Sarkozy, Wade), which seems to have the wind in its sails, sheds no light on the political outlook. Furthermore, given his background, Diabré does not appear to embody social justice. He himself has said, 'I am not afraid or ashamed to say that I am a neoliberal…today, the world belongs to us neoliberals; we have won and conquered it[…], the more

---

27 Groups close to Blaise Compaoré (FEDAP/BC, Amis de Blaise Compaoré, etc.) regularly organise marches. For instance during election campaigns or periods of social tension; the aim is generally to stage a portrayal of the supposed 'popularity' of the president.
28 *L'Observateur Paalga* (2013) 'Zéphirin Diabré : 'La pression sera maintenue si le gouvernement persiste', 5 July

I observe the state of the world, the more I am in phase with it.'[29] This proves that the economic crisis of capitalism has left his capitalist values intact and that he is certainly not 'in phase' with the majority in Burkina and beyond. It also shows that the 'lumpen-development recommended by the World Bank and supported by Europe and France, generating social and economic regression and unlimited pauperisation'[30] will not be questioned if he takes the reins of the country. For the moment, it seems that no ideological orientation has been defined within the apparent united front of the political opposition. The CFOP explains that if the opposition comes to power it will propose a consensual programme, since it is made up of heterogeneous currents. The UPC itself - despite its three years of existence - does not seem to have a programme for the time being. To the question: 'The Senate, the high cost of living and Article 37 surely cannot make up an alternative programme, as I am sure you will agree. What are your concrete proposals beyond that?' he answered, 'We are thinking about it.'[31]

Diabré was in fact inspired by another politician, Senegal's Macky Sall, whose formula he intends to use: 'In Senegal, there was a holy alliance between the neoliberal Macky Sall, the liberal Idrissa Seck, the socialist Tanor Dieng, the social-democrat Moustapha Niass, communist groups and civil society. It was a pluralistic coalition, but that did not stop the change of government from taking place and, as far as I know, Senegal is not in a state of disorder!' Indeed, it may not be in a state of disorder, but the question is how the people who supported Sall by default view the situation. Although we can certainly not apply a situation from one country to another in cookie-cutter fashion, we can certainly learn some lessons, and particularly the fact that, 'To get rid of the system of exploitation, young people across Africa should no longer settle for being "watchdogs for the change of government"' (Fall-Barros 2012).

29 Press conference, 25 July 2013
30 We are quoting the translation of the neoliberal offensive described by Samir Amin (2013).
31 *L'Observateur Paalga* (2013) 'Zéphirin Diabré : 'La pression sera maintenue si le gouvernement persiste', 5 July

The socio-political situation on the eve of the next presidential election is ideally configured to serve the political ambitions of Diabré, who has used the senate and Article 37 like a Trojan horse. The fact that he has tackled these issues in the street has set the CFOP apart in a political arena teeming with dozens of opposition parties without any personality embodying a credible alternative. It should be noted that the sudden explosion of the opposition took place in the urban environment, giving free rein to the CDP in the rural world, which is the party's true base, particularly through customary organisations and peasant organisations. According to Diabré, the role of opposition members is to 'deal a death blow, democratically, to the government', which they succeeded in doing. As mentioned above, the march initiated by the opposition on 29 June marked a turning point: the opposition no longer merely settled for attempting to recuperate street demonstrations launched by others, such as the masses, and civil society organisations. The march drew a crowd including every social class, younger and older people, and members and non-members of political and civil organisations. On 28 July, the day of the senatorial elections,[32] another march was organised, drawing thousands of demonstrators. The issue of the senate was the focus of the marches, but popular discontent was much broader. Demonstrators brandished signs with slogans such as: 'No to the Senate, we want jobs'; 'No to 89 vampires in the Senate, we are tired and have no blood left for them'; 'Better a lecture hall than a Senate'.

The repression of the march showed that the regime was on the defensive. Before it even took place, the CDP called for a 'mobilisation against the destabilising actions of certain opposition parties'.[33] 'First, the party (the CDP) and its arm, Fedap/BC, stepped up to the plate. Party thank-you rallies in the cities of Ouagadougou and Bobo-Dioulasso after the combined elections (six months afterwards), a meeting of the political bureau, a press conference for the party leadership, and a big interview with the executive

32 Only six parties presented candidates.
33 Press statement of 19 June 2013 by Assimi Kouanda, CDP National executive secretary, and president of the National Political Board, published by *Lefaso.net*, 21 June 2013, 'Situation nationale: Le CDP appelle à la vigilance et à la mobilisation face aux actions déstabilisatrices de certains partis d'opposition'.

secretary granted to a local daily; the party sought to hold its own in this competition where the battle of public opinion is a vital concern.'[34]

The CDP called for a march on 6 July on the theme of 'Social peace, consolidation of democracy and development'. This did not keep party leaders from using a rhetoric of division. Assimi Kouanda, national executive secretary, spoke of 'the other side'[35] and 'those who want violence, those who seek to organise a Donnybrook'. The CFOP and numerous observers described this march as a 'counter-march' intended as a retort and as proof of the popularity of the senate. Diabré condemned the presidential party marches organised by 'dint of CFA 1000 notes drawn from the public purse'.[36]

That day, the signs showed the will of the members of the CDP to amend Article 37 of the constitution: 'Blaise in power forever!'; 'We prove our love for our President [...] we say yes to the amendment of Article 37'. François Compaoré spoke out for the first time on the subject: 'Blocking a man or a party with an article doesn't make sense. When the people has no need for you, there's really no need for an article to hold you back. All you have to do is tell them to vote, and they will choose the person they want. That is why we think that that article may not be necessary.'[37]

A 'republican front' was developed to contend with the front formed by the opposition parties around the CFOP. It included the Fedap-BC, the parties in the presidential camp and various associations supporting Blaise Compaoré. This set-up, irresistibly reminiscent of the origins of the Fourth Republic, is proof that the rot has set in. In the early 1990s, the debate over whether it was necessary to hold a sovereign national conference before the 1991 presidential elections was stormy. The opposition - which called for the conference - joined together in the Coordination of Democratic Forces

34 *Mutations* (2013) 'Marche de l'opposition. La frilosité du pouvoir', 1 July
35 *APA-Ouagadougou* (2013) 'Le CDP, parti au pouvoir, se félicite de la réussite de sa marche-meeting à Ouagadougou', 6 July
36 *Le Pays* (2013) 'Marche-meeting du CDP - Le chef de file de l'opposition appelle à un boycott', 5 July
37 *L'Observateur Paalga* (2013) 'Marche-meeting du CDP: La réponse du berger à la bergère' 8 July

to stand against the supporters of Compaoré forming the Alliance for the Respect and Defence of the Constitution. The latter won the day. Today, the bipolarisation of Burkina's political parties seems to have made a comeback.

As was the case in 2011,[38] when the streets had already been seething for several weeks, the president spoke from abroad, in Côte d'Ivoire, in late July 2013. On the debates over the senate, he said, 'In France, or in America, laws have never been changed by marches.'[39] 'In a legal State, the political authorities assume the jurisdiction to establish their own legality, which enables them to impose their order or their ideology, [...] Justice merely serves as an excuse' (Gaboriau 2003:34).

In formal terms, the fact that he has repeatedly spoken about the national situation from abroad has been criticised as evidence of Compaoré's preoccupation with enhancing his international image. In terms of substance, in addition to being inaccurate, his statements fanned the flames. Many put forward the examples of the reintroduction of the limiting clause in Article 37 in 2000 and the cancelation of the community development tax - a tax on vehicle owners to purportedly generate funding for local development in 2011 - as proof that laws had indeed been changed by marches. However, it cannot be denied that Compaoré was right: in these two cases, the laws were not changed by marches, but by the radical and violent nature of the protests. Furthermore, these two demands, each in their own time, were part of a set of demands focused on a radical change in the status quo and not on just one aspect of the situation. This is confirmed by the fact that the revolts did not stop once those concessions were made. Our intent here is not to make 'riots' the centre of attention, but to make one thing clear: marches in Burkina Faso, as elsewhere, can only be organised because the regime has allowed it, even

---

38 In 2011, the president only spoke on television after 18 days of rioting and six dead, and he spoke from Ethiopia. However, when the first mutiny broke out, he cut short his stay in Nigeria. In September 2013, in the United States, he returned to the subject of national debates in an interview with Voice of America. When questioned on the possibility that he might run in 2015, he said: 'I think the choice will be up to me. I know my physical and intellectual limits. It is up to me to choose. But, as I said, 2015 is still a long way away.'

39 On 11 July 2013, government spokesman Alain Edouard Traoré said of the marches 'They don't keep us awake at night.'

when it is backed into a corner. As long as these mobilisations remain in the classical schema of strict separation between struggle and march, the regime can be weakened, but not endangered.

It remains that the battle over the senate took place in the street and once again revealed the existence of two Burkina Fasos (both equally subject to internal tensions). Since 1998 and the rise of the popular struggles, the divide between the 'legal country' and the 'real country' has continued to widen (Halidou Ouédraogo, president of the Collective Against Impunity and the MBDHP at the time, was nicknamed the 'president of the real country'). In 2011, it was forcefully revealed: the country was in a 'situation of dual power'. The twin pillars of the state were revolting (the army and justice, the latter having gone on strike after being targeted by mutineers). The situation became one of 'calculation evasion' (Dobry 1992), or, in other words, one in which it was no longer possible to count on the reliable functioning of institutions.

The feeling that the serious, structural and multidimensional socio-political situation had plunged the country into 'times of uncertainty'[40] was pervasive, leaving the door open to any eventuality. In addition to the institutional situation that continued to divide the country, this feeling was further exacerbated by the 'social powder keg' generated by the high cost of living and the unfair distribution of wealth.

The letter from the bishops on 15 July, viewed as a 'counter state of the nation address',[41] had considerable impact. They called the government to account for the social tensions and agitation surrounding the creation of the senate. They observed that the state was blind to social realities and to the yawning social chasm between the governors and the governed and recalled

40 Title of an ICG report (ICG 2013)
41 L'Observateur Paalga(2013), 'Lettre pastorale : Contre-discours sur l'Etat de la nation'

that 'institutions are only legitimate when they are socially useful'. Although initially the government turned a deaf ear to their appeal, on 12 August, the president's office announced the suspension of the setting up of the senate pending a detailed report from the ministry of political reforms.

In terms of the social movement, a number of lessons can be drawn from this period of political and social turmoil. To take only two, we note the ability of the popular masses to organise and often to provide each other with mutual support, as well as the attitude of the counter-hegemonic organisations towards the political opposition.

Prior to the upsurge of the political opposition, citizen organisations were created to combat the amendment of Article 37. Since then, they have proliferated: *mouvement contre la révision de l'article 37 de la Constitution* (M37) was formed in January 2013; *M21: on n'est pas d'accord* (M21) was created on 21 April (both condemn the revision of Article 37, the creation of the senate and the high cost of living); the *front de résistance citoyenne*, was founded in July (it brought together some 20 civil society organisations that took a position against 'the confiscation of the sovereignty of the people for monarchic purposes'), *balai citoyen* (citizens' broom) was created in July by musicians Smockey and Sams K Le Jah and organised in neighbourhood bases in both rural and urban areas. Others included *Y en a marre-Burkina*,[42] and the *Collectif des femmes pour la défense de la Constitution*, formed in June. This multitude of organisations is revelatory of a certain 'narcissism of minor differences' (Freud 1930). However, their relations are not conflictual. Furthermore, their multiplicity reflects refusal to place themselves under the leadership of the political opposition, even though they shares some of the same watchwords. This is a major difference compared to the 2011 social movement, when the opposition parties were largely marginalised.

---

42   The Senegalese movement led by rap musicians and media figures, whose name is French for 'We've had enough' or 'We're fed up' seems to have become a model for the youth of French-speaking Africa: Burkina Faso, Togo, Mali, Benin.

Under the Fourth Republic, protest movements have been led by trade unions and associations, which have played a major role in the socio-political landscape of Burkina Faso. The General Confederation of Labour of Burkina (CGT-B, *Confédération générale du travail du Burkina*), founded in 1988, which identifies itself with the revolutionary class-struggle trade union movement, was one of the labour confederations behind the creation of CCVC following the riots against the high cost of living in 2008; and the MBDHP founded in 1989. There is a strong relationship of interdependency between these organisations, both of which are run by former members of UGEB, which was created in 1960. This explains the ideological consistency between the counter-hegemonic forces in the country (Loada 1999). Another association close to these organisations, the *Organisation démocratique de la Jeunesse* (Democratic Organisation of the Youth), was founded in 2000 in the wake of the mobilisations against impunity. Given the sudden presence of the political opposition in the streets, it is interesting to examine its relations with these social forces.

CCVC refused 'on principle' to associate with the march of 29 June led by the CFOP; on the other hand, the opposition called on the public to participate in the day of protest organised by CCVC on 20 July against the high cost of living and bad governance. Thousands of people responded across the national territory and their slogans revealed just how fed up the majority were: 'A midwife is worth more than a Senator'; 'When the people are Egyptianised, Blaise is Morsised'; 'Change salaries, not articles'.

For many observers, a conjunction of the struggles led by the political opposition and the other organisations seemed to be a *sine qua non* condition for Burkina Faso to find its way out of the political, economic and social situation in which it was mired. Accordingly, civil society organisations and trade unions - particularly those that were members of CCVC - were blamed by various observers for having placed 'minor contradictions' before the 'major contradiction', which was to keep Compaoré from running in

2015.[43] In short, they were reproached with putting out the wrong fire. In the view of some, their attitude was actually a godsend for the authorities.[44] This was undoubtedly due in part to historical reasons, as, several times in post-colonial history, associations, trade unions and political parties have agreed on specific demands. The fall of the First Republic, on 3 January 1966, was made possible by one such conjunction. In the early 1990s, the same applied again, until certain parties rallied around the regime. In 1998, the different types of organisations came together in a collective of mass organisations and political parties, but when the national union government was formed, certain parties entered the government.

Tolé Sagnon, secretary general of CGT-B, tried to explain this position:[45]

> We can replace Blaise Compaoré with someone else who will choose the same neoliberal policies. In this sense, we need to develop critical thought towards the various political forces that are attempting to present themselves as alternatives to the current government but which, for the most part, share the basic fundamentals of the neoliberal policies of the government in place.

He went on to say that the issues relating to the senate or 'attempts to revise Article 37, despite their relevancy and their importance, should not be the focus of all of the attention of the people of Burkina!'[46] According to UGEB, 'change does not mean "move over and let me take your place" [...instead] it is a matter of needing to put an end to the neo-colonial system that has been in force for the last 53 years.'[47]

---

43   *L'Evènement* (2013) 'Dr Ibriga: Nous sommes à une étape charnière de la vie politique du Burkina', 2 August
44   *L'Evènement* (2013) 'Burkina: Blaise a-t-il encore les ressorts pour rebondir ?', 2 August
45   *L'Observateur Paalga*, (2013), "Meeting contre la vie chère : 'Réviser les salaires et non les articles'", 22 July
46   Statement made by CCVC during the 20 July 2013 protest
47   *Burkina 24* (2013) 'L'UGEB à Zéphirin Diabré: "Le changement, c'est de mettre fin au système néocolonial"', 18 August

According to Diabré, the attitude of the trade unions is an 'expression of [their] will to conquer State power'.[48] In his view, the role of the unions is to 'defend specific interests, whatever the political party in power'. He feels 'it seems strange' to see a trade union wondering about the identity of the successor to the head of state.[49] Actually, 'it seems strange' that he finds that surprising. Trade unions in post-colonial history have played a major role that goes well beyond the issues involved in collective bargaining agreements, above all because they often served as a refuge for politicians in times when political parties were banned. In addition, under the Fourth Republic most of the opposition parties were not 'on the ground' except in the run up to the elections. Under this regime, the conjunction of political and social demands owes much to the unions, which broadened and politicised the protest movement (Chouli 2013). Thus, if anything should be deemed abnormal, it was rather the sudden presence of the political opposition in the streets. The dynamics of the current movement are not *sui generis*; they draw on previous protest experiences. This is an illustration of Verta Taylor's concept of '*abeyance*' (1989), which 'describes a process whereby these movements are sustained or remain dormant and manage to maintain themselves despite political environments that are no longer receptive, playing the role of a liaison between the two stages of mobilisation'[50] (Filleule *et al.* 2009:17).

However, it is undoubtedly reassuring that the counter-hegemonic organisations do not adopt an attitude in keeping with the dynamics of the moment, to wit: that they avoid opportunism, as part of the population may be tired of the lack of transparency and the succession of socio-political crises that always lead in the end to the re-establishment of the previous social order. Although they may be convinced of the need for organised action, they undoubtedly want it to be designed as a step towards a clear prospect. Furthermore, in this stage in history, it seems that the idea of emancipation

---

48   Counter-hegemonic organisations were systematically accused by the authorities, certain observers, and certain opposition parties of including members of the Voltaic Revolutionary Communist Party (PCRV) - a clandestine body since 1978. Behind every major struggle, the authorities see its 'spectre', which they view as an 'internal enemy' in the country. According to Bruno Jaffré (2013), 'This is one of the risks of destabilisation of the opposition.'
49   *Lefaso.net* (2013) 'Zéphirin Diabré sans détour: Tolé Sagnon et Assimi Kouanda sur la sellette', 28 July
50   *Our translation*

should avoid messianism. The question remains: if 'Blaise is to go […] who shall take his place?' The question is legitimate, but it has been turned into a crime of *lèse-majesté* through a dynamic according to which the best of all worlds is the one proposed by the opposition. A Burkina Faso without the Compaoré family? Perhaps. But it is time we found out what shape the post Compaoré era will take. Because not only does the struggling superpower that is the CDP worry its members, but the senate and Article 37 as the only guide for the opposition is also a cause for concern.[51] It is always dangerous to separate the struggle for a specific cause - in this case, peaceful change of government, whose legitimacy is unquestionable - from the ultimate goal, which is a liberating policy for all Burkinabè.

Student society labelled a 'dangerous class'

It has now become a habit in Burkina Faso during every major socio-political crisis to target students. In recent years, students have served as both a safety valve and a diversion, notably in times when the 'political situation was fluid' and there was a *'conjunctural de-sectoralisation'* of the social space (Dobry 1992).

Throughout post-colonial history students have always been perceived as being in conflict with authority, whether that of the university or of the state. In the context of the socio-political crisis that followed the assassination of Norbert Zongo, the decision to invalidate the 1990-2000 academic year and undertake an in-depth reform of the University of Ouagadougou (U of O) amounted to the government taking control of the university, which was perceived as the main source of socio-political protest (Bianchini 2002). In 2011, the march organised by ANEB on 11 March was viewed by the government, which was worried by the geographic and social spread of the demonstrations, as an opportunity to put an end to the protests. The authorities used the strategy of claiming that the protests where restricted to

---

51 *Lefaso.net* (2013) 'Opposition burkinabè : Il y aura quoi après Blaise ?', 16 August

the academic sphere. And yet it was the involvement of other social categories that made the social movement a mass movement. Campus residents were evicted as the students of the U of O had been in 1990, 2000 and 2008. Again, in 2013, students at Ouagadougou and Ouaga ll universities were subjected to economic repression. Beyond the official justifications, we can imagine that the strategy was aimed at turning media attention away from protests against the senate and focusing it on the students, and discouraging them from engaging in further mass demonstrations against the senate. The use of repression (be it symbolic or forceful) and of justice against students always works very well: protests against the repression overshadow the original demands and protest is diverted from those demands to focus on repression.

Students say that they were only informed on 29 July of the decision by the *Centre national des œuvres universitaires* (CENOU, the national student services body) to close all university residences and cafeterias as of 1 August, leaving them with barely 48 hours to pack and leave. The measure impacted 7,000 people. The justification given was that the school year was over, and yet, since the reform of 2000, the academic year had been behind schedule every year.

Students used a variety of forms of action to protest the closing of student services: power cuts to force staff out of the office of the president of the U of O, blocking traffic, confiscation of government and NGO vehicles (several were burned after interventions by law enforcement) and confrontations with law enforcement. Faced with repression, students came out in support of their classmates. However, repression by the CRS and the BAC took a heavy toll: a dozen were wounded, 50 taken into custody, and all of the campus residents thrown out into the streets. Some of them, who had nowhere to go, gathered at the African Union roundabout to sleep. During the night, the BAC took action. From that time onwards, the students had to look for individual solutions and count on public goodwill.

It seems that in Burkina Faso more than elsewhere, the expression 'spare the rod and spoil the child' is literally applied. The director of the CENOU, having explained that on certain campuses students had awaited law enforcement officers with machetes and sticks, added that 'they know I care about them very much and defend them as best I can'.[52] In a similar situation in 2011, when the universities and student services were closed, Minister of Security Jérôme Bougouma had stated that talks were to be held with students (meanwhile, however, the first wave of mutiny had paralysed the authorities). He informed a local paper, *L'Evènement*, about the 'surprise': 'They don't know yet. You see, a government cannot be unkind to its own people.'

To everyone's surprise, the Ministry of Social Action and National Solidarity offered to house the students evicted from Ouaga and Ouaga II universities in the stadium (Stade du 4-Août), proving the government's schizophrenic attitude. The students refused, describing the minister's offer as 'locking the stable door after the horse had bolted', and reminded him that they were not 'football players or athletes or even less cyclists' who should be housed in a stadium. The list to collect the names of students wishing to be housed remained desperately empty. ANEB/OUAGA told the press that it felt that the minister's offer was ironic.

According to the minister, although few students accepted his helping hand, it was because they were held back by the others: 'It's completely normal: I can't go sign up if people want to throw stones at me [sic].'[53] The students denied the allegations and said that people who had not been evicted had been paid to pass themselves off to the press as rehoused students.[54]

52 *Sidwaya* (2013) 'André Batiana, DG du Cenou, "Les œuvres universitaires accompagnent l'activité académique"', 2 August

53 *Lefaso.net* (2013) 'Mesure gouvernementale de relogement des étudiants expulsés des cités : "12 à 13 inscrits à la date d'hier", selon le ministre Alain Zoubga', 10 August

54 *Lefaso.net* (2013), 12 August, 'Expulsés des résidences universitaires : Non à l'aide du gouvernement', 12 août

The support the students received, particularly from the opposition, drew criticism from some. The CDP's national assistant secretary in charge of youth mobilisation said: 'By refusing the helping hand offered by the government [...] and by accepting offers of room and board from opposition leaders and political parties, students have unwittingly placed themselves in a position of "indebtedness" that will involve them in a struggle that has nothing to do with defending their moral or material interests.'[55]

The whole issue of the relationship between students and the political apparatus lies in the way the latter apprehends its mission towards the former: it seems that it is a matter of charity. In 2008, during a similar situation, a teacher offered free meals to interested students following the closure of student services. The prime minister at the time, Tertius Zongo, made a contribution.[56] The fact that he made a donation towards solidarity intended to make up for the fecklessness of his own government was disconcerting in itself, yet edifying. In 2004, the then minister of education stated in an interview that: 'Certainly, in human terms, I can be sensitive to the fate of a student left up to his own devices, but people need to know that the State is not an apparatus that produces pity and messianism.'[57] He added that, 'if he were Bill Gates' cousin, he could have drawn sums however he wanted to satisfy everyone.'[58]

Solidarity with the students was manifested in a variety of ways (statements of support, offers of room and board, creation of fixed and mobile solidarity funds, hotlines and Facebook pages) and by a variety of stakeholders (associations, political parties, mass movements, ordinary citizens and trade unions). The MBDHP, for its part, set up a pool of lawyers to defend students who had been arrested. Fifty people, including one young woman and eight

---

55 *Le Pays* (2013) 12 August, 'Crise à l'Université de Ouagadougou. L'opposition opte pour la stratégie de la terre brulée'
56 *L'Evènement* (2008), 'Les restos du cœur de Madame Sangaré', 30 August
57 *Le Pays*, 31 May 2004, quoted in Barry (2005)
58 *L'Observateur Paalga* (2004) Interview with Laya Sawadogo. 'Je reçois mes instructions du PM, pas du CDP', 27 May

non students, were prosecuted. The 'trial strategy'[59] is very commonly used during social movements in general and student protests in particular, where it is a constant. Members and sympathisers of the U of O's ANEB were arrested during major crises and sometimes taken to court, as in 2002 and 2008, or in 2009 at the University of Koudougou. In 2011, after a march organised by ANEB on 11 March, 19 people were arrested. When the mutinies began, they were released. The students arrested in this year were immediately brought before a judge, which is proof that the justice system can act rapidly. In 2011, the 'two-tier justice system' and the 'justice of the powerful' were repeatedly criticised. Certain public opinion coups may have given the impression that the situation was going to change, but the regime soon reverted to its old habits. Indeed, the justice system was not so swift to react when economic or blood crimes were directly or indirectly linked to the authorities, as in the Ousmane Guiro case, that of the victims of repression in Boulkiemdé in 2011, and the Thomas Sankara and Norbert Zongo cases.

The people arrested on 2 August 2013 appeared in court on 13 August for vandalism and assault against law enforcement agents, charges that fell within the scope of the law of 23 June 2008 on the repression of acts of vandalism (a law adopted after the riots against the high cost of living). The defence counsel felt that the law was not in compliance with the constitution and raised an objection on grounds of unconstitutionality. They requested the release of the accused pending trial.

The Constitutional Council was asked to decide on the question of unconstitutionality. However, provisional release was not granted. On 20 August, the criminal chamber decided that it did not have jurisdiction to grant provisional release. Three days later, the public prosecutor requested provisional release 'to preserve and consolidate social peace and public order'. According to the defence 'the case was based on values other than justice',

---

59   In the university environment, the same cycle of crisis management by the authorities seems to have been repeating itself since 1997: student demonstrations (whatever their mode of action), physical violence, arrests of protesters, trials, disqualifications (subversion, manipulation) and negotiations and calls for mediation.

which would explain why the prosecutor changed his mind within ten days. 'The rule of law [is still definitely] a pipe dream' as the secretary general of the Burkinabè Magistrates' Union said in May 2011.[60]

On 30 August 2013, the political reform monitoring committee submitted its detailed report to Compaoré, marking the resumption of the setting up of the senate with a few adjustments (a reduction of the number of senators, taking account of youth and openness to other political opinions). The head of state urged the government to extend the consultations to all social and political constituencies in order to solidly establish the relevance of the senate. During the first Council of Ministers meeting following summer holidays (11 September 2013), a series of social measures was announced involving support for the elderly, young people and women, wage increases, income tax relief and price cuts on certain products. In a gesture towards students, the Council of Ministers decided to reinforce 'university infrastructure by building university centres, classroom facilities and a university cafeteria to seat 300'[61] and to increase the amounts of student aid and student loans. Although the government had increased the price of electricity and gas just months before, the measures were perceived by numerous observers and by the opposition as a way to reduce social tension and break the opposition to the senate.

Conclusion

Interpreting the social and political changes affecting Burkina Faso as a whole has rarely been so risky an undertaking. Blaise Compaoré's longevity in power has demonstrated that he is a talented strategist. He has always been able to defuse protests with a combination of repression and institutional reform. However, in this phase of history, which is already marked - well beyond the

---

60   *Bendré* (2011): According to René Bagoro, 'There is a circular letter from the Ministry of Justice asking that cases involving military personnel no longer be tried', 21 April
61   Report of the Council of Ministers, 11 September 2013

borders of Burkina Faso - by uncertainty, threats to the future and sudden upheavals in numerous countries, it is highly unlikely that this strategy can be maintained. The type of political domination that seems to be envisaged —combining political power, economic interests and filiation, or in other words, replacing one Compaoré by another, despite François Compaoré's unpopularity—would indubitably carry dangers. In Africa, dynastic transmission of power seems to be a thing of the past, as demonstrated by the thwarting of the presumed nepotistic intentions of Egypt's Hosni Mubarak and Senegal's Abdoulaye Wade, even though Jean Salem (2012) has counted some 20 electoral dynasties currently active around the globe.

The social movements of Burkina Faso are part of a global trend in which social movements are on the rise and citizens participate much more directly than before in political affairs. Rioting can be an indicator of such 'participation'. Globally, according to estimates by Alain Bertho, there were 547 riots in 2009; 1238 in 2010; 1781 in 2011; and 1839 in 2012.[62] 'The last decade [2000-2010] has experienced more civil unrest than the 1960s' (Bertho and Luret 2010). The spread of the phenomenon denotes a lack of faith in our institutions. It can also be linked with the hyper-institutionalisation of counter-powers such as trade unions and associations. Indeed, the notion that there is a crisis of representation - fuelled by economic and social failures, deregulations, unmet promises, defence of private interests and gradual dispossession by transnational bodies - is pervasive across all continents.

In Burkina Faso, since 1998, there has been a real increase in popular protest. The socio-political crisis and the protests against the high cost of living in 2008, and the socio-political crises of 2011 and 2013 all form part of the same historical sequence, which is to say that the Compaoré regime has already been senescent for a very long time.

---

62   Not all of these are necessarily directed against the authorities. For a report by Julie Jane Thoreau, see: http://berthoalain.com/2013/06/19/les-emeutes-dans-le-monde-en-2012, accessed 8 January 2014.

However, the main challenge of these social movements is offering a credible alternative to the system in place that goes beyond short-term 'gains' (no matter how important). In the current situation, a large mass of citizens is looking at the political system from the outside. Although they are increasingly sceptical, they are developing mobilisation for coordination and organisation - largely horizontal and independent from the parties - to channel civic energy. The will to claim ownership of the public space and become independent from political parties and structured organisations

in general reflects both maturity and radicalism; however, limitations soon appear, notably their inability to offer an alternative to the system in place, if that is indeed their role (see below). Furthermore, spontaneous revolts are often spurred by specific, concrete demands, and once these are satisfied (if they have encountered no other causes for discontent or if the issue is highly localised), then the movement is likely to stop there. However, when they overflow and spread socially and geographically, social forces can play an important role in politicisation and broadening of protest action. However, at the same time, they may also be an obstacle to spontaneous radicalism.

It remains that the social framework in Burkina Faso is powerful enough to orient decisions. Spontaneous revolts are on the rise and sometimes engender direct meetings between various social constituencies that do not necessarily meet under ordinary circumstances (young unemployed graduates, students, informal sector workers, labourers, wage earners and rural people). An insurrectional environment such as in 2011 or collective defensive reactions can lead to political change. In any case, their political impact is significant because repressive mechanisms - honed throughout the Fourth Republic - focus above all on social forces using conventional modes of political action and are ineffectual when faced with the exasperation of the population dealing with growing economic and social hardship and the arbitrariness and impunity of officials at all levels of the administration.

Therein lies the paradox: the ability of the authorities to disregard the institutional channels conveying political, social and economic demands is far from constructive outside of times of crisis. And, in the end, when spontaneous revolts take place, it is those channels that attempt to 'channel' them.

The upsurge of unconventional modes of political participation all around the world is doubtless linked to the fact that, at the present time, it is difficult to foresee a brighter future, which is a major political and perhaps a major anthropological turning point. The most glowing promises of the opposition are often abandoned once they come to power. At this stage of neoliberal capitalism, the state appears as a 'regulatory official' (Hermet, Kazancigil, Prud'Homme 2005), and may even seem superfluous. The 'crisis of the state', in the sense of the political apparatus, and its staff's inability to manage public affairs and maintain social peace, is visible virtually everywhere. In Burkina Faso, this is combined with a 'crisis of the regime', or the paralysis of the democratic institutions, which, it appears, have never actually been meant to be operative as demonstrated by the quasi systematic recourse to religious or traditional authorities whenever there is a crisis. Ultimately, the regime of the Fourth Republic has done everything to 'render institutionally possible the hopes [it seeks] to neutralise' (Hilgers 2010). Today, activism is no longer reflected by a will to take power; the masses who are mobilising on the side lines demand specific changes to the situation here and now. Hence the rejection of the political parties that try to recuperate or organise their movements, ranging from the movement in Burkina Faso in 2011, to the Occupy Wall Street movement, to the *Indignados*, and others. Their rejection of all representation or hierarchy of this kind is extremely interesting. The more offensive sectors are mainly located on the fringes of the social production and reproduction system (with a violent continuum), as that is what they are. The traditional practice of politics as being within a political party is also compromised in our current era; unlike in the 20th century, there is no longer a movement or utopia that provides an overall orientation.

In many recent experiences, the sufficiency/insufficiency of the simple slogan 'change' - whatever the ideological, theoretical or social orientation - seems to be a political panacea for organised parties. It is as if it has become superfluous to specify the basis for change, which is most often limited to changing the head of state (Sarkozy, Compaoré, Wade). In Burkina Faso, this slogan sacrifices concrete struggle in the present to events (marches) focusing on a demand (not amending Article 37) that is still for the moment no more than a hypothetical scenario, albeit an increasingly likely one. Not that it would not be useful to oppose it before it becomes a reality. But that is not enough if the protest does not extend to the struggle against social distress.

During social revolts, political opposition parties try to capitalise on the discontentment, and this extends well beyond the borders of Burkina Faso. The situation in 2013 was quite unusual in that the CFOP was one of the initiators of the protests against the senate and for peaceful political change, or at least spurred the movement. And yet, the CFOP does not seem to be offering a credible alternative, other than the 'normalisation' of capitalism so that it is not fettered by nepotistic management, as desired, for example, by the bourgeoisie in Tunisia. In the end, there was a consensus around the mobilisation against the senate and the amendment of Article 37, but class interests remained unchanged. Furthermore, the apparent unity observed during the latest mobilisation will have to last two years: will the opposition be able to achieve this?

2014 began with a day of protest called by the political opposition on 18 January 'to say NO to the revision of Article 37 of our Constitution, NO to the Senate and NO to government policy'. Above all, the presidential party was considerably weakened following the resignation, early in the year, of 75 members, including former party leader and former president of the National Assembly, Roch Marc Christian Kaboré and former mayor of the capital, Simon Compaoré, both founding members of the CDP, as well as Salif Diallo, formerly one of Blaise Compaoré's right-hand men and several times a minister. They explained their resignation on grounds that the founding democratic platform of the party had not been upheld, that there was no internal democracy within the CDP, that the senate had been set up by force and attempts were being made to amend Article 37. For the time being, doubts persist as to their intentions. Will they join the existing political opposition or will they found their own party? It remains that these resignations compromise Blaise Compaoré's plans for staying in power.

The current lack of a bright future (not only in Burkina Faso) is also evidenced by the fragmentation of political struggles into the mobilisation of a handful of social groups, with no signs that any of them may bring about social change. In a present marked by spontaneous popular mobilisation, this figure is embodied by a collective of subjectivities, by the 'class being' typified by marginalisation. This characteristic is both a strength—contributing to political intensity—and a limitation.

Today, belief in the democratic system is in decline: 'The betrayal is in the electoral form itself', (*editor's translation*) said Holloway (2002). This is supported by Rancière (2005), who reminds his readers that the expression 'representative democracy' was 'originally an oxymoron', and that, 'Universal suffrage is a mixed form, born of oligarchy, redirected by democratic combat, and perpetually reconquered by oligarchy, which proposes its candidates and sometimes its preferred decisions' (*editor's translation*).

While socio-historical environments are unique, it remains that at the global level there is currently a trend towards across-the-board criticism of all representatives of the traditional political class, and the political and economic elites. A number of reasons can be cited to explain this tendency, which is equally prevalent in Northern and Southern countries.

Perhaps the 21st century simply needs to stop believing that political time will be election time (in other words, with emulation during campaigns and then a wait until the next elections where we have our previous demands heard, along with the new ones that necessarily arise). Representative democracy can no longer deceive the masses; it has failed to honour its promise of benefitting the people.[63] In the economic crisis of capitalism, it seems that social revolts will proliferate, and election time will no longer have any meaning as a time of social change. This also means that those in power will have to deal with increased and endless infernal vigilance on the part of citizens. This is demonstrated by the social revolts taking place in the four corners of the earth (Bosnia, Brazil, Bulgaria, Burkina Faso, Turkey, Greece, Egypt, Tunisia). Although each arose from a unique situation, they share a common focus: exasperation with corruption and mismanagement of national wealth, democratic demands and the struggle against neoliberalism. It is furthermore significant when the head of state is called upon not to run again (Burkina Faso, Senegal, etc) or leaders are urged to resign (Bulgaria, Tunisia, Egypt, etc).

The contemporary situation in Burkina Faso demonstrates that the organisational capacity of the popular masses (who often form groups by affinities of condition) remains steadfast, as does the radicalism of the fringes. The representation of the latter is developed *en acte* through unconventional modes of action and gains - however minimal - in the present and enhanced experience. 'There are a hundred ways of being on the side of power,' said Raoul Vaneigem (1967), 'There is only one way to be radical.' Whatever the location, a large portion of the population has come to the conclusion that the authorities only understand the language of force. As Marcuse (1965) said of the environment in 1968, if the roads to democracy 'are blocked by methods of repression and indoctrination, then undemocratic means are the only way left to open them'.[64] Social movements are certainly one viable response to the crisis of political legitimacy. In any case, for the time being they are surely the only one.

63 Representative democracy is no longer in phase with 21st-century politics. To see the truth in this, it is enough to observe the energy deployed to try to deceive the popular masses with 'participatory democracy', at every level, through policy at the national level, but also through transnational organisations, such as the World Bank in particular.
64 *Our translation*

However, the future in Burkina Faso is also partially determined abroad. The country is at the heart of an extremely unstable regional sub-group in which it plays an important role. The emergence of armed groups in the region, the country's status as a support base for foreign military powers (US and especially French), and the role of Blaise Compaoré - the man himself and not his diplomats—as a mediator[65] leaves a degree of uncertainty as to the attitude of his allies. Several signs and observers seem to indicate that Burkina Faso could well be the next country in the sub-region to descend into chaos.

It cannot be forgotten that Laurent Bigot, former deputy director West Africa of the French Ministry of Foreign Affairs, explained in 2012[66] that:

> there are countries that are absolutely in the same situation as Mali. I think Burkina Faso is a good example and may be the next to collapse, as it came close to doing a year ago. There is no army, no political class, civil society is more or less organised and especially there is an economy that is systematically bled by the presidential clan, corruption beyond belief, and involvement in sub-regional trafficking that extends all the way to the close associates of the President.

External watchdogs, but especially national ones (human rights organisations, journalists, intellectuals) stress the blindness of Burkina's political regime and that the consequences of this are unpredictable. To quote Günther Anders (1987), 'there is no danger more serious than when the all-powerful are not serious'.

---

65 Shockingly for Blaise Compaoré, during the crisis over the senate, some people envisaged Macky Sall or Alassane Ouattara as mediators. On 9 January 2013, the latter sent Guillaume Soro to act as a mediator in the internal crisis within the CDP. This raises two points: firstly that the Ivorian government also seems to confuse Burkina Faso's presidential party with the state; secondly that the fact of freely choosing to leave one's party is now viewed as an act with dangerous consequences for the national situation. See Jaffré (2010, 2013).
66 Statements made during the IFRI (Institut français des relations internationales) Conference, 'Les défis du Sahel: focus sur la crise au Mali', 22 June 2012

References

Adorno, T. W. (1951) *Minima Moralia: Reflections from Damaged Life,* (English translation by Dennis Redmond, 2005), http://www. marxists.org/reference/archive/adorno/1951/mm/, accessed March 2014

Africa Mining Intelligence (2013) « Burkina Faso : l'eldorado des anciens ministres », Collection Insiders Mining, 16 avril

Amin, S. (2013) « Mali. Analyse de Samir Amin », 23 janvier, http://www.m-pep.org/spip.php?article3184, visité en mars 2014

Anders, G. (1987) « Une contestation non violente est-elle suffisante ? », première édition, *Tumultes*, n°28/29, 2007/1-2

Barry, S. (2005) *Les Déterminants sociopolitiques de la contestation Estudiantine à l'université de Ouagadougou de 1990 à 2004,* Mémoire de maîtrise de sociologie, Université de Ouagadougou

Bertho, A. and Luret, S. (2010) *Les raisons de la colère,* Arte-Morgane Prod., 52 mn

Bianchini, P. (2002), « La "refondation" de l'Université de Ouagadougou. Une mise en perspective », in N. Akam et Roland Ducasse (éd.) *Quelle université pour l'Afrique ?*, Bordeaux, Éditions Maison des Sciences de l'Homme d'Aquitaine

Centre Tricontinental (CETRI) (2013) *Industries minières – Extraire à tout prix*, Syllepse, collection Alternatives Sud

Chouli, L. (2012) *Burkina Faso 2011. Chronique d'un mouvement social,* Tahin Party

Chouli, L., 2013, « Les mouvements sociaux de 1998 et 2011 au Burkina Faso comme indices et réponses à la crise de la représentation politique », Actes du 4ᵉ colloque international de Dakar, 22 au 24 mai 2013, in *Le retour de la question politique : crise de la représentation et luttes démocratiques en Afrique*

Conseil National de Prospective et de Planification Stratégique (2005) *Étude nationale prospective. « Burkina 2025 », rapport général*

http://213.154.74.164/invenio//record/18783/files/burkina2025_ rapportgeneral.pdf, visité en mars 2014

Dobry, M. (1992) *Sociologie des crises politiques. La dynamique des mobilisations multisectorielles,* seconde édition, Paris, Presses de la Fondation nationale des sciences politiques

Fall-Barros, A. (2012) « Conjoncture politique : Tourmente idéologique ou opportunisme politique ? », 16 octobre http://www.m23juin. org/index.php/acceuil/10-opinions/73-qconjoncture-politique-- tourmente-ideologique-ou-opportunisme-politique (visité en mars 2014)

Fillieule, O, Mathieu, L. and Péchu, C. (2009) (dir.), *Dictionnaire des mouvements sociaux,* Paris, Presses de Sciences Po

Freud, S. (1930) *Civilisation and Its discontents,* Martino Fine Books, 2011

Gouiffès, P.F. (2007) *Margaret Thatcher face aux mineurs: 1972-1985 treize années qui ont changé l'Angleterre,* Toulouse, Privat

Gaboriau, S. (2003) « L'enjeu démocratique de la Justice », in S. Gaboriau, H. Pauliat, G. Canivet, *Justice et démocratie : Actes du colloque organisé à Limoges les 21-22 novembre 2002,* Presses universitaires de Limoges

Hermet, G., Kazancigil, A. and Prud'homme, J.F. (2005) (éd) *La gouvernance. Un concept et ses applications*, Paris, Karthala

Hilgers, M. (avec la collaboration de J. Mazzocchetti) (2010) « Semi-autoritarisme, perceptions et pratiques du politique », in M. Hilgers, J. Mazzocchetti, *Révoltes et oppositions dans un régime semi-autoritaire. Le cas du Burkina Faso,* Karthala

Holloway, J. (2002) *Change the world without taking power. The meaning of revolution today,* London, Pluto Press

IMF (2013) « *Burkina Faso : évaluation ex post de l'application de programmes sur longue période – actualisation* », Rapport du FMI, n°13/228 ;

http://www.imf.org/external/french/pubs/ft/scr/2013/cr13228f.pdf, visité en mars 2014

International Crisis Group (ICG) (2013) 'Burkina Faso: with or without Compaoré, Times of Uncertainty', *Africa Report* 205, July

Jaffré, B. (2010) « Le Burkina Faso, pilier de la 'Françafrique' », *Le Monde diplomatique,* janvier

Jaffré, B. (2013) « Au Burkina, le chaos, c'est Blaise Compaoré, tandis que l'opposition gagne en crédibilité », *Médiapart,* 14 août

Loada, A. (1999) « Réflexion sur la société civile en Afrique: le Burkina de l'après-Zongo », *Politique africaine,* n°76: 136-151

Marcuse, H. (1965) « Repressive tolerance », in R.P. Wolff, B. Moore, H. Marcuse (eds) *A Critique of pure tolerance pure,* Beacon Press

Negt, O. (2007) *L'Espace public oppositionnel,* translated from German by Alex Neumann, Payot & Rivages

Rancière, J. (2005) *Hatred of democracy*, second edition (translated from French), Verso, 2009

Salem, J. (2012) *Élections, piège à cons ? Que reste-il de la démocratie ?*, Paris, Flammarion

Sory, I. (2013) « *'Ouaga La Belle !' Gestion des déchets solides à Ouagadougou : Enjeux politiques, Jeux d'acteurs et Inégalités environnementales* », Thèse de géographie, Université Paris I Panthéon Sorbonne

Taylor, V. (1989) 'The Women's movement in abeyance', *American Sociological Review*, 54(5): 761-775

United Nations Environment Programme (UNEP) (2009) *From Conflict to Peacebuilding - the Role of Natural Resources and the Environment*, Nairobi, UNEP

Vaneigem, R. (1967) *The Revolution of everyday life* (translated from French), PM Press, 2012

CHAPTER: 8

THE CRISIS OF 'REPRESENTATIVE DEMOCRACY' AND NEW FORMS OF STRUGGLE IN MALI

Issa N'Diaye

The crisis of democratic representation appeared very early in Mali, in the years following the fall of the dictatorship in March 1991. Over the more than two decades since, it has been reflected in the low rates of participation in the various elections held subsequent to 1991. These rates of participation have rarely exceeded 30 per cent of the electorate. The progressive rise in social movements marks this break in trust between the population and elite governance. This break has become more pronounced over time, reaching into the various segments of society, including political, civil, military and religious. Between 2011 and 2013, social struggles have involved unions, in mining areas in particular, and peasants. This has led to the latter organising more autonomously, in contrast to being supervised by the state's structures. But it is mainly the social strata composed of women and the youth who were at the basis of the dynamics noted. They were at the forefront of the social movements that led to the fall of the Amadou Toumani Touré regime in 2012. Their struggle questions the system of democratic representation, which appears to provide them with little space in decision-making concerning their future.

Introduction

The 1990s have been touted, often mistakenly, as the years of democratisation in Africa. This has largely contributed to a failure to take into account the impacts of social movements and resistance struggles in the changes that have occurred. More than two decades have passed and the assessment of the democratisation years is far from positive. The expectations aroused by democratisation have failed to materialise, thereby causing a general disrespect for the political class due to its disastrous management of power. This situation raises a number of questions to which this chapter attempts to provide some insights:

- Has the declining legitimacy of elites led to new forms of democratic participation and expression?

- Is the surge of social movements an expression of the quest, or even the demand, for new forms of democratic expression and participation?

- Does it present new challenges to the issue of representative democracy?

- What form will these social struggles take?

- Which social categories will be their spearhead? What political impacts will they have?

- What responses will be provided by the elites? What will be their limits? What alternatives are needed?

A historical untruth

A historical untruth suggests that, like many African countries, Mali first experienced a multiparty system and democracy only in the 1990s, following the collapse of the Berlin Wall and the La Baule conference.[1] Developed by a number of Western analysts, this theory overlooks many important points.

First, it suggests that Africa has for decades, even centuries, been a sort of virgin continent or *tabula rasa* where the winds of democracy have never blown. Thus, throughout their long history, African societies have reportedly ignored democracy. They are said to belong to mankind's 'barbarian' period of history, from which they were brutally lifted out of by the thunderclap of La Baule, which imposed on them a forced march towards democracy.

One should remember the July 2007 speech in Dakar by former French President Nicolas Sarkozy, which was largely inspired by the theses of the German philosopher Hegel (1770-1831) in his *Lectures on the Philosophy of History* (1830). In these writings, he pronounced that Africa was outside of the history of mankind, because it had not been visited by 'Universal Reason'.

However, many Western writers like the German ethnologist Leo Frobenius (1873-1938) have strongly contested the ideological basis of the claim that Europeans had found in Africa truly savage peoples to whom they allegedly brought civilisation. During several expeditions between 1904 and 1920, Frobenius collected a wealth of data on African civilisations, which served as a basis for the theory of Negritude of the Senegalese Léopold Sédar Senghor (1906-2001).

Following the constituent congress of the *Rassemblement Démocratique Africain* (African Democratic Rally, RDA) held in Bamako between 18 - 21 October 1946, its Sudan section, *Union Soudanaise* (Sudanese Union -

---

1 At the 16th conference of heads of state of Africa and France held in La Baule, France, French President François Mitterrand, in his 20 June 1990 speech, placed as a condition of collaboration with and support of France that changes be made in terms of democratisation and consolidation of the rule of law. Therefore, some believe that the so-called democratic changes (multiparty and pluralistic elections) that occurred were primarily due to the pressure from France towards its former colonies.

African Democratic Rally, USRDA) was formed on 22 October. It was the product of the merger between Mamadou Konaté's *Bloc Soudanais* (Sudanese Bloc), Modibo Keita's *Parti Démocratique* (Democratic Party) and Fily Dabo Sissoko's *Parti Progressiste* (Party for Solidarity and Progress, PSP). These different political groups had themselves been previously formed by the merger of former political groupings.

Mali's political history, therefore, tells us that the constitution of USRDA, the party of Modibo Keita that led to the independence of Mali in 1960, was the result of a merger process. The analysis of the various documents and texts of the period of the First Republic (1960 - 1968) shows that this party was criss-crossed by currents which often gave rise to fierce internal debates, or even crises. All these facts question the simplistic reading that Mali's democratic era only started in the 1990s. Reality shows something completely different.

Mali, for its part, had therefore experienced the multiparty system on the eve of independence. It is the very process of anti-colonial liberation struggle that led to the alliance, and then the merger of parties within the RDA, on the national and African regional level.

Secondly, the theory of La Baule is silent about the fierce resistance struggles of African populations, in this case Malian, against oppression and dictatorship and the huge sacrifices made for the advent of democracy. In fact, it was precisely these struggles that led Western leaders, under pressure in their own countries from public opinion which stood in solidarity with the resistance struggles, to distance themselves from, or in some cases denounce, the serious violations of public liberties committed for decades by regimes they had previously supported.

These struggles created a new situation, thereby contributing greatly to Western leaders forcing their different protégés to either make concessions or be swept aside by the growing popular revolts, as was the case in Mali in March 1991.

The history of the advent of democracy

The Malian case was a textbook example. In the face of the stubbornness of an age-old dictatorship, popular struggles surprisingly overcame a bloodthirsty and despotic regime after several months of riots. But although this was an example for oppressed African people, it considerably disrupted established patterns. Mali's example gave too much freedom and initiative to African populations in democratic conquests, hence the need to remove any revolutionary potential that might call into question the neo-colonial order and constitute an example for other countries. This is amply illustrated by what has been occurring since then in Mali and elsewhere in Africa, despite all the propaganda and the benevolent image of Malian democracy conveyed by the Western media.

The history of the advent of democracy in Mali has not been sufficiently researched. It was a long conquest that required painful sacrifices and was mainly the work of underground political activists who, in the face of the ferocity of repression, had worn several masks. They were thus prompted to engage in union activity and many other organisations such as humanitarian associations, human rights associations, women's associations, village or community-based associations, cultural associations and the like. Often putting their own lives at risk, they also became involved in the media, theatre, music and literature; in short all kinds of activities that could help inform, organise and mobilise the population. This three-pronged approach at political, union and association levels made it possible to mobilise all social segments. But beyond this, one of the main questions about African democracy remains that of the model. It influences many analyses about the foundations and conduct of the democratic process and about the contradictions and impasses faced by African populations, whose thirst for democracy clashes desperately with the hard daily realities. African people hoped that the advent of the democratic era would at last enable them to put an end to their oppression, and to participate in shaping their own future. But they were soon disillusioned. They realised that they had little chance of seeing any change in their situation. It was a huge deception. In most cases, the issue of democratisation was dealt with as a mere question of pomp, a mere legal-electoral issue.

In the early 1990s, popular struggles in countries such as Mali led to a violent reversal of the established order. In countries like Benin we witnessed a peaceful regime change through the ballot box (even if it subsequently led to the return to power of the former dictator through the same ballot box). Unfortunately, there are many cases in which former one-party dictatorships rapidly gave themselves a veneer of democracy under pressure of events, national and international public opinion, and their Western guardians.

There are many examples like Togo, Cote d'Ivoire, Burkina Faso, Gabon and elsewhere, where new tailor-made constitutions decreed a multi-party system and where equally tailor-made electoral codes ensured victory in advance even when elections where highly questionable or simply rigged. Docile opposition parties were created to allay suspicion during dubious elections in which more credible opposition parties refused to participate. Sometimes, these docile parties were so unrepresentative that they had to participate in the elections on the list of the presidential party, as was the case in Mali in 1997. Yet, they continued to qualify as opposition parties.

Judges with little independence were established in the highest courts to endorse election results. Voters who were frightened or had no real choice were bought with embezzled public funds and money accrued through corruption. Vote rigging was institutionalised and became an electoral technique for remaining in power.

For many current African regimes, democracy comes down to the multiparty system and elections. In this context, creating a party quickly becomes a *leitmotiv*, as it is the shortest way to be associated with the sharing of the cake. Hence, this has led to the mushrooming of political parties. There are currently more than 120 parties in Mali. In most cases, these parties operate under the former one-party model, largely drawing upon the political culture inherited from the previous dictatorial regime. They have no strategic vision, no debate of ideas and no government programme worthy of a name. The parties then become sounding boxes for personal ambitions, or coalitions of more or less sordid private interests. So, the new multiparty system has in fact generated a plethora of single parties.

Furthermore, the proliferation of budget-eating institutions, despite their supposed democratic functions, appears to be more of a response to the concern to 'cut a niche' for accomplices, to whom excessive privileges are granted, than a real will to create institutional balance in the exercise of power. This is painfully evidenced by unilateral presidential power in Mali for two decades, the confinement of the National Assembly to its role as rubber-stamp of the government's will, the corruption of political elites and their collusion with the business community and the impunity guaranteed by an increasingly instrumentalised legal power. There is no significant change in the conduct of public affairs, or the breathtakingly fast enrichment of the ruling elite in the face of the tragic and continuous impoverishment of the population. Hollow verbiage is taken for democratic expression. Electoral campaigns give rise to a display of financial and material resources which is an insult to the populations. In the end, huge amounts of money continue to be ploughed into electoral operations to satisfy the needs for a democratic parade. Meanwhile, priorities are elsewhere.

Lack of ideological identity becomes a general feature of political groups. The notions of left and right no longer have real meaning, even though some African parties eagerly affiliate with Socialist International or Liberal International. In the face of the de facto two-party system in the West, a 'plural one-party system' was established in Africa, thus giving content to the theory of liberal fascism of Subcomandante Marcos of the Chiapas in Mexico.

But the present failure of democratic expression in Mali and Africa cannot be reduced to the sole issue of the state, even if it is largely due to the greed, incompetence and mediocrity of those who aspire to manage it. This repeated failure forces us to raise questions about the model of democracy advocated. It forces us as Africans to take a mirror, look at ourselves and think about our current situation. It imposes on us a necessary theoretical independence that could enable us to devise our own way. This would take into account, of course, the positive experience of all humankind, international solidarity and respect for the positive cultural values of all people. Above all, it would need to appeal to Africa's own creative genius.

Similarly, the decentralisation model currently implemented in some countries, like Mali, should be reviewed and corrected in the light of African realities. In many cases, decentralisation appears to be like a gadget, conceived, imported, financed and implemented without taking into account the history, culture and mind-set of populations. It also seems to be part of the democratic showcase, and to have caused in many cases the rude awakening of local feudalities that have confiscated local votes almost everywhere in the newly created communes. Despite all these weaknesses, it could undoubtedly renew the democratic experience in our countries, if it were rethought.

Furthermore, the Senegalese example, which seems to put an end to the blind strategy of boycotts hitherto applied by African opposition parties, strongly challenges us. It brings back into fashion the issue of alternation of power in Africa, which is now a prospect. But at the same time, it poses the dangers of electioneering in which ill-assorted, or even unnatural coalitions may be formed with the sole objective of seizing power, as in previous elections in Mali. Yet, the future may be painful if no long-term solution is found to the key issue of: 'what to do with power?'

The so-called democratic management of power

From 1992 onwards, the so-called democratic management of power has followed a fairly chaotic path. Under Alpha Oumar Konaré's term in office, popular enthusiasm and generous activism seemed to open the floodgates of hope. But very rapidly, it turned into wreckage. Instead of confronting the problems, this president manoeuvred and sidestepped them. He abandoned many of his former comrades and opened his party to militants and officials of UDPM[2], the sole party at the time of dictatorship. In the face of the ever intensifying popular protest and escalating threats, he established what he called the 'concerted management of power'. He offered ministerial and other high administrative positions in the state apparatus to his opposition, and established a plethora of institutions to meet the strong demand for the sharing of power.

He promoted the setting up of many small parties allied to presidential power. He created a so-called moderate opposition which was elected at the legislative and communal elections on the lists of the majority party. Money and corruption became the privileged means to ensure the submissiveness of the political class. He promoted men and women who were more or less corrupt and often had no activist track-record. Disappointed, even disgusted, many political activists left the battle field. He prompted the emergence of some sort of 'spontaneous generation', a new political class that was going to be sustainably entrenched in the mysterious workings of power, and be the source of all the distortions and excesses of democracy in Mali.

Power struggles and individual ambitions led almost all the first parties to multiple and repeated divisions. Thus, ADEMA[3], the majority party, mainly

---

2   UDPM: Union Démocratique du Peuple Malien (Democratic Union of the Malian People), a constitutional single party created under the dictatorship of Moussa Traoré
3   ADEMA: Alliance pour la Démocratie au Mali (Alliance for Democracy in Mali), the party of Alpha Oumar Konaré

generated the MIRIA[4], the RPM[5] and then the URD[6]. As for the other major political union at that time, the CNID[7], which symbolised the opposition, it generated successively the PARENA[8], the BARA[9] and the SADI[10], among others, thereby deepening the process of division within political parties and the explosion in the number of parties. The dilution of the political game obviously suited those in power, who secretly encouraged the proliferation of political parties.

The second phase of Konaré's term was marked by progressive militarisation of the state administration. In the face of the flourishing number of senior officers and the lack of command in the army, many were promoted without having the required qualifications. The state's authority was gradually weakening while political racketeering and impunity reached alarming levels.

The end of this term was marked by the progressive and continuous weakening of political and civil society. The balance of power, which had previously been in their favour, was tilting slowly but surely in favour of military society. The growing number of political parties, the divisions ad infinitum, the sometimes unnatural alliances and counter-alliances, the political nomadism, the collusion between politics and business, and the widespread impunity had discredited the political class in the eyes of the people. Hence the continued erosion of the rate of participation in elections, which hardly reached 30 per cent in successive elections.

---

4   MIRIA: Mouvement pour l'indépendance, la révolution et l'Intégration Africaine (Movement for the Independence, Renaissance, and Integration of Africa), a party born out of the dissent with ADEMA, led by Prof. Mamadou Lamine Traoré

5   RPM: Rassemblement Pour le Mali (Rally for Mali), a breakaway ADEMA party led by Ibrahim Boubacar Keita, current President-elect of Mali

6   URD: Union pour la République et la Démocratie (Union for the Republic and Democracy), a breakaway ADEMA party led by Soumaïla Cissé, unsuccessful candidate of the last presidential elections.

7   CNID: Congrès National d'Initiative Démocratique (National Congress for Democratic Initiative), second large party created at the fall of the dictatorship, led by Maitre Mountaga Tall

8   PARENA: Parti de la Renaissance Nationale (Party for National Renewal), a breakaway of CNID led by Tiébilé Dramé

9   BARA: Bloc des Alternatives et de la Renaissance Africaine (Bloc of Alternative for the Renewal of Africa), a breakaway of CNID and PARENA led by Prof. Yoro Diakité

10   SADI: Solidarité Africaine pour la Démocratie et l'Indépendance, the African Solidarity for Democracy and Independence

Similarly, trade unions could not escape the same abuses. The associative movement, in particular the civil society movement, finally became contaminated too. Under these circumstances, the better organised military profited from the general disrepute of other segments of society. Thus, the road to power Amadou Toumani Touré (ATT) was going to take during the 2002 elections was being extended little by little, with the blessing of those in power and support from the West. Tired of its political class, the people applauded and ensured the triumph of military society over political society.

However, the new hope was short-lived. The state apparatus was stormed by the military society. The wheeler-dealer fever seized the military hierarchy and gangrened it just as quickly as it had with civil society. The key levers of the state administration were entrusted to the military. Government contracts and the lucrative sectors of the national economy ended up in their hands. And, above all, they were actively involved in networks of trafficking in goods, arms, ammunition, fuel, drugs and hostages. The weakening of state authority went along with widespread corruption and impunity.

Faced with difficulties and protests, ATT used the famous notion of 'consensus' that was coined by Moussa Traoré's UDPM. This consensus consisted of inviting all of the political class to the power feast. While Konaré had made and maintained a formal opposition, though it was often elected through skilful combination of the electoral lists, ATT simply dissolved it into the presidential majority of which everyone was now a member. Already when running in the election, he did not present himself as the candidate of a party, but passed himself off as an independent candidate. He did not want to be adversely affected by the unpopularity of the political class. His populism and political demagogy provided him with the support he needed. The ATT consensus alleviated all the conflicts and emptied the democratic game of its content, based on corruption. Every protester received a share, even though the power remained mostly in the hands of the army.

Instead of contributing to pacifying the country, the political gluttony increased popular frustration. In the face of many cases of injustice, popular discontent grew stronger. The risky management of power turned everyone against the government. Successive crises occurred. None was appropriately dealt with. State failure became all too apparent. The days of the ATT regime were now numbered. The shortcomings and extreme fragility of the regime were hidden by extreme de-politicisation of the population, de-unionisation of workers, dilution of checks and balances, and the takeover of the media by ruling party hacks.

Social movements and union struggles

However, ATT's last term in office was marked by many social battles. Protests were aroused in the union sector, such as over the implementation of Compulsory Health Insurance (*Assurance Maladie Obligatoire*, AMO) plan. While the idea appeared to be generous, its implementation left much to be desired. Drastic cuts were directly made to civil servant salaries, without corresponding to real service provision. Furthermore, the establishment of the administrative structure in charge of implementing the AMO led to recruitments based on convenience and the payment of unjustified bonuses, while workers saw no implementation of the commitments made. Thus, in May 2011, many trade unions, grouped around the *Confédération Syndicale des Travailleurs du Mali* (CSTM), organised protest marches in the streets of Bamako. They demanded an immediate end to the deductions, which had taken place over a six-month period, and the repayment of these deductions. They denounced on that occasion the cavalier manner in which the state conducted the AMO project, without consulting trade unions. To justify its stance, the government argued that it lacked information. However, the trade unions remained unmoved as to the legitimacy of the cuts in the already meagre wage earnings of their members. Similar initiatives obliged the authorities to reconsider the compulsory nature of the AMO. Partial repayment was made but the dispute is not totally settled.

Following this, the main trade union confederation of the country, *Union Nationale des Travailleurs du Mali* (UNTM), threatened to go on a 24-hour general strike if the government did not take action against the policemen of the new dissenting trade union which aligned with the slogans of CSTM during the protests of 1 May, Labour Day.

Similarly, the *Syndicat de l'Enseignement Supérieur* (Higher Education Union, SNESUP), in February 2011 initiated a general strike which lasted several months. It called for a review of the laws on higher education teaching staff and researchers, and the alignment of their wages with those of their counterparts in the sub-region. It also called for a new hierarchy in the sector.

It was indeed difficult for the government to justify the low level of wages in Mali while the country was supposed to be the third largest economy in the West African Economic and Monetary Union (WAEMU) zone, after Cote d'Ivoire and Senegal. In poorer countries like Burkina Faso and Niger, teacher salaries were twice that of Mali. In order to ease the protests, the state undertook commitments that were, as usual, applied only in part.

For over a decade now, schools in Mali appear to have been engaged in an endless crisis. Between teacher strikes and wildcat student strikes, the collapse of the education system has reached tremendous levels. It has now reached such a level of deterioration that its reorganisation seems unavoidable. But instead of facing the challenges, the authorities seem to equivocate and adopt the tactic of avoidance. Academic years of barely four to five months are validated, for want of political courage. Corruption in the school environment has become institutionalised. There is a deficit of professional ethics and poor academic and pedagogical skills on behalf of teachers. The declining level of trainers and learners is a hard reality. As years go by, Mali's diplomas lose their value on the labour market. The decline in the quality of human resources is felt in all sectors of activity, up to the highest level of the state apparatus. The findings are overwhelming.

Popular struggles in the mining sector

In the vital sectors of the national economy, social movements experienced unprecedented growth in the period 2011-2013 following a mining boom that led to the widespread allocation of major concessions. Thus in Faléa, in the south-western part of the country, adjacent to the Guinea and Senegal borders, the total area of the mining concessions granted exceeds that of the commune. In the Circle of Keniéba, which belongs to the commune of Faléa, land pressure in favour of mining concessions is such that farmers are losing their farmland, thereby being deprived of their livelihoods. The dwelling places, the areas that hosted their historical, cultural or religious heritage, are also threatened by the expansion of mining concessions. Former inhabitants, who are now landless peasants, are compelled to turn into a cheap daily workforce for the neighbouring mines. The precariousness of their living conditions, therefore, has plunged populations previously self-sufficient in food crops into the infernal cycle of uncertainty about the future. Promises made to these communities have never been fulfilled by the mine owners or the state. Instead, claims and protests have been met with brutal police repression. Abandoned by local authorities and sometimes by their locally-elected representatives, who were bought by the mining companies, they organised into associations, as in the case of ARACF (*Association des Ressortissants et Amis de la Commune de Faléa*), thereby forging numerous solidarity links throughout the mining area of the Kenieba Circle and sometimes even further afield. Their resistance struggles were covered by the media and known both nationally and internationally. Thus, support from Eva Joly and members of the European Parliament forced ATT to publicly give the assurance that exploration work would end. This had been responsible for releasing mud from drilling operations into the environment. The practice was responsible for contaminating the environment and threatening the health of local people.

But once again, promises were not upheld. The sale of mining concessions was accelerated during the transition period after the fall of ATT in 2012. A new mining code even more unfavourable to national interests was voted on behind closed doors by the government and the transitional parliament. Mining concessions were allocated at an increased rate, leading to enrichment that was as fabulous as it was spontaneous and that served as a war chest during the last presidential and legislative elections.

In the Circle of Kati, close to Bamako, 93 peasant organisations in the rural commune of Yékébougou formed the *Union des Associations et des Coordinations d'Associations pour le Développement et la Défense des Droits des Démunis au Mali* (Union of Associations and Coordination for the Development and Vindication of the Rights of Destitutes in Mali) to re-appropriate their farmlands allocated to the Chinese company COVEC for quarrying purposes. In a collective letter addressed in January 2011 to the governor of the region of Koulikoro and the prefect of Kati, they called for an immediate end to unilateral boundary-marking by the Chinese company and compensation for all those whose fields had been affected by COVEC's operations.

In March 2011, they sent a report to the president which was attached to a memorandum on the status of the resolution of land issues, which had previously been filed with the government. Following this, they submitted a letter containing a declaration to march in all places where they had offices across the national territory. Faced with their determination, the government set up an ad-hoc commission with the ministry in charge of territorial administration. In June 2011, COVEC was called by the prefect of Kati and notified of the immediate halt of work for non-compliance with standards, the lifting of the ban on cultivating in the area, and the compensation for farmers whose fields had already been affected by the company's activities.

Social movements and peasant struggles

While peasant organisations in Kati achieved success, this was not the case elsewhere. It was quite the contrary. During the Forum of the People held in Niono in late October 2011, peasant associations in the *Office du Niger* area, region of Ségou, made a deplorable assessment of the situation in the country. Following the neoliberal mantra of the World Bank and International Monetary Fund, the government had already sold over 700,000 hectares of farmland to foreign companies, foreign states and national investors. Lands that were formerly reserved for food crops were turned into production areas for export and fuel crops. The elimination of food crops led to an endemic food crisis in the region. The country moved from being food self-sufficient to a reliance on imports. Now landless, the peasant populations concerned engaged in resistance against the grabbing of agricultural lands.

Thus, in February 2012, the dispossessed peasants of the villages of Saou and Sanamadougou in the *Office du Niger* area engaged in a fierce resistance struggle against the company Moulin Moderne du Mali (3M). Despite the allocation of their farmland to a private operator, they went to the land as usual to grow millet, which is their staple food. More than 400 families had been living there for generations and they had lost their only source of income overnight. The company had previously obtained 7,400 hectares 30km away from the area in question. Over time and with support from the state, it absorbed the lands of the peasants of Sanamadougou. On the request of the authorities, the police bluntly expelled the peasants from their land, molesting women, children and the elderly. The brutal repression caused casualties.

The customary law which is recognised in Chapter III of Mali's Land Tenure Code (*Code domanial et foncier*) allows peasants to retain the lands they have been farming since well before colonisation. In the worst-case scenario, it opens the way for compensation. However, the rights of local peasants, who had been living on the land from generation to generation in their centuries-old villages, did not count for much in the face of agribusiness investment. The agribusiness projects that were established in the region were mostly for the production of agro fuels made from sugarcane, jatropha, sunflower, soya or rice, and foodstuffs for export.

Previously, over 60 per cent of the rice consumed in Mali was produced by some 50,000 family farmers on the 100,000 cultivated hectares of the *Office du Niger*. Peasants in Saou and Sanamabougou produced surplus millet which enabled them to donate 60 tonnes to the state for the drought-affected northern regions of Mali. They were nevertheless brutally expelled from their land. They took the case to the Markala tribunal which, in March 2013, gave a verdict in favour of agribusinesses. The resulting massive exodus of the youth deprived the population of its workforce. In protest, the Malian Convergence against Land Grabbing (*Convergence Malienne contre l'Accaparement des Terres*) organised the establishment of a 'landless village' at the foot of the administrative city, the seat of the government. The land issue remains completely deadlocked in the *Office du Niger* area.

However, peasant social movements continued to gain momentum despite the repression. In the wake of popular resistance struggles against the steamroller of frenzied liberalisation of vital sectors of the national economy, dictated by structural adjustment programmes, a new peasants union was created in February 2012, the *Syndicat des Paysans du Mali/Terre-Travail-Dignité* (SYPAM/TTD). It was a major turning point in social struggles, especially those of the peasantry. Its fundamental objectives were, according to the statutes of the organisation, to ensure access to land, agricultural inputs, agricultural credits and strong and sustainable support to peasant women. Indeed, the creation of an autonomous union marked a change from the producer groups, village associations and other structures that were more or less supervised by state structures.

The political forces and even the press ignored or pretended to ignore these social struggles. Only Radio Kayira and some local media opened their airwaves and columns. The organic and sometimes underground link which had existed between political forces (except for some opposition parties like SADI), trade unions and civil society organisations, which had largely contributed to the fall of Moussa Traoré's dictatorship, was thus broken. The democratic fever that had swept across the country seemed to have stopped at the doors of the countryside.

The religious offensive

It is in the context of repeated social crises and an ever increasing school failure rate among the youth, that a third phenomenon, that of the religious society, appeared. First an interface during the crises within the political class, it became the natural arbitrator of conflicts between the state and its citizens. It was even entrusted with the presidency of the *Commission Electorale Nationale Indépendante* (Independent National Electoral Commission, CENI). Becoming increasingly aware of its influence because its meetings could fill stadiums whereas other political parties no longer mobilised, it raised its voice during the vote of the law on the Family Code. In the view of religious society, this gave too many rights to women. By mobilising the population, it forced the government to withdraw and review the new code.

This victory marked a political turning point which saw religious society emerge into the political arena. The vacuum left by the disrepute of political, civil and military society gave it wings, thereby providing it with a pretext for playing an increasingly pivotal role in the political arena. With the 'Arab Revolutions' and the accession to power of the Islamists in Tunisia, Morocco and Egypt, it thought that it could now play a major political role in Mali. State power seemed to be smiling on it in the run up to the 2012 elections. It was sure to have won the elections, had it not been for the 22 March 2012 coup following the Jihadist offensive. This and the French military intervention in January 2013 disturbed its projects and agenda.

It was during ATT's term in office that the religious associations achieved an unprecedented proliferation and grip on power. Faced with social crisis and growing discontent, ATT thought to use the religious people, first in political conflicts and then systematically. They became the regime's firemen. In return, he gave them free rein in taking control of the ideological outlook of the country. Associations representing young Muslims sprouted up everywhere. Consciences were systematically formatted. In the face of despair and lack of alternatives, the spiritual drug was effective. Koranic schools and Madrasas were established even in the remotest villages, often to the detriment of public schools.

The economic impasse and difficulties of everyday life threw into their arms youth left behind by the political class. The religious leaders recruited them on a large scale and made them their *talibés* (Koranic school pupils). From public spaces in the neighbourhood, they came to occupy stadiums. Every meeting was a show of force. Politicians who were jealous of their capacity to mobilise courted them. Political parties rushed to figure prominently at the side of religious leaders. They hoped to be able to take advantage and manipulate them. But it was a different story. They ended up absorbing the political class. As their appetite grew, they started to cast an eye on state power, with which they did not hesitate to cross swords with in January 2011, during the vote of the new Family Code. The government's retreat and the revision of a code already voted on by parliament consecrated their triumph. Power seemed to be smiling on them.

The occupation of the northern part of the country made them the sole interlocutors of the invaders. They were the only ones who could convoy humanitarian aid into the area. The head of the High Islamic Council became a privileged interlocutor at the national and regional level. His status of key political player was now recognised and accepted by all. The upcoming elections at the end of ATT's term in office seemed to be an easy ride for them. The future looked rosy.

The youth burst onto the stage

The 22 March 2012 coup threw youth and women into the street. In fact, it is the strong and repeated protests of these two categories that caused the fall of ATT's regime. Following the massacre of young soldiers at Aguelhok by joint MNLA, Ansar Dine and AQMI Islamist troops, the wives, children and parents of the defenceless soldiers who had their throats slit and were eviscerated, protested against the passivity or complicity of the regime. There were public denunciations directly blaming the head of state and the military high command. The Aguelhok massacre was the last straw that broke the camel's back.

The mutiny by young soldiers, which took place between 20-21 March 2012, brought to light their lack of wellbeing and the breakdown of the chain of command. Their march towards the Presidential Palace to protest and denounce the wheeling and dealing of their leaders led to the fall of the regime. They were the first to be surprised. Everywhere throughout the national territory they were applauded.

The youth followed in their footsteps and all the rancour that had accumulated over the years exploded. The spontaneity and scope of the demonstrations surprised many foreign observers. The population rapidly joined the putschists, who had succeeded in sweeping away the ATT regime without bloodshed and with disconcerting ease.

Youth groups organised in associations sprang up and monopolised public speaking without waiting for permission. Some camped in front of the seat of parliament and denied access to some deputies, who were considered as the accomplices of the defunct regime. Others burned down the labour exchange offices where the leaders of UNTM[11] and some leaders of political parties belonging to the presidential camp gathered to denounce the coup. They owed their salvation to their speed.

---

11 UNTM: Union Nationale des Travailleurs du Mali

The protest march against the power grab spoke for itself. A human tide invaded the streets of Bamako. It was obvious even for ECOWAS that the ATT page had to be definitively turned. Almost daily marches were the main feature of popular expression and took place against ECOWAS dictates, the threats of foreign military intervention and against the restoration forces. The break between the population and the political elites which were in its eyes the accomplices of the tragedy that occurred seemed to be an accomplished fact.

The much touted democratic model exploded in the face of those who had promoted it by showcasing it at the African level.

While political activists under Moussa Traoré's dictatorship had invested in the social movements, helping them build political awareness in the global context of the democratic struggles of that time, this is not the case today. The new political elites who came to power following the 1991 popular revolts have over time become the sometimes zealous advocates of the neoliberal policies they once criticised. Their betrayal, their staggering enrichment, impunity and their alignment with privatisation policies convinced social movements to organise their own space of autonomous thinking and action. Thus new organisations were born from the ashes of the hegemony of political elites who had betrayed popular expectations.

Outlining another alternative

But what should be done in the face of the current impasse? In Africa, we are condemned to thinking about these and many other issues, as we are obliged to conceive our own way. Inventing the future is the price to be paid for true democratisation of Africa. Partisan democracy seems to be losing ground throughout the world. In contrast, direct democracy, that of the grassroots, seems to still be in its infancy.

The West itself is also in need of democracy. This can be seen everywhere in the rampant corruption of the political class, the lack of ideals, the lack of leaders able to galvanise people, the growing lack of popular interest in electoral contests and the making of promises that are never kept. The global 'democratic' order is increasingly contested worldwide, and especially in the West itself, as evidenced by the *Indignados* movement /Occupy movement across Europe and elsewhere.

The present world situation forces us to ask lucid and insightful questions if we are to give humanity a chance to get out of its distressing situation. What matters most is correct problem-setting in developing a reflection that is both global and satisfactory. This should not be left solely to intellectuals. We should involve the masses in determining the conditions for reformulating the issues and alternatives to be outlined. They must be invited to initiatives aimed at acting together to change the world. Our creed should be 'think together to act together'.

However, no question can be formulated without shedding light on the status of the world as it is today in the North and South. In the early 21st century, humanity has experienced significant progress in science and technology, which in many respects has revolutionised the conditions of production. Today, there is sufficient wealth across the world to meet the fundamental needs of people everywhere. So why, despite all of this, does extreme poverty, destitution, disease and hunger continue to plague all of the continents?

In countries of the North, economies are constantly faced with growing crises, leading to the bankruptcy of an increasing number of businesses and causing the painful experience of unemployment and precariousness for households. Statistics show a high number of unemployed people across industrialised countries.

Men are feeling bad about their maleness. Women suffer by virtue of their femaleness. Men and women aspire to change their sex. Same-sex couples are formed and claim their right to legally establish a household and adopt children. The same applies for single-parent families. Similarly, one-childhouseholds are imposed by economic planners, thereby dooming society to ignore any feelings of brotherhood or solidarity.

Individualism, set up as the foundation of human rights principles, has profoundly dismantled the structure of society and created increasingly wide spaces of solitude and despair. Violence, drug usage and insecurity are growing in scale. High rates of suicide among young and elderly people attest to the scope of the human disaster to which recent progress has led. From bankruptcy to bankruptcy, Western states wage wars of aggression.

In the South, despite the world's immense wealth, poverty has increased, especially in African countries. This has obliged international institutions to launch urgent programmes for combating poverty, reducing or cancelling debt. The disintegration of the social fabric and loss of cultural identity has resulted in a lack of prospects and increasingly pronounced pessimism about the future. The situation in the North as well as in the South raises questions about the fate of human beings. What should be done in such circumstances?

There appears to be a strong need for the reconstruction of the world in a way that can allow human beings to dream again. In the construction of these new alternatives, Africa has a chance to be at the forefront and to lead the epic story of the theoretical reconstruction of a new and more promising world, owing in particular to the pressing challenges it faces.

Northern countries are relatively sleepy because of their material comfort and the 'rationalising' certainties they have reached, even if increasingly larger sections of their societies are protesting ever more violently against the imposed social order. As an example, a key indicator of this was the rejection in 2005 by the French and Dutch people of the project of a European constitution. It included the demand for social reconstruction of Europe on a more humane basis. The movement of the *indignados* throughout the

Northern countries has shown the limits of the present global system and the need for alternatives.

African countries are certainly faced with the same problems that are arguably more acute because of their material destitution. Failure of donor-imposed structural adjustment programmes, over-indebtedness beyond any ability to pay, privatisation policies that have thrown to the streets household heads upon whom the survival of many people often depended, difficult access to employment for many young graduates, accelerated plunder of raw materials, extreme poverty, injustice and oppression have all produced a potential for social explosion.

With the acuteness and urgency of the situation, we Africans are compelled to find new and smart responses that are likely to answer the questions of the day. But this is possible only with a break with the present global system. We do not pretend here to give ready-made and definitive answers but to contribute to outlining possible solutions. Building alternatives requires all existing models underlined with the framework of liberal globalisation to be rejected.

The current model of integration, the European one, seems to be unproductive and stalled. European integration has been achieved through the construction of a common market, because the problem here was not production, but organisation of the area in which produced goods were allowed to flow. The market issue had already led to two world wars. There was therefore a pressing need for Europe to organise the European market's exchange area.

As for African integration, while it is often formulated in terms of creating a solidarity-based area to face the challenges of globalisation, it actually offers no future prospect. All it offers Africa is for it to take an eternal position as a reservoir of cheap raw materials. This is because it fails to highlight the issue of the need to construct a protected area for the production of wealth based on in-situ processing of its own raw materials, no longer for the global market, but to meet the priority needs of its own populations.

Recent events in Africa, including successive constitutional restructurings aimed at quenching the thirst for power of civil-military cliques supported by Western governments and rigged elections making impossible any real alternation of power, all create the conditions for looming civil wars. The decentralisation models have also awakened the appetite of local potentates who try to take democracy away from the grassroots, if necessary through the use of weapons, like the warlords in Kidal.

In Africa and across the world, the model of liberal democracy is leaking. It has provided the foundation to an international 'mediocracy' that has seized state power everywhere. Nowadays, white-collar delinquency holds financial power throughout the world. The will to power in the North is increasingly reflected in all sorts of unilateral decisions, or even in military expeditions to subjugate peoples to the sole interests of multinational companies, as is the case today in Mali and Central Africa. Which country is next on the list?

Civil society action is increasingly faced with the arrogance of the powers in place. While it had aroused certain hopes, today the question of their ultimate purpose is relevant, particularly in Africa, where local policymakers do not care about the opinions of their own populations and only pay attention to the instructions of western sponsors. Acting on the field of social struggles is no longer enough. Civil society organisations are, of course, essential. They are the key locus of information, awareness, organisation and mobilisation of peoples.

Today, civil society in Africa and elsewhere runs into the wall of politics in their day-to-day activities. The question of political power, of state power and its nature, is then posed more and more clearly. Should civil society continue to refrain from political action, as it has done so far? Should it not consider other alternatives? The problems it faces are political in nature. Their resolution will necessarily entail political leverage. Increasingly, African civil society is becoming aware of the need for people to take control of political decision-making if they are to solve the problems they face. It has become urgent to think about how this will be done, and no longer make it the sole preserve of political parties.

Nowadays, political parties, the partisan model at the global level, are losing momentum. Their reconstruction will entail increasingly close collaboration with civil society. This imposes on them drastic changes. Political parties must no longer be more or less sordid coalitions for individual promotion. Politics itself must be changed into an instrument for addressing the questions citizens are asking themselves.

Examples in Latin America

In Latin America, new systems of democratic delegation have been imposed by the populations of some countries. The elected officials are no longer the representatives who decide on matters in the place of the people, who no longer want to entrust their destiny to a handful of elected officials, but want to decide their own fate. Highly innovative experiments in the democratic management of society have been put on the agenda by popular revolts. Venezuela, Bolivia and elsewhere make Latin America a very interesting social laboratory for countries in Africa, in the South or across the world.

The lack of interest in so-called democratic systems that are in place around the globe is more than obvious. But it is a historic necessity that populations enter onto the political stage. The day they are aware of the fact that it is their lack of interest, their indifference to politics that is the main cause of their problems, they will, once they start moving, be like the steamroller that will sweep aside the present world and impose a new, fairer and more humane world. In fact, today, only truly democratic creativity can positively and sustainably renew the democratic experience globally. It should not be left to the political elites, especially the Western ones. On the contrary, the people should appropriate the politics. To reinvent democracy or perish, such is the democratic challenge facing all of us today.

CHAPTER: 9

CRISIS, REPRESSION AND SOCIAL UNREST IN GUINEA-BISSAU

Fernando Leonardo Cardoso and Fodé Mané

Guinea-Bissau's history of resistance to colonial rule has played an important part in the development of contemporary social movements. These movements should be understood not only through an examination of large demonstrations, but also through an awareness of the different forms of resistance adopted by people whose rights and freedoms are violated.

Whenever social unrest is mentioned in Guinea-Bissau, our minds go back to the colonial period. Let us remember, for example, the Guinean League, set up in 1910, and the sporting and cultural club led by Amilcar Cabral in the early 1950s, the existence of which incidentally expedited his deportation to Angola. These two organisations were a warning to the colonial government of Lisbon: they signalled an organised protest against the state of oppression and poverty in which the average Guinean was living.

The struggle for independence against Portuguese colonial domination in the 1960s originated from several movements, which in the end merged into various national liberation movements. These were the PAIGC (*Parti Africain pour l'Indépendance de la Guinée et du Cap Vert*), which eventually came to lead the struggle for independence fought by Guinean and Cape Verdean nationalists that successfully resulted in the political independence of the two nations, and FLING (*Front de Libération Nationale de la Guinée*), which is currently confronted with problems of continuity as a political party in the context of multiparty democracy.

Guinea-Bissau's multi-ethnic nature and historical processes have influenced the evolution and dynamics of social movements in recent years. In his analysis of the different social groups and their contribution to the anti-colonial process, Cabral (1975) has shown that people's involvement in the struggle depended on their interests and social status. He united the different ethnic groups into two kinds of organisations, one that he described as a vertical society, and the other as a horizontal one. While in vertical or hierarchical societies, people act according to their class interests; in horizontal societies, apparently unstratified, the involvement in social movements is based on their internal organisation in relation to factors like age and disposal or ownership of land and cattle.

Nowadays, social movements are characterised by the diversity of the organisational forms and protests which concern social categories such as young people and the working class. By meetings and demonstrations or denouncing certain situations, vigils, radio debates, talks and conferences in youth camps, Guineans call for better living and working conditions. Women constantly speak out against the hardship of the political situation and the rising crime rate.

Socio-political context

We cannot understand the present socio-political context unless we reach into the past to analyse the crisis which undermined Guinea-Bissau at the end of the 1990s. That period was marked by the civil war which lasted almost a year and ended in the fall of João Bernardo 'Nino' Vieira and the setting up of a transitional government led by Francisco José Fadul. Due to the then economic and social crisis (characterised by a shortage of basic necessities, electricity shortages, widespread political instability, differences within the PAIGC and divergences between that political party and the army) the post-civil war period was marked by repeated claims demanding the normalisation of political life and the setting up of a legitimate government.

It was in such a context of social conflict that elections were organised, which were won by the PRS (Party for Social Renovation) of Kumba Yala, who set up a government legitimised by universal suffrage. Still, the economic and social crisis worsened, and consequently strikes and other forms of social unrest were rampant. Some years later, in 2003, Kumba Yala was overthrown by a coup, leading again to a transitional government headed by Henrique Pereira Rosa until new elections, this time won by Vieira, despite the fact that PAIGC backed Malam Bacai Sanhá as candidate.

Vieira's government was subject to strong social and political pressures, with waves of strikes and protests. What was outstanding during this period, with serious implications for the political, social and economic life of the country, was the 'cold war' between the president and the prime minister, Carlos Gomes Jr., who owed his legitimacy to his majority in parliament. It should be remembered that in the presidential election won by Vieira in 2005, the PAIGC had backed Malam Bacai Sanhá as candidate. The frequent disputes between the leaders of the two organs of sovereignty would have a tragic end. Vieira finally sacked the government led by Carlos Gomes Jr. on 31 October 2005. In 2009, a new wave of assassinations became rampant. Vieira was assassinated by unidentified men, a few hours after the chief of staff of the armed forces was murdered. This upsurge in violence was followed by popular uprisings demanding justice and social stability. Some relatives of Vieira called for clarification on his assassination while the widows of veterans who had fought during the national liberation struggles of 1963-1974 appealed for an end to assassinations. Many demonstrations were organised for peace and against impunity, the climate of prevailing violence and the persecution of citizens.

Following Vieira's assassination, new elections were organised in June 2009 and were won in the runoff by Sanhá. Physically weakened, he finally died in the middle of his term in 2011. Raimundo Pereira, who until then had served as chairman of the National People's Assembly, took over as interim president. The frequent political changes, fragility and instability of the different organs of sovereignty permitted the consolidation of power and influence of a portion of the armed forces, which, in turn, triggered the reaction of civil society through protest movements.

In this context, the stronger the power of the army became, the less respected human rights were. Violence and criminality were more and more rampant and the authority of the state was felt less and less. The head of state, acting *ad interim*, had limited constitutional powers. At the National People's Assembly, MPs did not agree because they had different views on how to deal with the political, economic and social crisis. The prime minister, without significant powers and with no authority, despite legitimacy derived from the elections, had made himself a hostage of the army. On many occasions they had defied him in public. In practice, power was in the hands of a dozen soldiers, which widened the disintegration of the state, making the social crisis more serious. It was at this period that Guinea-Bissau started to be labelled throughout the world as a narco-state, a country used as a route for drug smuggling and as a hideout for drug traffickers.

In these circumstances, social problems (such as youth unemployment, drug consumption, prostitution, lack of training opportunities and lack of social infrastructures) became more acute. Criminality, especially among young people, became rampant. In response to concerns around these issues, repression from the authorities has tended to increase.

Social movements and struggle between 2011 and 2013

There are different views on the dynamics of social movements. Marti i Puig, writing about the Latin American experience, refers to big rallies coordinated and organised around common goals. The vision of Habermas is perhaps more suited to the struggles seen in Guinea-Bissau, however, as he regards a social movement only as a way to guarantee the right of communication and political participation (Hamel 2009). The little room that representative democracy concedes to young people and women, notwithstanding the large number of voters among these two social classes, leads us to consider the different forms of organisation as an expression of political objectives based on common interests.

Social movements must be placed in a given context. There has to be a claim or an objective likely to reunite a social class or a group of individuals without taking the form of a conventional political organisation to consider that we are in the presence of a social movement. Nowadays, the best way of analysing social movements in Guinea-Bissau is to do so through the youth movements in view of the weight of their participation, their positioning and their reaction to political, economic and social crises.

According to the Guinean legal system, entities can group together into associations, foundations or companies. The classification of each of these groupings depends on the institutional model and the stated purposes. Civil service organisations take up as a kind of association in the light of the definition of a non-profit grouping sharing the same goals. On this basis, private law associations, which are development-oriented and involved in the protection of human rights and the environment, are called non-government organisations (NGOs), in opposition to those created by the government as forms of decentralisation and devolution of the administration. Remember that many organisations are the result of informal initiatives and have themselves been legalised by state institutions. Today, the main organisations of civil society are:

- The National Movement of the Civil Society for Peace and Development is a platform of many organisations created just after the 1998/99 civil war. It is a forum for consultation and enables civil society to speak with one voice;

- The Guinean League of Human Rights;

- The National Union of Teachers;

- The Association Against Female Genital Mutilations and Child Trafficking.

Officially and by definition, these organisations have no party affiliation. However, due to the heterogeneity of the militants, who come from every social background with sometimes divergent interests, it is no wonder that many actions are greatly impacted by the interests and positioning of leaders of the organisation or, if not, by natural opinion leaders who manage to manipulate or influence certain opinions.

Let us take as an example the issue of assassinations. Some assassinations benefitted from wide coverage. Demonstrations and waves of protests were organised, communiqués were issued and requirements were set out to the government. By contrast, others did not prompt any reactions (for example, the march organised by the relatives of victims of assassinations, the conflicts of competence between the Public Prosecutor'soffice and the Military Court, complaints filed by the families of late Helder Proenca and Baciro Dabo against the former Prime Minister Carlos Gomes Jr). There are cases where the attitude of organisations is clear-cut, whilethey have very little presence for others. It is as if certain actions of civilsociety are carried out according to the individual or government in power. The same applies to trade-unions. There are times when strikes and other protests are more frequent, giving the impression that they are ordered and well orientated.

Social movements can be in the form of strikes, political protests against assassinations, meetings and demonstrations against the disappearance of political personalities such as Roberto Cacheu (leader of PAIGC and a former member of the government), and uprisings against the army's harmful misbehaviour. The Civil Society Movement for Peace and Democracy, in the face of violations of fundamental rights and freedoms - especially the right to demonstrate - by the political and military authorities, has chosen other forms or struggle: meetings of various associations and organisations, direct contact with the authorities, issuing of communiqués, some in the form of leaflets, and broadcasts of images or sounds speaking out against cases of violations.

The increasing number of social struggles and the struggles of the working class during the last two years is also part of the vitality of social movements. Some of these struggles have a radical aspect, like the frequent and lasting strikes of teachers and healthcare professionals. Their main characteristic resides in their capacity to mobilise all the unions of one sector into a single movement aimed not only at claiming the payment of salaries and the improvement of working conditions, but also at revolting against the political situation.

We can better understand these struggles if we know that freedom of association and the right to strike are relatively new phenomena; they are contemporary with the advent of multiparty democracy in the early 1990s. The upsurge and diversity of socio-political struggles can also be interpreted as a token of the distrust and divergences between political parties and civil society. As a matter of fact, it is clearly discernable in the last few years the existence of a dividing line between the different segments of civil society on the one hand and the political and military circles on the other. These last two social segments, the political and the military one, are great accomplices and shoulder responsibility for the present context of social, political and economic crisis.

The radicalism of the social fights led by the above-mentioned unions does not refer to violence, but to the formalisation of a great number of claims. Between 20-30 requirements can be found in the memorandum of demands, some of which are difficult to meet in the stated timeframe. Protest strategies can therefore be seen as ways of hindering the authorities and fostering social revolts of many kinds against the same power, since it is sometimes obvious, in the very eyes of the trade unions, that it is impossible to satisfy the points laid down in their demands. A case in point is the salary scale in the public service, where the levels required by the trade unions are far beyond available funds. Many strikes of that kind were successful and have given expected results (payment of wage arrears, benefits, etc). Following these strikes, some student associations merged into a Confederation of Bissau-Guinean Students which staged various protest actions.

Among movements of a social nature, the general strike called by the syndicate affiliated to UNTG (The National Union of Workers in Guinea-Bissau/*l'Union Nationale des Travailleurs de Guinée*) in late 2010, is worth mentioning. This strike was the result of the stalemate in the Permanent Council for Social Concertation, a dialogue structure between the government, employers and trade-unions. It was a strike that essentially affected the health and education sectors while the strikes of CSI (*Confédération des Syndicats Indépendants*/Confederation of Independent Unions) have had more impact on telecommunications and transport.

It is worth noting that none of the general strikes called by unions in recent years took place over an extended period of time. They have been stopped after a round of negotiations that resulted in the signing of agreements between the unions and the government. Such a fact can be understood as an indicator of the strength and impact of labour movements, which manage to make the government yield on specific claims. Even in the case where the government seems to be indifferent, the claims end up showing positive results for the strike calls are not lifted, even though they last one month or more. The government then feels obliged to sit down at the negotiation table to satisfy all or part of the demands. A recent case that has marked the labour movement was the strike of the union of teachers of secondary schools. This strike lasted more than 30 days, between 17 September and 1 November 2012, and had to be extended until the government agreed to satisfy the demands. The strike, in addition to the review of the salary scale, promoted teaching careers and payment of distance allowances and newly recruited teachers, among other issues. Even though the strike did not reach all of its objectives, it was a serious warning for the government and the call to strike was lifted only for reasons related to the suffering of students' parents, according to the National Union of Teachers, headed by Luis Nancassa. Parents and education authorities spared no effort in offering to mediate between the government and the teachers, especially in cases where the situation threatened to become worse.

Social pressures can take more original forms. Television channels portrayed more and more citizens suffering from diseases. In these cases the government felt obliged to act through, for instance, the funding of medical evacuations or grants for treatment abroad.

It would not be an exaggeration to affirm that all these movements, expressing themselves through demonstrations, strikes and other claims by different socio-professional organisations, female associations and legal and natural persons, are embodied by the achievements of the Guinean League of Human Rights (GLHR), presently led by the jurist Luis Vaz.

The GLHR has taken on the role of championing human rights and putting pressure on the government. Its energetic intervention at the political as well as judicial and legal levels has sometimes seen it confused with that of a big opposition party. Its actions have changed many decisions and positions of the government, especially in cases of alleged political prosecutions and imprisonments.

Pressure on the government by the Association of Importers and Exporters and the Association of Merchants and Retailers has influenced trade policy and resale price policy in Guinea-Bissau. As an example, the successful commercialisation of the cashew nut, the main export product, or the setting of the sale price of rice, a staple food product, resulted from the agreement which the government and these organisations reached in order to avoid uprisings in 2011 when the trade ministry finally lowered the price of staples.

These examples emphasise the variety but also the plurality of social movements and political, social and economic struggles waged in Guinea-Bissau in the face of an adverse political situation.

Politicians find it difficult to understand the degree to which social movements and struggles evolve. That is why they think they can suppress them by restricting the freedom to demonstrate. Indeed they are not aware of the long political experience gained from the anti-colonial struggle where the harshness of the institutions and laws were not able to prevent the struggle of different social movements.

These social struggles also have a significant impact in rural areas where the population is bigger and thus the state of shortages of food products and drinking water more important. Demonstrations and other claims, such as those laid down by teachers and health technicians, have benefitted from the solidarity and support of the whole Guinean population, which confirms that movements are not restricted to the capital. Moreover, the main civil society organisations to which we have referred have local branches and deep roots throughout the country. Beyond local membership of struggle movements, the rural population itself is organised into associations for the defence of their interests.

Another form of popular participation in political life is related to parliamentary and presidential elections. On that occasion, different communities voice their claims and ambitions. There are real opportunities for the Guinean electorate to urge the different political parties to put forth their ideas and to defend their claims.

Slightly more than half of the 700,000 voters are sentimentally linked to a party, which means that nearly half of the population who are of voting age are not party members. Some communities threaten not to vote if their claims are not satisfied. Claims in general refer to road repair and road access, supply of basic goods and building of necessary facilities.

The assertion of these claims does not always produce the expected effects due to poverty levels, especially in rural areas. In exchange for a few francs, many end up selling their votes, forgetting the demands of the whole community. The buying of votes is widespread, so the pressure exerted by the population is very limited.

The 'bancadas' as a socio-political movement of the young

Socio-political struggles of the last three years cannot be separated from the forms of organisation prevailing among young people, forms in which the *bancadas* are very important. The *bancadas*, a Portuguese word meaning places equipped with steps where one can sit, are inspired by the tradition of meeting under big trees (the *bantabás*). People of different ages meet there to talk about subjects concerning the community. In this case, there are no marches and people get together at the same level and enjoy the same rights.

The *bancadas* appeared in the late 1990s and at the beginning of 2000. The country was then going through a difficult social, political and economic situation and the *bancadas* were spaces where idle young people met to discuss music and football. As time went by, the debates diversified and finally became more about issues related to the national political life. The *bancadas* have introduced new themes concerning the political and military crises in the country. These gatherings aim not only at bringing the young together, but also at discussing issues raised by the times of crisis. It is also a way of getting around restrictions laid down on freedom of movement and expression. Within the context of these dynamics, *bancadas* of young people with political orientations and positions started to appear. There were cases of persecution and the beating of young people because of the political attitudes they assumed. These youth movements did not go unnoticed by politicians, who soon tried to win their support by creating movements or small groups of independents, who became very active on the Guinean political scene.

At the end of 2011 and the beginning of 2012, a new strategy and form of social movement appeared. This consisted of a union of some *bancadas* and a setting up of an association which later led to an NGO platform that ensured a diversified and unbiased political intervention. A more concrete example of this strategy was the involvement of the National Network of Young People and a coalition of civil society organisations in demonstrations against the coup of 12 April 2012, and their participation in the National Front Against Coups.

Due to the constant threat that demonstrations would be cracked down on, these associations and platforms adopted other forms of struggle such as the organisation of meetings and talks, radio debates and the diffusion of messages on social networks.

Apart from *bancadas*, we can give the example of the inhabitants of Antula on the outskirts of Bissau, who protested against pollution caused by the building firm contracted to build the road that links their zone to the city centre. A similar example was the case of semi-urban transport drivers (toca-toca) from the district of Enterramento, who interrupted their service to protest against the deterioration of the roads. Another example is provided by the protest against garbage dumps and other waste created by the Bissau city council. Due to the vastness of the district, Antula, like in other districts of the capital, organised into associations, each dealing with a specific issue.

Conclusions

A history of more than a century of traditional resistance in Guinea-Bissau allowed the unification of many liberation movements around the PAIGC. That long period of collective consciousness building impacted on the development of contemporary social movements. Interests started to become more and more convergent while unions increased in size.

Today, organising and rallying people to a cause is no longer very difficult, as the regular mobilisations against the excessive harvestingof timber, especially in the eastern side of the country, have shown. A platform of civil society movements against timber exploitation has been set up with the massive participation of traditional authorities and religious leaders. Although the process of forest degradation and the practice of illegal timber export have not stopped, signs of improvement are starting to appear. The platform has resulted in more discreet logging operations so as to avoid frequent disputes at village level. In Bissau, programs and radio debates are organised on this subject. The results are so evident that even government structures are involved in discussions. In the cases of the director general of forests and the secretary of state for the environment, both have affirmed their determination to fight the plague of timber exploitation, under threat of losing their posts.

In spite of these examples, we have to conclude that social movements still act on a very small scale. This is essentially due to the socio-political context and the crackdown faced by those making claims. However, they gradually manage, through the platforms established, to develop into a more organised and participatory social movement. The different forms of expression of social movements show unequivocally that the forms of struggle depend on the kind of right involved. The different forms of expression of social movements reinforce the relationship between one form of struggle and the rights claimed. It is becoming more and more obvious that not all forms of struggle can have the same characteristics and that the union of efforts in one struggle depends on the collective character of the rights claimed. For that, the study of social movements must not be limited to big demonstrations and struggles. The movements must be analysed according to the way people react in the face of situations in which their rights and freedom are violated and affected.

References

Cabral, Amílcar (1975) *Unité et lutte 1. L'arme de la théorie; textes réunis par Mario de Andrade,* Paris, F. Maspero

Hamel, Marcio Renan (2009) Movimientos sociais e Democracia Participativa, May, http://gajop.org.br/justicacidada/wp-content/ uploads/Movimentos-Sociais-e-Democracia-Participativa-M%C3%A1rci-Renan-Hamel2.pdf, accessed March 2014

INEP (1997) *Estudos Nacionais Prospectivos a Longo Termo,* Instituto Nacional de Estudos e Pesquisa, Guinea-Bissau

Martí i Puig, Salvador (n.d.) Los Movimientos Sociales, http://campus. usal.es/~dpublico/areacp/materiales/Losmovimientossociales.pdf, accessed March 2014

PART: 3

THE AMBIGUITIES
OF CIVIL SOCIETY

CHAPTER: 10

NIGER: NEO-BONAPARTISM
AND SOCIAL MOVEMENTS

Souley Adji

Niger has experienced a period of political instability that culminated in the coup of 2010, the third one since the beginning two decades earlier of political liberalization. This chapter analyses the process of political mobilization that led President Tandja to stay in power in violation of the Niger Constitution, the ambiguities of civil society organisations and intellectuals, given their partisan and opportunistic public positioning, and the growing social malaise that is expressed through the intensification of social struggles.

Introduction

Niger was shaken by great political instability in 2009, which led the following year to the third military coup in the 20 years since the beginning of political democratisation in the country. While the first democratic break of 1996 can be seen as a democratic counter-revolution, and the second in 1999 as a palace revolution, the third was Bonapartist in orientation (Adji 2011).[1] Having inherited power not from a glorious patronymic lineage but from an inglorious and defunct brother-in-arms, Mamadou Tandja benefited from the complicity of the military elite in perpetrating his constitutional coup, and also from a multitude of elected officials, traditional chiefs (Garba 2009), association leaders and unrepentant defenders of neo-Bonapartism, which translates as *Tazarce*[2] in the Hausa language.

The coming together of internal struggles and pressure from the international community ended up creating a situation conducive to the coup of 18 February 2010. Having called in the armed forces, the accession to power led to spontaneous outbreaks of joy and pathetic scenes where political, trade union and civic leaders stood hand-in-hand, praising the 'heroic intervention' of the military (Adji 2010) as if to hide their inability to awaken the collective mobilisations of the 1990s, which had put an end to the second republic and led to a political transition controlled for the most part by active forces such as trade unions, political parties and NGOs opposed to the regime.

After this decade of chaotic democratisation however, the two mandates of the president were marked by a climate of relative stability and by the gradual restoration of the state's authority. An economic tremor was even noted, as illustrated by the substantial socio-economic achievements and the start of major development projects lauded by several social categories and even by the opposition itself.

From an economic perspective, Niger experienced a good year in 2008, with a 9.5 per cent GDP growth rate, the strongest recorded in Africa that year.

In spite of a food and energy crisis, the government achieved this result on the back of exceptional revenue gains, which came especially from

---

1 Making an analogy with Napoleon III is very tempting. Despite being ineligible after his second mandate ended in 1851, he undertook a referendum and extended his reign for another ten years. Carried away by plebiscite, he proclaimed himself emperor before later experiencing the worst humiliation

2 Tazarce means 'to march on' in Hausa, the dominant language in Niger. The president's supporters are commonly referred to as tazarcists

an agricultural campaign which resulted in a surplus of more than 25 per cent, according to *Le Sahel* of 23 June 2009. In 2008, the General Tax Administration and the Customs Services achieved a 113 per cent and 107 per cent surplus respectively by year end, as detailed by *Le Sahel*, this time on 24 June 2009.

In spite of this positive economic outlook, the candidate displaying Bonapartist tendencies was opposed first by the street and then became victim of a military coup that took place after he had been illegally in power only for 60 days.[3] These events were not without previously having held a referendum on the adoption of a new constitution that was officially approved by 92.5 per cent of votes, and with a participation rate estimated by the authorities at 68.3 per cent.

Thus, it is important to analyse political mobilisation processes from a sociological perspective, including the determinants and major positions of latent groups. Raymond Boudon (1984, 1983) famously suggested that we focus on analysing the properties of the interaction system and the intentionality and rationality displayed by actors, rather than the structural constraints. To what extent did the specificities of the interaction system, first under the fifth republic and then under successive regimes, tend to encourage the emergence of a Bonapartist-like situation in the context of which an in-depth reshaping of civil society structures occurred across party boundaries and personal motivations? After briefly describing the properties of the interaction system, with a particular emphasis on its socio-political dimensions, we shall describe the process leading to the emergence of neo-Bonapartism before we analyse the positions adopted by the various mobilised groups. We shall also give an overview of the political mobilisation process.[4]

---

3 From 22 November 2009, the expected end of Mamadou Tandja's mandate, to 10 February 2010, amounts to 56 days.
4 We have the same understanding of this concept as François Chazel (1975:516): 'The creation of new commitments and new identifications - or sometimes the reactivation of forgotten loyalties and identifications - as well as the coming together on that basis of actors or groups of actors in the framework of a social movement, if necessary through direct, or possibly violent clash with existing authorities, aiming at promoting and sometimes restoring collective goals.' (*editor's translation*)

Souley Adji

The interaction system

On the birth of the fifth republic in 1999, several historic figures of the National Sovereignty Conference, including a plethora of intellectuals and several association and political party leaders[5] chose to form an alliance with the former party of state.[6] Even two main unions, the Teacher Union of Niger (USN) and the Workers Trade Union (USTN) gathering moved to rally to the adversary of yesteryear, even facilitating in the process the re-election of the outgoing president in 2004. We shall consider the types of interaction reports involving these major actors.

A dormant civil society

By finally taking over the highest office, the National Movement for the Society of Development (MNSD-Nassara) enjoyed unprecedented political stability, only interrupted in 2010 by a new coup. The latter took place in the wake of a political mobilisation wave initiated mainly by associations and political parties in the hope of counteringPresident Mamadou Tandja's *Tazarce* party. Until 2004, the relations between the associative intelligentsia and the regime in power were either of sheer connivance, or marked by embryonic, though always temporary, tension.

First of all, regarding social forces and in particular intellectuals in organisations, their activist commitment had started waning as their acquaintance with the political class remained strong. There has indeed been massive mobilisation, organised by a few committed structures, including civic associations and worker trade unions. However, in the beginning years of the 2000s, one must recognise that the energy of yesteryear was no longer there. The year 2005 revived the tradition of impressive collective actions, especially

5   We can mention Professor Andre Salifou of the Union of Democratic and Progressive Patriots (UPDP-Chamoua) and former chairman of the High Table at the National Conference, or the Social-Democrat Gathering (RSD-Gaskiya) of Cheffou Amadou, former prime minister of the very first political changeover of 1992.
6   In our article entitled 'La trahison des clercs', we argue that 'one must admit that this generation of officials and intellectuals was not quite up to the task and the hopes that they generated amongst the population. Is this then the Sahelian stew, the new treason of the clerks that Julien Benda was referring to? (Adji 2004).

during the 'struggle against the high cost of living' and the existing budget law. In Niamey, tens of thousands of citizens had taken part in the social movement led by civil society organisations. Like a single being, civil society forces had held consultations with a view to successfully organising the massive collective action. The ensuing success was due not to the charisma of actors, but to a combination of objective circumstances and actors. On the one hand was the failure of the Tandja mandate, whose promises remained unfulfilled, the recurrence of scandals linked to the public procurement process and to over-billing by civil servants. On the other hand, there was the determination, experience and expertise of strongly implanted associations, trade unions and non-governmental organisations that were able to further demonstrate, through a meticulous communication strategy, the iniquity inherent in the said law and the unequal opportunities in terms of access to the benefits of education and health. Several leaders were jailed after a mock trial.[7]

Since then, human rights associations and organisations, rather than trade unions and their federations, have attempted with some difficulty to launch actions seeking to mobilise the population in favour of causes as diverse as the anti-slavery movement, the fight against the indifference of authorities regarding starvation and the fight for the protection of the education system. These trade unions and humanitarian associations have subsequently experienced difficulties initiating meaningful large-scale action by citizens.

Thus was the interaction context in which civil society entities rose against Tandja's desire to extend his mandate for a further three years. It is therefore possible to state with a great deal of certainty that the decade spent by Tandja at the highest office enabled conservative forces to reorganise themselves, to desensitise any potential force of protest and to consolidate themselves in

---

7   Thus, Marou Amadou from United Front for the Preservation of Democratic Achievements (FUSAD), Nouhou Arzika from the Citizen Movement, Kassoum Issa from the National Union of Teachers of Niger (SNEN), Moustapha Kadi from SOS Energie and Moussa Tchangari from Alternative Espaces Citoyens, were transferred into prisons close to the capital after a rushed trial. They were freed about one month after being arrested. On another occasion, the latter was also jailed by the authorities at the Niamey civilian prison for three months.

order to seize control of the revenue from the underground wealth of Niger. In light of these elements, the struggle against this authoritarian endeavour therefore seemed much more arduous than all previous political struggles, especially as the leadership of these struggles was made up of a composite plethora of insufficiently charismatic and sometimes controversial figures.

The resources of neo-Bonapartism

The president's real fortune remained mining and oil revenue, providing him with tremendous autonomy of action. Indeed, in 2007, Niger started attracting interest from Western and Chinese multinationals, who were fighting for the country's mining and oil resources. In this sense, as argued by Gregoire (2010), the renewed interest for this wealth is no stranger to the political crisis, as control of these dividends represents one of the major stakes of the current struggles and a way of doing away, in appearance at least, with the traditional assistance provided by Niger's financial partners.

In order to gain the trust of the middle classes, the president and his cronies undertook to take a number of self-serving economic measures in a departure from financial orthodoxy. This was the case with the forceful adoption of a law granting financial advantages to traditional chiefs (from province chiefs to district chiefs), the exponential increase of the military budget and the implementation of economic measures in favour of the military and of the families of soldiers throughout the territory. The 10 per cent increase of civil servant salaries, the granting of more than half a billion FCFA to students, the building of campus accommodation, the full reimbursement of deposits made at the defunct National Savings Fund or by micro-credits granted to poor rural women; there is a long list of actions seeking to win the loyalty of supporters or extend the base of the regime.

Such supporters were then quick to constantly narrate that as Tahoua prefect in the 1980s, Colonel Tandja had already shone with a vast rural project in favour of the Ader populations. The local and regional media and brokers then undertook to give the widest exposure and backing to all of the 'flashy' initiatives of his mandate, namely the building of a refinery in Zinder, the establishment of a dry dock in Dosso, the building of the Kandadji dam and the start of operations on the Imouraren site.

Thus, the illusion of a popular regime was built and the myth perpetuated of a builder ready to launch long-term projects, even when using illegal means (Grégoire 2010). It ought to be pointed out that many of these initiatives received the backing of the intelligentsia, including political opponents, who all and sundry praised the worth[8] of Tandja. Notwithstanding the idyllic relationship that the president entertained with these interest groups in particular, he and his clan had felt it necessary to put up safeguards, in case resistance was shown when the neo-Bonapartist project came into effect. In this respect, he launched a so-called 'clean hands' operation, which involved conducting a general inspection of public funds within all state institutions in order to identify perpetrators of financial malpractices or other similar wrongdoings.[9]

The associative movement

In the past, civil society structures acted as a strong barrier against any authoritarian attempts from the regime. But representatives of this trend, the Citizen Movement, United Front for the Preservation of Democratic Achievements (FUSAD) and Alternative Espaces Citoyens, adopted different stances during the neo-Bonapartist phase.

---

8   The MP Sanoussi Jackou, president of the Niger Party for Self-Management (PNA), went as far as describing Tandja as a 'great socialist'.
9   Several MPs were arrested for benefit overpayments; the shortfall for the state was several hundred million CFA. As *L'Actualité*, the biweekly newspaper, stated in its 8 September 2009 issue: 'Since Thursday, September 3, nearly thirty members of the 5th Republic are sequestered by the personal power of the dictator who seeks to establish, Mamadou Tandja. Three charges are invoked to justify such detention: unequal treatment in the award of public procurement, embezzlement of public funds, forgery and use of forgery. According to the indictments, an amount of nearly eighteen (18) billion CFA francs is apparently involved!'.

Previously, these organisations were led by former figures of the student movement whose activism was very much in line with intellectual and citizen debates. They were regularly involved in activism with significant intellectual dimensions through public statements on national and international issues, production and editing of studies and reports, coordination and participation in seminars, round tables and conferences, radio broadcasts, and audio-visual and multimedia programmes.

Those at the helm of FUSAD and Alternative Espaces Citoyens, both former student leaders, also had in common the joint organisation of a large-scale protest event against the government in 2005 over the high cost of living. They ended up being jailed and also gained exposure throughout the country. What was the stance adopted by these organisations during the neo-Bonapartist period?

FUSAD

At the time, FUSAD was led by Marou Amadou, a law specialist by training without a civil servant position and one of the leading figures of the historic movement of 2005 mentioned above.[10] He was one of the leading figures of the anti-*Tazarce* movement and was therefore involved in all related activities such as protests, conferences, public statements and international meetings. He was also jailed due to his commitment and his occasional verbal excesses. Already a member of the electoral commission set up by the regime in power, he did not hesitate to resign to signify his refusal of Bonapartism. There were few other similar actions during that period, when many movement leaders continued to hold strong institutional positions and to enjoy prebends. For a long time, trade union leaders, politicians and association actors held an ambiguous position, in sharp contrast with their readiness to oppose the regime.

---

10   He was later appointed chairman of the Consultative Council, the legislative arm of the military transition, before holding the position of justice minister in the wake of the opposition coming to power.

With the exception of Amadou, and of the vice-chairwoman[11] of the same electoral commission, very few opponents to the presidential plans adopted the same stance.

However, the views expressed by the association did not always have a federating effect. In fact, as the regime made post-referendum statements on radio and television, FUSAD spontaneously condemned the support received by Tandja in the Diffa region, his home turf, before realising that this ploy had been used by the regime in all regions of the country.[12] This reaction was then insisted on in the public statement made by FUSAD on 9 August 2009. Reference was made to Tandja's ties, as he allegedly 'fell back on those from his region', as if the head of state's entourage was mainly visible and identifiable through this specific feature. The debate on the defence of democracy, the rule of law and good governance had thus been raised in terms of regional, ethnic or geographic visibility. In a country constantly seeking national unity, a major issue which all heads of state in Niger have heeded and valued, the adoption of such a philosophy in the context of a democratic struggle front undeniably revealed the limits of intellectuals in organisations. Under the guise of the struggle for democracy and the rule of law, many activists rather seemed to be pursuing antinomic or even ethno-regionalist goals.[13] It seems clear that the speaker perhaps had in mind the foreign origin of Tandja's parents, even though he himself was born in Niger.

Organisational intellectuals, even when fighting for democratic values, can sometimes lose their clarity and send out messages that hardly unite nor are worthy of their status as opinion leaders. Exacerbation of the national sentiment and reference to ethnicity or regionalism are not the best arguments in the intellectual world. But it still remains true that FUSAD

11 The vice-chairwoman of the Niger National Independent Electoral Commission (CENI) and representative of the Order of Lawyers, Aissata Zada, resigned on 7 July 2009 as soon as her organisation spoke against the referendum of 17 June.
12 Public statement issued by the Front for the Defence of Democracy (FDD).
13 According to one of his advisers, he in fact became confused during his speech by trying to express two ideas at once; the oral nature of this misfortune made the muddle easier (personal interview with a National Assembly adviser, February 2013).

was strongly committed to the fight against the *Tazarce* and this resulted in several arrests and jail terms for their leaders.

Alternative Espaces Citoyens: a collective intellectual

Led by Moussa Tchangari, a philosopher by training, this association[14] is one of the few to have maintained a consistent position of autonomy vis-à-vis the successive political regimes of the country, whereas many other structures, associative and media-based, underwent several changes. It brings together intellectuals from various backgrounds and generations while promoting alter-globalisation, of which it is the lead representative in Niger.[15] Thus, in the case of the Human Rights Protection Association of Niger (ANDDH) in particular, it led several autonomous activities, such as workshops, seminars, conferences and radio programmes and debates. In fact, well ahead of the start of political struggles, Alternative Espaces Citoyens had already adequately assessed the threat.

Indeed, as early as 2007, based on a contextual and institutional analysis, officials from the association had identified the strong probability of a third and illegal presidential mandate. They had then attempted to inform public opinion on the risks of political instability and encourage a thus far apathetic political opposition to fully grasp the threat in order to prevent the fulfilment of a Bonapartist wish.[16] Unfortunately, the strategy of gaining power through a tactical siding with the president seems to have been the strongest motivation at the time. But in response to daily campaigns from supporters of the president, a gathering of 20 trade unions and NGOs (like FUSAD) was formed in 2008 in order to push the latter to clarify his personal stance, and if needed, fight any extension of his mandate.

14 The Alternative Group, a cultural and media cooperative, was created in 1994 by young, committed intellectuals with the goal of safeguarding the democratic framework, preventing any change to it, and for the defence and promotion of human and environmental rights.
15 In addition to its frequent involvement in all alter-globalist fora, it coordinated the Niger Social Forum in 2006 in Niamey.
16 Invited to a local television station on the very day that the parliament was dissolved, the author of these lines made reference to the expression 'Bonapartism'.

Alternative Espaces Citoyens was also one of the signatories to this campaign. On 21 December, some of the president's faithful supporters created support committees in favour of a third mandate and submitted a proposal to parliament for a three-year political transition, described as a 'national union' government under the leadership of Tandja Mamadou.[17]

With the coming into play of political parties in the campaign against *Tazarce*, the very diverse and at times unorthodox mix of struggle leaders and the lack of a credible alternative[18] for the poorest classes, Alternative Espaces Citoyens gradually shifted away from the strategies deployed by the campaign, which was essentially made up of different sections of the bourgeoisie, whose prebendalism and unrelenting search for power had often been condemned by the media. While encouraging dialogue and consultation, Alternative Espaces Citoyens followed an alter-globalist or revolutionary approach, leading it to radically distance itself from political parties on both sides, who were known for their worship of neoliberalism and political mismatches. Overall, the association adopted a rather civic approach, taking part in the forum of West-African Civil Society Organisations (FOSCOA) in Abuja that was concerned with finding a positive way out[19] and also co-organising reflection, sensitisation and advocacy activities. Furthermore, it showed prowess in co-organising with the National Customs Trade Union (SNAD) a historic public conference[20] in Niamey that was attended by supporters of the two opposing fronts.

---

17 The media reported that thousands of people, including Prime Minister Seïni Oumarou as well as members of the government 'spontaneously' asked parliament on 21 December to grant the president a three-year extension.
18 In 2004, many of the members taking part in the anti-Tazarce front had had the oppotunity to achieve a political changeover. They chose to back the MNSD-Nassara candidate against the 'changeover candidate', as Mahamadou Issoufou defined himself. In 2009, even Prime Minister Hama Amadou, with his new-found commitment to democracy, hesitated between joining the pro-governmental Alliance for National Reconciliation (ARN) and the pro-opposition Coordination of the Forces for Democracy and Republic (CFDR), before eventually joining the latter, seemingly against his wish.
19 These associations met between 31 July and 1 August 2009 in Abuja, Nigeria. They were signatories to an open letter to Tandja. They stated the following: "Thus, we are convinced that the only solution remaining for your country is to immediately put an end to the illegal referendum project of August 4th 2009, a return to the normal constitutional order, starting a dialogue with all actors and holding the local and general elections planned in 2009.'
20 The public conference was co-hosted by Alternative Espaces Citoyens, ANDDH and SNAD. Three presentations were made by the following: Bazoum Mohamed, a MP from the Niger Party for Democracy and Socialism (PNDS-Tarayya), Abdoulkarim Mamalo, president of the Mass Party for Labour (PMT-Albarka) and by the Alternative Espaces Citoyens representative.

The involvement of Niger's various partners, including ECOWAS, in the political dispute, supported this stance, even when dialogue between the protagonists had finally been made possible in Niamey. But the intra-Niger dialogue did not last long, as supporters of the president became increasingly allergic to the idea.

A coup put an end to the search for a peaceful solution. Let us point out that as soon as negotiations collapsed, the theory of a coup was supported, as some political groups were only too eager to see the military step onto the scene.[21] Officials and structures in the know therefore pre-positioned themselves by showing all the more determination to fight the *Tazarce*. This opportunistic stance took the shape of unexpected public statements, the distribution of anti-*Tazarce* leaflets and resignations from institutional positions. At the height of the political crisis, thus far undecided associative and political actors chose to speak up publicly in the hope of enjoying some of the benefits linked to a likely regime changeover.

Notwithstanding the creation of struggle fronts combined with strong political and democratic mobilisation, a new republic came about in 2009. The numerous international envoys and the involvement of several regional organisations did not achieve any more success.

Public intellectuals

At the other extreme of the clerks favourable to neo-Bonapartism, there was a category of intellectuals, academics in particular, who had taken a firm or even activist stance and often had a clear grasp of the implications of the extension of the presidential mandate. And if they themselves stayed clear of the political struggle, they were often called upon by the opposition movement to provide their scientific input.

---

21   Personal interviews with associative and professional political leaders, Niamey, February 2013.

Academic intellectuals

With the dissolution of the parliament and of the Constitutional Council, the debate on the illegal nature of the president's decision remained for a long time a legal joust. Legal experts and political scientists in particular were called upon by struggle fronts to enlighten public opinion. Modes of action mostly took the form of public conferences, debates and reports on televised events. Unimpressed with such legalese,[22] some political analysts[23]suggested that the fight against Bonapartism should privilege the sphere of political mobilisation rather than that of the law. Therefore, the modes of action chosen consisted of the publication of political articles in newspapers or in the search for synergy with committed associations in order to generate a collective debate and define alternative strategies, such as speaking on radio and television debates and interviews.[24] Other modes of commitment by intellectuals in their civic struggle included holding public conferences attended by both *Tazarce* supporters and opponents, launching petitions and taking part in national and sub-regional round tables.

At the same time, some free thinkers generously shared their critical thoughts, including against opponents, whose shortcomings and limitations they gladly highlighted. Some journalists were seemingly thrown off by this behaviour.[25] The contribution from these committed intellectuals was essentially quite enriching, due to the fact that they opposed arguments made by supporters of the regime, while enlightening the population on the nature of the regime.[26]

---

22 To this list, it is worth adding that of former attorney general Soli Abdouramane. Some of these contributors were called upon by FUSAD to speak at a series of conferences in the region. This association had just received financial support, namely from the Open Society Initiative for West Africa (OSIWA), in order to conduct sensitisation activities.
23 For example, we wrote: 'Threats of all kinds, namely the "mentoring phenomenon", that of "responsible participation", endemic poverty, civil wars and sometimes Bonapartism like in Niger, can tend to adjourn, alter or simply remove pluralist democracy to make way for a new State system, which is necessarily backward and reactionary. In fact, the real fight is perhaps less that which is waged on the legal sphere than in terms of political and civic mobilisation' (Adji 2009).
24 Some academics were regularly called upon by the media and civil society associations.
25 Professor Djibo Hamani, Dr Bagué Hima and S. Adji fully exercised their critical spirit, boldly pointing out the errors of the mobilised actors, especially as they did not objectively belong to any of the existing fronts.
26 We can also mention the case of diaspora intellectuals, such as Nasser Ary Taminoune, professor at the University of Ottawa, Gazibo Mamoudou, professor at the University of Laval, Farmo Moumouni, consultant historian in Quebec, and Issoufou Adamou, doctoral researcher and lecturer at the Faculty of Legal and Political Science (Cheikh Anta Diop University, Dakar). They published extensively in the Niger media and on the Internet to inform the world.

Thus, Djibo Hamani (2009) helped to identify the real initiators of Tandja's suicidal undertaking:

> In this adventure, even the MNSD, the President's party, disappeared from the group of initiators. The barons of the regime kept quiet and remained hidden. Those who orchestrated this national misadventure are unknowns that have come out of nowhere, youngsters, some minors, 'tchali-tchali'[27] from the 'civil society', marginals from the Bar Association and a few traditional chiefs forced to express their support.[28]

As for the type of regime planned in the *Tazarce*, academics were able to explain similar historical precedents and the features which had defined these regimes.[29]

From a media perspective, independent intellectuals also played an important role by providing greater visibility and legitimacy to the fight against the *Tazarce*. While we can recognise the courage of this category of intellectuals, can we say that their involvement in the political struggle was always selfless? Are there not other reasons that explain their commitment? In fact, notwithstanding the nature of the regime, intellectuals were never targeted through arrests or threats. None of them were called by the police, nor physically attacked because of the views they expressed. In this sense, we can argue that in the Tandja-Bonapartist context, purely intellectual activity, as described above, was not in itself seen as a genuine threat to the regime in place, at least not to the point of having public intellectuals monitored. As with the political crisis of 1996, it was mostly journalists who experienced abuses.

---

27 A Hausa word meaning 'clown'
28 Professor Djibo Hamani 'hopes that the forces which provided President Tandja Mamadou with a way out through dialogue shall succeed before it's too late. Let Mamadou Tandja get rid of the charlatans and influence pedlars surrounding him, the corrupt intellectuals, perpetual brown-nosers and unrepentant freeloaders hiding at the Presidency and elsewhere, and who are driving us right against the wall.' (*As-Salam* 2009, July-August).
29 On 26 May 2009, the date when the National Assembly was dissolved, we described the president's illegal undertaking as 'Bonapartism'.

Niger Trade Union of Teachers and Researchers (SNECS)

Since the start of Tandja's second mandate, the Niger Trade Union of Teachers and Researchers (SNECS) had adopted an ultra-corporatist approach, privileging the fulfilment of material demands. These were namely a special status for lecturers and the increase of salaries, research stipends and mortgages. Such an approach, while legitimate from a trade union's point of view, appeared intellectually inconsistent in so far as it neglected the protection of the moral and professional interests of its members.

Thus, the SNECS decided to project the image of a good partner of the government, overlooking national issues and the massive withdrawal of other civil society entities. In order not to give a bad impression to the regime, there were no loud public statements, no denunciations of acts of bad governance, no involvement with social movements protesting against the government and no public debates. Like in May 2008, there even came a point where if some of its members spoke publicly on the salaries of parliamentarians, SNECS would explain to them that they had spoken on their own behalf and not in the name of the union. With the advent of Bonapartism, and as SNECS had not had all its demands met, it stayed undecided for a long time, refraining from condemning or approving publicly the dissolution of republican institutions and the establishment of a new republic. In fact, two wings emerged inside SNECS: supporters of the 6th Republic, whose demands were of a more material than partisan nature, including officials from the chancellor's office, and the regime protagonists, driven as much by ethical as by political issues. If initially and alongside the so-called non-affiliated trade unions,[30] the SNECS co-signed a very neutral public statement, in which the words of the national anthem were literally used, it was later forced to set up an editorial committee with members from both currents. The statement thus produced did not shine in terms of originality or boldness.

---

30 These are trade unions that are not affiliated to the federations. SNECS, SNAD and the Autonomous Union of Magistrates of Niger (SAMAN) are such examples.

The authors simply presented a genesis of the democratic process while calling for dialogue. This strategy, consisting of bridging the gap with the decisional centre, seems to be a trademark of new trade union leaders. In this respect, the union leadership did not stand out against neo-Bonapartism in terms of boldness or intellectual independence. The same cannot be said of some members of the trade union who, by putting forward their own personal views and speaking on their own behalf, departed from the official line.

The student movement

Over time, the posture of students changed considerably. From a quasi-revolutionary and independent posture in the 1990s, student leadership gradually became depoliticised, going as far as backing the coup. The specificity of the interaction system produced a clear degradation of the living and studying conditions of students and the influence of centrifugal forces on the campus, since the phasing out of communist ideology undoubtedly led to the student movement somewhat losing its bearings.

In 2001, the forced exile of the legitimate executive leadership of the Union of the Niger Students of the University of Niamey (UENUN) completed the process of increasing uncertainties within the student movement, where proletarianised and clueless pupils and students fell easy prey to political parties and Islamic associations. The institutional crisis of 2008-10 occurred when USN was still finding its bearings. The leadership was quick to succumb to the charms of the president and his supporters.

The loss of its ideological bearings translated into the progressive emergence of various rifts, namely ethno-regionalist, partisan and religious. In some cases this reached the point of clashes. All vying for control of the movement, political parties[31] infiltrated the campus while Islamists also multiplied their

31 According to Tcherno (2006), '...each party uses every means possible to impose "its" candidate at the helm of UENUN. The immediate consequences of the stubbornness of each side are actions of intolerance.'

visits in order to introduce religious science. From then on, political party programmes and religious booklets substituted the Marxist and revolutionary books previously found on the night stands of students.[32] The critical mind became blunter and the organisational framework was weakened.

The description of the interaction system shows that when the *Tazarce* occurred, students were unable to resist the temptation of forging an alliance with political authorities. This was all the more the case since on the one hand their leaders had been jailed or fired by university authorities,[33] and on the other, civil society activists had set up shop on campus.[34] The relations between student leaders and the government were excellent, to the point that already in 2008, the steering committee had extended a motion of thanks to the minister of secondary and higher education, research and technology. Its secretary general Bio Abdourahmane[35] had underlined 'the resolution of school problems, including regulation over the issue of scholarships and student transport' and lauded 'the sincere partnership with the authorities, more than ever determined to restore the higher status of Niger schools' (*Le Canard Déchaîné*, 10 September 2009). Having gradually become very close to a movement initiated by a civil society actor[36] close to the regime, they became staunch supporters of the president. Thus, they did not express any objection when the issue of organising a referendum in order to usher in a new republic (in violation of legislation) was raised.

In the fifth republic's context of interaction, the political crisis revealed that students experiencing hardship had good historical and material reasons to

32 'Today, the majority of them are more interested in rap music than in reading the works of Lenine, Che Guevara and Mao. Whereas in the 80s and 90s, ideological debates were all the rage between Maoist, Guevarist, Trotskyst, Leninist, Sankarist and Lumumbist students in the name of proletarian internationalism and anti-imperialism, today, disputes oppose the pro-Ousmane (Speaker of the Parliament) and the pro-Hama (Prime Minister)' (Tcherno, 2007).
33 The general secretary and the secretary of academic affairs were sent to the civil prison of Niamey in March 2007. The Democratic Coordination of the Civil Society of Niger (CDSCN) claimed that the university council illegally expelled a group of students accused of being frontrunners, with the unavowed aim of weakening the Union of Niger Students at the University of Niamey (UENUN).
34 The president of the Patriotic Movement for the Defence of the Nation and the People (MPDNP) seemed very close to student circles. Founded in July 2009, this association gave its full support to President Tandja's project.
35 On 16 December 2009, during a public rally in support of the president, he claimed: 'Niger has become the victim of a plot by the international community.'
36 Nouhou Arzika, former leader of the Equity-Quality Coalition, was one of the most fervent supporters of the *Tazarce*. In this perspective, he created the Citizen Movement for Peace, Democracy and the Republic (MCPDR).

want to see the regime remaining in power, especially as trade union unity had become highly eroded. By the same token, the values of Pan-Africanism, secularism and independence cultivated by the USN became but a distant memory, relics from a long-gone era.

The era of political transition

Political transitions in Niger are invariably perceived as periods when political and social demands are shelved. New authorities are often given a free hand so that they can put the state and its administration back on track and produce new texts, heralding a new democratic regime. Then a strong consensus settles in political and civic society, in particular within the social movement, of which trade unions and human rights organisations are the backbone. However, if like in 1996, the junta leading the transition shows any desire to cling to power, there follows an outcry from all strong forces, including trade unions and political parties. Perhaps already scalded by a transition experience which ended with the death of General Mainassara Baré in 1999, the Supreme Council for the Return of Democracy (CSRD) eventually accepted a short transition, as demanded by the international community and the political class (International Crisis Group 2013). For this reason, the political transition turned out to be a long and quiet river, as the government enjoyed a state of grace from both trade unions and from other major actors. Nevertheless, some unions did show a degree of resistance.

The interaction context

The coup perpetrated by squadron leader Salou Djibo occurred following the failure of the ECOWAS mediation effort held in Niamey under the auspices of former Nigerian head of state, General Abdul Salami Aboubakar. The facilitator had invited both parties to consider a plan that consisted of maintaining Tandja in power, appointing a prime minister from within the opposition and establishing a national unity government that included the various political and civil society actors involved in the negotiations. The party of government rejected this process, which in their eyes deprived the president of his core prerogatives as head of state. The takeover therefore had the effect of comforting some and destabilising others, while at the same time institutionalising the political loyalties of trade union federations as well as other civil society associations. Some continued to cultivate their closeness with the junta, the new ally, and with their former partners, the CFDR and FUSAD. Thus, the political transition did not face strong adversity from opposition parties and social movements.

The careerism of public intellectuals

As members of the struggle front against neo-Bonapartism, union federations considered the junta a natural ally, especially as some leaders had strong links with political parties close to the new regime, from which they inevitably expected rewards. They did not undertake any strike action, even though improving the worsening living and working conditions of their members was one of their recurring demands. Likewise, some NGO chairs with a reputation for their commitment in political struggle or who enjoyed an international audience also decided to stop their fight as soon as they were appointed in positions of responsibility by the junta. The most emblematic case was undoubtedly that of the FUSAD chairperson, who was successively appointed president of the National Transitional Council[37] and justice minister under the new republic.

More broadly, sharing the same goals as the military junta, most human rights association leaders who had previously spearheaded social movements, took up official positions, including as the chairpersons of some institutions. At any rate, in light of the dividends gained by some protest figures, this position of intellectuals was at odds with that of 1996, when those who moved into

---

37   In charge of producing legal texts, including the new constitution, and which convened for a whole month.

state organs were few and far between once stability was recovered. This time around, academic intellectuals laid siege to the administration by occupying official positions.

Thus, academics were especially well provided for in the transition period that resulted from the political crisis. They chaired the Committee of Fundamental Texts (CTF), joined the Transitional Constitutional Council (CCT) and became advisers of the prime minister or of the Council for National Reconciliation (CNR). Others, such as Amadou Bounty Diallo, a teacher of philosophy at the University of Niamey, even went as far as to openly protest against exclusion from ministerial positions, arguing that their fellow countrymen from abroad[38] were not necessarily in a better position to lead the political transition[39] and therefore to hold ministerial positions.

Unlike those keen to move into political office, others remained steadfast. This was the case of Alternative Espaces Citoyens, whose members continued to denounce violations committed by the regime. In this respect, public conferences, reflection workshops and input to written and audio-visual media occurred.

In fact, knowing full well that the transition would be fairly short, the military authorities did not hesitate to appoint a plethora of agents emotionally close to their families or to the barracks. This was jokingly described by the press as 'parents, friends and acquaintances (PFA) politics'. At the presidency in particular, advisers and official representatives were intensively hired. No particular technical skill was required. This fashion was in fact born with Tandja Mamadou's presidency, when no one had known the exact number of advisers of all sorts. Lacking imagination, squadron leader Salou Djibo found the idea brilliant and a useful way of promoting kin: he recruited a host

---

38   The junta had intellectuals flown in from Europe or America and given administrative responsibilities. The press widely covered the arrival of Gazibo Mamadou from Canada, who was invited thanks to his elder sister, then secretary general of the government in charge of the military transition agenda.
39   Suspected of having made unorthodox comments during a television debate, he preferred to step down from his position as a presidential adviser due to the general outcry that followed, especially from certain political groups. Since then, he has been very critical vis-à-vis the regime.

of advisers – street accountants estimated the number of known promoted at 125; they felt frustrated when the government media suddenly stopped listing such appointments, which ended up being done more discreetly. It should be pointed out that public opinion always had mocking comments to make on the frenzy.

Indeed, anyone could be appointed adviser of anything, provided that they were on the contact list of an influential CSRD member or that they showed some zeal at flattering the rare genius of these gentlemen. Wagging tongues did not tire of telling the story of this mere visitor to the palace who went out with the undreamed of title of official representative, to the amazement of the usual circle of friends at his club: he was allegedly a pimp. If the regime paid so little attention to the ethical character of those it promoted, it is because these were rewarded for services rendered.

The syndrome of the black car and of the spirit of profit had thus ended up chewing away at the activist fibre of many civil society actors, thus proving right those who had condemned early on the purely opportunistic and selfish nature of their commitment. Others still enthusiastically praised the military uniform, before realising then and there that the republican nature of the military continuously deteriorated as rapidly as clanism and mismanagement was eating away through all its pores. Never before in a political transition was such looting of public resources undertaken with such a level of indecency than under the latest experienced by Niger, at least based on media reports referring to tens of billions of CFA francs that had surreptitiously vapourised. In 2010, the illusion of the restoration of democracy by a military elite, always true to its values and greedy for promotion, found its limits here.

It is therefore not surprising that such political leadership, civic actors, and especially trade unionists, suddenly turned into politically-minded men and women, thus turning away from their traditional missions of protecting citizen rights and interests.

Since the advent of the junta civil society seems to have lost its tongue. Personalities whose harsh criticism against the Tandja regime had amazed many Niger people have now lost the language. In support of the transition, actors of civil society stubbornly refuse to criticize the shortcomings of the current system. No denunciation concerning the policy of parents, friends and acquaintances, no reaction on appointments disorders of certain personalities troubled past at the head of several institutions, and even the famous debate on the promotion of head of state…The silence of civil society is serious.[40]

After a 20-year democratisation process, civil society had failed to consolidate itself.

Uproar amongst teachers

Notwithstanding the treason committed by new clerks due to their new political allegiances, the transition nevertheless went through a period of social unrest. Thus, contractual teachers occasionally organised strikes with a significant impact on the sector, given that they represented 75 per cent of the teaching staff. Organised within the National Coordination of Contractual Teachers (CNCE), they had focused their demands on the issue of incorporating contractual teachers into the public service, namely by hiring the 8,000 contractual teachers as planned in 2010.

Faced with major social unrest barely a month after coming to power, the regime found no other response but to confirm the contract termination as decided by the previous regime. Yet the claims, bonus payments and other benefits alone linked to the teaching profession amounted to around 11 billion CFA. The decision was emphatically implemented in spite of the union's willingness to engage in legal proceedings. Several contract teachers were therefore

---

40   *L'Evénement* (2010) 'Société civile pro démocratie: le virage à 180', 25 May

discharged without pay, while new selection criteria were implemented. At the time, this governmental decision ended up shattering the movement, as some had miraculously escaped the purging. But, now reorganised, contract teachers demanded from the CSRD and the government that they put an end to arbitrary appointments, intimidation, contract termination and abuses of all kinds, as well as that they enjoy their rights (*La Griffe* 13 April 2010). The authorities promised that the issue would be resolved at the earliest, but as they did not keep their promise, there was a new outcry very quickly thereafter.

In addition to this category of staff, other civil servants also made themselves heard. These were mostly researcher-lecturers and physicians and pharmacists. A series of strikes was organised by the Niger Trade Union of Researcher-Lecturers (SNECS) on the issue of the decree of 7 October 2010 pertaining to university reform. This was the start of a wrestling match with the government. In addition to boycotting academic activities, general assemblies were held on a regular basis as well as debates in the media in order to enlighten public opinion on the consequences of such reform on the quality of teaching and research. As stated by a newspaper, the trade union:

> which launched a campaign to explain the grounds for its strike action gradually managed to convince the Niger people of the validity of its demands. Even the students who initially condemned any behaviour they considered an obstacle to evolution ended up understanding the procedural flaw or even the violation of the texts that lay at the foundations of the University's autonomy.[41]

There was indeed a great risk that if the government persisted in its position, the academic year would be declared void and the baccalaureate examinations would not take place in normal conditions.

---

41   In an article, the author mentioned an open letter that we had personally written to General Salou Djibo in order to explain the ins and outs of this reform. See *La Griffe* (2010) 'Réformes de l'enseignement supérieur : la crise s'accentue à l'Université de Niamey', 10 December

Legal proceedings were even initiated, as the government had filed a complaint against the trade union following the latter's request for the resignation of the relevant minister. As a result of this decision, some researcher-lecturers resigned from their administrative positions out of solidarity for their colleagues. Therefore, the prime minister's legal adviser also resigned. On the day of the trial, most researcher-lecturers were present in the court room. The judge declared that he had no jurisdiction over the case, but it was the later negotiations that led to sanctifying the university's autonomy and thus persuading researcher-lecturers to resume their activities.

Towards the end of the transition, in March 2010, the Trade Union of Pharmacists, Physicians and Dentist Surgeons of Niger (SYNPHAMED) suddenly launched strike action in order to secure an autonomous status within the civil service. Threatening to radicalise the movement and after it presented notice for a new 10-day strike action, the union was invited to meet the head of the junta. But far from fulfilling their expectations, the latter instead found their demands out of place. According to him, they amounted to no more than speculation and blackmail and he did not give in.[42] However, the issue of autonomy was once again brought to the fore with the advent of a new government.

In spite of its near-holy nature, the political transition of 2010 was no less the object of an approach by social forces concerned with promoting their own corporatist interests. It is however worth pointing out that for the most part, these were not so much lower social categories, but rather members of the country's intellectual elite whose living standards were more consistent with those of the middle class. Under the new republic, there was an increase in upheavals led by unions not affiliated to federations close to the regime.

---

42 He stated: 'I did not invite you here to negotiate, but to listen to you and to put an end to speculation and blackmail, so that we can look at each other in the eyes and tell each other the truth.' See *Xinhua* (2011) 'Niger : Djibo Salou dénonce le chantage au sujet de la grève des blouses blanches', 9 March

The seventh republic: the era of philosopher-kings

The Niger Party for Democracy and Socialism (PNDS-Tarayya) finally accessed power after being in the opposition for 20 years. But this rise was greatly facilitated by the military junta which weighed on the electoral process so that the barons of the former regime would not retain power. Facilities were granted to the PNDS-Tarayya candidate so that he could lead a pre-electoral campaign: escorted by a heavily armed military unit, he travelled across the whole country and the electoral lists of opponents were tampered with so as to prevent adequate representation in some regions of the country. Besides, some trade union federations and civic associations decided to free themselves from the regime while others consolidated their ties with the CFDR. Many civic activists turned into politicians or advisers of the president. Others, such as Alternative Espaces Citoyens, as usual, neither went for the money or opposition parties.

The republic of advisers

The party of intellectuals, from which a shift from previous practices had been expected, also chose continuity by providing the president with a cabinet filled to the brim with dozens of different types of advisers: special advisers with the rank of minister, main advisers and technical advisers, not to mention the armada of special representatives. However, the president provided his special touch, filling the cabinet with academics.

After the collapse of Athenian democracy, where excessive freedom, licentious behaviour and widespread instability prevailed, Plato, far from a democrat, had already advocated that the city be governed by philosophers, the holders of knowledge and wisdom. Did Mahamadou Issoufou, the new president of Niger, perpetuate this classic illusion of sentient power or did he simply take the idea of rewarding allies and parents instated by his predecessors to its extreme? In fact, if a leader should hear the opinion of so many advisers before taking a decision, he would never have to decide for himself and would be unable to separate the wheat from the chaff, as many are the courtiers who will only tell what the prince wants to hear. The fear of losing privileges or falling into disgrace sometimes forces one to cosy up with the latter. This is one of the reasons why some intellectuals prefer technocracy to academic research.

With the advent of the socialist party coming to power, many of the civic actors previously mentioned were kept in their positions, or promoted.[43] In truth, there was an unprecedented rush of intellectuals into the state's decision-making apparatus. A flurry of academics could thus be seen in the president's office, the like of which Niger had never experienced before, not to mention a plethora of colleagues holding positions in other high spheres of power. With respect to this impressive rush of lecturers, senior lecturers, associate professors and professors, not to mention all the clerks deserting their faculties, the media were quick to speak of the creation of a new institution, namely the 'Palace University', by far better endowed in teaching staff than the new universities of Maradi and Zinder combined.

In a context of so-called good governance, we can ask ourselves if the creation of new budget lines goes not only against any form of viable economic rationale, but also, and mostly, against the very development of the university as an institution. Indeed, when deserting faculties, the newly-promoted still served as part-time lecturers, paid by the hour, and with expressly guaranteed salaries. According to public opinion, the very image of academics has thus become that of prebenders who accumulate salaries and benefits linked with their appointment to technocratic positions, but whose usefulness and performances remain to be demonstrated.

In addition to the opportunity cost incurred by the university, one can also have doubts as to the latter's independence. Other major risks are

---

43 Amongst the most visible, we can mention the new justice minister, Marou Adamou, formerly the president of the Consultative Council, and the new general secretary of the government, the teacher-researcher Zakara Gandou, formerly the adviser of the prime minister of the 2010 political transition.

politicisation and alienation. With the creation of an *ad hoc* university extension project piloted by the president's office, the risk indeed appears significant that the university, or even research, would suffer from alienation and politicisation. When the issues are imposed or generated, academics are likely to be called in as token intellectuals to execute, via their trade union, activities and funding that they neither understand nor can control.

Most importantly, the policy of having academics hold positions of responsibility at the top of the civil service risks making their trade unions inactive and passive. Just like in the era of neo-Bonapartism, they remain absent from public debates, with no public statements to reassert their position of principle on issues of national interest, nor synergy of action with other trade unions, nor criticism or denunciation of acts of bad governance. It ought to be said that in the wake of political change, some bureau members chose to work with new institutions, with strong prebends attached.

Emergence of social movements

Not without some difficulty, the political transition managed to postpone the tackling of specific social issues. It is now up to the new government to commit to meeting latent social demands. Long suppressed by allied trade union federations, the desire for resistance that was felt by social groups ended up being expressed openly. New actors burst onto the scene of social struggle.

Multi-sectoral mobilisation

Education contract staff organised within the CNCE and quickly resumed the struggle. On 8 November 2011, the CNCE had initiated a series of strikes, including a first strike of 48 hours and two other strikes of 72 hours. Since then, it has continued to initiate diverse modes of action. Thus the press reports that 'activities undertaken in the framework of the strike were marked by a sectoral general assembly, marches in other regions of the country as well as a group prayer to implore the Lord so that the problems faced by contractual teachers would be resolved quickly'.[44] This approach seemed to raise concerns within the government. While it initiated an integration process, promising to consider in urgency all pending issues on the basis of new criteria, the regime was mostly seeking to decapitate the movement.

Its leaders were appointed at educational inspectorates or in recently-created offices,[45] more for the sake of rewarding the faithful than to wage a merciless fight against corruption. This operation had the effect of defusing the social movement, but also tended to awaken several teacher unions. For greater efficiency, these gathered within the Permanent Framework for Reflection and Action of the Teacher Unions in Niger (CPRASE).

Following up on the defunct CNCE, this new structure was quick to show more determination in the protection of the material and moral interests of its members. Thus several unlimited strikes were launched in order to back their standing demands related to the payment of salary arrears and teacher benefits for those who had been hired in 2011, and to the management of the careers of contractual teachers who represented nearly 80 per cent of the teaching staff. Notwithstanding the signing of a memorandum of understanding in April 2012, for a long time the government either kept its head in the sand or suppressed public protest. This stance encouraged CPRASE to reconsider its struggle methods, namely by adopting a hard line in state-run schools with the threat of a two-week strike, the boycott of administrative duties and the retention of student marks (Tcherno 2013).

The same strategy was adopted by teachers in institutes whose status seemed ambiguous or uncertain. To this end, they started a movement to demand that the government adopt an implementation decree relative to the law

---

44 *L'Evénement* (2011) 'La grève des enseignants contractuels reconduite de 72 heures', 12 December
45 We can mention la Ligne Verte (Green Line) and Halcia (High Authority for the Fight against Corruption and Related Offenses). Established in May 2011, Ligne Verte is a ministerial process allowing citizens to report cases of attempted bribery. Victims or eyewitnesses of the events constituting corruption can also email the justice ministry.

on the status of teaching staff in Technological University Institutes (TUI), which had been passed by the parliament on 15 May 2012. Thus, teachers in the Maradi, Tahoua and Zinder TUIs and at the School of Mining and Geology (SMG) of Niamey decided to maintain 'the interruption of all academic activities (lectures, lab work, practical work, supervision, vivas, etc.) in the TUIs and at SMG until a final resolution is found' (Boukar 2013). They ended up asserting their rights, especially with the support of students, whose mobilisation risked creating an even greater situation of instability in urban centres.

The extension of social unrest

The wait-and-see and occasionally restive attitude of the government even caused the anger of trade unionists close to the regime. Faced with the discontent of their members, four union federations created a struggle front in July 2012. They blamed Brigi Rafini's government for not complying with the implementation calendar pertaining to specific points of the memorandum of understanding of 7 February 2012. For the most part, the demands centred around the adoption of a decree introducing tax reductions as well as another on a minimum six per cent industrial wage increase in the parastatal and private sectors, the widespread implementation of bonus pay and benefits, payment linked to promotions and the increase of January and February salaries.

In addition to the rise of the Niger Interunion of Workers, four other union federations belonging to the Union of Free and Democratic Federations (UCLDN) also decided to come out. The latter demanded from the government the payment of state subsidies and for measures to be taken against the high cost of living. As if the state of grace had indeed come to an end, several trade unions made themselves heard. Thus, the National Union of Magistrates in Niger also initiated a series of strikes in order to obtain better living and working conditions for its members. The student members of the UENUN were not to be left behind (*La Griffe* 30 July 2012). College students in particular occasionally held large-scale protest events in all the main towns in order to express their discontent about their studying conditions. They complained of overcrowded classrooms, a shortage of classrooms and a shortage of teachers. Such protests were usually violent and they systematically clashed with the police. As argued by a keen observer:

> The violence of school protest should awaken the consciousness of all our citizens on the fate of our country. Obviously, beyond the lip service paid by the current authorities on their willingness to make the improvement of schools an absolute priority and to devote a quarter of the national budget to training the Niger youth, one is forced to acknowledge that unfortunately, this will has not materialized, if only in the various budget laws adopted over the two years of governance of the 7th Republic.[46]

The issue of the quality of teaching is obviously nowhere near being resolved.

The government was also shaken by the revolt to obtain a reduction of oil and gas prices. This movement was sparked in Zinder, around 1,000 kilometres away from the capital. Given that a refinery is situated there, local associations demanded a reduction of the price per litre of gas. Interurban and periurban transporter trade unions then took up this issue. Unions of taxi drivers and owners in Niamey[47] came on board by organising a series of strike actions which had a devastating impact. In October 2012, after a number of strikes to demand that the government reduce by 30 per cent the price of oil and gas products produced in Niger, the collective of taxi owners and various unions of taxi and minibus drivers unilaterally decided to increase urban and interurban fares.

---

46 *Xinhua* (2012) 'Grève des scolaires: L'école nigérienne en péril', November
47 The main actors were the Niger Collective of Trade Unions in the Sector of Transport (CSSTN), the Niger National Union of Road Drivers (SNCRN) and the Union of Taxi Drivers (Syncotaxi).

With this decision, the taxi fare went from 200 to 300 FCFA, which amounts to a 50 per cent increase, and the fare for minibuses from 125 to 200 FCFA. This social issue is still a source of concern for the government, which is reluctant to change its oil and gas pricing policy.

Conclusion

Commitment by the intelligentsia to fighting neo-Bonapartism seems to respond to specific concerns, sometimes individual, but never as some may think for the single purpose of defending democratic values and human rights.[48] It is rarely a matter of volunteering. For a significant part of the actors, political conflicts seem to present major opportunities to boost their institutional or international visibility. In case of 'success', they would be rewarded with positions of power or possibilities for acquiring wealth. For opposition political actors, the opportunity was ideal to disqualify the existing elite or remove them by force, as was the case of the gesture made by the opposition leader towards the military. They thus find an opportunity to access power, as the military have always had a tradition of sweeping away tenants of the state. We can reasonably assume that this objective comes second to the protection of good governance, given the silence of the opposition following the many acts of bad governance committed by the authorities. Public intellectuals and academic intellectuals were totally absent from social struggles under the political transition and the regime of the seventh republic. Thus, in the space of four years, they adopted different stances. Increasingly cut off in the corridors of the presidential palace and ministries in their role as advisers, university professors have become less and less involved in public debate that would enlighten public opinion and denounce or criticise political practice. Their personal ambitions, including self-advancement, obviously took over from the protection of common values.

---

48   CFDR (2009) Memorandum on the national political situation, Niamey, November

The opportunistic rallying of traditional social actors such as trade union federations and civic associations did not create widespread apathy, however. New actors have emerged. Emerging social categories, generally not yet integrated into the civil service, have attempted to implement often original modes of action, such as prayer sessions or collective fasting days, in order for their demands to be met. Dominant in some spheres of administration, these new structures can undermine at will the normal running of schools, or even create a year of no teaching. Outside of these action frameworks, non-affiliated trade unions also enjoy scope for manoeuvre, as a result of which they ignore the instructions given by established federations.

Other organisations also advocate from the perspective of genuine political change, through revolutionary means if need be, without expecting any returns from major actors and institutions for their commitment against Bonapartism. Few and far between, they are usually of alter-globalisation or Trotskyst leanings and have been characterised by unfaltering commitment. In this respect, their leaders are renowned for being fierce intellectuals who are active in social movements and in the media. Contrary to other categories of actors, such as the collective intellectual that is Alternative Espaces Citoyens, they were always keen to keep their distance from the various political regimes, whether in the fifth republic, the political transition or the seventh republic. Because of this stance, they earned the trust of the public and of those disappointed with fluctuating organisations such as FUSAD, and of the permanent focus on governmental positions.

Nevertheless, political mobilisation still represents a powerful political involvement mechanism or one for non-constitutional political succession when dialogue fails. In response to this permanently hostile presence in the public arena, the government generally resorts to intimidation and repression before agreeing, sometimes later on, to start negotiations under the pressure of the street and more so from Western nations and international institutions. Thus, both General Baré Mainassara's regime and that of Tandja paid a price for having under-estimated the importance of the international advocacy developed by social movement activists, whose networks and transnational contacts contributed to isolating or broadly undermining the government's legitimacy in the eyes of public opinion (Keck and Sikkink 1998). The study of political mobilisation in Africa can therefore not eschew this important strategic dimension, especially as new communication strategies are actively used to connect with the international sphere. The 'Arab Spring' experience is a telling example of this.

References

Adji, S. (2002) 'Globalization and Union Strategies in Niger' in Jose, A.V. (ed) *Organized Labour in the 21st Century*, Geneva: International Institute for Labour Studies

Adji, S. (2004) « La trahison des clercs », *Hebdomadaire Alternative*, 13 décembre

Adji, S. (2009) « Réforme constitutionnelle et bonapartisme au Niger », *Hebdomadaire Alternative*, 9 juin

Adji, S. (2010) « Quelle transition pour quelle démocratie ? », *Hebdomadaire Alternative*, 2 avril

Adji, S. (2011) « Armée et instabilité politique », in Actes du Colloque « *Armée et pouvoir politique dans la gouvernance démocratique au Niger* », Niamey, 29-31 mai

Alou, M.T. (2008) « Les militaires politiciens » in K. Idrissa (dir.) *Armée et politique au Niger*, Dakar, Codesria

Boudon, R. (1984) *La place du désordre. Critique des théories du changement social*, Paris, Presses universitaires de France

Boudon, R. (2003) *Raison, Bonnes raisons*, Paris, Presses universitaires de France

Boukar, H. (2012) « Grève illimitée dans les IUT et à l'EMIG », *Hebdomadaire Alternative*, 13 octobre

Chazel, F. (1975) « La mobilisation politique : problèmes et dimensions », *Revue française de science politique*, 25 (3): 502-516

Garba, A. A. (2009) « Le « Tazarcé » et la chefferie traditionnelle : la complicité invisible », Cetri, 10 décembre, http://www.cetri.be/spip.php?article1460, visité en mars 2014

Gazibo, M. (1997) « Gloires et misères du mouvement syndical nigérien », *Politique Africaine*, n°69 : 126-134

Grégoire, E. (2010) *Rentes minières et coup d'État constitutionnel au Niger*, Institut Français de Géopolitique, février

Idrissa, K. (2008) « Introduction » in K. Idrissa (dir.) *Armée et politique au Niger*, Dakar, Codesria

International Crisis Group (2013) 'Niger: another weak link in the Sahel?', *Africa Report*, no. 208, 19 September, http://www.crisisgroup.org/fr/regions/afrique/afrique-de-louest/niger/208-niger-another-weak-link-in-the-sahel.aspx, accessed March 2014

Keck, M.E, Sikkink, K. (1998) *Activists beyond borders: Advocacy networks in International Politics*, Ithaca, Cornell University Press

Marx, K. (1852) *The Eighteenth Brumaire of Louis Bonaparte*, http://www.marxists.org/archive/marx/works/1852/18th-brumaire, accessed March 2014

Tcherno, H.B. (2006) « 'Guerre des gourdins' au campus universitaire », *Hebdomadaire Alternative*, 7 février

Tcherno, H.B. (2007) « Gloires et misères du mouvement étudiant », *Hebdomadaire Alternative*, 7 mars

Tcherno, H.B. (2013) « L'école publique en danger », *Hebdomadaire Alternative*, 5 mars

CHAPTER: 11

BETWEEN REPRESENTATION CRISIS, SOCIAL MOVEMENTS REPRESENTIVITY CRISIS AND MEDIA PROPAGANDA: WHAT ROLE FOR SENEGALESE CITIZENS?

Modou Diome

While social movements have usually been involved in the development of elite governance oversight by citizens, between 2010 and 2013 they risked losing all legitimacy through their insistence on pushing Senegal into a revolutionary state inspired by the Arab Spring. For the majority of social movements observed during the period, instead of the much-heralded citizen, frustrated and conspiring elite inserted themselves onto the protest scene under the benevolent gaze of an alarmist media hostile to the regime in place. Therefore, caught in a vice between the crisis of political representation and the legitimacy crisis of social movements, the silent majority of the people, through self-preservation instinct or through mere calculation, chose individual survival strategies that included abstention and withdrawal from the slogans of protesters. This chapter not only describes the scope, but also the critical flaws of social movements, whose fate, as we witnessed, remains for the most part failure, compromise and surrender.

Introduction

Senegal experienced its first democratic changeover when the *Sopi*[1] beat the Socialist Party (SP) with 58.1 per cent of votes in the second round of the elections of 19 March 2000. Seven years later, President Abdoulaye Wade was re-elected despite unfavourable predictions. Although he was re-elected, however, the pressure from unmet social demands led to the rise of social movements, or in other words collective actions targeted at the state whose single most significant goal was to control the direction of historicity in order to drive a social change project (Touraine 1973, Fillieule et al 2010). After the 'unemployment riots' (2007), the 'hunger riots' (2008) and the campaigns to boycott SENELEC (the national electricity company) bills (2008-2009), 'electricity riots' broke out in Dakar in 2009, 2010 and 2011. From the latter date and particularly as the 2012 presidential elections drew closer, social struggles took on an increasingly political dimension amid controversy on the unconstitutional nature of the outgoing president's decision to run for a third term. New movements such as *Y'en A Marre* and the Living Forces Movement of 23 June 2011 (M23) seized the baton of protest and, by the same token, federated the frustrations accumulated by community self-defence collectives over more than a decade of liberal rule (Diome 2013).

The resurgence of social movements nevertheless raises a central question that must be addressed: did social movements emerge as a result of a crisis of representative democracy in Senegal? Indeed the political representation crisis, decried for decades, is generally seen either as a cause, or as a symptom, which first translated into a considerable increase in abstention and also into

---

1   *Sopi,* which means change in Wolof, was Abdoulaye Wade's slogan. This movement was backed by the *Front pour l'Alternance*/Front for a Changeover (FAL) coalition.

a growing abandonment of politics, with the frustration expressed through collective protest in the street and the outpouring of dissident views through the media (Denquin 2010). From this perspective, we can assume that the social movements observed in Senegal during the period 2010-2013 derived not only from a crisis of political representation, but were also linked, for the most part, to an oligarchic struggle in which a frustrated elite, under the benevolent gaze of alarmist media hostile to the regime in place, claimed that it represented the people and defended the constitution against authoritarian abuses. Building mainly on an analysis of newspaper articles, audio and video recordings and interviews, this chapter first redefines the background and then continues to analyse the emergence of major social movements, before finishing with an in-depth discussion of the social movements observed between 2010 and 2013.

Background to the emergence of social movements

Historically, Senegalese political life has been marked by large-scale social movements. The 1944 revolt of the Senegalese '*tirailleurs*' against the colonial administration, the 1948 strike by rail workers, the sign bearers 'No' to General De Gaulle in 1958, the May 1968 student uprising, the 1987 police revolt and the 1988 *Sopi* revolt are just some of many milestones that, in many respects, bear the mark of social and political struggles (Zucarelli 1988, Diop and Diouf 1990, Bathily 1992, Diome 2013). This groundswell culminated with a democratic changeover on 19 March 2000, instilling in Senegalese the huge hope of seeing social demands, left unresolved by the defunct Socialist Party, finally met. Re-elected for a second term in 2007 with 56 per cent of votes in the first round, Wade's regime nevertheless failed to favourably respond to popular aspirations and to introduce the necessary change in the running of public affairs. The failure to separate powers, the wastage of resources and the social inequalities denounced by private radio stations were relayed by social movement leaders, who gave a central place to the issues that were 'mishandled' by the regime. During the 2011-2012 school year, teacher trade unions[2] went on strike demanding that agreements signed by the government be respected. There were fears that the academic year would be lost, especially with college and university student strikes. These students felt that it would be unreasonable to sit for final exams without having reached the time quantum.[3] Yet the education sector seemed privileged, as the regime always claimed that it allocated 40 per cent of the state budget to education. In the area of health, people criticised the poor quality of services, the high cost of care and the remoteness of health facilities which meant that due to the lack of ambulances in some rural communities, as media reported, women sometimes delivered on horse-drawn carts as they were being taken to the closest maternity ward.

As for electricity, it is the area in which people were the hardest hit. In spite of bill increases and the issue of double-invoicing, which was unilaterally imposed by SENELEC, the *Takkal*[4] plan proved ineffective against power outages and rationing. Households and small and medium enterprises (SMEs) not equipped with a power generator incurred significant losses. This is without mentioning the security risks caused by power cuts in districts where gangs of thieves committed crimes under the cover of darkness.

Low income households were unable to afford basic commodities, while constant stock-outs caused exasperation. Access to drinking water remained difficult in poor areas, while an end to recurring water shortages were at the heart of demands. To this list, one should add the issue of unusable roads, the conditions of which prevent the movement of goods and people. Meanwhile, the state built a 'sea road for the rich' in the capital. In this context, accusations

---

2   This was mainly the Unified Framework for Secondary Education Trade Unions (CUSEMS). This coalition later split, leading to the creation of two new trade unions: the CUSEMS and the SAEMSS-CUSEMS.
3   Compliance with time quantum refers to the effective realisation of the time allotted for teaching in the classroom. With disruption of the school year (absences, delays, strikes), the actual time achieved is often less than the time quantum. This reflects on academic performance and credibility of diplomas awarded by the educational system.
4   In the wake of the energy sector crisis, especially the sub-sector of electricity, the minister for international cooperation, air transport, infrastructures and energy created a Committee for Restructuring and Boosting the Sector of Energy (CRRSE), whose main mandate was to draw up an emergency plan for restructuring and boosting the sector: the *Takkal Plan*. See SAR (2013).

poured in. Some of the dissatisfied youth presented '1000 complaints against the Government of Senegal' (*Y'en A Marre 2011b*).

> I am a citizen; I lose days of work; I live in the dark because of power outages. Yet I pay my bills. I am sick and have no access to basic health care, although this is my right. I am a father, but my salary no longer covers the needs of my family. I am a mother, but my basket is empty. Yet 2000 filled me with dreams. I am a pupil, but my schooling is compromised. I passed my Baccalaureate, but have not been oriented; I am a student, but have no scholarship. I am a teacher, but my meagre salary is late. I wonder where the 40% of the national budget went. I am a farmer; I had faith in the GOANA and the REVA.[5] Yet, I no longer have seeds, no longer sell my harvest and am still owed 22 billion. They promised me a house in Jaxaay and because of that, they postponed the elections till 2007. And my family still lives through the hell of floods. I am a street seller, I am constantly hounded. Yet I just need a little space to earn a living [...] Through this complaint, I cry out my pain, express my rage and my revolt [...] Through this complaint finally, I say Stop to corruption, to demagogy, to political deception and I demand the right to a simply more decent, more humane life (*Y'en A Marre 2011b*).

In this context of unmet social demands, the corrupt nature of the ruling elite was brought to the fore with the 'Alex Segura' affair, named after the former International Monetary Fund (IMF) resident representative in Dakar. As he left Senegal in October 2009, Wade allegedly gave him a briefcase containing 100 million CFA Franc as a 'farewell gift'. In addition to corruption, those in power were accused of nepotism and clientelism due to the lack of transparency and objectivity in public procurement processes, marked by an over-reliance

---

5   Goana and REVA refer to plans made by the Senegalese government to booster agriculture and food self-sufficiency. Jaaxay plan was designed to house poor and middle class households at affordable conditions in Jaxaay commune.

on private arrangements. Subjective recruitments were also denounced. The ruling elite's appetite for quick and illicit wealth was even described as 'financial and estate bulimia' by the so-called independent media. The regime was discredited for grabbing arable land from communities (Mbane, Gnith, Fanaye, Sangalkam, Kedougou etc) and selling it to foreign agribusiness operators, despite popular protest. During an interview in Kedougou, the journalist Fode Camara dissected the looting of mining resources, organised under the guise of a so-called prospection operation, in a story of a state caught in the act of granting licenses on land owned by local communities.[6] This was all done at the expense of the population and particularly the youth, who faced endemic unemployment. Beyond these material complaints, there was a sense of impunity stemming from the treatment of some cases where partisans of the regime were involved. The changeover regime seemed to be encouraging or covering up for perpetrators of death threats, insults, physical violence, etc, and targeting journalists or political actors considered too critical. This climate of insecurity partly discredited the institutions in charge of upholding the law, while some of its members were suspected of being corrupted by the regime. Some of the private media felt that they were the victims of a censorship system intentionally activated to thwart its development and diversification policies, as it alone spoke with a conflicting voice that disturbed those in power. The above-mentioned factors served as a launch pad for social movements.

Social movements and the assault on the ruling elite

Collective actions against the state

Immediately after Wade's re-election in February 2007, the opposition boycotted the June 2007 legislative elections after alleging that there was a likelihood of fraud due to the unreliability of the election roster. It rallied

---

6   The interview builds on ideas developed in a newspaper article published in 2003.

around the *Front Siggil Senegaal* (FSS) coalition in the process. Absent from parliament, FSS members were forced to join forces with protest movements in order to exist politically. For this reason, the changeover regime suspected that the manipulating hand of this ailing opposition was hiding behind the large-scale protest. In November 2007, street sellers set Dakar on fire because they refused to be moved out in efforts to unclog a city about to host the Islamic Conference Organisation (ICO) for the second time in its history. In March 2008, under the leadership of consumer organisations, 'hunger riots' broke out in Dakar. Its initiators protested against the high cost of living. In December 2008, the town of Kedougou became the scene of deadly riots in the wake of complaints over the management of the mining social program (MSP) and of the mining social fund (MSF) created to support local communities based in mining areas. The rioters accused the state of alienating community land in favour of foreign agribusinesses and of 'importing labour from other regions of the country, whereas Kedougou is full of skilled suitable for these positions'.[7]

In this tense context, the FSS convened all Senegalese to a national forum, organised under civil society stewardship. The Senegalese National Forum was held between 1 June 2008 and 24 May 2009, and gathered more than 140 actors from Senegalese public life, political parties and civil society representatives, as well as various personalities. It was chaired by Professor Amadou Mahtar Mbow, former UNESCO managing director. Though invited, members of the presidential majority—mainly the Senegalese Democratic Party around Wade—chose to stay clear. For organisers, the aim was to find a consensual, comprehensive, effective and lasting solution to the serious multidimensional crises (ethical, political, economic, social and cultural) that gripped the country. Civic consultations launched across the country and abroad (France, United States, Canada) helped to draw a complete picture of the political, social and economic situation of Senegal, at a time when political dialogue had reached a deadlock. The conclusion of the

---

7   Interview with a youth leader from Kedougou, August 2010

forum was delayed, so that consideration of its findings did not interfere with the local elections of March 2009. Officially completed on 24 May 2009, a 50-page synthesis report was drafted, addressing most of the problems faced by the country.[8] Having intentionally stayed away from the event, the state refused to adopt the democratic governance charter produced by the forum.

A few weeks before the 2008 Kedougou riots, a new organisation calling itself the Collective of Imams and Residents of the Guediawaye Districts (CIRQG) fought a relentless battle against the state and SENELEC. Indeed, the CIRQG started its protest action against high electricity bills, double invoicing and power outages with a major protest march on 6 December 2008. Attended by people from the suburbs, the march ended with a decision to boycott electricity bills in order to force the state to the negotiation table. The success of this first campaign encouraged CIRQG to launch a second boycott in July 2009 in order to block a unilateral attempt to increase electricity prices (by eight per cent). The specificity of this movement is that it was more inclusive, as it involved members of civil society, the clergy, consumer associations, and trade unions. Better still, through their efforts, Imams also wished to play a major role in the debacle of the *Sopi* coalition at the 2009 local elections. This coalition was beaten by the opposition in the suburbs and therefore in the capital (Diome 2010).

But in spite of its popularity and achievements (an extension of the social band from 50 to 150 KW/h for example),[9] the structure began waning in 2010. Indeed, co-opted as a member of the Committee for Restructuring and Boosting the Energy Sector (CRRSE) initiated by the state in 2010, its coordinator Imam Youssoupha Sarr was harshly criticised by some members of the movement who considered this a form of collusion with the regime. He was forced to stand down from this framework aimed at finding solutions to the desperate issue of electricity. However, this resignation did not prove

---

8   Wikipedia (2012) 'Assises Nationales du Sénégal', accessed 5 January.
9   Out of a total of 750,000 SENELEC subscribers, the social band applies to 482,000 users with a bi-monthly consumption under 150KW/h. Its extension amounts to a 2.69 per cent drop in the price of electricity for its beneficiaries, while those consumers not included incurred an eight per cent increase.

to be an effective response. This waning of popularity paved the way for 'electricity looters' and new movements such as the Initiative for Security in Guediawaye (ISEG) and the like (2010-2011).

Henceforth, electricity, thus far the main cause of CIRQG, was taken on by angry youth, who started the violent electricity riots in 2009, 2010 and 2011 in Dakar and its suburbs. The example of the electricity riots which broke out on the night of 27 June 2011 is telling. Indeed, that night was punctuated with violent protest, seemingly in response to power outages. Under the cover of darkness, uncontrolled groups engaged in looting and burning, targeting mainly SENELEC branches, public buildings and goods, as well as the homes of ministers and personalities close to the state. According to Superintendent Arona Sy of the Dakar police headquarters, these riots, given their intensity and scope, took the greatest toll on security forces, according to *L'Observateur* on 12 April 2012. In fact, on 14 July 2011, the president, while admitting his surprise and concern, described the riots as 'a brutal operation planned by groups of thugs and destabilization specialists' (Wade 2011).

As for struggle movements against the grabbing of arable land and their leasing or sale to agri-businesses, these gained in intensity in October 2011. In Fanaye (Podor) for instance, the rural council decided to grant 20,000 hectares of land to the 'private Italian financial group Tampieri, associated to the Senegalese operators Senethanol and Senhuile' (Ndiaye 2011). This move was endorsed by the central authorities. Threatened with expropriation, the mainly agro pastoralist populations organised themselves and created a collective for land protection in the Thille sub-district and the Fanaye rural community. In a statement dated 21 October, their spokesperson Youssouf Barro rang the alarm bell, taking an opposite stand to that of the president of the Karass Kane rural community, who had praised the benefits and community buy-in of the project in the media.

Barro said that it was neither participatory, nor inclusive. He went on to reveal some of its immediate harmful effects: the displacement of more than 60 villages and hamlets; the large-scale destruction of cattle, sheep, goats and horses; the destruction of several thousand hectares of protected forest; the desecration of cemeteries and mosques; and the loss of employment by thousands of farmers living on the site. Through a variety of actions, people demanded the discontinuation of an initiative which they considered, as stated by their spokesperson, disastrous, opaque and illegal, as it was likely to sow the seeds of 'violence and destruction in this very peaceful area of Senegal'. These pleas fell on the deaf ears of the central and local authorities. As a consequence, clashes broke out on 26 October between rural councillors in favour of the project and members of the collective. The community house was set on fire, with three deaths during the clashes (Amadou Bassirou Toumbou, Oumar Abdou Ba and Djabira Tall) and several injured amongst the security forces who stepped in during the clash (*Seneweb* 26 October 2011).

Under pressure from the collective and following the violence, the state came to its senses. At the council of ministers of 1 December 2011, Wade gave up on the Fanaye project. Nevertheless:

> Noting the major interest that populations express in large-scale agricultural projects due to their strong economic and social impact, [the Council of Ministers] advises initiators of the agricultural project [...] to move it to Nianga Edy, in the Podor Department [...] It strongly advises them to engage with religious and traditional chiefs as well as populations of this area in order to secure the endorsement of the Rural Council and adequate project localization (*Seneweb* 2 December 2011).

However, notwithstanding the importance of the social movements reviewed thus far, we have to refer to the first fortnight of June 2011 to see the emergence of the most significant post-2000 social movement, which sought from its inception to control the direction of historicity.

The rise to power of Y'en A Marre and the M23

According to its leaders, *Y'en A Marre* is a movement whose backbone is made up of rap artists and journalists, as well as urban youth and students. It was born on 16 January 2011 in the Dakar suburbs and more precisely at Parcelles Assainies, Lot 16.[10] In its January 2011 manifesto, *Y'en A Marre* defines its motivations and mission as follows:

> At the beginning, he said, was despair! Long nights in the darkness. Days of work lost. Children passing away in hospitals, on surgery tables. Corpses rotting in the morgues. Fed up of seeing all this pent up frustration, held back day after day without doing anything! Fed up of being an accomplice of this wearisome passivity without lifting the smallest finger. Fed up of having run out of our capacity for outrage. Fed up of waiting for a hypothetical savior to solve our problems while we do nothing to change things ourselves. Fed up of seeing the other jeopardize our future! Fed up with broken promises! Canted projects! Fed up with shattered dreams! Fed up of seeing the changeover be canted, sinking in the abyss of indifference, just as the Joola cruiser sank. Fed up seeing the PO LI TI SHITE elite ride on the misery of the weakest, teasing a people struggling to survive (*Y'en A Marre* 2011a).

Aiming to lay the foundations of a new society, in other words the republic of citizens, *Y'en A Marre* sought to build on the NTS concept (New Type of Senegalese). Steeped in republican values, the latter would be a 'responsible, righteous and committed citizen able to fulfil the social transformation

---

10   Author interview with Fadel Barro, Caat and Kilifë, May and June 2011

project' (Y'en A Marre 2011b). To this end, *Y'en A Marre* organised concerts throughout the capital and the country to denounce the regime, sensitise the youth and develop in them a 'civic awareness' conducive to 'a feeling of political empowerment' (Havard 2004:26).

Shortly after, the '1000 complaints against the Government of Senegal' campaign was launched. In spite of the setbacks, police summons, prohibition and breaking up of its rallies, it gained strength, developed strategies and held press conferences.

On 19 March 2011, *Y'en A Marre* rallied the youth at the Place de l'Obélisque to heed the call launched by Sidy Lamine Niasse, managing director of the Walfadjri Multimedia Group,[11] to protest against the excesses of the regime. After this event, *Y'en A Marre* poised for its most crucial battle over the ballot, with the campaign '*daas fanaanal*' *(*my voting card, my weapon*).* Its name suggests that potential voters 'sharpen your knife and patiently wait until the time has come to use it'. In other words, people needed to register on the electoral roster in order to be in a position to vote (*Nouvel Horizon* 15-21 April 2011). In spite of limited means (sound system, logistics, and payment of artists) for the running of this campaign, the desire for independence remained strong. The slogan 'Politicians need not apply!' confirmed their initial outlook: 'Neither with the regime in power, nor with the opposition.' This off-centre stance seems to be the trademark of social movement components, at least in theory, and especially at the start of their action.

Some remain sceptical of the argument that power outages were the reason for the birth of *Y'en A Marre*, maintaining that their 'involvement' was first and foremost linked to frustration at the marginalisation of its core group of rap artists during the World Festival of Black Arts (FESMAN).

---

11 The press boss made this call to protest against the 'relentless hassling' of his media group by the regime, having repeatedly been asked for dues by the regulation authority.

Collusion between the youth initiative and media bosses hostile to the regime, such as Youssou Ndour[12] and Abdou Latif Coulibaly,[13] was denounced.

This connivance between a frustrated press and dissenting youth became more visible during the election period. In the eyes of its detractors, *Y'en A Marre* even deviated towards politics, when it transformed into a political support movement for the election of Macky Sall in the second round of the 2012 presidential elections. This gradual 'peopleisation' of politics was a striking feature of the sequence leading to this contribution, in so far as actors previously involved in entertaining people through music, dance or sport ended up taking advantage of their icon status, sought after by the masses and the media, in order to enter politics and push with all their weight for the future of the country. The launch of the slogan '*doggali*'[14] (finished off) by *Y'en A* Marre and '*wër ndombo*' (rounding up) by Youssou Ndour of the *Fekkee Ma Ci Boole* (literally 'my presence involves me') movement aimed on the one hand at giving the final blow to Wade's regime, and on the other, at backing up an opposition candidate.

Concerning M23, it is a social movement including *Y'en A Marre*, civil society organisations, journalists, opposition political parties, trade unions, etc. It was born in the simmering period of June 2011. To best define the background, let us look at the events. Indeed, on 17 June 2011,[15] the chief executive signed a decree to submit Bill #13/2011. Introduced as part of an

---

12   Youssou Ndour is a musician and lead vocalist of the Super étoile band. Having founded a media group, he entered politics by creating the political movement called *Fekke Ma Ci Boole* in 2009. Launched to force the state to grant him a television broadcasting frequency, he then used this movement as a stepping stone to run for the 2012 presidential elections. When his candidacy was thrown out by the Constitutional Council, he joined the M23 and took an active part in the 2012 pre-electoral protest. After Wade's defeat, he was appointed culture and tourism minister.
13   Abdou Latif Coulibaly was a journalist from Sud Communication Media Group and director of *La Gazette* magazine. Author of the first pamphlet against Sopi's regime (*Wade un opposant un pouvoir, l'alternance piégée, Sentinelle Editions*, Dakar, 2003), he presented his candidacy to the 2012 presidential elections, then withdrew it to support Moustapha Niasse. He was later appointed minister for the promotion of good governance by Macky Sall.
14   *Y'en A Marre* used several slogans. The 'fanaanee daas' (spending the night sharpening the knife) is nothing more than a development of the 'daas fanaanal'. It urges citizens to withdraw their voting card. Besides, on 23 December 2012, *Y'en A Marre* launched the 'faut pas forcer' slogan against President Wade's candidacy. On 22 January 2012, it organised a 'Problems Fair' at Obelisque Square, inviting several social groups to present their difficulties to the audience.
15   Two days before the riots of 23 June 2011, in other words on 21June, Member of Parliament Cheikh Bamba Dièye chained himself to the gates of the national parliament in complicity with *Walf TV* reporters to protest against the constitutional bill that was about to be passed.

emergency procedure, the constitutional reform project aimed, amongst others, at the simultaneous universal suffrage election of a 'ticket' with a president and a vice-president, who would replace the former in case of resignation, permanent impeachment or death of the president of the republic. A ticket would be declared winner if it led the polls and received at least a quarter of valid votes (the blocking quarter).

The draft bill provoked an outcry. The opposition, civil society, journalists, media bosses and trade unions saw it as nothing short of a plot to do away with the second round and one more action towards fulfilling the so-called 'monarchic devolution of power' project by Wade, 85, in favour of his son Karim, 42, who was then at the helm of no fewer than four ministerial departments.

On 23 June 2011, while the MPs of the majority party were about to vote on this bill, actors of the collective clashed with security forces in the city centre and managed to cling to the gates of the national parliament. With violence spiralling out of control and the intervention of religious guides and other social mediators, the regime renounced the draft modification under pressure from the street (Diome 2012). The next day, the collective that had waged this fight became the M23. In order to better coordinate its future actions, it formalised itself at a structuring and orientation seminar held on 13 August 2011. The new entity was co-managed by a civil society figure (Alioune Tine[16]) and by a political figure (Amath Dansokho[17]).

After the first objective was reached (withdrawal of the draft bill on the ticket), M23 adopted the war cry of the Arab Spring: 'Wade out!' The M23 waged a new fight against the third mandate sought by Wade by conducting ritual protest on the 23rd day of each month. Its leitmotiv was: 'Wade must not be a candidate, he cannot be a candidate and he shall not be a candidate.' Foreign

---

16 Alioune Tine is a very influential member of civil society. Former President of RADDHO (African gathering for human rights), he became the president of the Senegalese Human Rights Committee after Macky Sall came to power.
17 One of the most iconic figures of the Senegalese left and former president of the Independence and Labour Party (PIT), Amath Dansokho currently acts as minister of state for the president of the republic, Macky Sall.

and national constitutional experts engaged in legal bouts, which only further contributed to confusing public opinion. It planned to coordinate a gathering on 23 January 2012 in a Dakar suburb. This march against Wade's candidacy was initially forbidden before being authorised. On 24 January, Wade introduced his candidacy despite challenges by M23. The movement promised that if Wade's candidacy was validated, Senegal would lapse into a cycle of violence.

The Constitutional Council cut the Gordian knot in favour of the presidential side. Its decision ignited a fire and radicalised M23, which settled at Obelisque Square before attempting, unsuccessfully, to seize Independence Square and turn it into a Tahrir Square scenario.[18] This power struggle led to deadly political violence. Between January and February, eight deaths were recorded in Dakar and other regions of the country. Well organised protesters used motorbike helmets, balaclavas, hoods, gas masks and goggles, picking up teargas grenades and throwing them back at the anti-riot police.

M23 action units, including *Y'en A Marre* and opposition youth, adopted an urban guerrilla strategy. In small groups, they set up a communication system using mobile phones and a fearsome subversion mechanism. These combat units became extremely mobile in Kaolack (the town of origin of *Y'en A Marre* leaders) thanks to the use of Jakarta bikes and they hit strategic targets at speed, throwing projectiles and burning tyres, blocking off crucial roads and then disappearing to avoid a clash with police. This streamlining of political violence (Braud 2004) considerably undermined the coercive capacity of the regime.

The regime started seeking ways to break the secret of this unexpected resistance capacity. Intelligence services got on the task. Idrissa Seck, one of the M23 leaders, chief of the *Rewmi* party and a presidential candidate, was accused of being the mastermind behind the resistance (see for example

---

18 'Tahrir Square' literally means Liberation Square in Arabic. It is situated in Egypt and played a prominent role in the popular revolution against Hosni Mubarak's military regime in February 2011. By analogy, social movement actors first compared it to Obelisque Square, then to Independence Square (formerly Protest Square).

Dakaractu 20 February 2012). Concerned, the international community sent former Nigerian President Olusegun Obasanjo to first lead an election observation mission on behalf of the Economic Community of West African States (ECOWAS) and then to act as mediator in the crisis between the regime and the opposition. The latter not only stood against Wade's candidacy, but also generally felt that the context of crisis and violence was not suitable to hold elections.

The Senegalese were called to the polls on 26 February 2012. In spite of the fears and the tense pre-election context, the presidential election took place as normal. The call for restraint made by religious guides and mediators was heeded by the silent majority of the Senegalese people (Diome 2012). This being said, what role did the media play in the M23 protest?

Political violence amplified by alarmist media

It is difficult to analyse social movements in Senegal without addressing the position of the media (Neveu 2010), especially in the 2010-2012 period. Indeed, in its coverage of pre-electoral events, the media played the role of distorting facts in order to blame the regime in place. During that period, the media treatment of the social unrest described in the first phase of this article was very biased. The regime went as far as to say that the real opposition to their power was the private press. The numerous unbalanced commentary articles, editorials, television debates, biased protest coverage, alarmist and propagandist headlines, etc are ample evidence of this. *Walfadjri*, for instance, printed the following headline the day after the protest of 23 June 2011: 'Senegal: Bloodbath in Dakar: the Sun sets over a scene from the Apocalypse'.

Better still, the state authorities, namely the Ministry of the Interior and the Ministry of Armed Forces criticised the *Walfadjri* and *Futurs Médias* multimedia groups for not only 'giving the opportunity to the opposition and civil society to pour out their hatred on Wade and his government, but also for contributing to the success of the protest that led to violent clashes between disgruntled groups and security forces.' What the regime felt most upset by were 'the live shows produced for this purpose'. According to the authorities, these 'live shows' encouraged a large section of the youth to go out on the streets, 'with massive groups coming from the suburbs and moving towards the city centre to take part in the clashes'. *Walfadjri* was also blamed for organising studio broadcasts (by Sidy Lamine Niasse, its managing director) on Wednesdays and Thursdays, days of protest, and *Futurs Médias* for the debates organised with resource people who clearly took the side of protesters (*Rewmi* 30 june 2011).

The media coverage of the 2012 pre-electoral protest followed the same principle of sensational headlines announcing the worst. In the online media, the written press and the radio and television airwaves, the lexical register on chaos prevailed: 'Senegal lights up' (*Dakaractu* 18 February; *Le Populaire* 18-19 February), 'Downward spiral...Macabre blaze' (*L'As* 20 February), 'Wade's bloody breeze' (*Le Quotidien*, 20 February), 'Bloodbath in Dakar' (*Seneweb* 19 February; *Observateur* 20 February; *Le Populaire* 28-29 January), 'Senegal on the edge of apocalypse' (*Dakaractu* 20 February), 'Chaos in Senegal?' (*Huffington Post* 20 February). In response to this media propaganda, which sought to manufacture consent at all costs, the bureau of the 2012 Allied Forces (FAL-2012), the coalition that supported Wade, issued a statement on 1 February to denounce the manner in which Youssou Ndour's *Futurs Médias Group* 'resorted to archives featuring the events of June 23rd 2011 to attempt to manipulate public opinion, to win it over, by pretending that the country was on fire, and therefore to maintain it in a spiral of violence' (*Express News* 1 February 2012). The FAL-2012 also criticised the foreign media, namely *France 24* and *RFI*, whom they asked for 'equity and transparency in their treatment of information' (*Express News* 1 February 2012).

But why so much hatred, we are tempted to ask? International media coverage of the protests, the French media in particular, was not always neutral. The Wade regime, which France blamed for trying to diversify its economic partners, used this to its advantage by denouncing a western plot against his power. As for the Senegalese media, their hostility can be explained by a two-fold dispute with the government. On the one hand, the regime had always felt ill at ease with the free tone used by journalists in editorials, and it often attempted to silence them through physical violence, death threats, insults, intimidation and jail. On the other hand, an entrepreneurial spirit within the media opposed the regime. The latter hoped that the changeover was going to foster a spirit of entrepreneurship. Many had invested heavily in the media business, hoping that change would be conducive to a heightened development and diversification policy. They ended up being somewhat dissatisfied, financially asphyxiated, deprived of advertising resources and harassed by the tax administration. Frustration led journalists and media bosses closer to the opposition, to protest movements and to civil society, thus creating a large anti-government coalition.

But stuck between the rock of poor political representation and the hard place of social movements joining forces with the media and 'elitists' in their agenda how did people respond?

Between the representation crisis and the representivity crisis of social movements: defection as an alternative

The ballot test

After the vote of 26 February 2012, the final results were published by the Constitutional Council on 6 March 2012[19] showing two candidates clearly in the lead: Wade (34.81 per cent) and Sall (26.58 per cent). The rate of abstention was estimated at 48.42 per cent, a figure much higher than the score obtained

---

19   Temporary results were published by the Dakar Court of Appeal on 31 February 2012.

by either of the two successful candidates in the second round. The lack of vision and consensus among the political elite, the popular disaffection with political affairs and political violence no doubt withered any desire among citizens to go to the polls. Having partly lost the street protests and partly lost through the ballot box, the M23 recognised that the battle had been lost. None of its candidates qualified for the second round. To save face, the movement rallied around Sall, who qualified for the second round in a treacherous first round. Following the second round held on 25 March 2012, Sall won with 65.8 per cent. As for the outgoing president, he only received 34.2 per cent of the votes. Estimated at 51.58 per cent in the first round, the rate of participation slightly improved to reach 55 per cent. At 9:27pm, Wade phoned the winner to congratulate him.

Overall, the results of the first and second round appeared to be a strong disapproval of the strategy and approach of the M23 *tahririans*.[20] Rooted in ideals of democracy, peace and non-violence, the Senegalese issued 'a clear denial [...] of all those prophets of doom who hastily called out to the bedside of an agonizing Senegal' (Wade 2012). In the same way, Alioune Tine made revealing remarks after the elections. Indeed, following the pre-electoral protest, the M23 realised that 'the Senegalese do not like violence'. Their electoral behaviour was proof that they wanted 'Wade's departure through the ballots', but not in the Tahrir way. Resigned, Tine concluded: 'Bearing this in mind, the M23 cannot stand in contradiction with the message, the desire and the willingness clearly expressed by the Senegalese. This would be anti-democratic' (*Le Quotidien* 29 February 2012).

The bitterness of the main leader of the M23 reveals a deep trench within social movements at that time and raises the issue of their legitimacy. Do social movements still have the popular legitimacy that they have always claimed thus far? Between the daily fight for survival and the fight to protect the constitution, where did priorities lie for people which, before the M23,

---

20 Protesters inspired by the occupants of Tahrir Square in Cairo (Egypt).

had created collectives within their communities to protect their dignity (*suturë*) against the high cost of living, power outages and the unpopular policies of the regime?

Defection to the social movement slogans as the secret weapon of the Senegalese against usurpers

Throughout its struggle, the opposition claimed that it defended the people and protected the constitution. This claim led it to first of all organise a national forum. With the benefit of hindsight, we can say that the actors of the national forum failed on two accounts: a pre-electoral failure, and its immediate consequence, the electoral failure. The first debacle is linked to the inability of the opposition political class to rally around a single candidate. The coalition was split into two currents in the absence of a unanimous figure: *Bennoo Siggil Senegaal*, which supported Moustapha Niasse,[21] and Ousmane Tanor Dieng's[22] *Bennoo ak Tanor*. The consequences of this first failure spilled over into the second, as they were negatively sanctioned by the people. When it comes to making an assessment, the forum program did not grab the attention of Senegalese. After the first round of voting, poor results came out: Moustapha Niasse with 13.2 per cent and Ousmane Tanor Dieng with 11.3 per cent. Overall, the cumulative percentage of these two candidates only represented 24.5 per cent of the vote, which amounted to less than the respective scores of Wade (34.8 per cent) and Sall (26.6 per cent).

This low popular buy-in of the national forum program was apparent in the lack of legitimacy of the M23 and of all its members who signed the pact of 2 February 2012 through which they unanimously decided to organise common protest activities during the electoral campaign in order to ensure

---

21 Moustapha Niasse was the leader of the Alliance for the Forces of Progress (AFP) and of the *Bennoo Siggil Senegaal* (BSS) coalition during the presidential elections of 2012. He is the current speaker of the national parliament.
22 Ousmane Tanor Dieng is a former minister of state in charge of presidential affairs under President Abdou Diouf; he is the current secretary general of the Socialist Party and was leader of the *Bennoo Ak Tanor* coalition during the 2012 presidential elections.

compliance with the constitution and the electoral code. The more radical members of this pact, also called 'Independence Square candidates', laid daily siege to Obelisque Square, and then to Independence Square, under the cameras of national and international media, leading to the most brutal scenes of violence imaginable. However, in spite of their ongoing presence in the theatre of operations where they claimed to defend the people and in spite of their tremendous exposure to the benevolent coverage of media hostile to the regime, these radical candidates ended up with poor results in the first round. Idrissa Seck (7.9 per cent), Cheikh Abiboulaye Dièye (1.9 per cent), Ibrahima Fall (1.8 per cent) and Cheikh Tidiane Gadio (0.98 per cent) are all evidence of this.[23] Amongst these political actors, only Seck reached a percentage that would secure him a refund of the 65 million CFA Franc[24] deposit.

Looking at such results, one understands better why the M23 did not want elections to take place. Indeed, without a candidate strong enough to face off against Wade and in the absence of enough guarantees on the electoral defeat of the outgoing president, some M23 leaders refused to take part in elections where the Senegalese Democratic Party (SDP) main candidate would run. While some bandied about a strategy of boycott, others theorised about recourse to the military, to a parallel government or to a national transitional council. Certainly convinced of this unpopularity, which they refused to admit, Wade challenged them several times through the media, saying: 'If I am as unpopular as you claim, let us go to the polls and beat me democratically.'

One must admit that it is between 2011 and 2012 that the M23, which had just been born, capitalised with a great sense of timing on all the frustrations

---

23 Idrissa Seck was former prime minister under Wade and number two of the Senegalese Democratic Party (SDP); he currently leads the Rewmi Party. Cheikh Abiboulaye Dièye, aka Bamba Dièye, is the leader of the Front for Socialism and Democracy, *Bennoo Jubël* (FSD BJ), and currently minister of communication under Sall. Ibrahima Fall, professor of public law, former under-secretary general of the United Nations Organisation for Human Rights, he is the president of the *Taxaw Temm* (standing firmly) political movement. Cheikh Tidiane Gadio is a former minister of state for foreign affairs and current leader of the *Luy Jot Jotna* (MPCL) political and civic movement.
24 Candidates who obtain less than five per cent of votes do not get a refund of their deposit.

individually aggregated by the self-defence collectives in districts and communities during more than a decade of struggle. Having quickly become the main organised political force in the country, the M23 revealed a gradual and often brutal infiltration of so-called civil society in order to conquer political power directly or indirectly, on the streets or, if all else failed, through the polls. Their stubborn efforts to push the country into an insurgency that would have justified the establishment of a national transitional council, as had been the case in Libya, failed before a people fearful of chaos. But it was revealing of the lengths to which some leaders of social movements were ready to go in order to not only access power using an indirect route, but also to achieve a post-revolution constitutive assembly, thus speeding up the process of modernising a society which, out of conservatism or caution, still resisted the lure of any kind of change.

In the final analysis, M23's insistence in trying to reproduce a Tahrir Square scenario only heightened suspicions that often weighed on the movement. It was variously suspected of 'working Senegalese society' on behalf of homosexual, Freemason and alter-globalist lobbies, whose secret plan was to redefine the overall standards and orientations of society. The dissemination through the media of the New Type of Senegalese (NTS) concept and the attacks perpetrated on brotherhood religious guides seemed to suggest that these social movements denied the 'Senegalese social contract'.[25] In its declaration of 19 March 2011 for instance, *Y'en A Marre* started speaking out against a patronage system, 'using the power of the religious leaders as vector of social control' (*Y'en A Marre* 2011b). This anticlerical vision perfectly reflected the stance of M23, which, through the whole duration of its fight against the regime, mainly targeted its religious supporters by trying to spitefully deconstruct the discourse presenting Senegal as a land blessed by its religious guides, and which, by virtue of this blessing, was shielded from

---

25 In Senegal, the state has historically been confronted with two major obstacles: first of all, the difficulty of establishing institutional links between state and society, and secondly, the lack of sociological legitimacy at the root of political power. Faced with these two obstacles, Senegalese brotherhoods have habitually provided an effective link between state and society (O'Brien 1992).

scourges such as civil wars, coups and revolutions. As a result, its coordinators were unable to do away with the negative image still associated with them. What the polls showed partly confirmed that the fight of the frustrated elite gathered around M23 did not receive the support expected from Senegalese. If the people had indeed risen on 23 June 2011, its vote should have reflected this stance of protest not only against Wade's regime, but also against the by-products of Wade's[26] regime, including Sall. The consistency of the popular vote has even been challenged, in so far as Sall belongs to the liberal family, which did not favourably meet the expectations of the people. So how can we explain that voters chose to sanction Wade in person rather than the regime that he built?

In fact, one can say that the Senegalese vote of 2012 was 'a crisis vote' to tell apart the elites fighting over power and ready to burn the country down to achieve their goals. Rather than being motivated by ideological debate and the relevance of programs, their choice was based on the need to regain peace and security. They had to elect someone and quickly turn the page, as since Senegal has been voting, elections have merely been a ritual for rotating elites at the helm of the state. In this case, as many Senegalese say, given the situation of emergency which prevailed during the electoral context of the time, Sall can be considered as a president by default (*yaafi sës mooy taxa falu*). The same discourse was used against Wade in 2000, then in 2007.

We need to insist on this point, as elections are a process for preserving the socio-political order. Therefore, it is difficult for citizens, in light of their political experience, to hope for a radical break within a political class in which all are alike. As is sometimes said, the number 6 and the number 9 are identical; you simply turn one upside down to obtain the other. Such is the popular perception of political actors. So people did not vote to change a system that will perpetuate itself at every election anyway, nor did they radically sanction a regime while pouring acclaim on one of its offshoots.

---

26 'No to Wade, no to Wade's by-products' was the slogan of Mor Dieng, candidate to the 2012 presidential elections.

However, they engaged in a ritual aimed at expiating the violence which periodically erupts during bouts between elites at the top of the political game. We can see therefore that an oligarchic struggle hides behind this seemingly democratic joust, because in order to protect the constitution, the elite claims to be ready for the supreme sacrifice ('*Sama constitution, sama bakka*', or 'hands off my constitution').

Having understood the habitual approach of the elite that loses its cool during electoral processes, many Senegalese were reluctant to answer the calls of social movements. This begs the question as to whether the fight is the same for the people and for the M23. Do they speak the same language? In fact, do people fight for modified or infringed constitutions? In reality, 'people do not fight for Constitutions. They fight first and foremost for their dignity, justice and better living conditions. They do not fight for a Constitution that was modified more than a dozen times in as many years, which they have never read and will never read in their lives' (Sylla 2012:2).

Confronted with an ailing representative democracy, with social movements whose concerns were far removed from their own and with media propaganda on political violence, Senegalese found other alternatives. For example, when their tables were smashed up and thrown into the fire by M23 rioters, the street sellers from Sandaga, Ponty and neighbouring areas remained concerned with their own survival and defected from M23 slogans, creating a counter slogan in the process: 'Hands off my table.' This concept revealed that the working masses felt excluded and unconcerned by a fight that they did not identify with, and which was led on their behalf by social movements in dire need of credibility.

> Indeed those 'tables' represent an important capital for the millions that are excluded from the Senegalese modern sector. As protesters took it out on the working tools of the poor, it was normal that they were reminded that for the neediest, 'tables' are

more sacred than 'Constitutions'. Their tables are their property and they do not feel that the existing judicial superstructure was designed for the purpose of their emancipation. The paradox lies with the fact that when burning or damaging their working tools, protesters cause significant loss of earnings for them. In other words, the victims of the system are the ones paying the highest price for the damages caused by oligarchies and the protest they generate (Sylla 2012:3).

Wanting to ease their conscience, M23 leaders ironically stated after 23 June 2011 that the people had fought valiantly to defend the fundamental charter against the presidential ticket project, and had therefore shown unprecedented maturity by demonstrating that they no longer fought only for concrete or material gains (such as bread, water and electricity), but also for formal and abstract things such as the constitution. This populism, which consists in portraying elite concerns as being the concerns of the people, in giving the people a political competence it does not have, serves the interests of an oligarchy that hides behind social movements in order to destroy regimes. The discrete existence of these oligarchic struggles also demonstrates the obvious connivance between social movement actors, journalists and multimedia group bosses, disgruntled with the regime in place. The representation crisis of the social movements in question is borne out of this discrepancy with the people, because when they steer clear from popular aspirations, when they are unable to decipher the message sent by the silent majority of the people, social movements lose all legitimacy or even control over the direction of historicity; in other words control over the models of behaviour based on which a society produces its practices (Touraine 1973).

Social movements and the test of power

Where is the much heralded shift?

In the insurgency context of 2011-2012, marked by a declining legitimacy of the political class, members of civil society who led M23 were convinced at a given point that they controlled the direction of historicity. But their rushed entry into politics exposed them to a game in which they eventually felt tricked by politicians. Thus after the second changeover, aware that they simply played the role of 'beaters', some ended up being tamed into a strategic alliance where their former role as 'righteous champions of citizens' was tested by power.

This coalition, named *Bennoo Bokk Yaakaar* and essentially made up of members of the national forum and of the M23, was criticised for doing 'the same as Wade without Wade'. The promised reforms failed to materialise. Instead of a lower cost of living, citizens noted an increase. The start of the 'hunt for ill-gotten wealth' is perceived by some commentators as 'a witch hunt', a justice of victors using the judiciary, which is supposed to be independent, to destroy an opposition gradually regaining strength. This highly publicised recovery campaign became increasingly akin to a communication campaign aimed at hiding their inability to meet social demands and to provide an effective remedy since accessing power. The promises for 'sober and virtuous governance' made during the campaign and the 'country before party' slogan were prematurely marred by the president's wealth declaration, estimated at around eight billion CFA francs. His opponents felt that this amount was unjustified and that the Court for the Suppression of Ill-gotten Wealth (CREI) should start its investigations there. Far from disappearing completely, the nepotistic and patronage practices much condemned under Wade's rule resurfaced in the era of the so-called 'Faye-Sall dynasty' (that of the president and in-laws, according to the press).

The regime co-opts social movement leaders

The powerful and very influential media bosses, formerly suspected of conspiring with the opposition against the regime in power, have been co-opted by the current regime. This is the case of Abdou Latif Coulibaly and Babacar Touré from the Sud Communication Group and its offshoots, of Bara Tall from the 7 Com group and of Youssou Ndour, managing director of the Futurs Médias Group. This co-optation resulted in a softening of their editorial lines towards the regime, especially when we compare their editorial stance before and after Wade's governance. The same phagocytosis strategy has been used with civil society leaders and intellectuals who have now been promoted to leadership positions, as exemplified by Alioune Tine, Penda Mbow, Abdoul Aziz Diop, Amadou Mahtar Mbow and Amsatou Sow Sidibé.[27]

Facing a situation of unmet social demand that President Sall's *'Yoonu yokkuté*[28] program had nevertheless pledged to resolve, M23 leaders embedded in the state apparatus remained walled up in suspicious silence. Today, the structure seems to have become but a shadow of its former self. Marred in conflicting interests and directions, it witnessed the emergence from its flanks of a dissenting voice named 'Authentic M23', essentially made up of youth who refused to be tamed by power. As for *Y'en A Marre*, after *'daas fanaanal'* and *'fanaané daass'*, and after the promises of the new regime, it went back in its sheath, just like a knife - perhaps waiting to run for the next local elections in 2014 with the *Ci Laa Bokk* (I'm also involved) citizen initiative. According to *Y'en A Marre* and *Ci Laa Bokk* members, an anomaly

---

27 Penda Mbow is a history professor, a feminist, member of civil society and leader of the Citizen Movement. Abdoul Aziz Diop is a political scientist, lecturer at the Higher Institute for Information and Communication Sciences (ISSIC), former civil society member and currently member of the Alliance for the Republic (APR, majority party) and advisor to Sall. Amadou Mahtar Mbow was formerly minister under President Léopold Sédar Senghor, a former UNESCO secretary general and is currently president of the Senegalese National Forum Bureau. Amsatou Sow Sidibé is a professor of private law, civil society member and leader of the *Caar Leneen* political movement as well as candidate in the 2012 presidential elections.
28 *'Yoonu yokkuté'* means the path to development in Wolof. But according to Fou-malade, a rap artist member of *Y'en A marre*, we should rather speak of *Yoonu yokk lepp*, which means the path of total increase.

in the electoral code should be corrected, as it prevents many Senegalese, especially independent candidates, from running in local elections.

Social movements resurface

In a state of latency since Sall's accession to power, popular discontent has gradually built up in spite of a state of grace period. Social movements have been created. After the first 'riots of the *Cantaakoon*'[29] in April 2012, a second series of riots took place in October of the same year[27] when angry *Cantaakoon* ransacked the capital to protest against the jailing of their religious guide, following the murder of two of his *talibe* in Medinatou Salam (Mbour).[30] Protesters accused the new regime, whose leaders were outspokenly hostile to their *marabout* during the presidential elections, of manipulating justice in an attempt to politicise this case. In this context, the opposition is currently regrouping around the Senegalese Democratic Party (SDP) and is causing serious problems for the regime, with large-scale street protests. This was the case on 23 April 2013, with a protest to defend democratic freedoms, fight against the high cost of living and demand the liberation of those jailed as part of the hunt for ill-gotten wealth.

The Senegalese are growing impatient and their perceptions of the regime are beginning to change for the worse, according to the *Afrobaromètre* surveys published in 2013. These revealed that after 15 months of Sall being at the helm of state, 51.5 per cent of Senegalese felt that the economy was badly managed, against 43 per cent who felt the opposite. The study also revealed that eight out of ten Senegalese people have a negative view of government policy aiming at reducing the gap between the rich and the poor, against 17 per cent who gave a positive assessment of the efforts (*Dakaractu* 11 July 2013).

Resentful of the regime, the youth disapprove of the narrow policy space given to the issue of employment by the new regime. The growing lack of

29 Name given to the talibe of the marabout Cheikh Béthio Thioune.
30 The two murders occurred in April 2012.

popularity of the current holders of power is reflected in repeated attacks by the movement of unemployed graduates, which was born during Wade's era.

The movement was reborn after the change of regime and has become the Gathering of Unemployed Graduates of Senegal (RDSES), led by the young Babacar Ndour. Given the stakes, a link was quickly established between social movements fighting for the recruitment of youth in the civil service and job creation for the youth. Thus, the National Coalition for Employment was born, which includes the RDSES, the National Collective of Graduates in Fishing and Aquaculture, midwives and state nurses, graduates from the School of Health and Social Development, the Maurice Delafosse Vocational and Business Centre, the Association of Unemployed Physicians, technicians in mechanics and related crafts, and disabled students (*Senenews* 20 March 2013). With electoral pledges not being given sufficient prominence by the government in its agenda, the movement is growing restless and speaking out in the media and on the streets.

> Now that the regime has been in power for 15 months [...], says Babacar Ndour, we must point out with much sadness and bitterness that a status quo prevails around the issue of employment in our country [...] The youth must take their responsibilities vis-à-vis this cheating regime. The pledge of creating 5,500 jobs in the Civil Service made by the Head of State during his address to the Nation on December 31st, 2012, of which Macky Sall himself said that it had become effective as at January 31st, 2013, [is but] trickery engineered by this regime. From top to bottom, we see only dithering, spiked with unfulfilled promises and manoeuvres towards the politicization of the issue of youth employment (*Sud Quotidien* 27 July 2013).

In his *Yoonu Yokkute*, Sall had indeed promised the youth 500,000 jobs. Later on, this figure was cut to 300,000 jobs with a project aiming at reducing the presidential term from seven to five years. However, when the 2012 recruitment program was launched, a much lower number (namely 5,500 positions) was opened up for competition to 120,000 job applicants registered at the civil service ministry.

> We are almost at the end of July [2013], and there's still nothing, says Babacar Ndour. [They came back] to tell us that the FONGIP [Priority Investments Guarantee Fund - ed.] has 6 billion CFA Francs to fund employment and youth projects. They even promised that we would be admitted as observers in the FONGIP. In this quality, we would have been able to obtain credit lines for our members. As it turns out, there is nothing at the FONGIP (*Djoloffactu* 26 July 2013).

Tired of waiting, the young unemployed graduates increased their presence in the media and organised various collective actions (against unfulfilled promises), amongst which was their sit-in on 21 August 2013 at Obelisque Square (*Leuksenegal* 22 August 2013). This rise of the marginalised seems at the same time to be a way of departing from the social movements, which supported the new regime in its quest for power. *Y'en A Marre*, for example, while not intent on leaving the initiative to the rising juvenile forces, is struggling to impose itself on the ground due to the involution of its legitimacy. This perception proved correct during the above-mentioned and hastily organised sit-in, where its representatives were almost beaten up by protesters who blamed them for the current situation of youth unemployment.[31]

Demands in favour of youth employment have become entangled with popular uprisings against the lease or even the sale of arable land to foreign agribusinesses. Following the deadly clashes of October 2011 in Fanaye, the

---

31 'We do not have to listen to you. We do not believe a word you say. You have taken advantage of the youth. We know everything! You received your slice of the cake just like the others [...] We have no lesson to take from you, *Y en a marre*. You led the country to chaos, with your moralizing speeches. Look at where we are today. It is because of you that the youth are in this situation' (*Pressafrik* video published on *Seneweb* on 22 August 2013).

controversial project was moved to the Gnith rural community, near Lac de Guier, following an unexpected decision by Sall and in spite of popular protest. To oppose the state, the Gnith populations, just like those of Fanaye, created a collective for the protection of the Ndiaël avifauna (Gnith rural community). According to Ardo Sow, spokesperson of the collective: The project cleared 20,000 hectares to produce ethanol destined for Europe; 37 villages are affected, 9,000 people are threatened with exodus, 100,000 cattle heads are in danger, schools, mosques and cemeteries risk being wiped out, thousands of trees and flora are threatened with extinction, millions of litres of fresh water are wasted, corruption is threatening social peace, solidarity and stability in Senegal. (*Rewmi* 12 June 2013)

In spite of the forced establishment of the farm, populations continued resisting by immobilising tractors of the project as a form of protest and sabotage. The risk that the unfortunate events of Fanaye will occur again is not unlikely.

To prevent this, 'gendarmes are watching over workers day and night' (*Rewmi* 12 June 2013) and 'armed guards have been stationed around the project boundaries, forcing women to walk dozens of kilometres to reach the well' (*Leral* 13 June 2013). The authorities and the project developers seem to have chosen heavy-handed tactics instead of consulting with communities. The events of Fanaye and Gnith, which took place under the blessing of the central authorities,[32] seems to suggest that public communication (or territorial public relations) is still not sufficiently working in favour of local governance. Started by the previous regime, this trend towards expropriating land continues with the new authorities, although they had promised citizens a change before being elected.

On the face of it, the much promised shift has up until now proven to be more of a slogan than a concrete achievement. The 'thirst and water riots'

32 The minister in charge of decentralisation invited rural communities to 'accelerate the process of allocating land to all the Senegalese who might request it', while pointing out that 'the land should be allocated only to those able to develop it and who have the means to do so (see IPAR 2013).

(September and October 2013) following a 20-day uninterrupted water cut suffered by the populations of the Dakar region are a perfect illustration of this. These disruptions in public services and the political violence that resulted reveal at least three clear weaknesses in our political systems. First of all, it shows the inability of the state to adequately manage water, a sector of national importance that has been placed under the control of a French subsidiary, the Sénégalaise Des Eaux (SDE). These seditious events and the water shortage that triggered them are also symptomatic of the crisis caused by privatisation, previously presented as a miraculous solution and imposed on our states by donors. In addition, following unsuccessful attempts by SDE and local technicians to repair the damage on the Keur Momar Sarr pipe (Louga region), the authorities were forced to call on French expertise.

Finally, let us underline the inability of the government and presidential communication team to speak to citizens/consumers in a credible fashion. The 'pipe of lies', as journalists described it, brought to the fore deceitful political communication, which many actually consider a trademark of the successive leaders at the helm of the state.

Conclusion

This contribution highlights the central role of social movements in terms of citizen oversight on political action and in creating awareness among citizens for deeper involvement in democracy. Two types of social movements were identified in Senegal during the historical period analysed: on the one hand, collective action that sought to curb the excesses of neoliberal governance, and on the other, social movements with a radical social change project. However, it ought to be said that even though social movements can result from a crisis of representative democracy, the samples examined have often been narrowed down to a mere tool for oligarchic struggles. Instead of the much-heralded people, the frustrated and conspiring elite inserted themselves into the scene of protest under the benevolent gaze of an alarmist media hostile to the regime. Often elitist when it came to their concerns, social movements have thus widened the gap between themselves and ordinary citizens. In response to this crisis of representation and legitimacy, citizens turned to individual survival strategies, defection from social movement slogans, electoral abstention and resignation.

Beyond this, the analysis of the period in question reveals that communities which social movements seek to mobilise, whatever the stakes, are not always prepared to commit to protest, much less use any means to see their demands met. The fear of destabilising the country has a dampening effect on the choice of protest strategies. The reason for this is that on the one hand, the Senegalese are relatively unwilling to sink into chaos. On the other hand, they are still convinced of the 'power of the last word' (Hastings 1996) provided by the polls, which, from a different perspective, can be seen as a simple process for preserving peace. Thus, the fate of the M23 as a whole shows that even if political involvement of an oppositional type is accepted due to its relative impact on public decisions, one must acknowledge that insurgent social movements, such as those in the Tahrir Square example, are disapproved of and do not, for now, have a bright future in Senegal.

References

Bathily, A. (1992) *Mai 68 à Dakar : ou la révolte universitaire et la démocratie,* Paris, Chaka

Braud, P. (2004) *Violences politiques,* Paris, Seuil

Cruise O'Brien, D.B. (1992) « Le 'contrat social' sénégalais à l'épreuve », *Politique Africaine,* n° 45: 9-20

Denquin, J.-M. (2010) « Pour en finir avec la crise de la Représentation », *Jus Politicum* n°4

Diome, M. (2010) « L'Islam contestataire au Sénégal : le cas de la révolte des Imams de la banlieue de Dakar », Mémoire DEA, Section Science Politique, UFR Sciences Juridique et Politique, Université Gaston Berger de Saint Louis

Diome, M. (2012) « Les guides religieux mourides et les crises politiques au Sénégal : la communication califale face à la dissidence », Communication au Forum du Grand Magal 2013, Dakar

Diome, M. (2013) « Médias, Mouvement Populaire et Violence Politique : Le Contrat Social Sénégalais à l'épreuve de la contestation et des urnes (2000-2012) », Thèse de Doctorat de Sociologie de l'Université Gaston Berger de Saint-Louis

Diop, M.-C. and Diouf, M. (1990) *Le Sénégal sous Abdou Diouf : État et Société*, Paris, Karthala

Fillieule, O., Agrikoliansky E. and Sommier, I. (2010)(éd.), *Penser les mouvements sociaux,* Paris, la Découverte

Gurr, T. R. (1970) *Why Men Rebel?,* New Jersey, Princeton University Press

Hastings, M. (1996) *Aborder la science politique*, Paris, Seuil

Havard, J.-F. (2004) « De la victoire du 'Sopi' à la tentative du 'nopi' : 'Gouvernement de l'alternance' et liberté d'expression des médias au Sénégal », in *Politique Africaine*, n°96: 22-38

IPAR (2013) « Note d'alerte sur les transactions foncières à grande échelle au Sénégal : impulser un large débat inclusif pour construire un consensus national sur la réforme foncière ! », http://www.ipar.sn/IMG/pdf/IPAR_note_d_alerte_sur_le_foncier.pdf (accessed 23 August 2013)

Lafargue, J. (1996) *Contestations démocratiques en Afrique. Sociologie de la protestation au Kenya et en Zambie,* Paris, Karthala et IFRA

Mamdani, M. and Wamba-dia-Wamba, E. (1997) « Mouvements sociaux et démocratie en Afrique », in GEMDEV, *Les avatars de l'État en Afrique,* Paris, Karthala, 1997: 41-76

Ndiaye, B.J. (2013) « Heurts fonciers dans la vallée Fanaye, mon amour et mon péché », 12 novembre 2011, http://www.seneweb.com/news/ Contribution/heurts-fonciers-dans-la-vallee-fanaye-mon-amour-et-mon-peche-decryptage-par-babacar-justin-ndiaye_n_54201. html (accessed december 2013)

Neveu, E. (2010) « Médias et protestation collective », in Fillieule O. et al, *Penser les mouvements sociaux,* Paris, La Découverte

Société Africaine de Raffinage (SAR) (2013), *Plan Takkal,* http://www.sar. sn/3-PLAN-TAKKAL.html (accessed 12 July 2013)

Sylla, N.S. (2012) « Le Sénégal à trois jours des élections : la démagogie au service des oligarchies », http://www.rosalux.sn/wp-content/uploads/2012/02/ d%C3%A9magogie_Senegal.pdf (23 février 2012); (accessed 22 August 2013)

Touraine, A. (1973) *La production de la société,* Paris, Seuil

Wade, A. (2011) « Discours du Président de la République », 14 juillet, Hôtel des Almadies, Dakar

Wade, A. (2012) « Message à la Nation », February 26

Y'en A Marre (2011a), Manifeste janvier 2011

Y'en A Marre (2011b), Mémorandum janvier 2011

Y'en A Marre (2011c), Déclaration 19 mars 2011

Y'en A Marre (2011d), Déclaration 27 juin 2011

Zucarelli, F. (1988) *La vie politique sénégalaise (1940-1988)*, Paris, CHEAM

Online articles

Dakaractu, « Le Sénégal s'embrase », http://www.dakaractu.com/Le-Senegal-s-embrase_a13843.html (18 février 2012 ; page consultée le 24 août 2013)

Dakaractu, « Idrissa Seck est le maître d'œuvre de toutes les émeutes, selon le pouvoir », http://www.dakaractu.com/Idrissa-Seck-est-le-maitre-d-oeuvre-de-toutes-les-emeutes-selon-le-pouvoir_a14058.html (20 février 2012 ; page consultée le 20 février 2012)

Dakaractu, « Le Sénégal au bord de l'apocalypse » (éditorial de Cheikh Yérim Seck), http://www.dakaractu.com/Le-Senegal-au-bord-de-l-apocalypse-L-Editorial-de-Cheikh-Yerim-Seck_a14052.html (20 février 2012 ; page consultée le 24 août 2013).

Dakaractu, « Exclusif : Ababacar Sadikh Niang, le colonel soupçonné avec Idy d'orchestrer les émeutes », http://www.dakaractu.com/Exclusif--Ababacar-Sadikh-Niang-le-colonel-soupconne-avec-Idy-d-orchestrer-les-emeutes_a14176.html (21 février 2012 ; page consultée le 22 février 2012).

Dakaractu, « Abdoulaye Wade à Macky Sall : 'M. le Président,…' », http://www.dakaractu.com/Abdoulaye-Wade-a-Macky-Sall-M-le-president-Par-Cheikh-Yerim-Seck_a17255.html (26 mars 2012 ; page consultée le 26 mars 2012).

Dakaractu, « Enquête Afrobarometre & Gestion économique, un mauvais point pour Macky », http://www.dakaractu.com/Enquete-afrobarometre-Gestion-economique-Un-mauvais-point-pour-Macky_a47821.html (11 juillet 2013 ; page consultée le 12 juillet 2013).

Djoloffactu, « Emploi : les diplômés-chômeurs tapent sur Macky Sall et exigent la suppression de l'ANEJ, le FNPJ, l'AJEB », http://www.djoloffactu.com/emploi-les-diplômés-chômeurs-tapent-sur-Macky-Sall-et-exigent-la-suppression-de-l'ANEJ,-le FNPJ,l'AJEB (26 juillet 2013 ; page consultée le 20 août 2013).

Huffington Post, « Le Sénégal dans le chaos ? », http://www.huffingtonpost.fr/ong-a-dakar/senegal-chaos_b_1288853.html (20 février 2012 ; consultée le 24 août 2013).

Le Quotidien, « Candidature aux Locales : *Ci laa bokk* dénonce l'exclusion des indépendants », http://www.lequotidien.sn/index.php/politique/item/20495 (page consultée le 12 juillet 2013).

Leral, « Projet Sen-huile/Sen-éthanol de Nguith : la tension monte entre éleveurs et les autorités locales », http://www.leral.net/Projet-Sen-huile-Sen-Ethanol-de-Nguith-La-tension-monte-entre-les-eleveurs-et-les-autorites-locales_a86256.html (13 juin 2013 ; page consultée le 16 août 2013).

Leuksenegal, « Sit-in des diplômés chômeurs : les membres de *Y'en A Marre* ont failli se faire tabasser », http://www.leuksenegal.com/component/k2/item/20400-sit-in-des-jeunes-diplômés-chômeurs-les-membres-de-yen-a-marre-ont-failli-se-faire-tabasser (22 août 2013 ; page consultée 27 août 2013).

Pressafrik, « Manifestation des diplômés chômeurs : La bagarre évitée de justesse entre Fou Malade et des jeunes de Bokk Gis Gis, Kilifeu insulté », document vidéo : http://www.seneweb.com/news/People/video-manifestation-des-diplomes-chomeurs-la-bagarre-evitee-de-justesse-entre-fou-malade-et-des-jeunes-de-bokk-gis-gis-kili_n_103699.html (22 août 2013 ; page consultée le 27 août 2013).

Rewmi, « Média et émeutes : Walf et RFM dans le collimateur de l'État », http://www.rewmi.com/ _a42404.html (30 juin 2011 ; page consultée le 30 juin 2011).

Rewmi, « Saint-Louis- Affaire Sen huile/Sen Ethanol : Les populations de Gnith avertissent 'Pour faire quitter le projet dans le Ndiaël, nous sommes prêts à mourir' », http://www.rewmi.com/Saint-Louis-Affaire-Sen-huile-Sen-Ethanol-Les-populations-de-Nginth-avertissent-Pour-faire-quitter-le-projet-dans-le_a79075.html (12 juin 2013 ; page consultée le 16 août 2013).

Senenews, « Dakar à feu et à sang, un mort dans les manifestations de ce dimanche », http://www.senenews.com/2012/02/19/dakar-a-feu-et-a-sang-un-mort-dans-les-manifestations-de-ce-dimanche_23216.html (19 février 2012 ; page consultée le 24 août 2013).

Senenews, « Problématique de l'emploi au Sénégal : les jeunes chômeurs fédèrent leurs forces », http://www.senenews.com/2013/03/20/problematique-de-lemploi-au-senegal-les-jeunes-chomeurs-federent-leurs-forces_56184.html (20 mars 2013 ; consultée le 20 août 2013).

Seneweb, « Affaire des terres de Fanaye : un affrontement dans la communauté rurale fait trois morts, http://www.seneweb.com/news/Politique/affaire-des-terres-de-fanaye-un-affrontement-dans-la-communaute-rurale-fait-trois-morts_n_53323.html » (26 octobre 2011 ; page consultée le 16 août 2013).

Seneweb, « Wade conseille aux porteurs du projet de Fanaye de procéder à sa délocalisation », http://www.seneweb.com/news/Societe/wade-conseille-aux-porteurs-du-projet-de-fanaye-de-proceder-a-sa-delocalisation_n_55207.html (02 décembre 2011 ; page consultée le 16 août 2013)

Sud Quotidien, « Face à l'échec et la politisation de l'emploi des jeunes par l'actuel régime : les diplômés chômeurs dans la rue le 20 août prochain », http://mobile.sudonline.sn/les-diplomes-chomeurs-dans-la-rue-le-20-aout-prochain_m_14838.htm (27 juillet 2013 ; page consultée le 20 août 2013).

Wikipedia, « Assises nationales du Sénégal »,
http://fr.wikipedia.org/wiki/Assises_nationales_du_Sénégal (page consultée le 05 janvier 2012).

CHAPTER: 12

SOCIAL MOVEMENTS IN CABO VERDE: PROCESSES, TRENDS AND VICISSITUDES

Cláudio Alves Furtado

In the context of a two-party political system that provides little scope for contrary political views, two social movements have come to the fore in recent years and raised the issues of high youth unemployment and regionalisation. In the absence of counter-hegemonic social movements, they have both highlighted the existence of a certain lethargy in the process of effectively consolidating democracy, and in particular the inability of the state to fulfil the political, social and economic rights of citizens, as guaranteed by the constitution.

Introduction

The socio-political dynamics that marked most African countries at the beginning of the 1990s have left a strong and indelible impact on their political systems as well as on the relationship between the state, political parties and citizens. The political changes that swept across the African continent largely resulted from urban and rural social movements that led to the rise of a process of restructuring an increasingly autonomous and active public sphere.

It is true however that the unifying and centrifugal power of public authority structures, gained by co-opting individual actors or social movements and organisations, ended up, in several contexts and through various movements, overshadowing the liberating dimension of several social movements.

More recently, the closed nature of existing political systems and the gradual contraction of spaces for enjoying and exerting social, political, economic and cultural rights has led to a resurgence of social movements almost all over the African continent, with varying degrees of visibility. Another factor is the increasingly difficult access to essential goods and services by specific social groups, especially the youth.

In this context, the so-called 'Arab Spring' (Brandes and Engels 2011) led to significant political changes in Morocco, Tunisia, Libya and Egypt (but not Algeria) which were analysed and scrutinised by the media. It can be seen as an indicator of the new rise of social movements, mostly urban, taking advantage of the creative possibilities provided by the new technologies of information and communication. Social networks and the use of the internet proved to be significant tools for social mobilisation and for the structuring and planning of demands.

In sub-Saharan Africa, social movements started flourishing again with varying degrees of dynamism.[1] The crystallisation of political participation and decision spaces, in other words a limitation of possibilities for involvement and influence on decision-making processes by citizens and civil society organisations, is not unconnected from this awakening.

---

1 The movement of the women of Rufisque (Senegal) who fought to secure land access (Hainard 2008), the fight of young citizens against the constitutional reform project which would have led to a change in electoral rules and to a new mandate for President Abdoulaye Wade (Dalberto 2011, Diop 2013), as well as the courage shown by the Burkina youth who opposed the existing political order and fought for its transformation (Bargo 2011), are but a few examples of several ongoing forays into African public spheres by actors or organisations challenging the regime in power and/ or promoting greater autonomy and the possibility to become involved in decision-making processes (Mamdani and Wamba-dia-Wamba 2000).

In addition, one can note the actual and/or perceived weakness of the state when it comes to meeting social demands, especially in terms of access to employment, income and basic social services. This is not to mention the swelling of the feeling of indignation and revolt felt by citizens in the wake of an increase in cases of corruption and harmful management of public goods. These were all relayed and amplified by the relatively free and pluralist press.

In Cabo Verde, very few studies over the last few decades focused on social movement trends. Attention was rather given to research which, on the basis of the neoliberal swell that reached African states and the rest of the world, insists on the emergence of NGOs and associative and grassroots movements that seek answers to issues previously under the responsibility of public institutions (Furtado 2002, Fonseca 2007, de Pina 2008, Jesus 2012). However, discussions with various degrees of depth and impact took place in the country and were reflected in the press. Debates have been conducted on the importance of the old social movements such as trade unions, professional associations and peasant movements and the emergence of associations and social groups claiming a new public development agenda.

Like what happened in other African countries and, more particularly, in the West African region, the emergence of social movements in Cabo Verde has been felt more strongly in the 1990s, in the context of the democratisation and restructuring of the political system. These movements were still present over the following years, at a time when public institutions proved unable to efficiently and effectively meet growing social demands, especially from the youth and urban dwellers.

Until then, analysis focused rather on civil society organisations, their emergence and organisation, activities conducted and their (lack of) independence vis-à-vis the state and transnational organisations (international NGOs). Very few studies focused specifically on the protest, and possible emancipating and anti-hegemonic dimensions of these movements. Most insisted less on their durability and more on the relevance of their demands and their capacity for mobilisation and influence on the public sphere. In the case of Cabo Verde, the approach promoted by McSween, however, seems more heuristic and meaningful:

> Indeed, a scope of analysis using protest episodes as entry points focuses the researcher's gaze less on the structural determining factors of the emergence of specific organized movements than on the social conflict dynamics within these episodes. Therefore, the consequence of such a scope of analysis is to shift social actors, their interactions and their interrelations (back) at the center of the analysis. Thus shifting the angle of analysis of organizations towards protest episodes helps to move out of the deadlock of theories on the civil society by approaching the African civil society as an empirical rather than a theoretical question (McSween 2010:14).(*Our translation*)

In this respect, we shall seek to provide an interpretative analysis of the fundamental reasons for the resurgence of social movements in West Africa in general and in Cabo Verde in particular. We shall also attempt to explore the scope of the impact of these movements, in spite of their alleged small quantitative significance. This approach requires that we analyse the links between economic crisis and the crisis of political representation, as well as the several disconnects between the political and social spheres preventing citizens, individually and collectively, from accessing material and symbolic resources and keeping them away from the process of influencing the development of a public agenda.

This analysis seeks to position itself primarily within the context of the dynamics leading to a process of social movements emerging over the 2010-2013 period, based on the assumption of the reappearance of social movements in Cabo Verde, and seeking to understand (i) their rationale; (ii) their organisational forms; (iii) their impact and (iv) the ability of these movements to present themselves as a response to the issue of political representation in the framework of representative democracy.

The analysis that follows focuses on two social movements which, and this is not random, originate in Mindelo, where they have their largest support base. Mindelo is the second largest urban centre in the country. During the last century of the colonial era, this town was a major economic and cultural centre, thanks to the role played by Porto Grande de São Vicente (Correia e Silva 2010) and to the establishment from 1917 of what was to become the sole secondary education establishment until 1960, and of the Technical and Business School in the middle of the 1950s, the former being the only school of the archipelago until the independence of Cabo Verde in 1975.

Indeed, although Praia, the country's capital, was and still continues to be the political base, the elite, particularly the administrative elite, were for the most part from Mindelo and neighbouring islands of the North. Therefore, during the colonial period and the first few years after independence, they dominated the administrative and political structures, and, to a lesser extent, held economic power. They also claimed intellectual hegemony, seeking to establish themselves as the country's intelligentsia. Gradually, independence contributed to reducing the weight and relative centrality of São Vicente Island and the city of Mindelo, its administrative centre, as well as that of their leadership, at the expense mainly of Santiago Island and the city of Praia. This increased political rifts and raised the issue of political representation mechanisms, as well as their mandate of distributing public investments and other symbolic goods.

The regained dynamism of social movements in Cabo Verde was made possible by the social, political and economic tensions experienced over the last few years. The tensions have arisen from the crisis of unemployment, especially amongst the youth, many of whom are educated, and the declining purchasing power of the middle classes, which has changed their consumption habits. To this must be added the strong reliance of citizens on the state. In a society where the state remains highly hegemonic, this takes the form of direct dependency through public employment, and indirect dependency through financing mechanisms, remittances and the distribution of resources and other goods.

It is worth pointing out that, beyond community-based organisations and associations as well as non-governmental organisations, which experienced significant growth in the 1990s and during the last decade, social movements began to emerge, with varying degrees of structure, durability and impact. These movements are characterised by an essentially political agenda, seeking to influence the public agenda, even if - and without making any value judgment - they defend specific interests or, better still, the interests of specific social groups.

This flourishing of social movements, especially NGOs, was adequately described for the African continent. According to Miles Larmer (2010:256):

> The role of social movements, both in this transition and in the constrained democracies that resulted, has been evidently ambiguous. The substantial decline in state capacity and the redirection of external funding to NGOs strengthened some existing social movements with credible grassroots linkages, but simultaneously led to a proliferation of new NGOs, many of which owed their initial existence solely to the availability of donor funding and which were thereby accountable externally rather than to those they claimed to speak for or represent.

In the case of Cabo Verde, we should note the presence in rural areas as well as in urban centres of dynamic groups and associations seeking, with varying degrees of autonomy, to face the social demands of populations and to protest against political measures - or lack thereof. In the framework of this study, we shall keep our focus on two social movements whose analysis can prove fruitful. The first is a group of young university graduates, either unemployed or occupying jobs that do not match their expectations, aspirations and life objectives. Disillusion with public authorities has been the cornerstone of social and political mobilisation, either expressed individually or concurrently with other social movements. The former encouraged the development of life projects based on standards of living and consumption that demanded significant financial resources. These projects however failed to materialise or simply collapsed. From the perspective of the youth, this was the result of an absence of efficient public policies geared towards them.

The second movement, called Movement for the Regionalisation of Cabo Verde and the Autonomy of S. Vicente seeks, as stated in its manifesto, to reach a minimum goal of achieving regionalisation in Cabo Verde, while its ultimate goal is to achieve autonomy for S. Vicente.

As we are going to demonstrate, the key argument of this movement is that the independence of Cabo Verde and the concentration of political power on the island of Santiago led to the economic and social decline of S. Vicente and the loss of its political role. In this sense, independence has had an adverse effect on Cabo Verde, as stated in this extract from the manifesto entitled *Por um S. Vicente Melhor* (For a better S. Vicente):

> In a strange paradox, the start of S. Vicente's decline coincided with Cabo Verde becoming an independent nation, whereas legitimate expectations sought the opposite, in line with the values of freedom and the desire for progress always cherished by the populations.[2]

From a methodological point of view, we wish to explore, based on the above-mentioned cases and through an analysis of the context and process of their emergence, their social support base and objectives, and the impact of their actions in terms of social mobilisation and their influence on the public

---

2 http://www.petitiononline.com/mmscent/petition, html accessed March 2014.

decision-making process, or at least, on the public agendas of public policy platforms. In doing this, we shall seek to assess the degree of autonomy, the policy maturation process as well as the governance of social movements. Alongside their organisational features, we shall attempt to understand the nature of their protest. Indeed, as described by André Gunder Frank and Marta Fuentes (2008) in reference to social movements, 'what motivates us is this deprivation/oppression/injustice in relation to the "we", regardless of how "we" are defined or "we" are perceived'.

Cabo Verde: socio-political and economic context

Recent socio-economic developments

Cabo Verde is the only island state member of the Economic Community of West African States (ECOWAS). Indeed, it is a small archipelago with a 4,033 km² land area, and a maritime territorial stretch and exclusive economic area of 734,265 km². Due to its Sahelian situation, it is forced to periodically face droughts and desertification. Agriculture continues to be its largest source of employment, but remains at the mercy of climate uncertainties. The environmental issue and the consequences of its fragile ecology, as well as food security, remain the major challenges faced by this country.

Given its environmental frailty and relative poverty in terms of natural resources, the economic growth of Cabo Verde over the last few decades was driven by the service industry, significant remittances from migrants, public and private investment as well as public development aid.

For a major part of the 1990s and of 2000, Cabo Verde achieved relatively stable growth. Between 2001 and 2006, the average growth rate of the economy was 5.6 per cent in real terms, with a low inflation rate, a stable rate of exchange and a significantly reduced public debt.

The macroeconomic imbalances experienced in 2000 were gradually rectified during the period outlined above.

The ensuing 2008 financial crisis has had some impact on the economy of Cabo Verde, namely with a notable decrease in foreign direct investments. After reaching 5.9 per cent in 2008, the GDP growth rate dropped to 3.9 per cent in 2009. 2011 showed a recovery (five per cent). The growth rate was forecast at 4.8 per cent for 2013 and five per cent for 2014 (see table 1).

Although migrant remittances, a significant source of financing of the Cabo Verdean economy, remained relatively stable, with a 1.7 per cent increase in 2009, foreign direct investment significantly decreased, especially in the areas of tourism, housing for tourism and construction.

Table 1: Macroeconomic indicators

	2011	2012	2013	2014
Real GDP growth (%)	5	4	4.8	5
Real GDP growth per capita (%)	4	3	3.8	4
Inflation - CPI (%)	4.5	2.5	2.4	2.5
Fiscal balance (% GDP)	-7.5	-7.3	-8.9	-8.9
Current balance (% GDP)	-16.4	-14.1	-15	-16.4

Source: African Economic Outlook; Consumption Price Index 2012, estimates 2013 and 2014 forecasts; http://www.africaneconomicoutlook.org/en/countries/west-africa/cape-verde, accessed March 2014

However, the 2008 financial crisis led the government to launch a public investment program, which increased public debt and the fiscal deficit. The latter rose from 1.1 per cent of the GDP in 2008 to six per cent in 2009. According to estimates, this deterioration is set to continue (see Table 1).

The fiscal deficit was entirely financed through foreign loans, at a time when foreign direct investment declined and when public development aid will likely continue to decrease.

A recent report of the Cabo Verde Central Bank (2012) predicts a decline in fiscal revenue, along with an increase in the fiscal deficit in a context of increased investment spending. As indicated by the Cabo Verde Central Bank, the fiscal situation is proving unfavourable. Along the same lines, the World Bank (2013) notes that:

> Cabo Verde currently faces a difficult macroeconomic scenario, with high fiscal and foreign deficits, a slowdown in growth and an adverse external context, reflecting the European economic crisis. Fiscal deficit is high, at close to 10% of the Gross Domestic Product (GDP), debt has increased significantly, from 86% of the GDP in 2011 to 97%, and international reserves are low – covering just 3.4 months of imports.

According to the Cabo Verde Central Bank (2012), based on the conclusions of the International Monetary Fund (2013), the country's debt sustainability risk has increased. However, it adds that debt servicing remains manageable, considering the fact that most loans are concessional. There appears to be a growing need for fiscal discipline.

Furthermore, it seems crucial to implement economic policies conducive to rebuilding private investor trust. This is a prerequisite for an increase in private investment, economic growth and job creation. It is however true that given the strong reliance of the country's economy on those of Europe and North America, actual and sustained recovery will only be possible when these economies experience a lasting turnaround from the current situation. Effective African regional economic integration is also crucial for the economy of Cabo Verde.

In the long term, the economic performance of Cabo Verde and its social indicators in the areas of education and health, have proved significant factors in contributing to the reclassification of the country from the category of least developed country to that of middle-income country.

Indeed, the country's economic growth went hand in hand with large investments in the area of social policy. Statistics on education show that significant progress was made. According to UNESCO (n.d.), Cabo Verde ranks in fifth position amongst 28 sub-Saharan African countries in relation to the Education for All index. In terms of universal primary education, the completion rate is 97 per cent. Furthermore, both at the primary and secondary levels, the presence and success of girls is higher than boys. This is actually why the government was greatly concerned about the dropout and failure rate among boys and has taken steps in order to correct this situation.

According to the same source, the literacy rate (15 years and over) reached 72.3 per cent in 2012. In the first cycle of secondary education (four years of learning), the enrolment rate was 81 per cent, and in the second cycle (two years) it reached 52 per cent.

In the area of health, progress has been equally strong. According to data from the Ministry of Health (2012), the gross mortality rate (overall mortality) reached 5.1 per cent in 2011, with a child mortality rate of 23 out of 1000 and an under-five mortality rate of 26 out of 1000.

It must be pointed out that in the areas of education and health, Cabo Verde has already achieved the Millennium Development Goal (MDG) indicators. In fact, Cabo Verde is on a positive trend, according to the United Nations Development Program (UNDP) Human Development Index (HDI). Over the last three years, the HDI reached 0.581, 0.584 and 0.586 respectively (UNDP 2013).This means that it ranks as a medium human development level country.

However, challenges remain high in areas such as the purchasing power of households, education quality and health services. Purchasing power is closely linked to access to employment, which remains problematic especially for the youth and low-skilled people.

A quick glance at employment statistics shows that the rate of activity among youth (15-24 years) reaches 48.5 per cent for boys and 38.7 per cent for young girls, which indicates a 10-point gap (INE 2013). For all ages combined, the rate of activity reaches 57.1 per cent for men and 47.3 per cent for women, revealing a ten-point gap here also (INE 2013).

With regards to youth unemployment, it usually reaches very high levels, a trend confirmed over the last five years by the six-monthly surveys on employment conducted jointly by the Institute for Employment and Vocational Training and the National Statistics Institute (INE).

Table 2: Rate of activity (%) per jurisdiction, age group and sex in 2012

Jurisdiction	Specific age major groups				15 - 24 years per sex	
	15 - 24	15-34	35 - 64	65+	Male	Female
Ribeira Grande	28.3	46.2	50.9	7.4	32.9	22.2
Paúl	42.2	58.5	66.3	14.7	51.9	29.2
Porto Novo	35.5	54.2	68.8	4.8	44.4	25.8
S. Vicente	47.8	64.0	82.2	6.8	51.8	44.2
Ribeira Brava	37.0	49.0	65.3	5.7	38.5	35.3
Tarr. S. Nicolau	50.3	65.6	72.4	22.7	54.7	45.1
Sal	59.6	78.1	84.2	13.1	57.8	61.6
Boavista	51.7	74.1	84.3	8.4	49.2	54.4
Maio	34.1	48.2	67.7	11.6	45.7	9.8
Tarrafal	44.6	59.1	85.7	26.8	51.4	37.9
Santa Catarina	48.6	62.9	75.9	25.9	55.5	41.4
Santa Cruz	51.0	59.7	86.3	40.4	62.9	37.4
Praia	40.4	60.0	77.3	14.3	39.8	41.1
S. Domingos	29.6	46.8	71.3	11.5	36.2	21.7
S. Miguel	54.2	63.7	82.1	37.1	65.8	42.3
S. S. do Mundo	54.5	64.0	84.6	37.1	67.9	39
S. L. dos Órgãos	31.8	46.5	77.4	23.3	40.0	22.9
R. Gr. de Santiago	30.5	47.2	68.5	17.9	43.7	17.2
Mosteiros	30.1	42.5	61.1	10.7	48.3	9.2
S. Filipe	47.1	60.3	80.2	30.1	53.0	41.5
S. Catarina do Fogo	37.7	46.3	57.7	9.1	50.2	19.9
Brava	23.4	45.9	59.2	5.0	27.7	19
Cabo Verde	43.7	60.3	76.8	16.6	48.5	38.7

Source: National Statistics Institute, Continuous multi-purpose survey, Employment and labour-market statistics (2013:14)

In 2012, while the national rate of unemployment lay at 16.8 per cent - 17.2 per cent for men and 16.2 per cent for women (see table 3) - it was much higher amongst the youth. For the 20 - 24 age bracket, the unemployment rate reaches 33.7 per cent, or 15.9 points above the national average. This is similar for the 25 - 29 age bracket, where the unemployment rate is 22.9 per cent (INE 2013). In a global context hardly favourable to a small island nation, the major challenges faced by Cabo Verdean society are the following: (i) sustainable economic growth capable of creating a large number of jobs in such a way as to absorb the unemployed and new job seekers; (ii) realistic macro-economic policies that can build investor confidence and attract foreign direct investment in particular; (iii) political stability in the country; (iv) developing human capital.

Table 3 - Unemployment rate (%) by gender in 2012

Jurisdiction	Cabo Verde		
	Men	Women	Total
Ribeira Grande	22.1	18.7	21.0
Paúl	22.4	30.1	24.8
Porto Novo	17.3	23.7	19.5
S. Vicente	27.3	30.7	28.9
Ribeira Brava	18.3	19.6	18.8
Tarr. S. Nicolau	13.2	19.7	15.8
Sal	16.0	19.7	17.7
Boavista	16.3	11.2	14.3
Maio	8.2	9.3	8.7
Tarrafal	9.5	6.6	7.8
Santa Catarina	15.5	11.1	13.4
Santa Cruz	9.8	10.6	10.2
Praia	18.8	15.5	17.2
S. Domingos	16.4	17.0	16.6
S. Miguel	3.6	2.4	3.0
S. S. do Mundo	4.3	1.8	3.0
S. L. dos Órgãos	7.3	11.8	9.4
R. Gr. de Santiago	17.4	10.5	14.3
Mosteiros	0.9	2.8	1.5
S. Filipe	8.1	8.3	8.2
S. Catarina do Fogo	7.8	22.6	13.0
Brava	16.1	10.3	14.0
Cabo Verde	17.2	16.4	16.8

Source: National Statistics Institute (2013: 34)

Cabo Verdean citizens have many more demands today, especially concerning access to basic social services and decently paid employment, a source of social prestige. This seems problematic in light of the education level of the young unemployed. Even though the INE indicates that the number of youth with secondary and intermediate education has increased, the fact is that in 2012, the number of years of education amongst the unemployed was on average 8.2 (8.5 years in urban areas and 7.3 in rural areas) (INE 2013).

Overview of the recent political situation

Like most African countries, Cabo Verde underwent changes in its political system in 1990, the first time that multi-party elections were held. The political system is considered by some as moderate parliamentarian and by others as semi-presidential (Costa 2009). From a constitutional point of view, the parliament plays a central role in the political system. Even if the president holds no executive power, he is also elected by direct universal suffrage. He appoints the prime minister amongst parliamentary majority party leaders, following consultations with parties represented in the parliament, and jointly steers defence and foreign affairs policies.

At present, there are four political parties, including three with parliamentary seats, namely the African Party for the Independence of Cabo Verde (PAICV), the Movement for Democracy (MPD), the Independent and Democratic Union of Cabo Verde (UCID) and the Labour and Solidarity Party (PTS). A fifth party, the Social Democratic Party (PSD), no longer has any political and social visibility although it is legally recognised. The UCID has two seats in parliament (when at least five seats are necessary to form a parliamentary group) and have access to the related benefits.

In spite of the existence of four political parties, the Cabo Verdean political field is dominated by two major parties: the PAICV and the MPD, which have held power in rotation. In actual fact, it is a two-party system. On this point, it must be said that the political transition took place rather quickly. In a little over a year, the constitution was reviewed, laws on the electoral process were approved and presidential, legislative and municipal elections were organised. This rapid process did not allow some political parties to meet legal requirements and to raise funds in order to ensure their participation in elections. So, the MPD and PAICV, who were the protagonists of the democratic transition, quickly became hegemonic.

This two-party political system prevents other ideological visions, and other views of the world and of politics from organising themselves and forming political parties. It makes difficult the emergence of political projects and alternative visions of society. It is the weakness of the democracy. Since 1990, the country has held five presidential, legislative and municipal elections. A change at the highest level of power has been observed. From a strictly formal point of view, we can say that we are dealing with a consolidated democracy.

The results of the February 2011 legislative elections led to the following political situation. The PAICV obtained the absolute majority of seats and is therefore the ruling party. Thus, for the third time, this political force has enjoyed renewed trust from Cabo Verdean voters.

In the presidential election of August 2011, candidate Jorge Carlos Fonseca was elected, backed by the MPD, the main parliamentary opposition party. This was the first time that the president and the prime minister cohabited in the same government while belonging to different political currents.

This new cohabitation experience caused some clashes between the three organs of sovereignty: the president's office, the government and the parliament. The vetoes opposed to the government and parliamentary texts and the preventive request for constitutionality checks have, in some instances, led to political clashes between these actors. Likewise, disharmony in the political discourse was caused at times by certain political stances, most notably in terms of foreign policy, an area constitutionally shared by the government and the president. However, these clashes and misunderstandings did not create an atmosphere of instability or a genuine lack of political coordination and institutional collaboration, which can be construed as a hint of the maturity of political actors.

At the municipal level, Cabo Verde has 22 municipalities. The latest elections took place in February 2012 and the majority of city halls and municipal councils were won by MPD candidates and lists, thus strengthening the local weight of the party.

According to the constitution, the judiciary is a sovereign body not under the authority of other sovereign bodies (government, parliament and president). It has gradually consolidated itself, with its own governance provided by the Higher Council of the Judiciary for judges and the Superior Council of the Public Prosecution for prosecutors.

As for civil society, in spite of the tremendous dynamism observed over the last few years with the creation of several NGOs and community, recreational and cultural associations, the effective and frequent involvement of citizens in the decision-making process, and therefore in the public sphere, whether local or national, has hardly been significant. Indeed, this involvement has been limited to electoral contests and, to a lesser extent, to attending parliamentary sessions. This attendance mostly occurs when the themes being debated are divisive or during municipal council sessions, when there is an institutional space for participation, generally before the actual start of the working agenda. These moments are called 'periods before the agenda'.

In the Cabo Verdean political system, in particular with regards to electoral legislation, running in the elections as a candidate is not limited to political parties. Citizens can run in municipal elections, organising themselves into associations or movements. Many political movements ran in local elections and some won a number of mayoral and municipal councillor seats.

At the 2012 local elections, a political movement made up of citizens residing in the Sal Island municipality, won for the third time. This success was however achieved with support from one of the political parties (MPD). Indeed, many activists and leaders of this party were inscribed on the lists of locally elected officials.

In S. Filipe, on the island of Fogo, the United Independent Group for a Unified S. Filipe, led by the former mayor and PAICV leader, Eugénio Veiga, managed to secure the election of two councillors and five municipal deputies in the 2012 local elections.

In the same municipality, another group of citizens ran in the elections, with support from MPD. This was the São Filipe 'Abraçar' Independent Group (GIASF) led by Júlio Andrade, a physician. The group did not win the local elections, but managed to secure the election of two municipal councillors and six municipal deputies. This helped it gain the political ability to influence, or even change public policy bills in the S. Filipe municipality. Besides, the GIASF became the spokesperson for the opposition in the local and national governments. Likewise, so-called independent MPD lists sought to appear in a more acceptable light in the Sal and S. Felipe municipalities, where voters had systematically given victory to the PAICV since 1990.

In any case, many of the citizen movements which ran in the municipal elections were not actual offshoots of organised civil society; they were rather citizens who had not found a space in their respective political parties, or were a political ploy by parties who had lost all clout amongst their constituents.

In this sense, political participation platforms outside the partisan context are relatively few; we thus have a democracy of political parties, rather than a democracy of citizens. It seems that in the case of Cabo Verde, this would explain the existence of few essential, anti-hegemonic movements that challenge the *status quo*.

The next election contests will take place in 2016. Stability seems a given since the current government has a strong parliamentary base, with an absolute majority of members of parliament. However, the expected change in the leadership of the ruling party, with the announcement that the current prime minister would not run for a second term either as party leader or as prime minister in 2016, is likely to cause political strife within the PAICV in spite of the official 'unity' discourse.

The high rate of youth unemployment, especially among university graduates, as well as the ongoing debate on regionalisation, will be prominent in the rhetoric between political actors and civil society. The latter debate in particular has revealed strong rifts and might highlight the need for some serious thought about the unity of Cabo Verde.

Perceptions of corruption and the quality of democracy

In the case of Cabo Verde, it must be said that we are in a context where there are low levels of natural resources, and where the state, in its self-appointed role as promoter and regulator of economic activity, continues to play an important role in terms of investment and job creation. The weight of public investment, the mobilisation of foreign direct investment and development aid still provide it with a strong central role. It is therefore an important body for organising and (re)distributing economic, political and symbolic resources. For this reason, the ruling party ends up being a clientelist structure, strongly inhibiting any protest and anti-hegemonic tendencies, especially among the youth, who do not yet have access to capital and social networks that may serve for help and support. In a context of labour market contraction and high competition between jobseekers, those wishing to rapidly climb the social ladder are frequently co-opted. This is also the case for the main opposition party: through the current (and future) prebend promises in the constituencies where it leads, it also proves attractive for new members, recruited mostly amongst the youth.

In the first two decades following the introduction of the multi-party system, there were many cases of corruption, which were examined by the administration or in the politico-parliamentarian context, and discussed in Cabo Verdean society. On this issue, José Carlos dos Anjos (2009) argues that 'there is evidence, in the case of Cabo Verde, of a political culture of scandal', which produces vigilance and indignation against the illicit practices of rulers (Anjos 2009:27). In his analysis of the political and institutional situation of Cabo Verde, the same author argues that:

> [The] denunciation of corruption is an endeavor seeking to convince that it is indeed a scandal only if it departs from partisan polarization and ascertains itself durably, beyond media spheres, as quasi-expertise. The political scandal is, like all Cabo Verdean political institutions, an imported institution, a type of rapport with politics and a production strategy for an intense moment of politics (Anjos 2009: 31). (*Our translation*)

If the period between 1991 and 2000 was rich in scandals linked to corruption cases, the years that followed (2000-2013) saw fewer reports of corruption cases and the few cases that were brought to the fore could hardly have been called 'scandals', to quote Anjos. Indeed, some cases and situations were reported, but they did not receive broad coverage, nor did they take on a dimension which, politically or judicially, might have compromised the accused. As an example, we can mention the denunciations made in 2007 in relation to an alleged case of misuse of public funds by the then justice ministry known as the 'slush fund affair'. This case led to a reshuffling and to the stepping down of the minister under investigation. The construction of the private residence of the current prime minister also raised suspicions, as well as the case of the Angolan money implicating a former foreign affairs minister from the time of the single party system and also a former Cabo Verdean ambassador in Luanda.[3] This denunciation was made public on the eve of the latest legislative elections.

Although high-level politicians and leaders were not linked to cases of corruption, mid-level leaders of government structures were. Indeed, an embezzlement case involving close to 35 million escudos (nearly US$427,000) from the finance ministry coffers was made public in 2012, implicating mid-level leaders and officials from that division. Recently, the written press reported on the case of the likely issuance of fake driving licenses on the island of Santo Antão, involving the delegate to the General Directorate for Road Transport. A locally elected official, the latter is also the leader of the PAICV group at the Porto Novo Municipal Council. This first led to the resignation of the delegate, then to his arrest pending trial. Corruption cases are diffusely revealed by the customs administration and mayoral offices. In the latter cases, corruption cases are mostly related to the sale of land. In the same way, security forces are sometimes mentioned in corruption cases.

There have frequently been cases of denunciations made by the main opposition party. These complaints relate to the practice of patrimony or the privatisation of the state and the systematic recruitment of 'senior staff' around the ruling party. It is a system allegedly based on the 'jobs for the boys' principle, whereby activists and officials of the ruling party are hired to fill important positions in the state or government on the basis of their partisan affiliations, rather than their technical skills. These are cases of partisan practices rather than actual corruption.

In this context, the state's practice of the privatisation and appropriation of wealth is being attacked, echoing the same claims made in the 1990s, with admittedly broader media coverage and with more sensitive cases (Anjos 2009). However, we cannot neglect the fact that the publicity surrounding partisan

---

3   The press reported, based on the statement of a MPD leader, that an aircraft apparently landed at the airport in Mindelo with money to support the PAICV. Aboard, there was this former minister and other important Angolan figures.

practices can increase the lack of credibility of politics and politicians. In some contexts and for some social groups, this can heighten the apathy and 'lag' in exercising citizenship, and create, in other situations, a leitmotiv for the emergence of social movements that challenge the *status quo*.

Even if there have been very few concrete corruption cases revealed to the public over the last three years, a clear perception of corruption still prevails in Cabo Verdean society. Indeed, during a conference organised on the theme 'Prevention and Fight Against Corruption', the former president António Mascarenhas Monteiro said that:

> In our country, corruption tends to rise to critical levels; unfortunately, the fight against this phenomenon is failing. There have been no notable efforts in the fight against corruption. (*Our translation*)

Although Cabo Verde finds comfort in international corruption indicators, particularly in the Corruption Perception Index,[4] the fact is that it is a phenomenon which, as suggested by Mascarenhas Monteiro, will tend to grow if adequate measures are not taken to fight it and avoid the appropriation of state wealth.

Overview of major social movements

In the context of a deteriorating economic situation in the country marked by a decline in growth rates, it seems that rising unemployment rates, especially among the youth, governmental bodies and public institutions, as well as political parties, represents a major constraint which prevents the exercise of citizenship and a broader participation of citizens in the public sphere.

---

4 Transparency International's Corruption Perception Index gave 60 points to Cabo Verde in 2012, ranking it 39th out of 176 countries. On the African continent, Cabo Verde has the second highest score, coming second only to Botswana (65 points) and followed by Mauritius (57 points).

Possibilities for the emergence of social movements, namely those opposed to public policies considered as adverse to the interests of the majority of citizens or specific social groups, have been few. However, what is striking in its frequency is the appearance of community associations for local development and of non-governmental organisations. According to data from the platform of non-governmental organisations, Cabo Verde has a total of 446 civil society organisations, including mostly community-based associations, cultural and civic associations, cooperatives and NGOs (see Table 5).

Table 5. Distribution of CBA and NGO per island and per municipality

Islands/Municipalities	CBA/NGO	%
Boa Vista	11	2.5
Brava	17	3.8
Mosteiros	13	2.9
Santa Catarina do Fogo	7	1.6
S. Filipe	35	7.8
Maio	10	2.2
Sal	2	0.4
Praia	43	9.6
Ribeira Grande de Santiago	5	1.1
Santa Catarina	24	5.4
Santa Cruz	20	4.5
S. Domingos	23	5.2
S. Lourenço dos Orgãos	15	3.4
S. Miguel	16	3.6
São Salvador do Mundo	9	2.0
Tarrafal	15	3.4
Paul	21	4.7
Porto Novo	21	4.7
Ribeira Grande	34	7.6
Ribeira Brava	21	4.7
Tarrafal de S. Nicolau	10	2.2
S. Vicente	74	16.6
Total	446	100

Source: NGO Platform

Let us point out that in the case of rural areas, community-based and development associations play an important role not only in organising local communities, but also in the relations between local populations and local, regional and national public institutions. They generally turn into a channel of expression for demands and act as a resource mobilisation instrument for community development. For this reason, they are either courted or fought by political parties and by the structures of the state. Relations are therefore tenser with local authorities and locally elected officials, with whom they dispute, in a certain way, the prestige of community leadership.

In all cases, as stated by Jesus (2012) in his study on Santo Antão, community-based organisations and their leaders have developed a strong mobilisation and 'negotiation' capacity with their partners over the last few years. If necessary, they resort to political 'blackmail', especially ahead of elections. It is true however that this game of manipulation, or the attempt at manipulation, is reciprocal and sometimes leads to actual and/or potential gains.

Most community-based organisations - many it is true, have gradually acquired a degree of autonomy - were created as a result of a process initiated from the outside, namely by donors seeking local partners and actors that can impose themselves as privileged actors in the framework of the financing and execution of development projects. This new approach by donors results from a recognition of the inability of the government to efficiently and effectively manage development resources. Resources made available by public development aid or from loans, concessional or not, are allegedly mismanaged and generally used through corruption to encourage the illicit acquisition of wealth by national elites. It is assumed that the allocation of resources towards community-based organisations, associations and NGOs can reduce the likelihood of corruption and at the same time achieve a greater impact amongst beneficiaries.

This type of organisation has flourished, especially in the 1990s and the years 2000. They continue to emerge, especially in rural areas, and represent a privileged form for rural communities to access resources from the state and from international cooperation for community development. In several cases, this associative drive enables communities to acquire a significant capacity to organise themselves, develop and take important economic and social initiatives, and to build strong and capable leaderships. Better still, there are cases where community leaders manage to mobilise their communities to defend their interests, opposing local oligarchies and local and even national political leaders and in the process becoming actual social movements.

However, over the last two years, very few social movements have emerged. In the absence of studies on the retreat of social movements in Cabo Verde, especially since 2000, a number of assumptions can be made, some of which have already implicitly been put forward, and these can help to understand the current situation in Cabo Verde.

The first assumption pertains to the very pronounced partisan nature of the political system and of society in Cabo Verde: on the one hand, this has inhibited, through a strong ramification of partisan structures, the consolidation of small political parties able to break the two-party situation; on the other, the creation of spaces for political participation outside of the partisan system is made difficult, which undermines consolidation, in the public sphere, of movements and organisations which do not recognise themselves in the mode of operation of political parties.

The second assumption is based on the following idea: in spite of the clearly liberal nature of the state, state institutions and more particularly the ruling elite have a sprawling presence all over the economic and social fabric, which promotes the emergence of strong partisan networks. In a society with low resource levels, a narrow productivity structure, local businesses that are heavily dependent on more or less transparent arrangements with the state and where education alone no longer constitutes a guarantee of social mobility, political co-optation tends to gain weight, curbing in the process any attempts at playing a political role outside of the political frameworks. We cannot overlook the fact that public resources and offices are very often included in the process of distributing prebends and the taming of bodies and souls.

As for the third assumption, it can be described as follows: disillusion and scepticism towards politics and politicians, resulting not only from cases of corruption and suspicious wealth acquisition, but also from permanent obstacles to the individual, economic and social development of citizens, thus leading to apathy and a rejection of political, and even civic, participation.

Two social movements emerged however in the last two years, which help to test these assumptions. They are essentially regional movements seeking to mobilise and regroup the Cabo Verdean diaspora; hence their national and even international impact. This impact is linked to the sensitivity of the themes put forward on the one hand, and to the specificities of the main actors on the other.

The first movement is the self-titled Movement for the Regionalisation of Cabo Verde and the Autonomy of S. Vicente. The leader and ideologist of this movement is the political figure, writer and political analyst Onésimo Silveira, as well as other intellectuals of the island. The leitmotiv of the movement is the autonomy/regionalisation of the island, including the neighbouring islands of Santo Antão and S. Nicolau.This idea reflects a debate of a few decades ago, when one of the submissions was to envisage a North Eastern region, including precisely the above-mentioned islands.This movement managed to introduce discussion on the issue of regionalism/ autonomy/decentralisation into the public agenda. It received broad coverage in the Cabo Verdean press, thus forcing the main leaders of the state and of political parties to take a stance on this issue.

The second movement is called the Cabo Verdean Association of Young Professionals. It is essentially made up of youth from S. Vicente, who have a university education and are unemployed or in a precarious job. Here again, the driver for change is politically and socially sensitive: youth employment, in particular among university graduates who perceive education to be a fundamental instrument for entering the labour market. However, these youth end up facing difficulties, or the impossibility, of accessing the labour market. This reduces their chances of having access to an income that could have lifted them to a higher level, thus changing their social status. Eventually, disappointment triggered youth mobilisation that spread through social networks: they criticised and condemned the government's political opinions and called on other youth in the same situation to unite in order to channel their dissatisfaction and make their demands heard by public authorities.

It must be pointed out that the two social movements have their origin and their militant base in S. Vicente and show points of convergence, namely in their criticism of the tenets of economic policy, investment and the structuring of the state. Further still, the island of Santiago, and more particularly the city of Praia, has become the primary recipient of their criticism. We can therefore consider that these two social movements, although different from the perspective of their objectives and of the actors that carry them, in fact end up complementing each other.

Over the last two years, issues of regionalisation and unemployment have definitely been inscribed on the public agenda, not under the initiative of political parties and public institutions, but rather through the dynamism of citizens who have gradually become organised. The relative remoteness of the political and administrative capital of the country seems to have enabled actors of these two social movements to cast a critical and informed glance on governance and its impacts. They have also achieved greater ability to exert pressure on decision makers.

As already stated, the social movements selected for this analysis originated from and have their support base on the island of S. Vicente and more specifically its capital, the city of Mindelo. One must also take into consideration the fact that Mindelo sees itself as the cultural capital of Cabo

Verde, a view supported by voices and discourses generally emanating from Portugal, the former colonial power. On the other hand, it feels short-changed by independence. The central argument is that public investments essentially go to the island of Santiago which, according to one of the leaders of the regionalisation movement, has mutated into the 'Republic of Santiago'. It is worth noting that the strength of these arguments rests less on their truthfulness than on the political impact and mobilisation that they can generate. Indeed, for nearly a decade and a half after independence, the main criticism levied by some officials and opponents of the regime towards the current regime was based on the fact that the country's economic development strategy rested on a tri-polar process. In other words, investments, especially structural investments for economic development, were focused on three islands: Santiago, São Vicente and Sal. As the island of São Vicente was one of the main beneficiaries, it has no reason to back the criticism.

In the meantime, it is true that S. Vicente island has lost some of its economic, political and cultural centrality. Due especially to investment in education and training, independence gradually enabled people from other islands, especially Santiago, which has the largest population, to access decision-making positions in the political, administrative and economic structures. Those from S. Vicente therefore lost their hegemony.

In fact, in an online petition promoting a better S. Vicente, its authors argue that independence has had a negative impact on S. Vicente. This idea was on the front page of one of Cabo Verde's online publications, *Liberal online*, dated 28 February 2010. Amongst the arguments put forward by the regionalisation movement, a reminder of a glorious historical past is presented at the same time as the post-colonial stagnation. In a manner of speaking, nostalgia about the past is opposed to the frustrations of today.

Going back to the 19th century, the petition, signed by several eminent figures and sent to the main leaders of the country, namely the president, the speaker of the parliament and the prime minister, narrates the beginnings of development in Porto Grande Island (as S. Vicente is called because of its large port), with Porto Grande driving this development, at the same time as the industrialisation process started (Correia et Silva 2010). In the same way, the petitioners argue that the establishment of the Lycée in S. Vicente in 1917, the only secondary school in Cabo Verde until 1960, turned S. Vicente into the most important and most developed city in the country. They argue that:[5]

> In the past, S. Vicente Island was the economic, political, cultural and intellectual center of Cabo Verde. It was on this island that the first industrial and commercial units were implanted in the 19th century, with the start of the Second Industrial Revolution on the archipelago, thus ensuring a thriving economy in the former colony. S. Vicente thus became the heart of the archipelago. (*Our translation*)

This dynamic as well as the centrality of the island, it is argued, were later slowed down by independence, which leads to the idea that independence has not been beneficial for S. Vicente. On the contrary, it heralded a gradual process of economic, political and cultural regression:

> In a strange paradox, the start of S. Vicente's decline coincided with Cabo Verde's birth as an independent nation; the legitimate expectations were at odds, in line with the values of freedom and the desire for progress always protected by the populations. The development model implemented by the First Republic of Cabo Verde consisted in concentrating all authority and resources within the Capital; this option had extremely adverse consequences for S. Vicente in particular and for Cabo Verde in general; the island ended up in a situation of painful recession, with the hint of a lack of political relevance. All successive

5 http://www.petitiononline.com/mmscent/petition.html

governments followed the same asphyxiating trend, which even intensified over the last few years. (*Our translation*)

The Movement for the Regionalisation and the Autonomy of S. Vicente, created in 2012, built on the sentiment expressed by coordinators and main signatories of this petition.

Movement for the Regionalisation and the Autonomy of S. Vicente

In laying out its objectives, the movement's founding document quotes the content of the online petition almost *ipsis verbis*. A slight nuance is introduced to show that the victims of the existing political and development model, which has led to the hypertrophy of the city of Praia, the country's capital, are all the islands and towns of the country, *including* Praia itself. This is clearly a way of lending a national scope to a clearly regional or even regionalist movement.

In the preamble to the above-mentioned document, the movement's leaders argue that:

> Development models implemented since the 1st Republic and consisting in concentrating all the authority into the capital and relegating other pieces of the national territory to the status of peripheral regions violated the natural and rational organization of the national space. Besides, these models exacerbated national rifts and regional rivalries; at the same time, they heightened the sense of injustice in terms of the distribution of available means and resources. This model led to an atrophied and dysfunctional development in the country, causing other islands to lag behind.
>
> S. Vicente is clearly a victim of the centralization options of the country and has lost the core of its political relevance. Since

independence, the island has been suffering from a situation of socio-economic stagnation, while a genuine crisis is profoundly damaging three crucial sectors: economic, social and cultural.[6] (*Our translation*)

The movement suggests a regionalisation model that divides the country into four (1. S. Vicente, Santo Antão and S. Nicolau; 2. Sal and Boa Vista; 3. Santiago and Maio; 4. Fogo and Brava), but this is not the end goal. Indeed, as described by the movement, its main objective is in fact the autonomy of S. Vicente Island. Although this is not explicitly mentioned, what is sought is to give back to the island the 'centrality' it enjoyed during the colonial period and which it lost after independence. The document argues that S. Vicente Island:

> [...] had the best schools and the first middle school in the colony, was the cradle of almost all the Cabo Verdean 'intelligentsia', past and present, as well as the majority of the country's leading class. The island reveals the multiple idiosyncrasies of Cabo Verde and represents the national paradigm of syncretism. This is an example of tolerance and positive integration of universal values. It is in Mindelo that was born the first cultural movement leading to political awareness amongst the colony's population, and that is where the most crucial struggles for the future of Cabo Verde were waged. (*Our translation*)

Without challenging the merit of this historical reconstruction and a possible accusation of regionalism and 'racism', this analysis calls for a focus on the impact of this movement and of its ideas in the Cabo Verdean public space, impact that has given it the dimension of a large-scale social movement.

---

6 Ibid.

Indeed, the Movement for the Regionalisation of Cabo Verde and the Autonomy of S. Vicente managed to mainstream the theme of regionalisation into the public discourse. It managed to secure broad media coverage in the main newspapers (printed and online press), and on radio and television. In the same way, and with a sound strategy, its leaders started using the press to convey their ideas and arguments through opinion pieces. In this way, they sought to broaden their membership base and to exert pressure on public authorities so that their claims were taken into consideration.

Sometimes, political and governmental decisions are quickly turned into a leitmotiv to contest choices made and show to what extent they exacerbate the rifts between different regions of the country and in fact benefit the 'Republic of Santiago' at the expense of others.

The debates that have taken place thus far have shown that at least in appearance, a consensus exists on the need for regionalisation. However, few are those who criticised the proposals made. In an opinion piece published online by the *A Semana* newspaper on 27 June 2013, Fabio Veira questions the pace and the eminently political intentions of speeches and debates, although he does not oppose the principle of regionalisation:

> In this context of uncertainties and ambiguity, it is important to understand first and foremost what intentions underlie this urgency for meso-governance. Regionalization to provide concrete and immediate responses to the 'neighborhood' discourses recently conveyed by the media? Or regionalization to create new positions for friends and comrades, a model defended by a known opposition party? It is obvious that if regionalization is a means to this end, we would point to this, without a doubt, as a good example of political irresponsibility. (*Our translation*)

In fact, analysis of the regionalisation movement framework document or of articles and debates does not help to visualise the issues structuring or preventing regionalisation. Indeed, it is not easy to know whether they propose an administrative regionalisation (regionalisation and de-concentration of powers and resources in the framework of an administrative reform or even a reform of the state), or a change in the unitary government organisational system as it is enshrined in the constitution. Likewise, the issue of how to finance regionalisation is neither discussed, nor raised.

At any rate, the movement's actions have had a significant impact on the government, which, according to the minister for environment, housing and land planning, commissioned a study on the subject in order to inform the public debate and facilitate decision-making. Besides, well ahead of that, the prime minister had given signals by referring to concerns about regionalisation. According to him, the government is examining the issue. It is interesting to note that he spoke in favour of regionalisation at the taking of office of locally elected officials of the mayor's office and of the Municipal Council of Praia.

In the same way, the president spoke in favour of regionalisation, thus making his the objectives of the regionalisation movement; he argued that 'regionalisation is the best development path for Cabo Verde'. The pressure on the government and other public authorities (parliament and presidency) is revealed by the search for external legitimacy of the objectives sought, thus strengthening the assumptions of the movement from a political and academic perspective.

Indeed, looking to Portuguese politicians and intellectuals is part of this ongoing search for increased legitimacy. The Portuguese university professor and former foreign affairs minister, Freitas do Amaral, and the economist and mayor, Rui Rio, were invited in this framework. Thus, taking ownership of the demands of the movement, the mayor of S. Vicente invited the mayor of Porto in Portugal to speak at a conference on regionalisation in Cabo

Verde. It is interesting to note the arguments by Rui Rio, the invited speaker, as reported by the online journal *A Semana* on 26 February 2013:

> ...the debate on regionalization is more relevant in Cabo Verde than in Portugal; it is obvious that, as an archipelago, the islands are further away from the capital than the city of Porto is from Lisbon. Even if Portugal is a mainland country, I too, protest against centralism. I always argue that proximity is more efficient, because if we are far removed from the problem, we cannot even understand it. When one is far, one needs to have tremendous intellectual capacity in order to understand what is happening far away; therefore, proximity is always important in order for public resources to be managed more efficiently. (*Our translation*)

Analysing the movement for regionalisation shows that, at inception, it was a regionally-based movement seeking to provide a greater economic, political and cultural role in the national context. Gradually, through a frontal clash with the government, the parliament and political parties, it managed to broaden its social base to the Cabo Verdean diaspora, to mobilise opinion makers and to exert influence on the media. It has turned its agenda into a national agenda, in a way giving political parties and state institutions no choice but to line up with the objectives of the movement.

A regional agenda was turned into a national agenda, and any view to the contrary would amount to anti-patriotism. The specificities of the social movements described by André Gunder Frank and Marta Fuentes (2008) and by McSween (2010) are embodied by the movement.

It is also interesting to point out that by wanting to place itself outside of the framework of political parties, the movement also sought, for its own interests, to pave the way for future political participation. From its exercise of citizenship, it made public policy propositions in line with the interests of its members and, in this case, of its territorial space. This is therefore a social movement borne out of a dual disconnect leading to low institutional performance (resulting in a disconnect between the political sphere and the social sphere) and to low socio-economic performances (resulting in turn in a disconnect between the economic sphere and the social sphere).

Association of Cabo Verdean Young Professionals in S. Vicente

In the socio-economic characterisation of Cabo Verde, we underlined the fact that unemployment, especially amongst the youth, reached very high levels. Indeed, in 2012, the rate of unemployment in Cabo Verde was 16.8 per cent, against 28.9 per cent on S. Vicente Island. With regards to youth unemployment, it reached 28.9 per cent amongst the youth aged 15 to 19, 33.7 per cent for the 20-24 age group, and 22.9 per cent for the 25-29 age group.

Unemployment is high even amongst educated youth, which frustrates both their expectations and those of their families, as these invested into vocational training as a sure mechanism for access to the labour market and to an income.

It is in this socio-economic context marked by low economic performance and a deficit in communication channels with political and governmental decision makers (a democratic performance deficit), that a group of university graduates who were either unemployed or in precarious jobs decided to organise themselves to speak out against the failure of government economic policy to create jobs. A public protest was organised by young professionals in the city of Mindelo. It received support from parents and other citizens of Mindelo concerned with the plight of the youth. This was also an opportunity to sensitise and exert pressure on governmental and political decision makers so that active employment policies would be implemented. Mobilisation took place through social networks and, gradually, the movement ended up receiving attention from the media, thus giving more weight to its actions. On 7 May 2013, *A Semana Online* published a report on the association's activities and stressed that its members described themselves as:

> [...] a group of active citizens with a common cause: increasing the number of youth in employment. We want to put our skills at the service of our cause and have a direct impact on the number of youth securing job interviews. We also want to create a support and guidance center. (*Our translation*)

A manifesto was developed and submitted to the government through the prime minister and minister for youth and employment, and to the political parties represented in parliament. Formally, as indicated by the minutes from the first meeting, the association was created in November 2012 and has close to 2,308 members today. The association thus defines its objectives: 'Sharing useful information on labor market access in Cabo Verde and abroad. Sensitizing public and private institutions on the need to promote internships and employment for young Cabo Verdeans.' It asserts its non-partisan nature and its openness to all young professionals in the country and in the diaspora 'who wish to participate and make a meaningful and constructive contribution'.

It is interesting to note that the association, as its name indicates, has a regional basis, but seeks national legitimacy. There is clear political proximity with the regionalisation movement with regards to contesting the national strategic choices made by the government. The national dimension (Cabo Verde) appears precisely in order to concentrate and focus its action on the regional framework (S. Vicente).

The proximity of the association to the regionalisation movement is also revealed in the rationale for the creation of the movement and the validity of its objectives. Indeed, the economic and investment policies centralised in

Santiago, and the strong concentration and centralisation of authority, skills and resources, have heightened regional asymmetries on the one hand, and worsened unemployment on the other, especially amongst the youth.

From the perspective of these youth therefore, employment policies must be rectified, a crucial condition to address the economic and employment crisis. The summary of the main outcomes of the first meeting of young professionals held in November 2012 clearly focuses on the worsening of working conditions in S. Vicente, especially with regards to employment:

São Vicente Island is considered today as that with the highest rate of unemployment, with an average higher than the national average. According to the National Statistics Institute, that rate on the island nears 18.3% against 12.2% at the national level.

With this in mind, and standing apart from the regionalisation movement, the young professionals compiled new issues that tend to undermine youth access to the labour market and which go beyond employment policies. In fact, corruption and nepotism in the process of recruiting civil servants and the migration policy, or lack thereof, created tremendous obstacles for the youth, especially those living far from the political decision centres.

Reference to immigration is interesting, because it makes migrant communities responsible for the issue of unemployment, whereas in actual fact, migrants are active in areas where local professionals generally refuse to work. Whatever the case may be, the main problems raised in the document drafted by young professionals are the following:

- Power centralisation on Santiago Island;
- Importing labour rather than giving priority to national professionals;
- Insufficient number of internship offers;
- Lack of transparency in bidding processes;

- Lack of skilled human resources in organisations;

- Precarious employment;

- Difficult access to credit for young entrepreneurs;

- Difficult access to information on international calls for applications;

- Low visibility of the situation of young professionals;

- Undervaluation of the intellectual capital of young professionals;

- Gap between training offers and labour market needs;

- Experience required for positions advertised;

- Interns and service providers;

- Creation of training courses in saturated employment categories (such as education and psychology);

- Cumulative expenses;

- Positions filled without going through recruitment and selection processes;

- Positions granted on the basis of influence peddling;

- Disregard for merit in recruitment and selection processes;

- Lack of openness and coordination of employment centres;

- Inability to start a family and provide for it, due to a lack of income.

As stated in the regionalisation movement report, the association managed, to some degree at least, to inscribe its demands within the national public agenda. Debates in the media, at the parliament and amongst party leaders and government officials show the relevance and impact of the actions led by these youth. Besides, the dynamism and capacity for structuring and using social networks and new communication technologies gave their activities a particular scope and relevance in the public sphere, thus influencing political opinion.

As mentioned earlier, the Association of Young Professionals seems to be seeking new spaces for civic participation in a relentless quest for an ability to influence public policy linked to their projects. The association is also the result of a relative failure of political and governance institutions in terms of the demands of society as a whole, and of the youth in particular. In a certain way, we can say that this social movement plays a role that is all the more important since it seeks to break the public sphere inertia. It seeks to be a catalyst for individual wills, an emancipator of the youth vis-à-vis the establishment and to boost and rejuvenate the democratic experience.

This being said, the question is whether this movement, which does not explicitly seek to exercise power, nor to launch a new social project, shall be able, in a structured manner, to bring about in-depth political changes in Cabo Verde. The actual spaces where this organisation can mature and consolidate are rather narrow. In a society steeped in partisan politics, the spaces for political participation are few, not because of a lack of objective conditions or of willingness from citizens, but rather because, by design or by omission, political actors tend to co-opt those who seek to succeed as autonomous subjects in a dialogue that is critical and based on reflection.

Conclusion

In the 1990s, Cabo Verde experienced a peaceful democratic transition process, with a political changeover and stability. In the years 2000, a new changeover occurred without any profound breaks.

From a socio-economic point of view, in spite of the impact of the economic and financial crisis of 2008-2009 and the subsequent decline in development assistance and foreign direct investment, social indicators in the areas of health, education and social security, steadily improved. Although remaining positive, economic growth has experienced significant slowdowns. As for employment, statistics show that unemployment rates remained high, in the order of two digits, and have showed an increase over the last two years, with a special incidence amongst the youth, even those with technical and vocational training.

The privatisation of the economy in the 1990s and the subsequent withdrawal of the state deprived the latter of mechanisms it previously had at its disposal to implement specific public policies. Thus, the capacity for the provision of social services by public institutions gradually decreased and led to a trend of self-organisation by society in order to satisfy unmet demands. In this framework, a number of NGOs, associations and community-based organisations appeared almost all over the country to fight for access to goods and social services by populations. Some of these play the role of privileged dialogue and political pressure counterparts with public institutions; they seek to influence political decisions and the process of resource allocation and public investment.

The pronounced rift in the political scene, with a *de facto* two-party system, reduced the spaces for political participation on one hand and on the other, became a form of pressure and coercion on those who take on a political stance based on citizenship; in other words, a stance that lies outside partisan frameworks and political society.

From our point of view, the strong direct or indirect reliance of citizens, as well as civil society organisations and corporations, on public resources has slowed down, over the last few years, the emergence of social movements that are autonomous and effectively liberating and anti-hegemonic.

Our analysis reveals the emergence over the last two years of social movements which, through their agenda of demands, clearly opposed the policy choices of the government and conventional political organs at the national, regional and local levels. After their objectives were echoed in the press and among public officials, these two movements were able to mainstream their concerns into the public agenda. They remain active and watchful, and avoid co-optation and the dilution of their demands.

However, our analysis does not determine whether the two social movements were able to consolidate, nor whether their objectives were reached. We feel that the relative consensus observed around the objectives of the two movements studied can harbour, in the absence of permanent vigilance and pressure, a possible risk of lethargy.

In spite of this possibility, it is undeniable that these two movements introduced not only the issue of unemployment and regionalisation, but also the debate on the need to create spaces to enable citizens to take part in the development and structuring of the public agenda, outside of the conventional political participation spaces. In this manner, they shed light on the existence of a certain lethargy in the process of effectively consolidating democracy. They revealed the inability of the state to meet the demands of citizens and to enforce the principles laid out in the constitution in terms of citizen rights—namely political, social and economic rights—and the inability of the state to fulfil its duties as enforcer of these rights.

References

Anjos, J. C. (2009) 'Sobre o escândalo político em Cabo Verde' in *Lusotopie* XVI (1): 25-43

Banco de Cabo Verde (2012) 'Relatório de Politica Monetária', Praia, Banco de Cabo Verde, Maio

Banque Africaine de Développement, Fonds africain de développement (2012) Cap-Vert: un modèle de réussite, http://bit.ly/1lKYM8E, accessed March 2014

Bonneval (de), E. (2011) 'Contribution à une sociologie politique de la jeunesse: jeunes, ordre politique et contestation au Burkina Faso', Thèse de doctorat en science politique, Bordeaux, École doctorale de Science Politique

Brandes, N. and Engels, B. (2011) 'Social Movements in Africa', *Vienna Journal of African Studies*, 20(11): 1-15

Correia E Silva, A.L. (2010) 'Nos tempos do Porto Grande do Mindelo', Praia/Mindelo, Centre Culturel Portugais

Costa, D.O. (2009) 'Papel do Chefe de Estado no semi-presidencialismo cabo-verdiano, 1991-2005' in M.C. Lobo, O.A. Neto (orgs), *O Semi-Presidencialismo nos Países de Língua Portuguesa*, Lisboa, Imprensa do ICS: 105-138

Dalberto, S. A. (2011) 'Sénégal: les nouvelles formes de mobilisation de la jeunesse', Paris, *Les Carnets du CAP*, Octobre: 37-65

Diop, M-C. (2013) (dir) *Sénégal (2000-2012). Les institutions et politiques publiques à l'épreuve d'une gouvernance libérale*, Dakar/Paris, CRES, Karthala

Fonseca, M. D. D. M. (2007) 'Terceiro Sector, Governabilidade E Balanced Scorecard', Praia, ISCEE/ISCTE (Mémoire de maîtrise)

Frank, A. G. and Fuentes, M. (1989) 'Dez Teses acerca dos Movimentos Sociais', *Lua Nova* n 17: 18-48 (São Paulo)

Furtado, C. (2002) 'Peasant Organisations in the Cape Verde Islands: From individualism to Associative Forms of Organisation in the Rural World', in M. Ben Romdhane, S. Moyo (eds), *Peasants Organisations and the Democratisation Process in Africa*, Dakar, CODESRIA: 219-259

Hainard, F. (2009) 'Effervescences et mouvements sociaux en Afrique de l'Ouest', in Cahier de l'ARUC – ISDC, Série Documentation et diffusion, Université du Québec en Outaouais, Développement international de la CRDC, no. 9

IMF (2013) Country page: Cabo Verde, www.imf.org/external/country/cpv, accessed September 2013

INE (2013) Inquérito Multi-objectivo. Estatísticas do Emprego e do Mercado de Trabalho-2012, Praia, INE

Jesus, A.T. (2012) 'Associativismo, municipalismo e Desenvolvimento Local em Cabo Verde', Thèse de Doctorat, Praia, Louvain-la-Neuve, Universidade de Cabo Verde/Universidade Católica de Louvain-la-Neuve

Jovens Quadros de São Vicente (2012) Conclusão dos encontros do Grupo de Jovens Quadros de Cabo Verde em S. Vicente, Mindelo

Larmer, M. (2010) 'Social movement struggles in Africa', Review of African Political Economy, 37 (125): 251-262

Mamdani, M. and Wamba-dia-Wamba, E. (1995) (eds) African Studies in Social Movements and Democracy, Dakar, CODESRIA

McSween, N. (2010) 'Repenser l'analyse des mouvements sociaux africains', Québec, l'Alliance de recherche université-communauté/Innovation sociale et développement des communautés (ARUC/ISDC), Chaire de recherche en développement des collectivités (CRDC), Série: Recherches, no.32, mars

Ministério da Saude (2012) Relatório Estatístico da Saúde 2011, Praia, GEP/MS

Plataforma das ONG (n.d.) Guia das ONG de Cabo Verde, Praia, Plataforma das ONG

Pereira, R.A.P. (2009) 'Cabo Verde a caminho dos Objectivos do Milénio para o Desenvolvimento: o papel das ONG - estudo caso: Ilha de Santiago', Lisboa, ISCTE (Master Thesis)

Pina (de), R. M. (2008) 'Associativismo e Desenvolvimento Local em Cabo Verde: Notas sobre alguns Percursos de Revitalização Rural', Actas do III Congresso de Estudos Rurais (III CER), Faro, Universidade do Algarve, 1-3 Nov. 2007, SPER/Ualg

Transparency International (2013) *The 2012 Corruption Perceptions Index*, www.cpi.transparency.org/cpi2012/results/, accessed August 2013

UNESCO Regional Bureau for Education in Africa (n.d.), Profil EPT de Cabo Verde EFA, Dakar, UNESCO

UNDP (2013) *Human Development Report 2013. The Rise of the South: Human Progress in a Diverse World*, New York. UNDP

World Bank (2013) Cabo Verde. Aspectos Gerais', http://bit.ly/1gEqRqk, accessed August 2013

CHAPTER: 13

GUINEA: AT THE CROSSROADS

Alpha Amadou Bano Barry

After arousing hope and admiration through the unitary process and ideals of independence, followed by disappointment and bitterness due to autocratic civilian and military rule, Guinea has since 2010 been at a crossroads. With social movements a potential part of renewal, Guinea can come out on top by embracing political modernity. By the same token 'tribalisation' of its political class, debates and associations, could also lead to weakening, regression and even collapse. After a presentation of the economic and political situation, this chapter seeks to explore the struggle between backward-looking forces and progressive forces. At stake is the destiny of a country and a sub-region.

Introduction

The December 2010 presidential election was keenly awaited by Guineans and the international community as the beginning of the end of Guinea's long period of hardship. Three years after 2010, where does Guinea stand now? Several answers to this question are regularly put forward. For some commentators, who are often very close to the current government, Guinea's hesitant march towards democracy is 'normal' for a country which has previously only experienced autocratic single party and military regimes. For them, Guinea is experiencing, like many others countries, the transition from autocratic rule to the establishment of the rule of law. Accordingly, it is normal for this march to be chaotic.

For others, most often those in the opposition, or close to the opposition, Guinea is in a very bad state. Its current situation is sometimes described as worse than under the previous military regimes. For these critics, the challenges in building a real democracy are attributable to the regime of President Alpha Condé, who wanted to use a politically-driven strategy to control the state and all other levers of power, such as justice and the legislative system.

Finally, others see Guinea's current difficulties as stemming from the disintegration of the state as a result of the neoliberal policies of the 1980s, which saw a process of state withdrawal (*désétatisation*) that led to the rise of communitarianism to compensate for the absence of the state and its loss of control.

For us, and this is central to our argument in this chapter, Guinea is at the crossroads. By creating the required conditions, it can consolidate democracy and the rule of law. It can also collapse, and in this contribution we are going to demonstrate how this could happen through the combined effect of the political and social divide and the emergence of community-based elites grouped within so-called regional associations.

This Guinean political and social divide is Manichean and expresses first and foremost the dysfunctions of Guinean political parties. Political parties are usually instruments for the exercise of democracy. In Guinea, they are mostly 'political businesses' with autocratic internal governance structures financed from the resources of each leader and based on allegiance to one individual, namely the founder and owner of the political party.

Not surprisingly, therefore, the point of view of the founding president prevails. With banknotes and extravagant promises, he ensures the support and buy-in of some of his relatives who, very often, are not differentiated from the members of his own ethno-cultural community. The president thus acts as a CEO, with party life being punctuated by his sovereign wills and whims. This 'employers/employees' logic is all the more integrated as militants, or clients, come with their hands extended for cash, to applaud and to listen to orders. To ensure complete and total control of the political field, the founding president has not only the exclusive right to be the candidate of the party, but also the right to present chosen candidates for positions in parliament.

This collective failure of politicians has resulted in a reduction of the capacity of the state to deliver basic social services such as water and electricity, 'privatisation', infiltration and subordination of civil society (an appendage of partisan politics) and a split in global society between the 'us' and 'them' based on a predictable point of reference: ethnicity, with the ethnic-regional coordination units as mediators.

For the purpose in hand, this chapter will be structured in three parts. The first will provide an overall picture of the economic situation since 2010. The political situation will follow, before a presentation on one of the expressions of societal dysfunction, namely conflicts and the rise of 'regional coordination units' (*coordinations régionales*), which are the expression of the ethnicisation of the associative and political space in Guinea.

Economic situation

Economically speaking, the government which came to power following the 2010 presidential election has put in place structural reforms and macroeconomic stabilisation, with a credit-tightening policy and budget restriction marked by the execution of public spending based on revenues and less on borrowing. Macroeconomists generally agree that Guinea's economy has improved, at least when it comes to reducing imbalances. In a nutshell, budgetary discipline is observed and there is virtually no money printed to finance the state's activities. The beginning of a return to economic and financial orthodoxy in running the country has resulted in significant control over inflation and a substantial increase in the country's foreign exchange reserves. These and other measures such as cash control and reduction in monetary expansion enabled the economy to be stabilised, but did not allow the re-launch of investments or job creation, let alone an improvement of the living conditions of the population. Instead, there is serious deflation and a liquidity crisis, pushing up the prices of basic necessities.

Likewise, these macroeconomic reforms do not yet translate into the establishment of new businesses that can make an impact on the high unemployment rate. Moreover, the companies that supported towns like Fria have shut down. The same could be said for the national telecommunications company (SOTELGUI). Other private companies like Nestlé and multinationals like the Brazilian company Vale and Anglo-American BHP have withdrawn from Guinea.

The unstable and still corrupt legal environment, coupled with the 'country risk' and political events that reduce the length of the working week are undermining the business climate when it comes to creating new businesses and preserving the existing ones. As a consequence, businesses of all sizes, and their subcontractors, major providers of employment, have been shut down or put on hold. It is therefore correct to say that the number of jobs destroyed because of the shutdown of businesses largely exceeds the jobs the government claims to have created.

Efforts have been made in the field of infrastructure, mainly in the hotel sector. On the occasion of the inauguration of the head of state on 21 December 2010, Guineans realised the country's inability to host, accommodate and feed distinguished guests. The day after the ceremony, a vast campaign of renovation or construction of new buildings was launched, but only in Conakry, the capital city.

Efforts were also made in the area of road infrastructure. But, regarding the country as a whole, shortfalls are still noted globally, with accelerated degradation of main and secondary roads. The inland cities are virtually separated from each other by the impracticability of the roads linking them, and Guinea's prefectures at the borders of neighbouring countries turn to the latter for economic and even social exchanges.

The government has also displayed some voluntarism in the strategic area of electricity. This is reflected in the mobilisation of important resources for the start-up of the Kaleta working site. However, this voluntarism did not yield the expected outcome in terms of meeting the daily electricity demand. The most electrified city in the country, Conakry, is often in the dark, with less than eight hours of power supply per day. A similar situation occurs in the supply of running water.

Despite the significant investments, selective power cuts remain daily practice. 2012 witnessed the greatest number of demonstrations by youth from many neighbourhoods of the capital and inland cities who were demanding better access to running water and electricity. On many occasions, the youth took to the streets to show their rejection of the programmes for alternating water and electricity supply, especially when these were irregular and fanciful. The youth were also refusing to be deprived of watching major sports events on TV because of power cuts.

This is precisely what happened in February 2012 when Kindia youth violently reacted against power cuts during the Africa Cup of Nations. In their anger, the youth ransacked the premises of the regional gendarmerie and set fire to the headquarters of *Électricité de Guinée* (EDG), looting public and private properties on their way.

Generally, when protesting, the youth erect barricades and vandalise facilities and properties. They attack vehicles on the roads, thus creating psychosis among motorists. The police forces are forced to intervene to deter protesters from taking to the streets or vandalising public and private properties.

In the healthcare sector, free caesarean sections as well as free care for children aged 0 to five are both poorly implemented. Added to this is the dilapidated infrastructure as well as the very low quality of services. The medical personnel subject to the rules of free care pour out their anger at patients, from whom they extort money.

Political situation

In a context of pain and psychosis, Guinea held its legislative elections in 2013. These elections had initially been planned for June 2011. Therefore, the new parliament was established three years after the inauguration of the president and two years before the end (in 2015) of the mandate of the president. The election also followed a long political crisis that particularly affected national cohesion and put to a severe test the authority of the state.

The day following the announcement of the results of the second round of the 2010 election, Guinea entered a spiral of clashes between supporters of the two candidates - Alpha Condé and Cellou Dalein Diallo - that dragged in the Malinké and Peul ethnic communities to which the two belonged, as well as the repressive apparatus of the state.

The clashes began on 28 September 2011, the day when Diallo returned to Guinea after a long absence. Supporters of his party, the *Union des Forces Démocratiques de Guinée* (Union of Democratic Forces of Guinea, UFDG), who mostly belonged to his ethnic group, defied the prohibition to welcome him. The clashes left one dead on the side of the UFDG, Zakariaou Diallo, who was raised to the status of first martyr for this party.

Following this first death, the opposition, particularly UFDG and its militants, and the ruling party, turned Conakry into a battlefield with a cortège of deaths, wounded, and destruction of property. As a consequence, the working week was divided in the following way: 'Monday and Tuesday was allocated for those in power, Wednesday and Thursday for the opposition, Friday for prayer, Saturday for delinquents and Sunday for the innumerable social affairs.'[1] At the same time, clashes increased in the interior and were characterised by much brutality.

In Conakry, during the last days of February 2012 and after a march organised by the opposition, shops were set on fire in the main markets of Taouyah and Madina. A second moment of extreme tension was marked by a clash between the opposition and law enforcement authorities on 18 April 2013. UFDG has said that since 2010 it has recorded 1,162 arrests, 653 unlawful convictions and 53 people shot dead by police forces.

The interior of the country was not spared. All of the mining areas (Fria, Kouroussa, Siguiri, Dinguiraye) and other prefectures like Guéckédou and N'Zérékoré (Galappay, Zogota, Koulé) were shaken by violent clashes between law enforcement authorities and the local populations, and also sometimes between actors claiming a different ethnicity. Sometimes, dozens and even hundreds of deaths were recorded, and properties were destroyed.

There have also been uprisings of indigenous populations in areas where mineral resources are exploited, either against new population settlements, the militarisation of the locality, or environmental pollution. Sometimes, revolts have started with claims by workers from the mining companies. At times, the conflicts have also started through grievances against local authorities, because of the poor management of income generated from the exploitation of resources.

---

1   The division of the week was put forward by the author of this article during a broadcast on *Lynx FM* on 24 February 2014.

The most deadly of all conflicts since 2010 was unquestionably the one which started in Koulé (a few kilometres away from N'Zérékoré) with a banal story of attempted theft by apprentice vehicle mechanics in a gas station. After one of the presumed thieves died following alleged ill-treatment from the station's manager, young Konianké attacked the station manager and other people of his ethnic group (Kpélè) to avenge the death of the presumed thief, who belonged to their ethnic group. The day following this, N'Zérékoré was set ablaze by clashes between Kpèlè and Konianké. In three days, the violence claimed more than 100 lives on both sides.

This conflict, born in N'Zérékoré, had an impact on other localities in the region (Beyla, Lola and Yomou) with the same social structures as N'Zérékoré. The official estimates of the number of dead, injured and displaced persons are, according to many sources, largely below reality. Some sources indicate over 500 deaths and thousands of injuries.

The presence of a dozen foreign companies in the Guinea Forest Region, which has fostered an accelerated migratory flow to that region, has created adequate conditions for intensifying competition between political and economic stakeholders from different ethnic and religious groups. The indigenous populations are Kpélé, who are essentially animists and Christians, whereas the non-indigenous are Konianké, Malinké, Peul and Toma Mania, who are Muslims. Although the Kpélé are the first occupants of the town, the non-indigenous people hold the strategic sectors, especially transport and trade. Thanks to their higher purchasing power, the Konianké, Malinké, Peul and Toma Mania have bought most of the housing plots that formerly belonged to the indigenous Kpèlè.

The discovery of substantial natural resources in the region, the arrival of mining companies and the mass exodus of job seekers to N'Zérékoré have raised the economic value of the land that had been occupied for a long time by indigenous people. On the basis of customary law, the Kpèlè claim exclusive ownership of the land they themselves sold to the non-indigenous people. The latter are opposed to any idea of returning the occupied plots to the indigenous people because they hold all the legal evidence that they are the owners. This situation exacerbates tensions and provides fertile ground for politicians in need of social mobilisation.

Kalifa Gassama Diaby, the minister in charge of human rights and public liberties, in referring to clashes in the Guinea Forest Region, was categorical in stating that:

> All the violent acts that generated the killings, the massacres, are a national tragedy which requires a moment of silence by all the people of Guinea, as should be the case any time one of our citizens' life is taken by violence, hatred and all communitarian perversities. It is unfair and inacceptable to hurt someone simply because of his identity, political, social or religious singularity.[2]

For Diaby, these mass human rights violations are increasingly common and unjustifiable. Through these repeated violations of human rights, Guinea presents a country 'curled up in its ethnic and tribal obsessions [...] giving the rest of the world a degrading, inhumane and intolerable image of our society.'[3]

In fact, we are faced with a country in which the political situation during the last three years has been marked by constant violation of the constitution, sometimes by 'consensus' among the political actors, and punctuated with a denial of justice and violence as a mode of expressing claims and responding to political debates.

In the eastern part of Guinea, the country's main gold and diamond mining area, there are other issues at stake. Gold and diamonds are mainly found in Upper Guinea, gold in the Siguiri basin (in the prefectures of Siguiri,

2   *Lynx* (2012) no. 1243, 28 August 2012
3   *Lynx* (2012) no. 1243, 28 August 2012

Kouroussa, Mandiana, Dinguiraye, Kankan) and diamonds in the prefecture of Kérouané.

The region's gold and diamond deposits are mined using artisanal, semi-industrial and industrial methods. Large-scale gold mining is carried out by three industrial companies, namely:

- *Société Aurifère de Guinée* (SAG) was established in Siguiri in 1995 and is mining lode gold deposits;

- *Société Minière de Dinguiraye* (SMD) is mining the lode gold deposits in Lero, Fayalala and surroundings;

- *Société d'Exploitation Minière d'Afrique de l'Ouest* (SEMAFO-Guinea) has been mining the Kiniéro mine, near Kouroussa, since 2002.

Diamond mining on an industrial scale is carried out by Aredor-First City Mining Company (AFCMC), chiefly in the area of Banankoro and Gbenko, and on a semi-industrial scale by various companies set up under Guinean law. Thousands of other Guineans spend days digging in the hope of finding the 'stone' that will change their lives and those of their families. The presence of all these mining companies and the artisanal gold and diamond mining activities do not happen without generating conflict in the region. People living in the areas where mines are established sometimes oppose the mining companies. In other cases, conflicts arise between populations of neighbouring localities over the ownership of an artisanal mine. Sometimes the conflicts involve workers and employers who exploit the mines using semi-industrial or artisanal methods.

The peculiarity of these conflicts is that they are totally out of the purview of both political organisations and organised movements like trade unions and associations. More often than not, the conflicts are generated by a grassroots movement with local leaders who are making claims on behalf and for the benefit of their community, but who are prejudiced by local authorities politically close to the population who are funnelling local resources into primitive accumulation. This predation is opposed to partisan logics and/or close community relations, and raises the real issue of political power and its use in 'catching' public resources.

In 2012, another dynamic appeared as the population of the sub-prefecture of Kiniero came into conflict with SEMAFO to protest against a managerial decision made by the company. Before the establishment of SEMAFO, one of Kiniéro's nationals residing in Conakry had particularly distinguished himself by fully paying the annual village tax and participating in the socioeconomic and cultural development of the locality. When SEMAFO established itself in Kiniéro, the community's benefactor obtained a contract for hiring buses to SEMAFO for the transportation of the company's personnel. After some years, a new call for tender was issued and another transport company was awarded the contract. In order to express support to their 'benefactor son', the population in Kiniéro attacked the company's facilities and caused huge losses. After this incident, SEMAFO was forced to stop its activities and to leave the area.

This mechanism of manipulation of economic actors who use charity towards their community as a means for economic monopoly is also practiced in other parts of the national territory. The process is simple and is the same everywhere: accumulate, redistribute and control to ensure the possibility for more important accumulation.

In Kérouané too, it is the youth who often denounce their marginalisation during recruitment by the AREDOR company. They charge local authorities with favouritism in recruiting workers and executives who work in the mines. According to the youth, the local authorities only hire their family members or people who are able to pay money to access jobs. To make their voice stronger, they attack the public buildings of the town.

These revolts outside the system and sometimes against the established system may, therefore, have more than one face. In the case of Kérouané and N'Zérékoré, for example, access to jobs appears to be the core issue. Taking a closer look, it is the whole issue of training in general, and the adequacy thereof, especially in the interior, and the socio-professional integration of the youth, that is raised. The laws make the employment of local people a contractual obligation for mining companies, but the state does not fulfil its obligation to train youth. This contradiction and the lack of institutional mechanisms for the integration of the youth into the production sphere are the drivers of popular protests that are often fuelled and nurtured by a political class lacking federative projects.

Lower Guinea too, the coastal and bauxite-producing region par excellence, is not spared the violence related to mining, bad governance and discriminatory acts based on family and/or ethnic ties. In Lower Guinea, three mining companies are engaged in bauxite mining and processing:

- *Compagnie des Bauxites de Guinée*/Bauxite Company of Guinea (CBG) has been mining the deposits around the mining town of Sangarédi in the region of Boké since 1973;

- Alumina Company of Guinea (ACG) extracts bauxite from the deposits of Fria and processes it *in situ* into alumina. ACG took over this mining activity in 2000 from the former semi-public company Friguia, which had been mining the deposits since 1960;

- *Compagnie des Bauxites de Kindia*/Bauxite Company of Kindia (CBK) has been mining the deposits of the village of Débélé, in the sub-prefecture of Mambiya and prefecture of Kindia, since 1974.

Since 2010, many conflicts have arisen, opposing on the one hand the companies and their workers, and on the other hand the companies and the neighbouring populations of the mining areas. Another kind of conflict takes place between local authorities in the mining areas and local populations because of the mismanagement of funds allocated by mining companies in support of the development of the different localities.

Thus, in Mambiya, a sub-prefecture of Kindia, a conflict arose between CBK and the population in this locality. The latter attacked the company's property to protest against the mismanagement of the dividends paid by CBK to support the development of local communities. The same phenomenon can be observed in the prefecture of Boké, where youth are often in conflict with the local authorities because of the lack of transparency in the management of mining royalties.

The same causes having the same effects, Guinea has become a land of 'small braziers' fuelled by bad governance, impunity and lack of vision on the part of government policymakers (see the map below).

The Guinean social movement: between subordination and autonomy

From Guinea's accession to independence in 1958 up until 2005, political issues have been monopolised by political party leaders and military elites. It was not until the regime change in 1984 and, above all, the La Baule speech in 1990 that genuine civil society organisations appeared, with associations of internal migrants established in Conakry. These associations were mainly interfaces between their locality of origin and development partners, aimed at channelling actions for infrastructure improvement in their localities. To support this movement, the state established in 1986 a national service to assist cooperatives and coordinate NGO interventions (*Service National d'Assistance aux Coopératives et de Coordination des interventions des ONG*), commonly referred to as SACCO.

Regional distribution of conflicts in Guinea

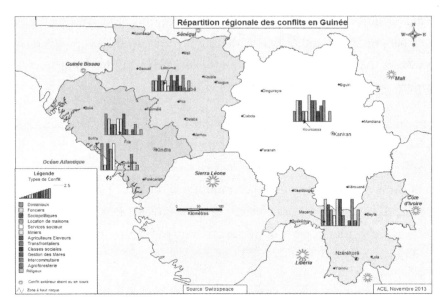

Source: Ministère de l'Administration du Territoire et de la Décentralisation (Ministry of Territorial Administration and Decentralisation), United Nations Development Programme and Swiss Peace Foundation (2013) 'Mapping of Conflicts in Guinea', Conakry, Guinea

It was only from 2006 that Guinean civil society truly invested in the governance field. Its institutional emergence resulted initially from a declining state undermined by poor governance and corruption. It also resulted from the changing paradigms of development partners in their development actions. Faced with the negligence of the state and its structures, and in order to bypass them, all development partners banked on civil society.

From this point, some structures, like the trade union federations,[4] joined forces with nongovernmental organisations (NGOs) by attending national consultations to form the social movement called *Forces vives* (Active

---

4 In Guinea, the major unions - Confédération Nationale des Travailleurs Guinéens (CNTG), Union Syndicale des Travailleurs de Guinée (USTG), Organisation Nationale des Syndicats Libres de Guinée (ONSLG) and Union Démocratique des Travailleurs de Guinée (UDTG) - resist being merged into the category of 'civil society' and demand a distinction between trade unions and other non-state actors considered to be part of civil society.

Forces). One year later, the unions launched a general strike leading to the establishment of the *Alliance Citoyenne pour le Changement* (Citizen Alliance for Change). The claims reached their climax with the obligation for the then president to nominate a prime minister, from a shortlist established by civil society.

The success achieved by the conduct and management of these events by the social movement under the leadership of eight of the major trade union federations of the country enabled civil society to build its reputation and become a legitimate force in the eyes of the population and the country's partners. Owing to this legitimacy, it played a major role in advancing the democratic process and participating in the management of the state from 2007 to the transition in 2008. However, immediately after the junta of President Moussa Dadis Camara came to power, disagreements appeared within the social movement, with some supporting the junta and others condemning it.

After the forced exile of Camara (first in Morocco and then Burkina Faso), the social movement became a major actor of the government team. Unfortunately, this participation in the management of the transition led to rapid politicisation of most of its leadership, in disregard of the citizen values in whose name it was fighting.

Weakened by corruption and the departure of its leaders, some of its structures no longer guaranteed exemplarity through alternation and transparency, two essential values of good governance. This has led to great alteration of the authority and the mediation and regulation capacity of the movement in the face of political abuses. Therefore, the social movement appeared in the eyes of a significant portion of the population as a backyard of those in power, as political party militants hidden behind civil society or as 'submarines of the political class'.

It was in these precarious conditions that Guinea engaged in the 2010 presidential poll, deprived of one of its main regulatory and social and political mediation forces. In the wake of these elections, one of the oldest trade union federations of the country, the *Confédération Nationale des Travailleurs de Guinée* (CNTG), found itself battling a contested internal election, with interference of the judiciary and the government in the handling of the dispute.[5] Even the *Union Syndicale des Travailleurs de Guinée* (USTG), the other major trade union federation of the country, narrowly escaped the same turmoil, with the willingness of its former leaders who were in the transition government to come back and reoccupy the positions they had left.

All of these frictions in the social movement sector, resulting from the readjustment process that followed the 2010 presidential poll, bring into sharp focus the question of the place of the social movement in Guinea, in a context somewhat characterised by a 'return to more normal democratic life'.

This place of the Guinean social movement in the period following the 2010 presidential poll shows several trends. The first is the growing power of the *Coordinations Régionales* which align with the political actors and divide society into communities and dominate the political field. The second is the remobilisation of the social movement around local and national development issues and 'renewed credibility' challenges. These two trends, which take opposite directions, attest to the dynamics opposing the dislocating forces of democracy and those of responsible citizen participation. In order to better understand the two dynamics, we will present them separately and then compare them.

---

5   After the departure of Rabiatou Serah Diallo as head, the CNTG held its congress. The regularity of the election of Ahmadou Diallo was contested by Yamoussa Touré. The battle took a political and judicial turn when a complaint was filed in court by the Touré camp. The current government initially lined up behind the loser. With the recognition of the regularity of the election of Diallo by the International Labour Organisation and by African and international trade union organisations, the government distanced itself from the Touré camp and confirmed their acceptance of the results. However, this recognition failed to address the fundamental question of political interference in the labour movement.

The regional coordination units: a community-based civil society?

Legally, the regional coordination units are community-based, apolitical and sociocultural associations. Thence, they are a component of civil society. Regional coordination units are supposed to be the guardians of the values of Guinean society. Normally, they are made up of wise men. They are rooted in all stateless and/or centralised state Guinean societies, as were the theocratic Fouta and the Manding. All these societies had a council of wise men to guide the decisions made by the authority and manage the city concerned.

But in reality, the regional coordination units are, in their structure, like a 'recycling plant' for retired former government executives who are permanently seeking to 'capture' state resources. Some of them started their career under colonial rule and continued it under the various successive regimes in Guinea. The state and its workings are their universe, and they obtained everything from the state.

Those responsible[6] for the coordination units are intermediaries of the executives in search of promotion and/or preservation of a lucrative position. Although they are associations open to all by the texts governing them, the regional coordination units promote the interests of people claiming to represent an ethnic group or a region.

The forerunners of the present coordination units originated from the last ten years of the colonial period (around 1944). Between 1944 and 1956, Guinea witnessed the emergence and expansion of a wide variety of ethnic associations like the A*micale Gilbert Vieillard* (Gilbert Vieillard Association of Friends) of the Fouta, *Union forestière* (Forest Union) in the Forest Region, *Comité de la Basse Côte* (Lower Coast Committee), *Union du Mandé* (The Manding Union) in Upper Guinea, *Union des Métis*, etc. The first

6 The president of the Fouta coordination unit is a founding member of the PDG and a Compagnon d'Indépendance, a description referring to those who walked alongside Sékou Touré in the struggle for independence and subsequently occupied positions of responsibility within the system of one-party rule. The current president of the Lower Guinea coordination unit (from the Soussou group) is a former president of the mayors of Guinea under Lansana Conté. The current president of the Forest Region coordination unit was a former education minister under Sékou Touré (head of state of Guinea from 1958 to 1984) and Lansana Conté (head of state of Guinea from 1984 to 2008).

political parties in Guinea emerged by building on these associations but also combating them. With the victory of the *Parti Démocratique de Guinée* (PDG) in 1956, the associations were vigorously fought and disappeared during the 26 years of PDG rule.

When it came to liberalisation of political life in 1990, the political actors called for former civil servants in the PDG era to act as facilitators in staffing the embryonic political parties. These resource persons who provided advice and meeting places would mostly become the leaders of the present coordination units.

As from 1993, the ruling power, *Parti de l'Unité et du Progrès* (Party of Unity and Progress, PUP), used fierce repression against the opposition to dominate the political arena. In the absence of an open political game, the only option left was to retreat into different ethnic groups through the coordination units in order to play the role of interface between power and the 'seekers' of administrative favour. The more opposition political parties were repressed and felt stifled under the yoke of police and military crackdowns, the more civil society and especially the regional coordination units gained importance in social regulation.

While the regime of Lansana Conté collapsed as his medical condition deteriorated and the nation felt the devastating effects of the drug trafficking in 'Rivières du Sud',[7] the coordination units were growing and superseding political parties in mobilising the population. Thus, it can be said that the current regional coordination units have emerged from the repression of opposition political parties and outside of any legal text, with no vision or mission stated before the nation.

During the 2010 presidential election campaign, the coordination units were called upon by the different candidates to support their candidacy and sometimes to put pressure on some of them so that they withdrew in their

---

7   Guinea's name under colonial rule.

favour.[8] But in the period between the two rounds of voting, the coordination units expanded and influenced those who were still uncertain, or forced the transition actors to support them. In the end, the second round appeared like a confrontation between ethnic blocks in which the number of votes depended on the demographic weight of Guinea's ethnic groups. Since then, Guinea is facing a strong trend, namely the omnipotence of structures like the regional coordination units which are aimed at speaking on behalf of an ethnic community without having the mandate or the legal authority to do so.

The most significant impact of the regional coordination units on political life is the fact that no reform is possible in Guinea. Indeed, all the reforms contemplated are hampered by all those who can rely on their coordination units to maintain the status quo. The state is losing its substance and citizens are turning to their community.

The other side of the coin is the interference of regional coordination units in the political game. Instead of political parties and social movements, the reality is that the regional coordination units take the state hostage, muzzling the executive and perverting the political game. Some in the presidential camp and others in the opposition denounce the phenomenon when it is in their favour, but subscribe to it tacitly when it suits them.

In the long run, the supremacy of the regional coordination units presents three possibilities:

- The first possibility, which is the most feared by all, is that their interference further breaks up the social fabric and leads to the partitioning of the country into several ethnic-regional entities or, in fact, several countries;

- The second possibility is that the interference of the coordination units heralds a new Guinea: a federal or confederate Guinea;

---

8   Between the two rounds of the presidential election, the Manding regional coordination unit demanded the victory of their 'son' Alpha Condé. Otherwise, the unit reserved the right not to recognise the results of the second round

- The third possibility is to see the interference of the coordination units as an indicator of the dysfunction of Guinea's political regime. In this case, it is hoped that their interference will wake up Guinean society, its elites and citizens, in order to put things right.

If the third scenario is to emerge, decisions need to be made and implemented immediately. The first and more urgent decision is to discuss the political model. If the coordination units must continue to have a legal existence, it appears necessary that Guineans define the outlines.

The new collective dynamics of the Guinean social movement: mines, human rights and unity

Since 2007, the Guinean social movement has made the mining sector (revision of contracts, establishment of a mining code and local royalties) and the respect of human rights the major challenges of its fight on behalf of citizens. It is within this framework that a symposium was organised in 2008 in Conakry on the exploitation of mining resources and the impact of mining on the lives and environments of the populations involved. The purpose of the symposium was to create a framework for exchange and reflection which could turn the 'mining resource curse' into a source of advancement and sustainable development, in a peaceful and stable environment.

To deliver on this, the social movement supported the formalisation of the 'Publish What You Pay' (PWYP) platform into an association in 2011. In July of the same year, at the initiative of the social movement and in order to widen the range of stakeholders in the sector, the PWYP platform adopted the multi-stakeholder consultation and exchange mechanism (involving civil society organisations, local, regional and national authorities, communities and elected people, and mining companies) at the national, local or regional level. It is through these engagements that improvements of the mining code were made and adopted on 9 September 2011.

Since 2010, the defence of human rights has been the second field of mobilisation of the social movement sector in Guinea. Indeed, the human rights issue is a recurrent one in the history of Guinea. This history is that of continued human rights violations and a culture of impunity for defence and law enforcement forces. For many, the end of the reign of Sékou Touré and the single party and, above all, the establishment of the multiparty system starting from the 1990s, was marked by a new era: that of respect for public freedoms. Unfortunately, human rights violations appear to have continued even after 2010, the year of the presidential poll, as evidenced by the events in the summer of 2013.[9] As concerns the human rights issue, leadership is offered by three civil society organisations: *Organisation Guinéenne des Droits de l'Homme* (OGDH)/Guinean Organisation for the Defence of Human Rights; *Mêmes Droits pour Tous* (MDT)/Same Rights For All; and *Association des Parents et Amis des Victimes du 28 Septembre 2009* (AVIPA)/ Association of Relatives and Friends of the Victims of 28 September 2009.

OGDH, the oldest human rights organisation in Guinea, was established in 1990 as a member of the Federation of Human Rights (FHR), with observer status before the African Commission on Human Rights.

MDT was established in 2004 by lawyers and law faculty lecturers in Guinean universities. MDT provides legal assistance to inmates but also training on prison management to law enforcement officers, perpetrators of torture in prisons, and prison staff.

AVIPA was recently created and resulted from the 28 September 2009 mass violations of human rights in the stadium of the same name. It gathers a membership of 300 people composed mainly of survivors. Its work consists in identifying the victims and compiling the complaints to the court, with

---

9   In August 2013, law enforcement forces fired at those protesting against the recruitment conditions of the Brazilian mining company Vale, leaving 30 people dead.

support from the Office of the High Commissioner for Human Rights and MDT.

Since 2010, the three organisations have put in place coordination of their activities for the defence of human rights, chaired by OGDH and supported at the African level by the *Rencontre Africaine de Défense des Droits de l'Homme*/African Meeting for the Defence of Human Rights (RADDHO). In order to improve their expertise and make human rights violations visible, the three organisations collaborated with *Action des Chrétiens pour l'Abolition de la Torture* (ACAT) in conducting a study on the situation of torture in Guinea.

This study was part of a European project aimed at taking stock of the situation of torture in several countries. One of the recommendations of the study was to reach a common CSO position in denouncing the violation of human rights and coming up with a bill on the criminalisation of torture.

To realise this synergy on the issue of human rights, the Guinean social movement sector put in place some mechanisms for action, such as: the formation of pressure groups; the establishment of a communication system; the setting up of human rights observation groups; capacity-building in human rights for civil society organisations; the revitalisation of traditional structures to get them involved in conflict resolution; and support in establishing a consultation framework at the level of the prefecture on conflict prevention and management practices.

On these two approaches, the Guinean social movement sector has made real achievements and created a real social mobilisation mechanism. However, what remains is the issue of the sustainability of these actions, given their dependency vis-à-vis funding and external support.

Since 2010, the social movement as a whole is therefore seeking a new lease of life. CNTG more or less succeeded in getting out of a turbulent zone, after several months of trial and political interference. The collapse of *Conseil national des organisations de la société civile guinéenne*/National Council of Guinean Civil Society Organisations (CNOSG), following the misappropriation of European Union funds and internal leadership quarrels, has given way to apex organisations such as the *Plate-forme des Citoyens Unis pour le Développement* and *Coalition des Femmes et Jeunes Filles pour la Paix.* These new organisations have recreated with their employers and the main trade union federations the second-phase social movement.

For the initiators of this new forum for the revival of the social movement, Guinea must be able to frame the political game with constructive citizen alternatives. According to this new approach, the social movement sector wants to:

- restore its legitimacy and credibility;

- revitalise the Guinean citizenship movement based on shared values, principles and mechanisms;

- define and adopt shared citizenship values;

- promote better communication between social and political players through the establishment of a permanent consultation framework.

The inclusive nature of future mobilisation, the clarity of debates and the relevance of the conclusions of this forum will determine what the dominant trend is when it comes to the issue of citizenship and tribalism in Guinea.

Conclusion

Three years after the 2010 presidential elections, where does Guinea stand now? Guinea is following a difficult path to democracy, because its present is severely handicapped by an undigested inheritance, with a political fight based on the principle of the 'zero-sum game'. The opening of the political game towards the end of the reign of President Lansana Conté, with the growing of a responsible social movement, did not translate into real democracy.

The Guinean social movement sector which spearheaded the protest against the military and autocratic rule of Conté has lost its soul and its credibility through participating in the various so-called transition governments. Coming out of a choppy, ill-prepared and foreign-led transition, with actors who had their own agendas, the Guinean social movement sector has lost ground. Instead of public service, the vast majority of Guinean civil society actors have been driven by opportunistic strategies based on improvisation. For people without employment prospects and idle civil servants, involvement in the civil society sector is part of a survival strategy. Through these practices, the citizen social movement has given way to new community-based and divisive actors, namely the regional coordination units.

More recently, with the disrepute of a significant part of the Guinean social movement sector, an underlying movement is taking shape with the emergence of new platforms. These new platforms are determined to break with the status quo, trigger a new momentum and put the regional coordination units back in their place.

If this trend continues, the Guinean social movement sector could regain its credibility and legitimacy while achieving sub-regional grounding. In these circumstances, and only these, the Guinean social movement sector could become a constructive force for the proposal of alternatives within the framework of a fair distribution of wealth, the eradication of inequalities and poverty, employment promotion and the dissemination of economic and political good governance practices. Otherwise, Guinean civil society will collapse, and Guinea with it.

References

ACAT-France, OGDH, MDT and AVIPA (2011) Torture. La force fait la loi. Étude du phénomène tortionnaire en Guinée, http://www.acatfrance. fr/medias/files/actualite/Rapport-Guinee-torture-ACAT-AVIPA-MDT-OGDH-novembre-2011.pdf, accessed March 2014

Bangoura, T. M. Bangoura, D. and Diop, M. (2006) *Quelle transition politique pour la Guinée?*, Paris, L'Harmattan

Barry, A. A. B. (2009) « Ethnicité et appartenance ethnique en Guinée », *Horizon* n°12 : 2-17

Barry, A. A. B. (2012) « La cartographie des conflits en Guinée », *Horizon Plus*, n°4 : 4-10

Barry, A. A. B. (2013) « Les violences politiques en Guinée : une pratique constante » in J.-P. Vettovaglia (dir.) *Déterminants des conflits et nouvelles formes de prévention, tome 3*, Bruxelles, Belgique, Bruylant

Doumbouya, O.S. (2008) *Les ONG féminines en Guinée. Instrument au service de la promotion féminine*, Paris, L'Harmattan

Faye, O.T. (2008) *Guinée, chronique d'une démocratie annoncée*, Paris, L'Harmattan.

International Crisis Group (2007) 'Guinea. Change on Hold', *Africa Briefing* no.49, http://www.crisisgroup.org/en/regions/africa/west-africa/guinea/B049-guinea-change-on-hold.aspx, accessed March 2014

International crisis group (2008) 'Guinea: Ensuring democratic reforms', *Africa Briefing* no. 52, http://www.crisisgroup.org/fr/regions/afrique/afrique-de-louest/guinee/B052-guinea-ensuring-democratic-reforms.aspx, accessed March 2014

International crisis group (2009) 'Guinea : Military rule must end', *Africa Briefing* no.66, http://www.crisisgroup.org/fr/regions/afrique/ afrique-de-louest/guinee/B066-guinea-military-rule-must-end. aspx, accessed March 2014

Lambert, A. and Barry, A. A. B. (2012) « Evaluation externe et finale du Programme Concerté des Capacités des organisations de la société Civile et de la Jeunesse Guinéenne (PROJEG 2008-2012) », Institut de Recherches et d'Applications des Méthodes de développement, Paris, France.

United States Agency for International Development and Tetra Tech ARD (2011) 'Democracy and Governance Assessment of Guinea', http:// frameweb.org/adl/en-US/8546/file/1164/DG, accessed March 2014

Printed in Great Britain
by Amazon

65204225R00281